CIMA

OPERATIONAL

PAPER P1

PERFORMANCE OPERATIONS

P
R
A
C
T
I
C
E

&

R
E
V
I
S
I
O
N

K
I
T

This Kit is for CIMA's exams in 2011.

In this Kit we:

- Discuss the **best strategies** for revising and taking your P1 exam

- Show you how to be well prepared for the **2011 exams**

- Give you **lots of great guidance** on tackling questions

- Demonstrate how you can **build your own exams**

- Provide you with **three** mock exams

FOR EXAMS IN 2011

LEARNING MEDIA

ii

First edition 2010
Second edition January 2011

ISBN 9780 7517 9459 5
(Previous ISBN 9780 7517 7524 2)
eISBN 9780 7517 8714 6

British Library Cataloguing-in-Publication Data
A catalogue record for this book
is available from the British Library

Published by

BPP Learning Media Ltd
BPP House, Aldine Place
London W12 8AA

www.bpp.com/learningmedia

Printed in the United Kingdom

Your learning materials, published by BPP
Learning Media Ltd, are printed on paper sourced
from sustainable, managed forests.

A note about copyright

Dear Customer

What does the little © mean and why does it matter?

Your market-leading BPP books, course materials and
e-learning materials do not write and update themselves.
People write them: on their own behalf or as employees
of an organisation that invests in this activity. Copyright
law protects their livelihoods. It does so by creating rights
over the use of the content.

Breach of copyright is a form of theft – as well as being a
criminal offence in some jurisdictions, it is potentially a
serious breach of professional ethics.

With current technology, things might seem a bit hazy
but, basically, without the express permission of BPP
Learning Media:

- Photocopying our materials is a breach of copyright

- Scanning, ripcasting or conversion of our digital
  materials into different file formats, uploading them to
  facebook or emailing them to your friends is a breach
  of copyright

You can, of course, sell your books, in the form in which
you have bought them – once you have finished with
them. (Is this fair to your fellow students? We update for a
reason.) But the e-products are sold on a single user
licence basis: we do not supply 'unlock' codes to people
who have bought them second-hand.

And what about outside the UK? BPP Learning Media
strives to make our materials available at prices students
can afford by local printing arrangements, pricing policies
and partnerships which are clearly listed on our website.
A tiny minority ignore this and indulge in criminal activity
by illegally photocopying our material or supporting
organisations that do. If they act illegally and unethically
in one area, can you really trust them?

Contents

Question index

The headings in this checklist/index indicate the main topics of questions, but questions often cover several different topics.

Questions set under the old syllabus's *Performance Evaluation (MAPE), Financial Accounting and Tax Principles (FATP) and Decision Management (MADM)* are included because their style and content are similar to those that appear in the Paper P1 exam.

Mixed Section B questions

Mock exam 1

Mock exam 2 (September 2010 resit examination)

Mock exam 3 (November 2010 examination)

Planning your question practice

Our guidance from page xiv shows you how to organise your question practice, either by attempting questions from each syllabus area or by **building your own exams** – tackling questions as a series of practice exams.

Topic index

Listed below are the key Paper P1 syllabus topics and the numbers of the questions in this Kit covering those topics.

If you need to concentrate your practice and revision on certain topics or if you want to attempt all available Section B and Section C questions that refer to a particular subject you will find this index useful.

Using your BPP Learning Media Practice and Revision Kit

Tackling revision and the exam

You can significantly improve your chances of passing by tackling revision and the exam in the right ways. Our advice is based on feedback from CIMA. We focus on Paper P1; we discuss revising the syllabus, what to do (and what not to do) in the exam, how to approach different types of question and ways of obtaining easy marks.

Selecting questions

We provide signposts to help you plan your revision.

- A full **question index**

- A **topic index**, listing all the questions that cover key topics, so that you can locate the questions that provide practice on these topics, and see the different ways in which they might be examined

- **BPP's question plan**, highlighting the most important questions

- **Build your own exams**, showing you how you can practise questions in a series of exams

Making the most of question practice

We realise that you need more than questions and model answers to get the most from your question practice.

- Our **Top tips** provide essential advice on tackling questions and presenting answers

- We show you how you can pick up **Easy marks** on questions, as picking up all readily available marks can make the difference between passing and failing

- We include **marking guides** to show you what the examiner rewards

- We summarise **Examiner's comments** to show you how students coped with the questions

- We refer to the **BPP 2010 Study Text** for detailed coverage of the topics covered in each question

Attempting mock exams

There are three mock exams that provide practice at coping with the pressures of the exam day. We strongly recommend that you attempt them under exam conditions as they reflect the question styles and syllabus coverage of the exam. To help you get the most out of doing these exams, we provide guidance on how you should have approached the whole exam.

Our other products

BPP Learning Media also offers these products for practising and revising the P1 exam:

Passcards	Summarising what you should know in visual, easy to remember, form
Success CDs	Covering the vital elements of the P1 syllabus in less than 90 minutes and also containing exam hints to help you fine tune your strategy
i-Pass	Providing computer-based testing in a variety of formats, ideal for self-assessment
Interactive Passcards	Allowing you to learn actively with a clear visual format summarising what you must know

You can purchase these products by visiting www.bpp.com/lm

Revising P1

The P1 exam

This will be a time-pressured exam that combines calculations with discussion. It is very important that you do not concentrate completely on the calculations at the expense of fully understanding the issues involved. You will need to be able to demonstrate the skill of explaining key ideas, techniques or approaches.

Topics to revise

You need to be comfortable with **all areas of the syllabus** as questions, particularly Question 1, will often span a number of syllabus areas. Question spotting will absolutely **not work** on this paper. It is better to go into the exam knowing a reasonable amount about most of the syllabus rather than concentrating on a few topics.

Cost accounting systems

- Traditional management accounting
- New alternatives
- Effect on inventory valuation and profitability

Standard costing

- Standard costs
- Variance analysis

Forecasting and budgeting

- Techniques

Project appraisal

- Evaluating long–term proposals using various investment appraisal techniques
- Inflation and tax
- Sensitivity analysis

Dealing with uncertainty in analysis

- Expected values
- Sensitivity analysis
- Decision trees

Managing short-term finance

- Working capital
- Cash requirements

Question practice

Question practice under timed conditions is essential, so that you can get used to the pressures of answering exam questions in **limited time** and practise not only the key techniques but allocating your time between different requirements in each question. It's particularly important to do questions from both sections of the paper in full to see how the numerical and written elements balance in longer questions.

Passing the P1 exam

Avoiding weaknesses

You will enhance your chances significantly if you ensure you avoid these mistakes:

- Lack of knowledge brought forward from earlier studies (particularly CIMA C1 and CIMA C3)
- Failure to read the question
- Lack of application of knowledge to scenario
- Lack of practice on discussion style questions
- Time management – spending excessive time on strong areas or too long on areas you struggle with
- Poor English, structure and presentation

Using the reading time

We recommend you spend the reading time looking at the compulsory Section B questions and planning your answers to these. Then look at Section C questions if you have time.

Choosing which questions to answer first

Choosing which questions to answer first is a matter of preference. You should practise different methods during your revision to decide which one suits you best.

Having read through the questions in Section B and C during the reading time you might feel quite confident about some of them. One option is to do these questions first. An alternative method is to do them in the order you have read them, that is, Section B, Section C and then Section A. The **most important** thing to remember is to spend **no longer** than 54 minutes on Section B, 90 minutes on Section C and 36 minutes on Section A!

Numerical questions

You are likely to see calculation questions covering:

- Marginal costing/absorption costing/ABC
- Variance analysis
- Throughput accounting
- Budgeting/forecasting
- Project appraisal including tax and inflation
- Cash management

Even if you do make a mistake on the numbers, you will gain credit for the correct approach in Sections B and C and in the objective test (non-MCQs) in Section A. A brief narrative explaining your approach to tricky calculations will help the marker.

You can expect to come across some difficult things in the questions. You must learn to move on and do as much of the questions as possible.

Present your numbers neatly in a table format with key numbers underlined and clear workings.

Discussion questions

As well as discussing the limitations of your calculations, you should expect to be asked to discuss their results.

One important aspect of time allocation is not to spend excessive time on the calculations at the expense of the discussion parts. You need to be strict with yourself in order to gain as many marks as possible.

Remember that the marking schemes for discussion questions will be fairly general, and you will gain credit for all relevant points. You'll gain higher marks if your explanations are clearly focused on the question and you can supplement your explanations with examples.

Gaining the easy marks

There are likely to be easier marks available for straightforward calculations, also for defining and explaining key topics in general terms when the question doesn't require you to link these definitions in with the question scenario. On some papers you may see a discussion question that doesn't link into a scenario and this type of question may well be easier than other scenario-linked questions on that paper.

Often the easier marks will be in the first part(s) of the question. If they are in subsequent parts, we would recommend that you do these parts first, in order to pick up the easy marks.

There will also be some easy marks available for answering using an appropriate format, for example a report.

The exam paper

Format of the paper

		Number of marks
Section A:	A variety of multiple choice and other objective test questions, 2-4 marks each	20
Section B:	6 compulsory questions, 5 marks each	30
Section C:	Likely to be 2 questions, approximately 25 marks each	50
		100

Time allowed: 3 hours, plus 20 minutes reading time

Breadth of question coverage

Questions in all sections of the paper may cover more than one syllabus area.

Knowledge from other syllabuses

You should also use your knowledge from other papers such as CIMA C1 and CIMA C3.

Sept 2010

Section A

1   8 objective test questions

Section B

2   Trade receivables, EOQ, backflush accounting, ZBB, ABC, ABB, decision trees

Section C

3   Operating statement, planning and operational variances

4   NPV, IRR

This exam is Mock exam 2 in this Kit.

May 2010

	Question in this Kit
Section A	
1 8 objective test questions	75
Section B	
2 Trade receivables, EOQ, MRP, ABB, budget preparation, decision trees	84
Section C	
3 Operating statement, standard costing and advanced manufacturing technology	17
4 NPV, IRR, expected NPV, standard deviation	45
Specimen paper	
Section A	
1 7 objective test questions	74
Section B	
2 Receivables, debt factoring, decision trees, forecasting, budgets, environmental costs	83
Section C	
3 NPV, ARR	46
4 Operating statement, planning and operational variances, standard costing	18

What the examiner means

The table below has been prepared by CIMA to help you interpret exam questions.

Learning objective	Verbs used	Definition	Examples in the Kit
1 Knowledge			
What you are expected to know	List	Make a list of	
	State	Express, fully or clearly, the details of/facts of	13b
	Define	Give the exact meaning of	42c
2 Comprehension			
What you are expected to understand	Describe	Communicate the key features of	
	Distinguish	Highlight the differences between	
	Explain	Make clear or intelligible/state the meaning or purpose of	12
	Identify	Recognise, establish or select after consideration	
	Illustrate	Use an example to describe or explain something	
3 Application			
How you are expected to apply your knowledge	Apply	Put to practical use	
	Calculate/compute	Ascertain or reckon mathematically	12f
	Demonstrate	Prove the certainty or exhibit by practical means	
	Prepare	Make or get ready for use	21a
	Reconcile	Make or prove consistent/compatible	14b
	Solve	Find an answer to	
	Tabulate	Arrange in a table	
4 Analysis			
How you are expected to analyse the detail of what you have learned	Analyse	Examine in detail the structure of	
	Categorise	Place into a defined class or division	
	Compare and contrast	Show the similarities and/or differences between	
	Construct	Build up or complete	
	Discuss	Examine in detail by argument	13d
	Interpret	Translate into intelligible or familiar terms	
	Prioritise	Place in order of priority or sequence for action	
	Produce	Create or bring into existence	
5 Evaluation			
How you are expected to use your learning to evaluate, make decisions or recommendations	Advise	Counsel, inform or notify	42
	Evaluate	Appraise or assess the value of	41c
	Recommend	Propose a course of action	

Planning your question practice

We have already stressed that question practice should be right at the centre of your revision. Whilst you will spend some time looking at your notes and the Paper P1 Passcards, you should spend the majority of your revision time practising questions.

We recommend two ways in which you can practise questions.

- Use **BPP Learning Media's question plan** to work systematically through the syllabus and attempt key and other questions on a section-by-section basis

- **Build your own exams** – attempt the questions as a series of practice exams

These ways are suggestions and simply following them is no guarantee of success. You or your college may prefer an alternative but equally valid approach.

BPP's question plan

The plan below requires you to devote a **minimum of 30 hours** to revision of Paper P1. Any time you can spend over and above this should only increase your chances of success.

 Review your notes and the chapter summaries in the Paper P1 **Passcards** for each section of the syllabus.

 Answer the key questions for that section. These questions have boxes round the question number in the table below and you should answer them in full. Even if you are short of time you must attempt these questions if you want to pass the exam. You should complete your answers without referring to our solutions.

 Attempt the other questions in that section. For some questions we have suggested that you prepare **answer plans or do the calculations** rather than full solutions. Planning an answer means that you should spend about 40% of the time allowance for the questions brainstorming the question and drawing up a list of points to be included in the answer.

 Attempt Mock exams 1, 2 and 3 under strict exam conditions.

6/8.

Syllabus section	2010 Passcards chapters	Questions in this Kit	Comments	Done ☑
Managing short-term finance	1-5	1	Answer in full. This question provides Section A practice	☐
		3	Answer in full. This question provides Section A practice	☐
		4	Answer in full. This question includes cash budget preparation.	☐
		5	Answer in full. This question provides Section A practice .	☐
		9	Answer in full. This is a very good practice question which includes several topics from the short-term finance part of the syllabus.	☐
		10		☐
		62.2	This is a narrative question on overhead under absorption	☐
Basic techniques, absorption costing and marginal costing	6a, 6b	12	Answer in full. This question tests your ability to write discussion answers as well as calculations.	☐
		14	Answer in full. This question gives you practice at reconciling marginal and absorption profits.	☐
Standard costing and variance analysis	7a-8	15	Answer in full. This question gives you plenty of variance calculation practice.	☐
		17	This is from the May 2010 exam.	☐
		18	This is from the Specimen paper.	☐
		30	Answer in full. This Section C question includes planning and operational variances	☐
		22	Answer in full. This Section C question includes mix and yield variances	☐

Syllabus section	2010 Passcards chapters	Questions in this Kit	Comments	Done ☑
Modern business environment	9-12	28	Answer in full. This question tests forecasts, ratio analysis and discussion of financial strategies.	☐
		29	Answer in full. This question requires lots of explanations.	☐
		30	Answer in full. This Section C question covers ABC	☐
		31	Answer in full. This Section C question covers throughput accounting.	☐
Budgeting and forecasting	13-14	34	Answer in full.	☐
Project appraisal, DCF, tax and inflation	15-17	38	Answer in full. Section A practice questions.	☐
		39	Answer in full. Section B practice questions.	☐
		40	Net present values and inflation question practice.	☐
		41	Do parts (a) and (b) in note form and then part (c) in full.	☐
		42	This question requires an explanation of real rate of return and money rate of return.	☐
Further aspects of investment decision making	18	43	Answer in full. This question provides Section A style question practice.	☐
		44	Answer in full. This question contains a good mix of discussion and calculation questions.	☐
		45	This is from the May 2010 exam.	☐
		46	This is from the Specimen paper.	☐
		51	Answer (a), (b) and (c) in full.	☐
Risk and uncertainty	19	53	Answer in full. This question provides Section A practice.	☐
		55	Answer in full. This questions requires you to prepare a two-way data table.	☐
		56	Answer in full. This questions requires you to prepare a decision tree.	☐
		83	Answer part (c). It's from the Specimen paper.	☐
		84	Answer part (f) which is from the May 2010 exam.	☐

Build your own exams

Having revised your notes and the BPP Passcards, you can attempt the questions in the Kit as a series of practice exams, making them up yourself or using the mock exams that we have listed below.

	Practice exams					
	1	2	3	4	5	6
Section A						
1	75	74	63	64	65	66
Section B						
2	84	83	78	79	80	81
Section C						
3	45	46	27	32	26	20
4	19	18	49	48	58	51

Whichever practice exams you use, you must attempt **Mock exams 1, 2 and 3** at the end of your revision.

QUESTIONS

2

WORKING CAPITAL AND CASH MANAGEMENT

Questions 1 to 4 cover working capital, the operating cycle and cash management, the subject of Chapters 1 and 2 of the BPP Study Text for Paper P1.

1 Section A: Working capital and cash management I   36 mins

1   An entity's working capital financing policy is to finance working capital using short-term financing to fund all the fluctuating current assets as well as some of the permanent part of the current assets.

The above policy is an example of

A   an aggressive policy.
B   a conservative policy.
C   a short-term policy.
D   a moderate policy.   **(2 marks)**

FATP 11/05

2   HMP has decided to adopt a moderate working capital policy. It has fluctuating current assets of $1m, permanent current assets of $5m, and non-current assets of $9m. Which of the following mixes of finance is the company MOST LIKELY to choose?

A   Short-term financing of $1m; permanent financing of $14m
B   Short-term financing of $0.5m; permanent financing of $14.5m
C   Short-term financing of $2m; permanent financing of $13m
D   Short-term financing of $4m; permanent financing of $11m   **(2 marks)**

3   The following figures are taken from the accounts of GRE:

	$
Inventories	400,000
Receivables	600,000
Cash	200,000
Payables	800,000
Loan stock redeemable in three years time	800,000

What is the quick ratio?

A   0.75
B   1.50
C   0.50
D   1.00   **(2 marks)**

4   The following figures have been extracted from the accounts of WI:

	$
Total sales	200,000
Cash sales	20,000
Credit sales	180,000
Year end receivables	25,000
Bad debts	5,000

What is the average debt collection period in days (based on 365 days per year)?

A   50.7
B   60.8
C   54.8
D   45.6   **(2 marks)**

5   A company has a current ratio of 2 :1. Due to having significant surplus cash balances, it has decided to pay its trade payable accounts after 30 days in future, rather than after 50 days, as it has in the past.

What will be the effect of this change on the company's current ratio and its cash operating cycle?

	Current ratio	Cash operating cycle
A	Increase	Increase
B	Increase	Decrease
C	Decrease	Increase
D	Decrease	Decrease

(2 marks)

6   DY's trade receivables balance at 1 April 20X6 was $22,000. DY's income statement showed revenue from credit sales of $290,510 during the year ended 31 March 20X7.

DY's trade receivables at 31 March 20X7 were 49 days.

Assume DY's sales occur evenly throughout the year and that all balances outstanding at 1 April 20X6 have been received.

Also, it should be assumed all sales are on credit there were no bad debts and no trade discount was given.

How much cash did DY receive from its customers during the year to 31 March 20X7?

A $268,510
B $273,510
C $312,510
D $351,510

(2 marks)

FATP 5/07

7   DX had the following balances in its trial balance at 30 September 20X6:

Trial balance extract at 30 September 20X6

	$'000	$'000
Revenue		2,400
Cost of sales	1,400	
Inventories	360	
Trade receivables	290	
Trade payables		90
Cash and cash equivalents	95	

Calculate the length of DX's working capital cycle at 30 September 20X6.   (4 marks)

FATP 11/06

8   DY had a balance outstanding on trade receivables at 30 September 20X6 of $68,000. Forecast credit sales for the next six months are $250,000 and customers are expected to return goods with a sales value of $2,500.

Based on past experience, within the next six months DY expects to collect $252,100 cash and to write off as bad debts 5% of the balance outstanding at 30 September 20X6.

Calculate DY's forecast trade receivables days outstanding at 31 March 20X7.   (4 marks)

FATP 11/06

(Total = 20 marks)

2 Section A: Working capital and cash management II   36 mins

1   A conservative policy for financing working capital is one where short-term finance is used to fund

     A   All of the fluctuating current assets, but no part of the permanent current assets.

     B   All of the fluctuating current assets and part of the permanent current assets.

     C   Part of the fluctuating current assets and part of the permanent current assets.

     D   Part of the fluctuating current assets, but no part of the permanent current assets.   **(2 marks)**

FATP 5/06

2   A company has a current ratio of 1.5:1. It decides to use surplus cash balances to settle 30% of its total current liabilities.

     The current ratio will

     A   Decrease by more than 30%

     B   Decrease by less than 30%

     C   Increase by more than 30%   –

     D   Increase by less than 30%   –   **(2 marks)**

3   A company buys goods on credit and then, before payment is made, it is forced to sell all of these goods on credit for less than the purchase price. What is the consequence of these two transactions immediately after the sale has taken place?

     A   Inventory decreases and cash decreases.

     B   Cash decreases and payables increase.

     C   Inventory decreases and receivables increase.

     D   Receivables increase and payables increase.   **(2 marks)**

4   A retailing company has an annual turnover of $36 million. The company earns a constant margin of 20% on sales. All sales and purchases are on credit and are evenly distributed over the year. The following amounts are maintained at a constant level throughout the year.

	$m
Inventories	6
Receivables	8
Payables	3

     What is the company's cash cycle to the nearest day (that is, the average time from the payment of a supplier to the receipt from a customer)?

     A   81 days

     B   111 days

     C   119 days

     D   195 days   **(2 marks)**

5   Working capital is MOST LIKELY to increase when

     A   Payments to suppliers are delayed.

     B   The period of credit extended to customers is reduced.

     C   Non-current assets are sold.

     D   Inventory levels are increased.   **(2 marks)**

6   EX is preparing its cash forecast for the next three months.

     Which ONE of the following items should be left out of its calculations?

     A   Expected gain on the disposal of a piece of land.

     B   Tax payment due, that relates to last year's profits.

     C   Rental payment on a leased vehicle.

     D   Receipt of a new bank loan raised for the purpose of purchasing new machinery.   **(2 marks)**

FATP 11/07

7   EV had inventory days outstanding of 60 days and trade payables outstanding of 50 days at 31 October 20X7.

EV's inventory balance at 1 November 20X6 was $56,000 and trade payables were $42,000 at that date.

EV's cost of goods sold comprises purchased goods cost only. During the year to 31 October 20X7, EV's cost of goods sold was $350,000.

Assume purchases and sales accrue evenly throughout the year and use a 365 day year. Further assume that there were no goods returned to suppliers and EV claimed no discounts.

Calculate how much EV paid to its credit suppliers during the year to 31 October 20X7.   **(4 marks)**

FATP 11/07

8   FR INCOME STATEMENT FOR THE YEAR ENDED 31 MARCH 20X8

	$'000
Revenue	270
Cost of goods sold	139
Gross profit	131

Assume all sales and all purchases are on credit and that there are no returns or discounts. All trade payables relate to cost of sales.

FR STATEMENT OF FINANCIAL POSITION AS AT 31 MARCH 20X8 (EXTRACT)

	$'000
Current assets	
Inventory	79
Trade receivables	52
Cash	25
	156
Current liabilities	
Trade payables	40
Accrued interest	21
Income tax	88
	149

Inventory balance at 31 March 20X7 was $79,000.

Calculate the number of days in FR's working capital cycle.   **(4 marks)**

FATP 5/08

(Total = 20 marks)

If you struggled with these objective test questions, go back to your BPP Study Text for Paper P1 and revise Chapters 1 and 2 before you tackle Section B type questions on working capital and cash management.

6\8

3 Section B: Working capital and cash management   54 mins

(a)   Extracts from the financial statements of PRT for the years ended 31 March are as follows.

	20X6 $'000	20X7 $'000
Raw material inventories	55	80
Finished goods inventories	185	185
Purchases of raw materials	600	850
Cost of sales	1,570	1,830
Administrative expenses	45	65
Sales	1,684	1,996
Trade receivables	114	200
Trade payables	50	70
Overdraft	400	950
Additions to non-current assets	700	900

Cost of sales includes all relevant production costs including manufacturing overheads and labour.

Required

Calculate the length in days of the company's operating cycle for the year ended 31 March 20X7.

(5 marks)

(b)   AAD is a newly-created subsidiary of a large listed company. It commenced business on 1 October 20X2, to provide specialist contract cleaning services to industrial customers. All sales are on credit.

More favourable credit terms are offered to larger customers (class A) than to smaller customers (class B). All sales are invoiced at the end of the month in which the sale occurs. Class A customers will be given credit terms requiring payment within 60 days of invoicing, while class B customers will be required to pay within 30 days of invoicing.

Since it is recognised, however, that not all customers comply with the credit terms they are allowed, receipts from customers have prudently been estimated as follows:

Customer type	Within 30 days	31 to 60 days	61 to 90 days	91 to 120 days	Bad debts
Class A		50%	30%	15%	5%
Class B	60%	25%	10%		5%

The above table shows that customers are expected either to pay within 60 days of the end of the credit period, or not at all. Bad debts will therefore be written off 60 days after the end of the credit period.

Budgeted credit sales for each class of customer in the first 4 months of trading are as follows:

Customer type	October $'000	November $'000	December $'000	January $'000
Class A	100	150	200	300
Class B	60	80	40	50

Assume all months are of 30 days.

Required

Prepare a statement showing the budgeted cash to be received by AAD from customers in each of the three months of November 20X2, December 20X2 and January 20X3, based upon the prudently estimated receipts from customers.   **(5 marks)**

(c)   AD, a manufacturing entity, has the following balances at 30 April 20X5:

Extract from financial statements:	$'000
Trade receivables	216
Trade payables	97
Revenue (all credit sales)	992
Cost of sales	898
Purchases in year	641
Inventories at 30 April 20X5	
Raw materials	111
Work in progress	63
Finished goods	102

Required

Calculate AD's working capital cycle.   **(5 marks)**

FATP 5/05

(d)   HRD owns a number of small hotels. The room occupancy rate varies significantly from month to month. There are also high fixed costs. As a result, the cash generated each month has been very difficult to estimate.

Christmas is normally a busy period and large cash surpluses are expected in December. There is, however, a possibility that a rival group of hotels will offer large discounts in December and this could damage December trade for HRD to a significant extent.

January is a poor period for the industry and therefore all the company's hotels will close for the month, resulting in a negative cash flow. The Finance Director has identified the following possible outcomes and their associated probabilities:

	$'000	Probability
Expected cash balance at 30 November 20X3	+175	1.0
Net operating cash flow in December 20X3	+700	0.7
	–300	0.3
Net operating cash flow in January 20X4	–900	1.0

Assume cash flows arise at month ends. ✓

After January 20X4, trade is expected to improve, but there is still a high degree of uncertainty in relation to the cash surpluses or deficits that will be generated in each month.

Required

Calculate the expected cash balance or overdraft of HRD at 31 January 20X4.

Explain why your answer may not be useful for short-term cash planning and outline alternative approaches that could be used.   **(5 marks)**

(e)   AM is a trading entity operating in a country where there is no sales tax. Purchases are on credit, with 70% paid in the month following the date of purchase and 30% paid in the month after that. ✗

Sales are partly on credit and partly for cash. Customers who receive credit are given 30 days to pay. On average 60% pay within 30 days, 30% pay between 30 and 60 days and 5% pay between 60 and 90 days. The balance is written off as irrecoverable. Other overheads, including salaries, are paid within the month incurred.

AM plans to purchase new equipment at the end of June 20X5, the expected cost of which is $250,000. The equipment will be purchased on 30 days credit, payable at the end of July. ✗

The cash balance on 1 May 20X5 is $96,000.

The actual/budgeted figures for the six month to July 20X5 were:

	Actual			Budgeted		
	Feb	Mar	Apr	May	Jun	Jul
	$'000	$'000	$'000	$'000	$'000	$'000
Credit sales	100	100	110	110	120	120
Cash sales	30	30	35	35	40	40
Credit purchases	45	50	50	55	55	60
Other overhead expense	40	40	40	50	50	50

Required

Prepare a monthly cash budget for the period May to July 20X5 and assess the likelihood of AM being able to pay for the equipment when it falls due. (Round all figures to the nearest $'000)   **(5 marks)**

FATP 5/05

(f)   FJ commences business on 1 April 20X8. Sales in April 20X8 were $60,000. This is forecast to increase by 2% per month.

Credit sales accounted for 50% of sales. Credit sales customers are allowed one month to pay; 75% of April credit customers paid on time. A further 20% are expected to pay after more than one month, but before two months. The remaining 5% are not expected to pay. All these percentages are expected to continue in the near future.

Calculate the total amount of cash FJ should forecast to be received in June 20X8. **(5 marks)**

FATP 5/08

+o do

(Total = 30 marks)

4 Section C: BB (FATP 11/05 – adapted) | 45 mins

BB is a private sector training entity, which provides short courses and various in-house courses for large employers.

BB's forecast financial statements for the year ended 31 December includes the following:

Forecast Statement of Financial Position at 31 December 20X5 (extract)

Current assets
Trade receivables: In-house training courses | $34,100
Bank | $12,460

Forecast Income Statement for the year ended 31 December 20X5 (extract)

Revenue: In-house training courses | $125,000

BB is preparing its budgets for the year 1 January 20X6 to 31 December 20X6, but the cash budget has not yet been completed. The Finance Director is concerned about the cash flow forecast for the first six months and has asked you, a trainee management accountant, to prepare a cash budget for the six months from January to June 20X6 from the budgeted information provided.

Budgeted revenue

Short training courses

Short training courses budgeted charge $100 per person per course.

Short courses are generally one night a week for four weeks commencing on the first of each month, except December and January.

Budgeted short course information:	Jan	Feb	Mar	Apr	May	Jun	Jul
Number of courses	0	2	3	3	4	4	4
Forecast students per course	0	10	12	12	14	13	15

BB expects to receive payment in advance of each course. Experience shows that, on average, one third of students pay one month in advance and the rest pay on the first day of the course.

In-house training courses

The exact number and type of in-house training courses is unknown at present but, during 20X6, BB is expecting to earn $130,000 spread evenly throughout the year. Based on previous experience, the following receipts are forecast:

	Jan	Feb	Mar	Apr	May	Jun
In-house training course fee receipts (including trade receivables at 31 December 20X5)	$5,000	$8,000	$10,000	$11,000	$12,000	$6,000

BB has previously experienced problems of slow payment from some large employers and is monitoring the trade receivables collection period.

Budgeted expenditure

BB employs permanent full-time members of staff to run the entity and provide key lecturing skills. Most of the trainers are part-time tutors at an hourly rate.

Budgeted wages 20X6	Jan	Feb	Mar	Apr	May	Jun
Part-time tutor wages	$0	$2,500	$4,000	$4,000	$5,000	$6,000

Permanent staff salaries are currently $4,000 a month. All full-time staff will receive an increase of 5% from 1 March 20X6.

BPP
LEARNING MEDIA

BB rents the premises for $2,500 a year, payable in quarterly instalments in January, April, July and October.

Teaching materials, printing and photocopying average $150 per short course (paid in the month of the course). The in-house courses cost, on average, $100 per month.

Budgeted payments in respect of overheads (electricity, telephone and so on) for January and April are $1,500 and for February, March, May and June are $600.

Capital expenditure in the first six months of 2006 is planned as follows:

(i)   New furniture for the managing director's office $5,000 payable in April.

(ii)   BB needs to replace all the IT equipment in one of its computer labs early in 20X6. This is currently planned to take place in April, with payment in May 20X6. The budgeted cost of the equipment is $40,000 for 20 top-of-the-range PCs and related equipment.

<u>Other information</u>

BB has negotiated an overdraft facility with the bank for an overdraft up to $5,000.

Required

(a)   Calculate BB's in-house training course trade receivables days outstanding

   (i)   according to the forecast at 31 December 20X5;

   (ii)   according to the projected figures at 30 June 20X6, assuming the revenue and cash flow budgets are implemented.   **(5 marks)**

(b)   Prepare BB's cash budget for the first six months of 20X6 (January to June) .   **(10 marks)**

(c)   Advise BB of any actions it can take to make sufficient funds available to purchase the new technology as budgeted in May 20X6.   **(5 marks)**

(d)   Explain the advantages of borrowing by means of a term loan rather than an overdraft.   **(5 marks)**

                                                                                                  (Total = 25 marks)

SHORT-TERM FINANCE

Questions 5 to 10 cover borrowing, investing, receivables, payables and managing inventory, the subject of Chapters 3 to 5 of the BPP Study Text for Paper P1.

Do Again

5 Section A: Short-term finance I   36 mins

1   DK is considering investing in government bonds. The current price of a $100 bond with 10 years to maturity is $88. The bonds have a coupon rate of 6% and repay face value of $100 at the end of the 10 years.

Calculate the yield to maturity.   **(4 marks)**

FATP 11/06

2   Which of the following could a company NOT use as a source of short-term credit?

    A   Trade credit from suppliers
    B   Bank overdraft
    C   Factoring of trade debts
    D   Mortgage on property   **(2 marks)**

3   Which one of the following statements about an overdraft facility is correct?

    A   An overdraft is a permanent loan
    B   Assets are always required as security
    C   Interest is paid on the full facility
    D   Compared with other types of loan it is quick and easy to set up   **(2 marks)**

FATP 5/08

4   Of what is the following statement a definition?

'A document issued by a bank on behalf of a customer authorising a person to draw money to a specified amount from its branches or correspondents, usually in another country, when the conditions set out in the document have been met.'

    A   Bill of exchange
    B   Export guarantee
    C   Banker's draft
    D   Letter of credit   **(2 marks)**

5   Which of the following is the LEAST IMPORTANT consideration when assessing how to invest a short-term cash surplus?

    A   Length of time for which the funds are available
    B   Maximising the return generated by the funds
    C   Ease of realisation
    D   Risk associated with calling in the investment early   **(2 marks)**

6   Which of the following services is LEAST LIKELY to be offered by a factoring company?

    A   Provision of finance by advancing, say 80% of invoice value immediately, and the remainder on settlement of the debt by the customer
    B   Taking over responsibility for administration of the client's sales ledger
    C   Deciding what credit limits customers should be given
    D   Non-recourse finance, ie taking over responsibility for bad debts   **(2 marks)**

7   KEN is awaiting the go-ahead to start its new building programme. This is likely to take place within the next 90 days, but the precise start date and timing of the cash flows are still uncertain. The company has $150,000 available in cash in anticipation of the investment. Which of the following is the LEAST APPROPRIATE use of the funds in the interim period?

    A   Investment in equities
    B   Treasury bills
    C   Bank deposits
    D   Local authority deposits   **(2 marks)**

8   BE has been offering 60 day payment terms to its customers, but now wants to improve its cash flow. BE is proposing to offer a 1.5% discount for payment within 20 days.

Assume a 365 day year and an invoice value of $1,000.

What is the effective annual interest rate that BE will incur for this action?   **(4 marks)**

FATP 11/05

(Total = 20 marks)

6   Section A: Short-term finance II   36 mins

1   A company with large amounts of surplus cash may decide to invest it in short-term money market instruments. Which of the following money market investments would carry the LOWEST interest rate?

    A   Sterling certificates of deposit (CDs)
    B   Treasury bills
    C   Finance house deposits
    D   Local authority deposits   **(2 marks)**

2   List **four** forms of short-term finance generally available to small entities.   **(2 marks)**

FATP 5/05

3   Which one of the following MOST APPROPRIATELY describes forfaiting?

    A   It is a method of providing medium-term export finance.
    B   It provides long-term finance to importers.
    C   It provides equity finance for the redemption of shares.
    D   It is the surrender of a share because of the failure to make a payment on a partly-paid share.   **(2 marks)**

4   Which of the following statements about certificates of deposit is FALSE?

    A   Certificates of deposit are negotiable instruments issued by banks.
    B   Certificates of deposit will typically have maturity periods of between three and five years.
    C   Certificates of deposit are non-negotiable.
    D   Certificates of deposit are issued in bearer form.   **(2 marks)**

5   Which of the following investments carries the highest level of risk?

    A   Local authority stocks
    B   Company loan stocks
    C   Convertible loan stocks
    D   Preference shares   **(2 marks)**

6   After a bill of exchange has been accepted, there are a number of possible actions that the drawer could take.

Which ONE of the following is NOT a possible course of action?

A   Ask the customer for immediate payment.
B   Discount the bill with a bank.
C   Hold the bill until the due date and then present it for payment.
D   Use the bill to settle a trade payable.   **(2 marks)**

FATP 5/06

7   FW holds a 91 day treasury bill, with a face value of $10,000. FW wants to sell the treasury bill, which has 40 days remaining to maturity.

The market yield for treasury bills is 6%.

Calculate the expected selling price of the treasury bill. (Assume 365 days in a year for interest calculation purposes.)   **(4 marks)**

FATP 5/08

8   A $1,000 bond has a coupon rate of 12% and will repay its face value on redemption in four year's time.

If the bond is purchased for $1,090 ex interest and held, what is its yield to maturity?   **(4 marks)**

FATP 5/08

(Total = 20 marks)

7 Section A: Short-term finance III   36 mins

1   Treasury shares are defined as

A   Equity shares sold by an entity in the period.
B   Equity shares repurchased by the issuing entity, not cancelled before the period end.
C   Non-equity shares sold by an entity in the period.
D   Equity shares repurchased by the issuing entity and cancelled before the period end.   **(2 marks)**

FATP 11/07

2   List FOUR advantages of forfaiting for an exporter.   **(4 marks)**

FATP 11/07

3   Which ONE of the following is NOT a stage in the credit cycle?

A   Negotiation of the price of the goods
B   Receipt of the customer order
C   Checking the credit limit
D   Goods despatched with delivery note   **(2 marks)**

4   DEN is considering whether to factor its sales ledger. It has been offered a 'without recourse' package by the factor at a cost of 2% sales, plus an administration fee of $5,000 per year. Annual sales are currently $1m, with bad debts of 1%. What is the annual cost of the package to DEN likely to be?

A $5,000
B $20,000
C $24,800
D $25,000   **(2 marks)**

5   GOR is considering changing its credit policy. It currently allows customers 90 days credit, but suffers bad debts amounting to 3% of its annual sales of $2m. It is proposing to reduce the credit period to 30 days, which should cause the bad debts to fall to 1% of turnover. However, it expects that this will result in a reduction in sales of 20%. This reduction will also be reflected in the level of purchases and inventory holding. What will be the effect of this on the annual financing cost? Current figures are:

Inventories (raw materials and finished goods)	$500,000
Annual purchases	$360,000
Payables	$30,000
Cost of capital	10%

   A   Saving of $46,000
   B   Increase of $46,000
   C   Saving of $36,000
   D   Increase of $36,000   **(2 marks)**

6   Z requires a rate of return of 13% each year.

   Two of Z's suppliers, Y and X are offering the following terms for immediate cash settlement.

Company	Discount	Normal settlement period
X	3%	3 months
Y	4%	4 months

   Which of the following discounts should be accepted to achieve the required rate of return?

   A   X's
   B   Y's
   C   Both X's and Y's
   D   Neither X's nor Y's   **(2 marks)**

7   The trade receivables ledger account for customer C shows the following entries:

		Debits $	Credits $
Balance brought forward		0	
10 June X6	Invoice 201	345	
19 June X6	Invoice 225	520	
27 June X6	Invoice 241	150	
3 July X6	Receipt 1009 – Invoice 201		200
10 July X6	Invoice 311	233	
4 August X6	Receipt 1122 – Invoice 225		520
6 August X6	Invoice 392	197	
18 August X6	Invoice 420	231	
30 August X6	Receipt 1310 – Invoice 311		233
7 September X6	Invoice 556	319	
21 September X6	Receipt 1501 – Invoice 392		197
30 September X6	Balance	845	

   Prepare an age analysis showing the outstanding balance on a monthly basis for customer C at 30 September 20X6.   **(4 marks)**

   FATP 11/06

8   AYS is a small domestic cleaning business. It has just acquired a new van for $12,750, which is needed urgently since the old one has been written off in an accident. The garage will not accept a company cheque on collection of the vehicle. Which of the following payment methods is the MOST APPROPRIATE for AYS to use?

   A   Cash
   B   Standing order
   C   Direct debit
   D   Banker's draft   **(2 marks)**

                                                                     (Total = 20 marks)

8 Section A: Short-term finance IV   36 marks

1   The economic order quantity formula includes the cost of placing an order. However, the Management Accountant is unsure which of the following items should be included in cost of placing an order'.

    1   Administrative costs ✓
    2   Postage ⁄
    3   Quality control cost ⁄
    4   Unit cost of products
    5   Storekeeper's salary

    Which **three** of the above would usually be regarded as part of the cost of placing an order?

    A   1, 2 and 3 only ·
    B   1, 4 and 5 only
    C   2, 3 and 4 only
    D   1, 2 and 5 only ·   (2 marks)

    FATP 5/05

2   SK sells bathroom fittings throughout the country in which it operates. In order to obtain the best price, it has decided to purchase all its annual demand of 10,000 shower units from a single supplier. RR has offered to provide the required number of showers each year under an exclusive long-term contract.

    Demand for shower units is at a constant rate all year. The cost to SK of holding one shower unit in inventory for one year is $4 plus 3% of the purchase price.

    RR is located only a few miles from the SK main showroom. It has offered to supply each shower unit at $400 with a transport charge of $200 per delivery. It has guaranteed such a regular and prompt delivery service that SK believes it will not be necessary to hold any safety inventory (that is buffer inventory) if it uses RR as its supplier.

    Using the economic order quantity model (EOQ model), calculate the optimal order size, assuming that RR is chosen as the sole supplier of shower units for SK.   (3 marks)

3   DS uses the Economic Order Quantity (EOQ) model. Demand for DS's product is 95,000 units per annum. Demand is evenly distributed throughout the year. The cost of placing an order is $15 and the cost of holding a unit of inventory for a year is $3.

    How many orders should DS make in a year?   (3 marks)

    FATP 5/07

4   KEN manufactures shopping trolleys. It produces 2,500 trolleys per year, each of which has four wheels. The wheels are purchased from a single supplier, and it costs $25 to place an order. The cost of holding a single wheel in inventory for a year is 50c. How many wheels should be ordered each time to minimise inventory costs (answer to the nearest 10)?

    A   350
    B   500
    C   710
    D   1,000   (2 marks)

5   FIN manufactures shopping trolleys. It produces 10,000 trolleys per year, each of which has four wheels. The wheels are purchased from a single supplier, and it costs $100 to place an order. The cost of holding a single wheel in inventory for a year is $2. How many orders should be placed each year to minimise inventory costs?

    A   3
    B   10
    C   14
    D   20   (2 marks)

6   STAN manufactures shopping trolleys. It produces 40,000 trolleys per year, each of which has four wheels. The wheels are purchased from a single supplier, and it costs $400 to place an order. The cost of holding a single wheel in inventory for a year is $8. How long is it between each order?

     A   1.3 weeks
     B   2.6 weeks
     C   3.9 weeks
     D   5.2 weeks   **(2 marks)**

7   Which of the following would NOT NORMALLY form part of the purchasing manager's responsibilities?

     A   Liaising with the R & D department to find suppliers for materials which are to the specifications required by the designers

     B   Locating and selecting suppliers

     C   Agreeing prices, discounts and lead times with suppliers

     D   Issuing payments to suppliers   **(2 marks)**

8   Which one of the following would NOT NORMALLY be considered a cost of holding inventory?

     A   Inventory obsolescence
     B   Insurance cost of inventories
     C   Lost interest on cash invested in inventories
     D   Loss of sales from running out of inventory   **(2 marks)**

9   Which of the following would be LEAST LIKELY to arise from the introduction of a Just-in-Time inventory ordering system?

     A   Lower inventory holding costs.
     B   Less risk of inventory shortages.
     C   More frequent deliveries.
     D   Increased dependence on suppliers.   **(2 marks)**

                                                       (Total = 20 marks)

> If you struggled with these objective test questions, go back to your BPP Study Text for Paper P1 and revise Chapters 3 to 5 before you tackle Section B and Section C type questions on managing short-term finance.

9   Section B: Short-term finance   54 mins

(a)   BH purchased a bond with a face value of $1,000 on 1 June 20X3 for $850. The bond has a coupon rate of 7%. BH intends holding the bond to its maturity on 31 May 20X8 when it will repay its face value.

     Required

     (i)   Explain the difference between the coupon rate of a security and its yield to maturity.   **(2 marks)**
     (ii)   Calculate the bond's yield to maturity.   **(3 marks)**

                                                    FATP 11/05

(b)   DH raised cash through an equity share issue to pay for a new factory it planned to construct. However, the factory contract has been delayed and payments are not expected to be required for three or four months. DH is going to invest its surplus funds until they are required.

     One of the directors of DH has identified three possible investment opportunities:

     (i)   Treasury bills issued by the central bank of DH's country. They could be purchased on 1 December 20X6 for a period of 91 days. The likely purchase price is $990 per $1,000.

     (ii)   Equities quoted on DH's local stock exchange. The stock exchange has had a good record in recent months with the equity index increasing in value for 14 consecutive months. The director recommends that DH invests in three large multinational entities each paying an annual dividend that provides an annual yield of 10% on the current share price.

(iii) DH's bank would pay 3.5% per year on money placed in a deposit account with 30 day's notice.

Required

As Assistant Management Accountant, you have been asked to prepare notes on the risk and effective yield of each of the above investment opportunities for use by the Management Accountant at the next board meeting. **(5 marks)**

FATP 11/06

(c) DF, a sports training equipment wholesaler has prepared its forecast cash flow for the next six months and has calculated that it will need $2 million additional short-term finance in three months' time.

DF has an annual gross revenue of $240 million and achieves a gross margin of 50%. It currently has the flowing outstanding working capital balances:

- $16 million trade payables
- $20 million trade receivables
- $5 million bank overdraft

DF forecasts that it will be able to repay half the $2 million within three months and the balance within a further three months.

Required

Advise DF of possible sources of funding available to it. **(5 marks)**

FATP 5/07

(d) Discuss:

(i) The significance of trade payables in a firm's working capital cycle
(ii) The dangers of over-reliance on trade credit as a source of finance **(5 marks)**

(e) *Required*

Explain the possible benefits and limitations of a Just-In-Time (JIT) purchasing system. **(5 marks)**

FATP 5/08

(f) The trade receivables ledger account for customer X is as follows:

Who owes us : (i.e. X

		Debits	Credits	Balance
01-Jul-X7	Balance b/fwd			162
12-Jul-X7	Invoice AC34	172		334
14-Jul-X7	Invoice AC112	213		547
28-Jul-X7	Invoice AC215	196		743
08-Aug-X7	Receipt RK 116 (Balance + AC34)		334	409
21-Aug-X7	Invoice AC420	330		739
03-Sep-X7	Receipt RL162 (AC215)		196	543
12-Sep-X7	Credit note CN92 (AC112)		53	490
23-Sep-X7	Invoice AC615	116		606
25-Sep-X7	Invoice AC690	204		810
05-Oct-X7	Receipt RM223 (AC420)		330	480
16-Oct-X7	Invoice AC913	233		713
25-Oct-X7	Receipt RM360 (AC615)		116	597

Required

(i) Prepare an age analysis showing the outstanding balance on a monthly basis for customer X. **(3 marks)**

(ii) Explain how an age analysis of receivables can be useful to an entity. **(2 marks)**

(Total = 30 marks)

10 Section C: CK (FATP 5/06 – adapted)   45 mins

CK is an entity that sells computer spare parts and peripherals to computer retail stores. The entity's sales and purchases accrue evenly throughout the year and inventory is managed in such a way as to give a constant inventory level throughout the year.

CK had the following figures for the year ended 31 March 20X6:

	$'000
Revenue from credit sales during the year	6,192
Purchases on credit during the year	4,128
Trade receivables balance at 31 March 20X6	1,083
Trade payables balance at 31 March 20X6	344
Inventory balance at 31 March 20X6	1,020
Cash balance at 31 March 20X6	622

50% m/p

The directors wanted working capital management improved and commissioned a consultant to prepare a report on working capital management in CK. The consultant's report indicated that efficiency savings were possible and, if the recommendations were implemented, the following changes in outstanding days would be achieved:

Trade receivables reduced to 45 days.

Suppliers would be willing to wait a total of 40 days for payment.

Inventory could be reduced by 40% (from 31 March 20X6 $ value levels) without having an adverse impact on sales.

The budgets for the year to 31 March 20X7 have been commenced, but are incomplete. Budgeted revenue from credit sales is based on the year to 31 March 20X6 figure, plus a price increase of 10% from 1 April 20X6 and a reduction of an estimated 3% in volume caused by the price increase.

Cost of sales is budgeted at the same percentage of credit sales revenue as the year to 31 March 20X6.

	$'000	
Salaries and wages are budgeted at	620	for the year
Other operating expenses budget is	432	for the year
Budgeted capital expenditure is	2,500	

The consultant's report recommended that $1,500,000 of the proposed purchase of non-current tangible assets could be leased instead of purchased. The terms of the lease would be five payments of $400,000 each, payable in advance of 1 April each year, commencing on 1 April 20X6.

The lease would be classified as a finance lease by IAS 17 *Leases*.

The implicit interest rate is 16.875%.

Required

(a) Calculate the following for CK at 31 March 20X6:

- Trade receivables days outstanding;
- Trade payables days outstanding;
- Inventory days outstanding.

(*Note*. You should base your calculations on a 365 day year)   **(3 marks)**

(b) Prepare a cash budget for the year to 31 March 20X7 based on the budgeted data and assuming CK implements the efficiency changes recommended by the consultant from 1 April 20X6.   **(10 marks)**

(c) Explain the effect on CK's cash budget if it decides to lease $1,500,000 of the non-current assets, instead of purchasing them.

(*Note*. You are **not** required to recalculate CK's cash budget)   **(2 marks)**

(d) Comment on any possible difficulties that CK may encounter when implementing the efficiency changes.   **(5 marks)**

(*Note*. All workings should be to the nearest $'000)

(e) Identify the services that may be provided by factoring organisations.   **(5 marks)**

(Total = 25 marks)

COSTING SYSTEMS

Questions 11 to 14 cover costing systems, the subjects of Chapters 6a to 7a in Part B of the BPP Study Text for Paper P1.

11 Section A: Costing systems 36 mins

1 A company operates a standard absorption costing system and absorbs fixed production overheads based on machine hours. The budgeted fixed production overheads for the company for the previous year were £660,000 and budgeted output was 220,000 units using 44,000 machine hours. During the year, the total of the fixed production overheads debited to the Fixed Production Overhead Control Account was £590,000, and the actual output of 200,000 units used 38,000 machine hours.

Fixed production overheads for that year were:

A   £90,000 under absorbed
B   £60,000 under absorbed
C   £20,000 under absorbed
D   £10,000 over absorbed

(2 marks)

MAPE 11/08

2 When comparing the profits reported under absorption costing and marginal costing during a period when the level of inventory increased:

A   Absorption costing profits will be higher and closing inventory valuations lower than those under marginal costing.

B   Absorption costing profits will be higher and closing inventory valuations higher than those under marginal costing.

C   Marginal costing profits will be higher and closing inventory valuations lower than those under absorption costing.

D   Marginal costing profits will be higher and closing inventory valuations higher than those under absorption costing.

(2 marks)

3 Summary results for Y Limited for March are shown below.

	£'000	Units
Sales revenue	820	
Variable production costs	300	
Variable selling costs	105	
Fixed production costs	180	
Fixed selling costs	110	
Production in March		1,000
Opening inventory		0
Closing inventory		150

Using marginal costing, the profit for March was

A   £170,000
B   £185,750
C   £197,000
D   £229,250

(2 marks)

MAPE 5/05

4   PH Ltd produces a single product and currently uses absorption costing for its internal management accounting reports. The fixed production overhead absorption rate is £34 per unit. Opening inventories for the year were 100 units and closing inventories were 180 units. The company's management accountant is considering a switch to marginal costing as the inventory valuation basis.

If marginal costing were used, the marginal costing profit for the year, compared with the profit calculated by absorption costing, would be:

A   £2,720 lower
B   £2,720 higher
C   £3,400 lower
D   £3,400 higher   (2 marks)

5   An attainable standard is:

A   A standard that is attainable under perfect operating conditions. No allowances are made for losses, waste and inefficiencies.   IDEAL.

B   A standard that is attainable under efficient operating conditions. Some allowance is made for losses, waste and inefficiencies, based on proper use of materials and machines.

C   A standard that is attainable under current operating conditions. CURRENT.

D   A standard that is kept unaltered over a long period of time.   BASIC

                                                                                (2 marks)

6   A company's normal output is 1,000 units each period and budgeted fixed costs are incurred evenly throughout the year. The following production levels and associated production costs were recorded for two recent periods.

Period no.	Production (units)	Production costs £
6	1,210	3,394
9	990	3,086

In a period when production volume was 1,040 units and sales volume was 1,200 units a profit of £8,160 was reported using marginal costing.

Calculate the profit that would be reported for the period using an absorption costing system.

                                                                                (3 marks)

7   A company produces and sells one type of product. The details for last year were as follows:

Production and Sales

	Budget	Actual
Production (units)	25,000	22,000
Sales (units)	23,000	20,000

There was no inventory at the start of the year.

Selling price and costs

	Budget $	Actual $
Selling price per unit	70	70
Variable costs per unit	55	55
Fixed production overhead	130,000	118,000
Fixed selling costs	75,000	75,000

Calculate the actual profit for the year that would be reported using:

(i)   Marginal costing;
(ii)   Absorption costing.   (4 marks)

MAPE 11/08

8   S plc produces and sells three products, X, Y and Z. It has contracts to supply products X and Y, which will utilise all of the specific materials that are available to make these two products during the next period. The revenue these contracts will generate and the contribution to sales (C/S) ratios of products X and Y are as follows:

	Product X	Product Y
Revenue	£10 million	£20 million
C/S ratio	15%	10%

Product Z has a C/S ratio of 25%.

The total fixed costs of S plc are £5·5 million during the next period and management have budgeted to earn a profit of £1 million.

Calculate the revenue that needs to be generated by Product Z for S plc to achieve the budgeted profit.

(3 marks)

MAPE 5/06

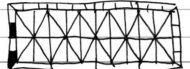

(Total = 20 marks)

If you struggled with these objective test questions, go back to your BPP Study Text for Paper P1 and revise Chapters 6a to 7a before you tackle Section B and Section C type questions on costing systems.

12 Section B: Costing systems   54 mins

(a)   Explain the advantages of using marginal costing as the basis of providing managers with information for decision making.   **(5 marks)**

(b)   Explain why absorption costing is usually considered to be unsuitable for decision making. Justify your answer.   **(5 marks)**

(c)   Y plc has two production departments, the Assembly and Painting and two service departments, Stores and Maintenance. Maintenance provides the following service to the production and service departments: 40% to Assembly, 45% to Painting and 15% to Stores.

Stores provides: 60% to Assembly and 40% to Painting.

The budgeted fixed production overheads for the period are as follows:

Assembly	£200,000
Painting	£300,000
Stores	£100,000
Maintenance	£80,000

The budgeted output is 100,000 units.

At the end of the year after apportioning the service department overheads, the total overheads debited to the Assembly department's fixed production overhead control were £360,000.

The actual output achieved was 120,000 units.

Calculate the over/under absorption of fixed overheads for the Assembly department.   **(5 marks)**

(d)   Explain the terms overhead allocation and overhead apportionment.   **(5 marks)**

(e)   Explain the term overhead absorption rate and briefly discuss how an entity may select a suitable absorption rate.   **(5 marks)**

(f)   Revenue and cost details for a company's single product are as follows.

	£ per unit	£ per unit
Sales price		27
Variable cost	15	
Fixed cost	8	
	23	
Profit		4

Fixed costs are absorbed based on the company's normal activity, which is also the company's budgeted sales value for each period.

Last period there were no changes in inventory and the company achieved a margin of safety of 20 per cent of the actual sales volume. Fixed costs were over-absorbed by £2,400.

(i) Calculate the breakeven point in units for each period.

(ii) Calculate the number of units to be produced and sold to achieve a profit of £6,600 for the period.

(5 marks)

(Total = 30 marks)

13 Section B: Costing systems   54 mins

(a) Explain the term standard costing and briefly discuss how you would set standards for material costs.

(5 marks)

(b) State and briefly explain the four types of standards and their behavioural implications.   **(5 marks)**

(c) State and briefly explain the four dimensions of McDonaldisation.   **(5 marks)**

(d) Discuss the similarities and differences between budgets and standards.   **(5 marks)**

(e) Briefly explain three limitations of standard costing in the modern business environment.   **(5 marks)**

(f) Explain how the use of diagnostic related groups enables the principles of standard costing to be applied in the health service.

(5 marks)

(Total = 30 marks)

14 Section C: Marginal and absorption reconciliation   45 mins

The following budgeted profit statement has been prepared using absorption costing principles.

	January to June 20X7		July to December 20X7	
	£'000	£'000	£'000	£'000
Sales		540		360
Opening inventory	100		160	
Production costs:				
Direct materials	108		36	
Direct labour	162		54	
Overhead	90		30	
	460		280	
Closing inventory	160		80	
		300		200
Gross profit		240		160
Production overhead:				
(Over)/under absorption	(12)		12	
Selling costs	50		50	
Distribution costs	45		40	
Administration costs	80		80	
		163		182
Net profit		77		(22)
Sales units	15,000		10,000	
Production units	18,000		6,000	

The members of the management team are concerned by the significant change in profitability between the two six-month periods. As management accountant, you have analysed the data upon which the above budget statement has been produced, with the following results.

- The production overhead cost comprises both a fixed and a variable element. The latter appears to be dependent on the number of units produced. The fixed element of the cost is expected to be incurred at a constant rate throughout the year.

- The selling costs are fixed.

- The distribution cost comprises both fixed and variable elements. The latter appears to be dependent on the number of units sold. The fixed element of the cost is expected to be incurred at a constant rate throughout the year.

- The administration costs are fixed.

Required

(a)   Present the above budgeted profit statement in marginal costing format.   **(10 marks)**

(b)   Reconcile each of the six-monthly profit/loss values reported respectively under marginal and absorption costing.   **(5 marks)**

(c)   Reconcile the six-monthly profit for January to June 20X7 from the absorption costing statement with the six-monthly loss for July to December 20X7 from the absorption costing statement.   **(5 marks)**

(d)   Calculate the annual number of units required to breakeven.   **(5 marks)**

                                                                                                              (Total = 25 marks)

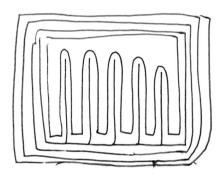

standards

cwculdoilily   human element.
control

efficiency   1 point to anothr --
predictability   Same outlet
                    everywhere

   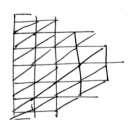

VARIANCE ANALYSIS

Questions 15 to 27 cover variance analysis, the subject of chapters 7b to 8 in Part B of the BPP Study Text for Paper P1.

---

15   Section A: Variance analysis   36 mins

1   The fixed overhead volume variance is defined as:

   A   The difference between the budgeted value of the fixed overheads and the standard fixed overheads absorbed by actual production.

   B   The difference between the standard fixed overhead cost specified for the production achieved, and the actual fixed overhead cost incurred.

   C   The difference between budgeted and actual fixed overhead expenditure.

   D   The difference between the standard fixed overhead cost specified in the original budget and the same volume of fixed overheads, but at the actual prices incurred. ✗   **(2 marks)**

MAPE 5/05

---

2   Which ONE of the following would **NOT** explain a favourable direct materials usage variance?

   A   Using a higher quality of materials than that specified in the standard. ✓

   B   A reduction in materials wastage rates. ✓

   C   An increase in suppliers' quality control checks.

   D   Achieving a lower output volume than budgeted. ✓   **(2 marks)**

MAPE 11/08

The following data are given for sub-questions 3 and 4 below

X40 is one of many items produced by the manufacturing division. Its standard cost is based on estimated production of 10,000 units per month. The standard cost schedule for one unit of X40 shows that 2 hours of direct labour are required at £15 per labour hour. The variable overhead rate is £6 per direct labour hour. During April, 11,000 units were produced; 24,000 direct labour hours were worked and charged; £336,000 was spent on direct labour; and £180,000 was spent on variable overheads.

---

3   The direct labour rate variance for April is:

   A   £20,000 Favourable
   B   £22,000 Favourable
   C   £24,000 Adverse
   D   £24,000 Favourable   **(2 marks)**

---

4   The variable overhead efficiency variance for April is:

   A   £12,000 Adverse
   B   £12,000 Favourable
   C   £15,000 Adverse
   D   £15,000 Favourable   **(2 marks)**

MAPE 5/05

---

5 AD Ltd manufactures and sells a single product, E, and uses a standard absorption costing system. Standard cost and selling price details for product E are as follows.

	£ per unit
Variable cost	8
Fixed cost	2
	10
Standard profit	5
Standard selling price	15

The sales volume variance reported for last period was £9,000 adverse.

AD Ltd is considering using standard marginal costing as the basis for variance reporting in future. What would be the correct sales volume variance to be shown in a marginal costing operating statement for last period? **(3 marks)**

The following data are given for questions 6 and 7 below

SW plc manufactures a product known as the TRD100 by mixing two materials. The standard material cost per unit of the TRD100 is as follows:

			£
Material X	12 litres @	£2·50	30
Material Y	18 litres @	£3·00	54

In October 20X3, the actual mix used was 984 litres of X and 1,230 litres of Y. The actual output was 72 units of TRD100.

6 Calculate the total material mix variance for October 20X3. **(3 marks)**

MAPE Pilot Paper

7 Calculate the total material yield variance for October 20X3. **(2 marks)**

MAPE Pilot Paper

8 D Limited manufactures and sells musical instruments, and uses a standard cost system. The budget for production and sale of one particular drum for April was 600 units at a selling price of £72 each. When the sales director reviewed the results for April in the light of the market conditions that had been experienced during the month, she believed that D Limited should have sold 600 units of this drum at a price of £82 each. The actual sales achieved were 600 units at £86 per unit.

Calculate the following variances for this particular drum for April:

(a) Selling price planning variance
(b) Selling price operating variance

(4 marks)

MAPE 5/05

(Total = 20 marks)

In you struggled with these objective test questions, go back to your BPP Study Text for Paper P1 and revise chapters 7b to 8 before you tackle Section B and Section C type questions on variance analysis.

BPP
LEARNING MEDIA

16   Section B: Variance analysis   54 mins

(a)   You are provided with the following information about product B

	Budget	Actual
Sales (units)	72,000	64,000
Selling price	£10 per unit	£8.40 per unit
Variable cost	£6 per unit	£6.20 per unit

Using a contribution approach, calculate appropriate variances and comment briefly on the possible causes of those variances.   **(5 marks)**

(b)   A company uses variance analysis to monitor the performance of the team of workers which assembles Product M. Details of the budgeted and actual performance of the team for last period were as follows:

	Budget	Actual
Output of product M	600 units	680 units
Wage rate	£30 per hour	£32 per hour
Labour hours	900 hours	1,070 hours

It has now been established that the standard wage rate should have been £31.20 per hour.

(i)   Calculate the labour rate planning variance and calculate the operational labour efficiency variance.

(ii)   Explain the major benefit of analysing variances into planning and operational components.

(5 marks)

`MAPE 5/07`

(c)   Briefly explain three factors that should be considered before deciding to investigate a variance. **(5 marks)**

`MAPE 5/07`

(d)   An analysis of past output has shown that batches have a mean weight of 90 kg and that the weights conform to the normal distribution with a standard deviation of 10 kg. The company has a policy to investigate variances that fall outside the range that includes 95% of outcomes. In September one sample batch weighed 110 kg.

(i)   Calculate whether the material usage variance for this batch should be investigated according to the company policy described above.   **(3 marks)**

(ii)   Discuss two other important factors that should be taken into account when deciding whether to investigate this variance.   **(2 marks)**

`MAPE 11/05`

(e)   A multi-national company manufactures and sells a wide range of digital equipment. The company is structured into three Divisions: Computers, Audio-visual and Photographic.

The manager of the Photographic Division was concerned that the Division was falling behind its competitors in terms of financial returns and market share, and has implemented strategies to improve the situation. An external benchmarking exercise was undertaken to try to establish the position of the Division in relation to its competitors in a number of key areas. It has now been suggested that the Division should also carry out an internal benchmarking exercise.

Explain **three** reasons why internal benchmarking may provide information that is more useful to the Manager of the Photographic Division, in terms of monitoring and improving performance, than that provided by external benchmarking.   **(5 marks)**

`MAPE 5/08 adapted`

(f)   B Ltd uses two grades of labour to manufacture product W. The standard labour cost of product W is as follows.

Labour grade		£ per unit
I	7 hours × £12	84
II	12 hours × £15	180
		264

During control period 3, 522 units of W were manufactured using 3,398 hours of grade I labour and 6,786 hours of grade II labour. ✓

Valuing mix variances at standard rates, what are the labour mix and yield variances that arose in control period 3? **(5 marks)**

(Total = 30 marks)

---

17 Section C: CP (5/10) 45 mins

A company manufactures a range of industrial cleaning products from its automated factory in Western Europe. The company has recently introduced a just-in-time system for raw material purchases.

The company uses a standard absorption costing system for planning and control purposes although this system is now under review.

The following budget data relate to the production of one of its major products CP1 for April. The product is manufactured by mixing two raw materials ETH1 and RXY2.

Standard cost per kg of Product CP1

	Quantity	Cost/kg	Cost
Raw material input			
ETH1	0.30kg	$18.00	$5.40
RXY2	0.70kg	$6.00	$4.20
Raw material cost per kg of input			$9.60
Yield			96%
Raw materials cost per kg of output			$10.00
Fixed production overheads per kg of output			$4.00
Total standard cost per kg of output			$14.00

Budget data for product CP1 for the period is detailed below:-

* Sales - 72,000kg ✓
* Production - 70,000kg
* Opening inventory - 2,000kg of CP1 (valued at $28,000)
* Selling price per kg - $20·00 ✓
* Fixed production overheads - $280,000

The fixed production overhead absorption rate is based on the budgeted number of kilograms produced.

Actual data for product CP1 for the period was as follows:

* Sales - 71,000kg
* Production - 69,000kg
* Selling price per kg - $20·30
* Fixed production overheads incurred - $278,000
* Cost per kg of ETH1 - $18·10
* Cost per kg of RXY2 - $5·80
* Input of ETH1 - 22,100kg ~
* Input of RXY2 – 47,900kg

Required

(a) Produce a statement that reconciles the budgeted and actual profit for CP1 for April showing the variances in as much detail as possible. **(19 marks)**

(b) Discuss three reasons why the use of a standard costing system is considered inappropriate in a company that operates in an advanced manufacturing technology environment. **(6 marks)**

(Total = 25 marks)

18   Section C: Hospital (Specimen paper)   45 mins

A hospital specialises in the provision of a particular surgical procedure. The hospital seeks to provide a value-for-money service. In order to do this it hires teams of specialist staff on a sub-contract basis and pays them only for the hours that they have worked. The hospital uses a standard marginal costing system.

Overhead costs are attributed to the procedures based on direct labour cost.

Budget for November

Budgeted number of procedures to be performed: 20 procedures

Standard marginal cost per procedure:

		$
Team fee	2 hours @ $1,500 per hour	3,000
Variable overheads	65% of team fee	1,950
		4,950

The budgeted fixed overheads for November were $48,000

Actual results for November Procedures performed: 22 procedures

Costs incurred:

   Team fees: the team worked 47 hours and were paid a total of $75,400. ⌊

   Variable overheads: $48,000 ⊢

   Fixed overheads: $46,000 ⊬

Required

(a)   Prepare a statement which reconciles the original budget cost for November and the actual costs incurred, in as much detail as possible.   **(14 marks)**

(b)   It has now been realised that the budgeted rate for the team should have been $1,625 per hour. Calculate the planning variance and the operational rate and efficiency variances for the team fees for November.   **(6 marks)**

(c)   Explain why budgetary control and standard costing are most effective when used together as a means of cost control in service-based organisations.   **(5 marks)**

                                                                                               (Total = 25 marks)

19   Section C: X & Y (MAPE 5/09 & 11/09 – adapted)   45 mins

A company manufactures many different products. Each product has a Product Manager. The company's management information system produces cost reports for each of the products that are made.

An analysis of previous reports has revealed the following information for Product X:

Units produced	Average variable cost per unit	Total product-specific fixed costs	Head office costs
	$	$'000	$'000
5,000	160	500	300
10,000	150	500	600
15,000	140	800	900
20,000	140	800	1,200
25,000	155	1,100	1,500
30,000	170	1,100	1,800

Required

(a)   Explain, for each of the three costs in the above table, possible reasons for the cost/volume relationships.   **(6 marks)**

Budgeting and actual information for Product Y for the previous period was as follows:

	Budget	Actual
Output	80,000 units	76,000 units
Direct materials	480,000 kg	430,000 kg
Direct labour	200,000 hours •	196,000 hours
	$	$
Direct materials	960,000	924,500
Direct labour	1,600,000 •	1,626,800
Fixed production overheads	640,000	590,000

The company uses standard absorption costing.

Required

(b) Produce a statement that reconciles the standard and actual total costs for the previous period's output and shows the variances in as much detail as possible. **(11 marks)**

(c) It has now been realised that the standard price of the direct materials used to manufacture Product Y in the previous period should have been $2.10 per kg.

   (i) Calculate the direct materials planning variance.

   (ii) Calculate the operational direct materials price and usage variances. **(4 marks)**

(d) Explain the importance to management, for planning and control purposes, of the differing definitions of "variable" costs offered by traditional costing methods and activity based costing. **(4 marks)**

(Total = 25 marks)

20 Section C: Chemical fertilisers (MAPE 11/08 – adapted)   45 mins

A company manufactures two types of fertilizer (FA and FB). The company uses a standard costing system for planning and control purposes. Standards are set annually but budgets and variance reports are prepared each period.

Chemicals

Three chemicals (C1, C2 and C3) are used to make the fertilizers. C2 and C3 can be input directly to the manufacturing process but C1 has to be treated before it can be used. The treatment results in a loss of 30% of the chemicals treated. There are no further losses in the manufacturing process.

Details of the standards for the chemicals are as follows:

	C1	C2	C3
Price per kg	$8	$15	$12
Treatment loss	30%		
Content of finished product:			
per unit of FA	0·20 kg	0·15 kg	Nil
per unit of FB	0·20 kg	Nil	0·25 kg

Inventory policies

Chemicals: end of period holdings must be equal to 50% of the following period's requirements.

Treated C1 is used immediately. There are never any inventories of treated C1 at the start or end of any period.

Fertilizers: no finished products are to be held.

Period 1: output and sales

	Budget	Actual
FA	40,000 units	38,000 units
FB	24,000 units	25,000 units

Periods 2 and 3: sales budgets

	Period 2	Period 3
FA	40,000 units	44,000 units

FB	24,000 units	33,000 units

Required

(a) During Period 1, the quantity of C1 used was 17,740 kg. Calculate for Period 1 for C1:

  (i) The materials usage variance for the whole process
  (ii) The treatment loss percentage **(6 marks)**

(b) In Period 1, the company purchased and used 6,450 kg of C3. The cost of this purchase was $94,000. It has now been realised that the standard price of C3 should have been $14·50 per kg for Period 1.

  (i) Calculate the planning variance, and the operational price and usage variances for C3 for Period 1. **(7 marks)**
  (ii) Explain two problems associated with the reporting of planning variances. **(3 marks)**

(c) 'Variance analysis presents results after the actual events have taken place and therefore it is of little use to management for planning and control purposes, particularly in a modern manufacturing environment'.

  Discuss the above statement. **(9 marks)**

(Total = 25 marks)

21 Section C: FX (MAPE 5/08)   45 mins

The newly appointed Managing Director of FX has received the variance report for Month 6, which is shown below.

Month 6 variance report

Output and Sales for Month 6. Budget 1,000 units. Actual 1,200 units

	£	£	£
Budgeted contribution			90,000
Budgeted fixed costs			70,000
Budgeted profit			20,000
Volume variance			18,000
Expected profit on actual sales			38,000
Sales price variance			12,000

Production variances	Favourable	Adverse	
Materials price		6,300	
Materials usage		6,000	
Labour rate	5,040		
Labour efficiency		2,400	
Variable overhead expenditure	–	–	
Variable overhead efficiency		1,200	
Fixed overhead		4,000	
	5,040	19,900	14,860
Actual profit			11,140

Background information (not seen by the Managing Director)

The report did not include any other information. Details relating to the company and the product that it makes are given below.

FX produces one type of product. It operates a standard marginal costing system.

The standard unit cost and price of the product is as follows.

	£	£
Selling price		250
Direct material (5 kg at £20)	100	
Direct labour (4 hours at £10)	40	
Variable overheads (4 hours at £5)	20	160
Contribution		90

The variable overhead absorption rate is based on direct labour hours.

The company has budgeted fixed overheads of £70,000 per month.

Budgeted sales and production levels are 1,000 units per month.

Month 6

The company has just completed Month 6 of its operations. Extracts from its records show:

1   1,200 units were produced and sold.
2   The actual direct materials purchased and used was 6,300 kg costing £132,300
3   The actual direct labour hours worked were 5,040 hours.

Required

(a)   Prepare a report for the Managing Director of FX that explains and interprets the Month 6 variance report. The Managing Director has recently joined the company and has very little previous financial experience.

(17 marks)

(b)   The Managing Director was concerned about the material price variance and its cause. He discovered that a shortage of materials had caused the market price to rise to £23 per kg.

In view of the additional information calculate for Direct Materials:

- The total variance
- The planning variance
- The two operational variances   **(8 marks)**

(Total = 25 marks)

---

22 Section C: Product P (MAPE 11/06 – adapted)   45 mins

X Ltd uses an automated manufacturing process to produce an industrial chemical, Product P. X Ltd operates a standard marginal costing system. The standard cost data for Product P is as follows:

Standard cost per unit of Product P

Materials				
A	10 kgs	@ £15 per kilo	£150	
B	8 kgs	@ £8 per kilo	£64	
C	5 kgs	@ £4 per kilo	£20	*Budget*
	23 kgs			*1 space.*
Total standard marginal cost			£234	*421.2*
Budgeted fixed production overhead			£350,000.	

In order to arrive at the budgeted selling price for Product P the company adds 80% mark-up to the standard marginal cost. The company budgeted to produce and sell 5,000 units of Product P in the period. There were no budgeted inventories of Product P.

The actual results for the period were as follows:

Actual production and sales		5,450 units
Actual sales price		£445 per unit
Material usage and cost		
A	43,000 kgs	£688,000
B	37,000 kgs	£277,500
C	23,500 kgs	£99,875
	103,500 kgs	
Fixed production overheads		£385,000

Required

(a)   Prepare an operating statement which reconciles the budgeted profit to the actual profit for the period. (The statement should include the material mix and material yield variances.)   **(12 marks)**

(b)   The production manager of X Ltd is new to the job and has very little experience of management information. Write a brief report to the production manager of X Ltd that:

(i)   Interprets the material price, mix and yield variances.
(ii)   Discusses the merits, or otherwise, of calculating the materials mix and yield variances for X Ltd.

(8 marks)

(c)   The variances are not always calculated immediately at X Ltd. Explain the advantages of calculating the material price variance at the time of purchase.   **(5 marks)**

(Total = 25 marks)

ction C: RBF Transport Ltd   45 mins

Transport Ltd, a haulage contractor, operates a standard costing system and has prepared the following report for April 20X9.

Operating statement

	£	£	£
Budgeted profit			8,000
Sales volume profit variance			880 (A)
			7,120
Selling price variance			3,560 (F)
			10,680

Cost variances	(A)	(F)	
Direct labour – rate		1,086	
– efficiency	240		
Fuel – price	420		
– usage	1,280		
Variable overhead – expenditure		280	
– efficiency	180		
Fixed overhead – expenditure		400	
– volume	1,760		
	3,880	1,766	2,114 (A)
Actual profit			8,566

The company uses delivery miles as its cost unit, and the following details have been taken from the budget working papers for April 20X9.

- Expected activity   200,000 delivery miles
- Charge to customers   £0.30 per delivery mile
- Expected variable cost per delivery mile:

Direct labour (0.02 hours)	£0.08
Fuel (0.1 litres)	£0.04
Variable overhead (0.02 hours)	£0.06

The following additional information has been determined from the actual accounting records for April 20X9.

- Fixed overhead cost   £15,600
- Fuel price   £0.42 per litre
- Direct labour hours   3,620

Required

(a) Calculate the following for April 20X9.

    (i) The actual number of delivery miles
    (ii) The actual direct labour rate per hour
    (iii) The actual number of litres of fuel consumed
    (iv) The actual variable overhead expenditure   **(16 marks)**

(b) Prepare a report, addressed to the transport operations manager, explaining the different types of standard which may be set, and the importance of keeping standards meaningful and relevant. **(9 marks)**

                                                     (Total = 25 marks)

24 Section C: POC Ltd   45 mins

POC Ltd has one product which requires inputs from three types of material to produce batches of product S. Standard cost details for a single batch are shown below.

	Materials		Labour	
				Standard
	Standard	*Standard*	*Standard*	*rate per*
Material type	*input*	*price per kg*	*input*	*Hour*
	Kgs	£	Hrs	£
S1	8	0.3	1	5.00
S2	5	0.5		
S3	3	0.4		

Standard loss of 10% of input is expected. Actual production was 15,408 kgs for the previous week. Details of the materials used are as follows.

Actual material used (kg)

S1	8,284
S2	7,535
S3	3,334

Total labour cost for the week was £6,916 for 1,235 hours worked.

Required

(a)   Calculate the following.

    (i)   Total material mix, yield and usage variances   **(10 marks)**

    (ii)   Labour rate and efficiency variances   **(4 marks)**

(b)   Write a report to management which explains and interprets your results in part (a). The report should pay particular attention to the following.

    (i)   Explaining what is meant by mix and yield variances in respect of materials

    (ii)   Possible reasons for all the results you have derived   **(11 marks)**

                                                      (Total = 25 marks)

25 Section C: NFL Ltd   45 mins

NFL Ltd produces three models of desk. The company's financial controller prepared the following statements for the month of June 20X3.

	Model 1	*Model 2*	*Model 3*
Standard labour (hours)	16	20	24
	£	£	£
Unit selling price	220	290	400
Material costs	44	60	87
Labour costs	80	100	120
Overheads	100	125	150
Profit/(loss)	(4)	5	43

Budget for June 20X3

	£
Sales revenue	14,660
Material costs	3,030
Labour costs	5,000
Variable overheads	1,250
Fixed overheads	5,000
Profit	380
Model 1 unit sales	30
Model 2 unit sales	14
Model 3 unit sales	10

Note. Overheads are absorbed on a labour hour basis.

In June 20X3 the actual results were as follows.

Operating statement for June 20X3

	Notes	£
Sales revenue		17,480
Material costs	(i)	3,538
Labour costs (1,180 labour hours)	(ii)	5,900
Variable overheads		1,600
Fixed overheads		6,200
Profit		242
Model 1 unit sales		40
Model 2 unit sales		12
Model 3 unit sales		15

(i)   During June 20X3 all sales were at standard price with the exception of sales of Executive desks (Model 1) which were all at a unit selling price of £200 under the terms of a special promotion.

(ii)   At the start of June 20X3, management negotiated a job security package with the workforce in exchange for a promised 5% increase in production efficiency – that is, that the workers would increase output per hour by 5%.

Required

(a)   Calculate the following variances for inclusion in the financial control report – sales volume, selling price and labour efficiency (split into operational and planning components).   **(12 marks)**

(b)   Explain the meaning, significance and use of the planning and operational variances you have calculated in your answers to part (a) above.   **(8 marks)**

(c)   FG Ltd budgeted to produce 2,800 units of product A during the latest period. The standard labour cost of product A was set at £15 (3 hours at £5 per hour). After a labour dispute during the period, the average hourly rate for labour was increased. During the period, 2,800 units of product A were produced and the labour cost was £50,032 for 8,480 hours worked.

In retrospect, management decide that a more realistic standard rate for labour would have been £6 per hour.

What are the total planning and operational variances relating to labour?   **(5 marks)**

(Total = 25 marks)

26   Section C: M plc   45 mins

M plc uses a standard absorption costing system and values its inventories of raw materials and finished products at standard cost.

M plc produces and sells two products. The standard cost and standard selling price details are as follows.

	Product X $ per unit	Product Y $ per unit
Direct material ($5 per kg)	62.50	27.50
Direct labour ($8 per hour)	24.00	40.00
Fixed production overhead *	36.00	60.00
Total production cost	122.50	127.50
Standard profit	30.90	33.50
Standard selling price	153.40	161.00

* Absorption rate based on standard labour hours

Budgeted and actual production and sales units for October 20X3 were as follows.

	Budget Product X	Budget Product Y	Actual Product X	Actual Product Y
Production	8,500	11,500	9,000	9,500
Sales	7,600	11,000	8,300	9,000

The budgeted output and the budgeted fixed production overhead costs for October were both expected to be one-twelfth of their annual totals.

Actual data for October were as follows.

		$
Direct material purchases	180,000 kgs costing	1,150,400
Direct materials used	174,500 kgs	
Direct labour hours	82,500 hours costing	690,320
Fixed production overhead		1,200,780
Sales revenues:		
Product X		1,260,000
Product Y		1,430,000

An analysis of the direct labour hours shows that of the 82,500 hours that were paid for, 2,670 were idle time due to a machinery breakdown.

There were no inventories of direct materials or finished products (planned or actual) at the start of October.

Required

(a)   Calculate the budgeted profit/loss for October.   **(2 marks)**

(b)   Calculate the actual profit/loss for October.   **(4 marks)**

(c)   The management accountant has started to reconcile the budgeted and actual profits and has already calculated the following variances.

Direct material price variance $250,400 Adverse
Direct material usage variance $48,750 Adverse
Direct labour rate variance $30,320 Adverse

Required

Prepare a statement that reconciles the budgeted and actual profit/loss for October, showing the variances in as much detail as possible from the information provided.   **(19 marks)**

(Total = 25 marks)

27   Section C: RJ (MAPE 5/07 – adapted)   45 mins

RJ produces and sells two high performance motor cars: Car X and Car Y. The company operates a standard absorption costing system. The company's budgeted operating statement for the year ending 30 June 20X8 and supporting information is given below:

Operating statement year ending 30 June 20X8

	Car X $000	Car Y $000	Total $000
Sales	52,500	105,000	157,500
Production cost of sales	40,000	82,250	122,250
Gross profit	12,500	22,750	35,250
Administration costs			
Variable	6,300	12,600	18,900
Fixed	7,000	9,000	16,000
Profit/(loss)	(800)	1,150	350

The production cost of sales for each car was calculated using the following values:

	Car X		Car Y	
	Units	$000	Units	$000
Opening inventory	200	8,000	250	11,750
Production	1,100	44,000	1,600	75,200
Closing inventory	300	12,000	100	4,700
Cost of sales	1,000	40,000	1,750	82,250

Production costs

The production costs are made up of direct materials, direct labour, and fixed production overhead. The fixed production overhead is general production overhead (it is not product specific). The total budgeted fixed production overhead is $35,000,000 and is absorbed using a machine hour rate. It takes 200 machine hours to produce one Car X and 300 machine hours to produce one Car Y.

Administration costs

The fixed administration costs include the costs of specific marketing campaigns: $2,000,000 for Car X and $4,000,000 for Car Y.

Required

(a)   Produce the budgeted operating statement in a marginal costing format.   **(7 marks)**

(b)   Reconcile the total budgeted absorption costing profit with the total budgeted marginal costing profit as shown in the statement you produced in part (a).   **(5 marks)**

The company is considering changing to an activity based costing system. The company has analysed the budgeted fixed production overheads and found that the costs for various activities are as follows:

	$000
Machining costs	7,000
Set up costs	12,000
Quality inspections	7,020
Stores receiving	3,480
Stores issues	5,500
	35,000

The analysis also revealed the following information:

	Car X	Car Y
Budgeted production (number of cars)	1,100	1,600
Cars per production run	10	40
Inspections per production run	20	80
Number of component deliveries during the year	492	900
Number of issues from stores	4,000	7,000

Required

(c)   Calculate the budgeted production cost of one Car X and one Car Y using the activity based costing information provided above.   **(13 marks)**

(Total = 25 marks)

MODERN BUSINESS ENVIRONMENT AND COSTING SYSTEMS

Questions 28 to 32 cover costing systems and the modern business environment, the subject of Chapters 9 to 12 in Part B of the BPP Study Text for Paper P1.

28 Section A: Modern business environment and costing systems
36 mins

1   MN plc uses a Just-in-Time (JIT) system and backflush accounting. It does not use a raw material inventory control account. During April, 1,000 units were produced and sold. The standard cost per unit is £100: this includes materials of £45.

During April, conversion costs of £60,000 were incurred.

What was the debit balance on the cost of goods sold account for April?

A   £90,000
B   £95,000
C   £105,000
D   £110,000   **(2 marks)**

2   Definition A: 'A technique where the primary goal is to maximise throughput while simultaneously maintaining or decreasing inventory and operating costs.'

Definition B: 'A system whose objective is to produce or procure products or components as they are required by a customer or for use, rather than for inventory.'

Which of the following pairs of terms correctly matches the definitions A and B above?

	Definition A	Definition B
A	Manufacturing resource planning	Just-in-time
B	Enterprise resource planning	Material requirements planning
C	Optimised production technology	Enterprise resource planning
D	Optimised production technology	Just-in-time

(2 marks)

`MAPE 5/05`

3   Which of the following statements is/are true?

(i)   Computer-integrated manufacturing (CIM) brings together advanced manufacturing technology and modern quality control into a single computerised coherent system.

(ii)   Flexible manufacturing systems (FMS) are simple systems with low levels of automation that offer great flexibility through a skilled workforce working in teams.

(iii) Electronic data interchange (EDI) is primarily designed to allow the operating units in an organisation to communicate immediately and automatically with the sales and purchasing functions within the organisation.

A   (i) only
B   (i) and (ii) only
C   (i) and (iii) only
D   (ii) and (iii) only   **(2 marks)**

`MAPE 5/05`

The following data are given for sub-questions 4 to 6 below

SM makes two products, Z1 and Z2. Its machines can only work on one product at a time. The two products are worked on in two departments by differing grades of labour. The labour requirements for the two products are as follows:

	Minutes per unit of product Z1	Z2
Department 1	12	16
Department 2	20	15

There is currently a shortage of labour and the maximum times available each day in Departments 1 and 2 are 480 minutes and 840 minutes, respectively.

The current selling prices and costs for the two products are shown below:

	Z1 £ per unit	Z2 £ per unit
Selling price	50.00	65.00
Direct materials	10.00	15.00
Direct labour	10.40	6.20
Variable overheads	6.40	9.20
Fixed overheads	12.80	18.40
Profit per unit	10.40	16.20

As part of the budget-setting process, SM needs to know the optimum output levels. All output is sold.

---

4   Calculate the maximum number of each product that could be produced each day, and identify the limiting factor/bottleneck. **(3 marks)**

MAPE 5/05

---

5   Using traditional contribution analysis, calculate the 'profit-maximising' output each day, and the contribution at this level of output. **(3 marks)**

MAPE 5/05

---

6   Using a throughput approach, calculate the 'throughput-maximising' output each day, and the 'throughput contribution' at this level of output. **(3 marks)**

MAPE 5/05

The following data are given for questions 7 and 8 below

DRP Limited has recently introduced an Activity Based Costing system. It manufactures three products, details of which are set out below:

	Product D	Product R	Product P
Budgeted annual production (units)	100,000	100,000	50,000
Batch size (units)	100	50	25
Machine set-ups per batch	3	4	6
Purchase orders per batch	2	1	1
Processing time per unit (minutes)	2	3	3

Three cost pools have been identified. Their budgeted costs for the year ending 31 December 20X4 are as follows:

Machine set-up costs	£150,000
Purchasing of materials	£70,000
Processing	£80,000

---

7   Calculate the annual budgeted number of:

   (a)   batches
   (b)   machine set-ups
   (c)   purchase orders
   (d)   processing minutes   **(2 marks)**

---

8   Calculate the budgeted overhead unit cost for Product R for inclusion in the budget for 20X4.   **(3 marks)**

(Total = 20 marks)

If you struggled with these multiple choice questions, go back to your BPP Study Text for Paper P1 and revise Chapters 9 to 12 before you tackle Section B and Section C type questions on the modern business environment, modern costing systems and activity based costing.

---

29   Section B: Modern business environment and costing systems
54 mins

(a)   State and briefly explain five main features of a JIT production system.   **(5 marks)**

(b)   State the financial benefits of JIT.   **(5 marks)**

(c)   Give FOUR reasons why the adoption of TQM is particularly important within a Just-in-Time (JIT) production environment.   **(5 marks)**

(d)   Explain why Activity Based Costing may be better attuned to the modern manufacturing environment than traditional techniques.   **(5 marks)**

(e)   Critically appraise the reported claim that ABC gives better information as a guide to decision making than do traditional product costing techniques.   **(5 marks)**

(f)   Explain what is meant by environmental costs and how activity based costing techniques may be more effective than a traditional absorption costing system in the management of environmental costs.
(5 marks)

(Total = 30 marks)

30   Section C: F plc (MAPE 5/05)
45 mins

F plc supplies pharmaceutical drugs to drug stores. Although the company makes a satisfactory return, the directors are concerned that some orders are profitable and others are not. The management has decided to investigate a new budgeting system using activity based costing principles to ensure that all orders they accept are making a profit.

Each customer order is charged as follows. Customers are charged the list price of the drugs ordered plus a charge for selling and distribution costs (overheads). A profit margin is also added, but that does not form part of this analysis.

Currently F plc uses a simple absorption rate to absorb these overheads. The rate is calculated based on the budgeted annual selling and distribution costs and the budgeted annual total list price of the drugs ordered.

An analysis of customers has revealed that many customers place frequent small orders with each order requesting a variety of drugs. The management of F plc has examined more carefully the nature of its selling and distribution costs, and the following data have been prepared for the budget for next year:

Total list price of drugs supplied	£8m	
Number of customer orders	8,000	
Selling and Distribution Costs	£'000	*Cost driver*
Invoice processing	280	See Note 2
Packing	220	Size of package – see Note 3
Delivery	180	Number of deliveries – see Note 4
Other overheads	200	Number of orders
Total overheads	880	

Notes

1   Each order will be shipped in one package and will result in one delivery to the customer and one invoice (an order never results in more than one delivery).

2   Each invoice has a different line for each drug ordered. There are 28,000 invoice lines each year. It is estimated that 25% of invoice processing costs are related to the number of invoices, and 75% are related to the number of invoice lines.

3   Packing costs are £32 for a large package, and £25 for a small package.

4   The delivery vehicles are always filled to capacity for each journey. The delivery vehicles can carry either 6 large packages or 12 small packages (or appropriate combinations of large and small packages). It is estimated that there will be 1,000 delivery journeys each year, and the total delivery mileage that is specific to particular customers is estimated at 350,000 miles each year. £40,000 of delivery costs are related to loading the delivery vehicles, and the remainder of these costs are related to specific delivery distance to customers.

The management has asked for two typical orders to be costed using next year's budget data, using the current method, and the proposed activity-based costing approach. Details of two typical orders are shown below:

	Order A	Order B
Lines on invoice	2	8
Package size	small	large
Specific delivery distance	8 miles	40 miles
List price of drugs supplied	£1,200	£900

Required

(a)   Calculate the charge for selling and distribution overheads for Order A and Order B using:

   (i)   The current system; and
   (ii)   The activity-based costing approach.   **(10 marks)**

(b)   Write a report to the management of F plc in which you:

   (i)   Assess the strengths and weaknesses of the proposed activity-based costing approach for F plc; and   **(5 marks)**

   (ii)   Recommend actions that the management of F plc might consider in the light of the data produced using the activity-based-costing approach.   **(5 marks)**

(c)   Explain why an organisation's product range and customer base may make the use of activity-based techniques particularly useful.   **(5 marks)**

(Total = 25 marks)

31 Section C: Bottlenecks   45 mins

F plc makes and sells two products, A and B, each of which passes through the same automated production operations. The following estimated information is available for period 1.

- Product unit data

	A	B
Direct material cost (£)	2	40
Variable production overhead cost (£)	28	4
Overall hours per product unit (hours)	0.25	0.15

- Original estimates of production/sales of products A and B are 120,000 units and 45,000 units respectively. The selling prices per unit for A and B are £60 and £70 respectively.

- Maximum demand for each product is 20% above the estimated sales levels.

- Total fixed production overhead cost is £1,470,000. This is absorbed by products A and B at an average rate per hour based on the estimated production levels.

One of the production operations has a maximum capacity of 3,075 hours which has been identified as a bottleneck which limits the overall estimated production/sales of products A and B. The bottleneck hours required per product unit for products A and B are 0.02 and 0.015 respectively.

Required

(a)   Calculate the mix (in units) of products A and B which will maximise net profit and the value (in £) of the maximum net profit.   **(8 marks)**

(b)   F plc has now decided to determine the profit-maximising mix of products A and B based on the throughput accounting principle of maximising the throughput return per production hour of the bottleneck resource.

Given that the variable overhead cost, based on the value (in £) which applies to the original estimated production/sales mix, is now considered to be fixed for the short/intermediate term:

   (i)   Calculate the mix (of units) of products A and B which will maximise net profit and the value of that net profit.   **(8 marks)**

   (ii)   Calculate the throughput accounting ratio for product B.   **(3 marks)**

   (iii)   Comment on the interpretation of throughput accounting ratios and their use as a control device. You should refer to the ratio for product B in your answer.   **(6 marks)**

(Total = 25 marks)

32   Section C: ZW plc and Z Ltd   45 mins

(a)   (i)   Explain the term backflush costing and discuss its advantages and disadvantages.   **(9 marks)**

        (ii)   ZW plc uses backflush costing with two trigger points (when materials and components are received and on transfer to finished goods). 980 units were transferred to finished goods during the period and 950 units were sold. There were no opening inventories of raw materials, finished goods or WP. The standard cost per unit is made up of £80 for materials and £90 for conversion costs. Assume no variances arise during the period and that under-or over-absorbed conversion costs are not written off.

                Record the accounting entries and find the balance on the finished goods inventory account at the end of the period.   **(6 marks)**

(b)   Z Ltd produces signs and labels for a number of businesses. Some of the signs are produced on vinyl and then fixed to vehicles and display panels whereas others are produced on metal and fixed to machinery and equipment to indicate how they are to be operated safely.

        Presently Z Ltd holds inventories of raw materials (vinyls, metals and inks) and controls the level of inventory using a inventory control system that involves the setting and monitoring of minimum, maximum and re-order levels for each item. There are also some specialist materials that are bought from suppliers as required.

        Z Ltd uses a number of suppliers, some of whom are based overseas. The Purchasing Manager of Z Ltd is responsible for negotiating prices and contracts with suppliers for all of the materials used by the company. The performance of the manager is monitored as part of Z Ltd's responsibility accounting system.

        The Managing Director has recently returned from a conference on best practice where one of the speakers mentioned the use of Just-in-Time (JIT). The Managing Director seeks your advice, and has asked you to prepare a report that can be discussed at the next Board meeting.

        Required

        Prepare a report which:

        (i)   Describes the key features of a JIT system both for purchasing a raw materials and for their conversion into finished items for customers.   **(3 marks)**

        (ii)   Explains the changes in working practices that would be necessary for a JIT system to succeed.
                                                                                                                                              (7 marks)

(Total = 25 marks)

BUDGETING AND FORECASTING

Questions 33 to 37 cover budgeting and forecasting, the subjects of Chapters 13 and 14 in Part C of the BPP Study Text for Paper P1.

33   Section A: Budgeting and forecasting   36 mins

1   Which of the following definitions best describes 'Zero-Based Budgeting'?

A   A method of budgeting where an attempt is made to make the expenditure under each cost heading as close to zero as possible.

B   A method of budgeting whereby all activities are re-evaluated each time a budget is formulated.

C   A method of budgeting that uses the previous year's budget or actual results as a base for preparing the current year's budget.

D   A method of budgeting where the sum of revenues and expenditures in each budget centre must equal zero.   **(2 marks)**

2   BDL plc is currently preparing its cash budget for the year to 31 March 20X8. An extract from its sales budget for the same year shows the following sales values.

	£
March	60,000
April	70,000
May	55,000
June	65,000

40% of its sales are expected to be for cash. Of its credit sales, 70% are expected to pay in the month after sale and take a 2% discount; 27% are expected to pay in the second month after the sale, and the remaining 3% are expected to be bad debts.

What is the value of sales receipts to be shown in the cash budget for May 20X7?   **(2 marks)**

3   Based on the last 15 periods, the underlying trend of sales is $y = 345.12 - 1.35x$, where y is the number of items sold and x represents the period number. If the 16th period has a seasonal factor of -23.62, assuming an additive forecasting model, then the sales forecast for that period, to the nearest whole unit, is:

A   247 units
B   300 units
C   324 units
D   347 units   **(2 marks)**

4   A regression equation $y = a + bx$ is used to forecast the value of y for a given value of x. Which of the following increase the reliability of the forecast?

A   A large sample used to calculate the regression equation
B   Forecasting for values of x outside the range of those in the sample used to calculate the equation
C   Working to a higher number of decimal places of accuracy
D   A correlation coefficient numerically close to 0   **(2 marks)**

5   Each unit of product B uses 6 kg of raw material. The production budget and inventory budgets for December are as follows.

Opening inventories	– raw materials	21,000 kg
	– finished goods	15,000 units
Closing inventories	– raw materials	24,400 kg
	– finished goods	11,400 units

Budgeted sales of B for December are 18,000 units. During the production process it is usually found that 10% of production units are scrapped as defective. This loss occurs after the raw materials have been input.

What are the budgeted raw materials purchases for December?   **(3 marks)**

---

6   BW Ltd recorded the following total costs over the last three years.

Year	Volume of production Units	Total cost £	Average price level index
0	160,000	2,770,000	100
1	140,000	2,551,500	105
2	110,000	2,092,800	109

What are the expected costs (to the nearest £'000) in year 3 when output is 120,000 units and the average price level index is 112?   **(3 marks)**

---

7   Q Ltd has prepared the following regression equation as a basis for estimating sales (Y) in units for period X.

$Y = 27X – 24$

Quarterly seasonal variations affecting Q Ltd's sales levels are as follows.

Q1	Q2	Q3	Q4
–25%	–25%	+15%	+35%

Period 12 is in quarter 4. What is the forecast sales level for period 12?   **(3 marks)**

---

8   The overhead costs of RP Limited have been found to be accurately represented by the formula

$$y = £10,000 + £0{\cdot}25x$$

where y is the monthly cost and x represents the activity level measured as the number of orders.

Monthly activity levels of orders may be estimated using a combined regression analysis and time series model:

$$a = 100,000 + 30b$$

where a represents the de-seasonalised monthly activity level and b represents the month number.

In month 240, the seasonal index value is 108.

Required

Calculate the overhead cost for RP Limited for month 240 to the nearest £1,000.   **(3 marks)**

(Total = 20 marks)

If you struggled with these objective test questions, go back to your BPP Study Text for Paper P1 and revise Chapters 13 and 14 before you tackle Section B and Section C type questions on budgeting and forecasting.

34 Section B: X plc (MAPE 11/06 – adapted)   54 mins

The following scenario is given for sub-questions (a) to (f)

X plc manufactures specialist insulating products that are used in both residential and commercial buildings. One of the products, Product W, is made using two different raw materials. The company is now preparing its budgets for the next four quarters. The following information has been identified for Product W:

Sales

Selling price	£220 per unit

Sales demand

Quarter 1	2,250 units
Quarter 2	2,050 units
Quarter 3	1,650 units
Quarter 4	2,050 units
Quarter 5	1,250 units
Quarter 6	2,050 units

Materials

A	5 kgs per unit @ £4 per kg
B	3 kgs per unit @ £7 per kg

Inventory holding policy

Closing inventory of finished goods	30% of the following quarter's sales demand
Closing inventory of materials	45% of the following quarter's materials usage

The management team are concerned that X plc has recently faced increasing competition in the market place for Product W. As a consequence there have been issues concerning the availability and costs of the specialised materials needed to manufacture Product W, and there is concern that this might cause problems in the current budget setting process.

Required

(a)   Prepare the following budgets for each quarter for X plc:

   (i)   Production budget in units;
   (ii)   Raw material purchases budget in kgs and value for Material B.   **(5 marks)**

(b)   X Plc has just been informed that Material A may be in short supply during the year for which it is preparing budgets. Discuss the impact this will have on budget preparation and other areas of X plc.
                                                                                          (5 marks)

(c)   X plc currently uses incremental budgeting. Explain how zero based budgeting could overcome the problems that might be faced as a result of the continued use of the current system.   **(5 marks)**

(d)   Discuss the factors that X plc needs to consider when preparing sales forecasts.   **(5 marks)**

(e)   Briefly explain how linear regression analysis can be used to forecast sales and briefly discuss whether it would be a suitable method for X plc to use.   **(5 marks)**

(f)   Discuss briefly some of the problems that X plc is likely to face when preparing forecasts as the basis for a budgetary plan.   **(5 marks)**

                                                                                          (Total = 30 marks)

35 Section C: Cash budget (MAPE 5/09 – adapted)   45 mins

A company manufactures and sells a single product. Next year's budgeted profit (based on absorption costing) on the projected sales of 810,000 units is £1,611,000. In view of this figure the company is thinking of investing in new machinery at some time in the forthcoming year.

The company is preparing its cash budget for next year. The company divides the year into four periods, each of thirteen weeks. Sales and production will occur at even rates within each period. Details are as follows:

Sales budget (810,000 units)

The selling price is £30 per unit. All sales will be on credit and payment will be received five weeks after the date of sale. It is expected that 2% of all sales will become bad debts. The budgeted sales units are:

Period	1	2	3	4
Sales (units)	150,000	200,000	180,000	280,000

The product incurs variable selling costs of £1.60 per unit. These are paid in the period in which they are incurred.

Production budget (860,000 units)

Period	1	2	3	4
Production (units)	210,000	210,000	220,000	220,000

Production cost per unit

	£	Notes
Raw materials	9·50	Purchased on credit. Paid for four weeks after purchase.
Production wages	8·20	Paid one week in arrears. These are variable costs.
Production expenses	7·00	See below.
	24·70	

Raw material inventory

The company wishes to increase inventory to six weeks of forward production by the end of Period 1 and then to seven weeks by the end of Period 2. Purchases will occur evenly throughout the periods.

Production expenses

The production expenses of £7·00 per unit are detailed below:

	£	Notes
Variable expenses	1·10	Paid in the period incurred
Depreciation	2·70	This is an annual fixed cost that is absorbed on a per unit basis by the budgeted production of 860,000 units
Fixed expenses	3·20	Absorbed on a per unit basis based on the annual production of 860,000 units. Paid in two equal instalments at the beginning of periods 1 and 3.

Long term borrowing

The company has a long term loan. The balance on this loan at the start of the year will be £10m. Interest on this loan is charged at 9% per annum on the amount outstanding at the start of the year and is to be paid in two equal instalments at the end of period 2 and at the end of period 4. The loan is "interest only": there are no capital repayments due.

Opening balances

	£	
Raw materials inventory	710,000	(all purchased at the current price)
Trade receivables (net of bad debts)	2,430,000	
Bank and cash	76,000	
Trade payables	612,000	
Unpaid wages	130,000	
Loan	10,000,000	

Required

(a)   Calculate, in units, the budgeted break even point and margin of safety for the next year.   **(6 marks)**

(b)   It is now thought that the price of raw materials could range from £7·50 to £11·50 for each unit produced.

Produce a diagram that shows the sensitivity of the budgeted profit to changes in the price of the raw materials.   **(4 marks)**

(c)   Prepare, showing all cash flows, a cash budget for period 1 and a cash budget for period 2 (assume the price of raw materials is £9·50 for each unit produced).   **(15 marks)**

(Total = 25 marks)

---

36   Section C: Zap plc   45 mins

(a)   Sales are often considered to be the principal budget factor of an organisation.

Explain the meaning of the 'principal budget factor' and, assuming that it is sales, explain how sales may be forecast, making appropriate reference to the use of statistical techniques.   **(6 marks)**

(b)   You are the assistant management accountant of Zap plc. Preliminary discussions concerning the company budgets of the year ended 30 June 20X9 have already taken place, and the sales and production directors have produced the following forecasts.

Sales Director:

'I forecast that the total sales for the year will be 24,000 units of product A.

July – September	7,200 units
October – December	3,000 units
January – March	4,800 units
April – June	9,000 units

This represents a 20% increase over our present quarterly sales targets, and I expect that within each quarter the monthly demand will be equal. We can also sell up to 2,000 units of product B per month. This is a less profitable product, so we should concentrate on product A.'

Production Director:

'Our maximum capacity is at present limited by the available machine hours. Each unit of product A requires 2 machine hours, and on this basis we can usually produce 2,000 units per month. However, because of employee holidays in August, the number of machine operators is reduced, and in that month we can produce only 1,000 units. We have placed an order for new semi-automatic machines which are being installed in August 20X8. These should be capable of producing a further 2,000 units per month starting on 1 September 20X8.

Product B requires 4 machine hours per unit. The quantity that we can produce is limited because of the demands on the available machine time by making product A.'

(i)   Calculate the extent of the limiting factor during the budget period.   **(4 marks)**

(ii)   Prepare monthly sales and production budgets, expressed in units, for the period *July to December 20X8*, based upon the limiting factor you determined in (i) above. Assume that inventories of products A and B cannot be held, and that Zap plc wishes to concentrate on production of product A.   **(6 marks)**

(iii)   Prepare monthly sales and production budgets, expressed in units, for the period *July to December 20X8*, based upon the limiting factor you determined in (i) above. Assume that inventories of products A and B can now be held, and assume that Zap plc decided to sell equal quantities of product A and product B each month.   **(9 marks)**

(Total = 25 marks)

37 Section C: List price   45 mins

(a)   Explain the differences and similarities between zero based budgeting and activity based budgeting

(10 marks)

(b)   XYZ Ltd has the following forecast sales at list price for the nine months to 29 February 20X6.

June	£40,000	September	£48,000	December	£44,000
July	£44,000	October	£40,000	January	£42,000
August	£50,000	November	£45,000	February	£50,000

60% of the company's sales are on credit, payable in the month after sale. Cash sales attract a 5% discount off list price.

Purchases amount to 40% of selling price, and these are paid for two months after delivery.

Inventory is maintained at a level equal to 50% of the following month's sales except that in November inventory is to be increased by £2,000 (at cost prices) to ensure that XYZ Ltd has a safety inventory during the period when its major supplier shuts down. This safety inventory will be released in March.

Wages comprise a fixed sum of £2,000 per month plus a variable element equal to 10% of sales; these are payable in the month they are incurred.

Fixed costs amount to £7,500 per month, payable one month in arrears, of which £1,500 is depreciation.

XYZ Ltd has capital expenditure/receipts scheduled as follows.

	£
Acquisitions	
September	15,000
November	10,000
February	4,000
Disposal	
October	8,000

Corporation tax, payable in November, amounts to £44,000.

The bank balance on 1 September 20X5 is expected to be £5,000.

Required

(i)   Prepare a cashflow forecast for XYZ Ltd for each of the six months from September 20X5 to February 20X6, using a row and column format.   **(9 marks)**

(ii) Explain briefly, using your answer to (i) above, how a spreadsheet may be used to assist in the preparation of cash forecasts.   **(6 marks)**

(Total = 25 marks)

PROJECT APPRAISAL, DCF, TAX AND INFLATION

Questions 38 to 42 cover project appraisal, DCF, tax and inflation, the subjects of Chapters 15, 16 and 17 of the BPP Study Text for Paper P1.

---

38   Section A: Project appraisal, DCF, tax and inflation   36 mins

1   B Ltd has identified two mutually exclusive projects which have an equivalent effect on the risk profile of the company. Project 1 has a payback period of 3.7 years, an NPV of £16,100, an internal rate of return of 15% and an average accounting rate of return of 16%. Project 2 has a payback period of 4.7 years, an NPV of £14,900, an internal rate of return of 19% and an average accounting rate of return of 17%. The cost of capital is 10%. Assuming that the directors wish to maximise shareholder wealth and no shortage of capital is expected, which project should the company choose?

     A   Project 1 because it has the shorter payback period
     B   Project 1 because it has the higher net present value
     C   Project 2 because it has the higher internal rate of return
     D   Project 2 because it has the higher accounting rate of return   **(2 marks)**

---

2   In a comparison of the NPV and IRR techniques, which of the following statements is true?

     A   Both methods give the same accept or reject decision, regardless of the pattern of the cash flows.
     B   IRR is technically superior to NPV and easier to calculate.
     C   The NPV approach is superior if discount rates are expected to vary over the life of the project.
     D   NPV and accounting ROCE can be confused.   **(2 marks)**

---

3   What is the present value of £5,000 in perpetuity at a discount rate of 10%?

     A   £500
     B   £5,500
     C   £4,545
     D   £50,000   **(2 marks)**

---

4   What are the disadvantages of the payback method of investment appraisal?

     I   It tends to maximise financial and business risk.
     II   It is a fairly complex technique and not easy to understand.
     III   It cannot be used when there is a capital rationing situation.

     A   None of the above
     B   All of the above
     C   I only
     D   II and III   **(2 marks)**

The following data relates to questions 5 and 6

A company is considering investing in a manufacturing project that would have a three-year life span. The investment would involve an immediate cash outflow of £50,000 and have no residual value. In each of the three years, 4,000 units would be produced and sold. The contribution per unit, based on current prices, is £5. The company has an annual cost of capital of 8%. It is expected that the inflation rate will be 3% in each of the next three years

---

5   Calculate the net present value of the project (to the nearest £500)   **(3 marks)**

---

6   If the annual inflation rate is now projected to be 4%, the maximum monetary cost of capital for this project to remain viable is (to the nearest 0.5%)

   A   13.0%
   B   13.5%
   C   14.0%
   D   14.5%   (2 marks)

7   The details of an investment project are as follows.

Life of the project	10 years
Cost of asset bought at the start of the project	£100,000
Annual cash inflow	£20,000
Cost of capital, after tax	8% each year

   Corporation tax is 30% and is paid in equal quarterly instalments in the 7th and 10th months of the year in which the profit was earned and in the 1st and 4th months of the following year.

   Writing down allowances of 25% reducing balance will be claimed each year.

   (Assume the asset is bought on the first day of the tax year and that the company's other projects generate healthy profits.)

   (Round all cash flows to the nearest £ and discount end of year cash flows.)

   Calculate the *present value* of the cash flows that occur in the *second* year of the project   **(4 marks)**

8   IM Ltd hopes to purchase a machine for £80,000 on which it can claim writing down allowances of 25% on a reducing balance basis. The machine will have a life of four years and will be sold for £20,000. Corporation tax is 30% and is paid in equal quarterly instalments in the seventh and tenth months of the year in which the profit is earned and in the first and fourth months of the following year. On the assumption that the investment occurs on the first day of the tax year and that IM Ltd's other projects generate healthy profits, what tax savings will the investment produce in years 3 and 4?   **(3 marks)**

(Total = 20 marks)

If you struggled with these objective test questions, go back to your BPP Study Text for Paper P1 and revise Chapters 15 to 17 before you tackle Section B and Section C type questions on Project appraisal.

---

39 Section B: Project appraisal, DCF, tax and inflation   54 mins

(a)   A company is currently appraising a major investment in an IT project which will revolutionise its business. The company intends to use the net present value method as the basis of the appraisal.

       Discuss the difficulties associated with the net present value method when appraising this type of investment.   **(5 marks)**

The following information relates to questions 39(b) and 39(c)

JLX plc is a well-established manufacturing organisation that has recently expanded rapidly, by a series of acquisitions, in a period of favourable trading conditions. The need to integrate the management information and control systems of the rapidly expanding group has imposed a very large workload on the managerial and accounting teams. Consequently, some of the normal procedures at JLX plc have been neglected.

The company uses net present value (NPV) to assess and select investment projects. It used to be standard practice to assess and review all projects after implementation by a post-completion appraisal (PCA). However, PCA has been one area that has been neglected because of the increased workloads, and recently PCA has been applied only to those projects which have been considered unsuccessful.

PRO35 is a major project recently implemented by division X. This project was controversial because of its large capital requirement and high risk level. The group finance director has stated that his department is now considerably under-staffed and that he requires more resources to operate effectively. In particular, he is using the need to carry out a PCA on PRO35 as a lever to gain more funds. He has told the group chief executive that he thinks that PRO35 should be subjected to a PCA as he considers that it should be generating a greater return given the continuing favourable trading conditions.

The group chief executive has responded to this by saying that he feels that a PCA for PRO35 is unnecessary as it is generating the predicted net cash flow.

Required

(b)   Explain why it is advisable for JLX plc to carry out PCAs.   **(5 marks)**

(c)   Discuss whether a PCA should be carried out on PRO35, a project that appears to be performing satisfactorily.   **(5 marks)**

(d)   M plc is evaluating two possible investment projects and uses a 10% discount rate to determine their net present values.

Investment	*A*	*B*
	£'000	£'000
Initial Investment	400	450
Incremental cash flows: Year 1	100	130
Year 2	120	130
Year 3	140	130
Year 4	120	130
Year 5*	100	150
Net present value	39	55

*includes £20,000 residual value for each investment project.

(i)   Calculate the payback period of investment A.   **(2 marks)**
(ii)   Calculate the discounted payback period of investment B.   **(3 marks)**

(e)   Investment C generates the following cash flows.

	£'000
Initial investment	350
Incremental cash flows: Year 1	50
Year 2	110
Year 3	130
Year 4	150
Year 5*	100

* Includes residual value of investment

(i)   Calculate the net present value of the investment using a 10% cost of capital (to the nearest £'000)

                                                                                                    (2 marks)

(ii)   Calculate the Internal Rate of Return (IRR) of the investment.   **(3 marks)**

(f)   An investment project with no residual value has a net present value of $87,980 when it is discounted using a cost of capital of 10%. The annual cash flows are as follows:

Year	$
0	(200,000)
1	80,000
2	90,000
3	100,000
4	60,000
5	40,000

(i)   Calculate the Accounting Rate of Return of the project using the average investment value basis.

                                                                                                    (2 marks)

(ii)   Calculate the Internal Rate of Return of the project.   **(3 marks)**

                                                                                       (Total = 30 marks)

40 Section C: Household products (MADM 5/08)   45 mins

H is a well-established manufacturer of household products. It produces its accounts to 31 December each year.

The machinery that is currently being used to manufacture one of H's products will have to be scrapped on 31 December 20X8, because H can no longer obtain a safety certificate for it. H is considering investing $500,000 in new machinery on 1 January 20X9 in order to continue manufacturing this product If the project does not go ahead H will no longer be able to manufacture the product.

The new machinery will have sufficient production capacity to meet the expected sales demand levels for the next five years. It will have a life of five years, and at the end of that time it will be sold for $100,000. It will qualify for tax depreciation at the rate of 20% per annum on a reducing balance basis.

Sales revenues and production costs for the current year, which ends on 31 December 20X8, are predicted to be as follows.

	$,000
Sales revenue	540
Production costs	
Variable production costs	240
Fixed overhead*	120
	360
Fixed non-production costs	80
Profit before tax	100

*Fixed production overhead cost includes $20,000 for depreciation of the existing machinery.

Sales

The following table of index numbers (20X8 = 100) shows the predicted levels of sales volume.

	20X9	20Y0	20Y1	20Y2	20Y3
Sales:					
Volume	103	105	109	107	110

Assume there are no changes in the selling price other than those caused by selling price inflation which is expected to be 4% per year.

Costs

Production costs are not expected to change as a result of investing in the new machinery, but production cost inflation is expected to be 5% per year. Non-production cost inflation is expected to be 3% per year.

Taxation

H is liable to pay tax on its profits at the rate of 30%. Half of this is payable in the year in which the profit is earned and the remainder is payable in the following year.

H has a post tax money cost of capital of 14% per annum.

Required

(a) Calculate the Net Present Value (NPV) of the project (to the nearest £'000).   **(15 marks)**

(b) Calculate the post tax money cost of capital at which H would be indifferent to accepting/rejecting the project.   **(4 marks)**

(c) Explain your treatment of inflation in your solution to part (a) above and describe an alternative method that would have provided the same NPV.   **(6 marks)**

(Total = 25 marks)

41   Section C: X (MADM 5/07 – adapted)   45 mins

X operates in an economy that has almost zero inflation. Management ignores inflation when evaluating investment projects because it is so low as to be considered insignificant. X is evaluating a number of similar, alternative investments. The company uses an after tax cost of capital of 6% and has already completed the evaluation of two investments. The third investment is a new product that would be produced on a just-in-time basis and which is expected to have a life of three years. This investment requires an immediate cash outflow of $200,000, which does not qualify for tax depreciation. The expected residual value at the end of the project's life is $50,000. A draft financial statement showing the values that are specific to this third investment for the three years is as follows:

	Year 1 $	Year 2 $	Year 3 $
Sales	230,000	350,000	270,000
Production costs			
Materials	54,000	102,000	66,000
Labour	60,000	80,000	70,000
Other*	80,000	90,000	80,000
Profit	36,000	78,000	54,000
Closing receivables	20,000	30,000	25,000
Closing payables	6,000	9,000	8,000

* Other production costs shown above include depreciation calculated using the straight line method.

The company is liable to pay corporation tax at a rate of 30% of its profits. One half of this is payable in the same year as the profit is earned, the remainder is payable in the following year.

Required

(a)   Calculate the net present value of the above investment proposal.   **(10 marks)**

(b)   Explain how the above investment project would be appraised if there were to be a change in the rate of inflation so that it became too significant to be ignored.   **(5 marks)**

The evaluations of the other two investments are shown below:

Investment	Initial investment $	Net present value $
W	300,000	75,000
Y	100,000	27,000

The company only has $400,000 of funds available. All of the investment proposals are non-divisible. None of the investments may be repeated.

(c)   RAD Enterprises (RAD) has signed a contract with LPC to supply accounting packages. However, there has been a fire in one of the software manufacturing departments and a machine has been seriously damaged and requires urgent replacement.

The replacement machine will cost £1 million and RAD is considering whether to lease or buy the machine. A lease could be arranged under which RAD would pay £300,000 per annum for four years with each payment being made annually in advance. The lease payments would be an allowable expense for taxation purposes.

Corporation tax is payable at the rate of 30% of profits in two equal instalments: one in the year that profits are earned and the other in the following year. Writing-down allowances are available at 25% each year on a reducing balance basis. It is anticipated that the machine will have a useful economic life of four years, at the end of which there will be no residual value.

The after-tax cost of capital is 12%.

Required

Evaluate the lease or buy considerations for acquiring the new machine from a financial viewpoint, assuming that RAD has sufficient profits to claim all available tax reliefs.   **(10 marks)**

(Total = 25 marks)

42 Section C: JK plc (MADM 11/06)   45 mins

JK plc prepares its accounts to 31 December each year. It is considering investing in a new computer controlled production facility on 1 January 20X7 at a cost of £50m. This will enable JK plc to produce a new product which it expects to be able to sell for four years. At the end of this time it has been agreed to sell the new production facility for £1m cash.

Sales of the product during the year ended 31 December 20X7 and the next three years are expected to be as follows:

Year ended 31 December 20X7	20X7	20X8	20X9	20Y0
Sales units (000)	100	105	110	108

Selling price, unit variable cost and fixed overhead costs (excluding depreciation) are expected to be as follows during the year ended 31 December 20X7:

	£
Selling price per unit	1,200
Variable production cost per unit	750
Variable selling and distribution cost per unit	100
Fixed production cost for the year	4,000,000
Fixed selling and distribution cost for the year	2,000,000
Fixed administration cost for the year	1,000,000

The following rates of annual inflation are expected for each of the years 20X8 – 20Y0:

	%
Selling prices	5
Production costs	8
Selling and distribution costs	6
Administration costs	5

The company pays taxation on its profits at the rate of 30%, with half of this being payable in the year in which the profit is earned and the remainder being payable in the following year. Investments of this type qualify for tax depreciation at the rate of 25% per annum on a reducing balance basis.

The Board of Directors of JK plc has agreed to use a 12% post-tax discount rate to evaluate this investment.

Required

(a)   Advise JK plc whether the investment is financially worthwhile.   **(17 marks)**

(b)   Calculate the Internal Rate of Return of the investment.   **(3 marks)**

(c)   Define and contrast *(i)* the real rate of return and *(ii)* the money rate of return, and explain how they would be used when calculating the net present value of a project's cash flows.   **(5 marks)**

(Total = 25 marks)

FURTHER ASPECTS OF INVESTMENT DECISION MAKING

Questions 43 to 52 cover further aspects of investment decision making, the subject of Chapter 18 of the BPP Study Text for Paper P1.

---

43 Section A: Further aspects of investment decision making
36 mins

1   A Ltd can invest in three out of the following four projects. The company's cost of capital is 8%.

Project	1	2	3	4
Investment (£)	66,000	72,000	60,000	43,000
Life (years)	3	6	8	4
Annual receipts (£)	31,000	20,000	16,000	17,000

Which project should be rejected? Show your workings.   **(4 marks)**

---

2   L Ltd is considering a project. The present value of the initial investment of the project is £714,000, the present value of the project's variable costs is £290,000, the present value of its cash inflows is £1,250,000 and the present value of its net cash flows is £246,000.

Required

Calculate the change required in the value of the initial investment to make L Ltd indifferent between accepting and rejecting the project.   **(3 marks)**

---

3   B plc has purchased equipment which has the following costs and disposal values over its four-year life. The initial cost is £28,000. B plc's cost of capital is 8%.

Year	1	2	3	4
Operating costs (£)	(12,000)	(14,000)	(15,000)	(17,000)
Year-end disposal value (£)	20,000	18,000	12,000	6,000

How frequently should the equipment be replaced?   **(4 marks)**

---

4   R Ltd is considering a project. The present value of the initial investment of the project is £32,000, the present value of the project's variable costs is £27,000, the present value of its cash inflows is £130,000 and the present value of its net cash flows is £71,000. The cost of capital is 10%. The project's IRR is 17%.

The change required in the cost of capital to make R Ltd indifferent between accepting and rejecting the project is 17%. *True or false?*   **(3 marks)**

---

5   A company is evaluating a new product proposal. The proposed product selling price is £180 per unit and the variable costs are £60 per unit. The incremental cash fixed costs for the product will be £160,000 per annum. The discounted cash flow calculation results in a positive NPV.

		Cash flow £	Discount rate factor	Present value £
Year 0	Initial outlay	(1,000,000)	1.000	(1,000,000)
Year 1-5	Annual cash flow	320,000	3.791	1,213,120
Year 5	Working capital released	50,000	0.621	31,050
	Net present value			244,170

What percentage change in selling price would result in the project having a net present value of zero?

A   6.7 per cent
B   7.5 per cent
C   8.9 per cent
D   9.6 per cent   **(2 marks)**

---

6   R Ltd is deciding whether to launch a new product. The initial outlay for the product is £20,000. The forecast possible annual cash inflows and their associated probabilities are shown below.

	Probability	Year 1 £	Year 2 £	Year 3 £
Optimistic	0.20	10,000	12,000	9,000
Most likely	0.50	7,000	8,000	7,600
Pessimistic	0.30	6,400	7,200	6,200

The company's cost of capital is 10% per annum.

Assume the cash inflows are received at the end of the year and that the cash inflows for each year are independent.

Required

Calculate the expected net present value for the product.   **(4 marks)**

(Total = 20 marks)

If you struggled with these objective test questions, go back to your BPP Study Text for Paper P1 and revise Chapter 18 before you tackle the Section B and Section C type questions on further aspects of investment decision making.

44   Section B: Further aspects of investment decision making
54 mins

(a)   Define the term 'profitability index' and briefly explain how it may be used when a company faces a problem of capital rationing in any single accounting period.   **(5 marks)**

(b)   Explain the limitations of using a profitability index in a situation where there is capital rationing.
                                                                                              (5 marks)

The following information relates to questions 44(c) and 44(d).

A manager is evaluating a three year project which has the following relevant pre-tax operating cashflows:

Year	1 $000	2 $000	3 $000
Sales	4,200	4,900	5,300
Costs	2,850	3,100	4,150

The project requires an investment of $2m at the start of year 1 and has no residual value.

The company pays corporation tax on its net relevant operating cashflows at the rate of 20%. Corporation tax is payable in the same year as the net relevant pre-tax operating cashflows arise. There is no tax depreciation available on the investment.

The manager has discounted the net relevant post-tax operating cashflows using the company's post-tax cost of capital of 7% and this results in a post-tax net present value of the project of $1·018m.

Required

(c)   Briefly explain sensitivity analysis and how the manager may use it in the evaluation of this project.
                                                                                              (5 marks)

(d)   Calculate the sensitivity of the project to a change in the cost of capital.   **(5 marks)**

(e)   A company operates a fleet of three canal boats that provide cruises for tourists around the canals of a city. The company seeks your advice as to whether it is better to replace its boats every year, every two years or every three years. The company has provided the following data:

Purchase cost of each boat $400,000

Operating costs, which include maintenance, servicing, and similar costs are paid at the end of each year. Operating costs and end of year trade-in values vary depending on the age of the boat and are as follows for each year of the boat's life:

Year	Operating Costs $	Trade-in values $
1	300,000	240,000
2	400,000	150,000
3	600,000	80,000

The company uses an 8% cost of capital for its investment decisions.

Required

Produce calculations to determine the optimum replacement cycle of the boats and state clearly your recommendations. Ignore taxation. **(5 marks)**

(f)   Explain and provide examples of non-financial considerations that should be incorporated into project appraisals. **(5 marks)**

(Total = 30 marks)

45 Section C: Airport (5/10)   45 mins

A small regional airport is modernising its facilities in anticipation of significant growth in the number of passengers using the airport. It is expected that the number of passengers will increase by 10% per annum as a result of a "low cost" airline opening new routes to and from the airport.

At present, the airport has only one food outlet selling sandwiches and other cold food and drinks. To improve the facilities available to customers, the management of the airport is considering opening a restaurant selling a range of hot food and drinks. The cost of fitting out the new restaurant, which will have to be fully refurbished after four years, is estimated to be $350,000. These assets are expected to have a residual value of $30,000 at the end of four years.

A firm of consultants carried out an extensive study in relation to this project at a cost of $30,000. The key findings from their report, regarding expected revenue and contribution from the restaurant, are as follows:

*   Average revenue: $9·00 per customer
*   Average variable cost: $5·00 per customer
*   Demand in year 1: 500 customers per day

Future demand for the restaurant is expected to rise in line with passenger numbers.

The airport operates for 360 days per year.

Other relevant information from the consultants' report is listed below:

1.   **Staffing of the new restaurant:**

*   Number of employees (Years 1 and 2): 4
*   Numbers employees (Years 3 and 4): 5
*   Average salary per employee: $20,000 per annum

2.   **Overheads**

*   The annual budgeted fixed overhead of the airport which will be apportioned to the restaurant is $80,000.

*   The annual overheads apportioned to the cold food outlet will be $30,000.

*   The airport's overheads are expected to increase by the following annual amounts as a direct result of the opening of the restaurant:

    –   Electricity: $40,000
    –   Advertising: $20,000
    –   Audit: $10,000

3.   **Cold food outlet**

The average contribution from the sale of cold food is $2·50 per customer. If the restaurant is not opened it is expected that the cold food outlet will sell to 1,200 customers per day in the coming year and in subsequent years the customer numbers will rise in line with passenger numbers.

If the restaurant is opened, the consultants expect sales from the existing cold food outlet to initially reduce by 40% in year 1 and then to increase in line with passenger numbers.

The airport's Financial Director has provided the following taxation information:

- Tax depreciation: 25% reducing balance per annum.

- The first year's tax depreciation allowance is used against the first year's net cash inflows.

- Taxation rate: 30% of taxable profits. Half of the tax is payable in the year in which it arises, the balance is paid the following year.

- Any taxable losses resulting from this investment can be set against profits made by the airport company's other business activities since the airport company is profitable.

The airport company uses a post-tax cost of capital of 8% per annum to evaluate projects of this type. Ignore inflation.

Required

(a)   Calculate the net present value (NPV) of the restaurant project.   **(16 marks)**

(b)   The Managing Director of a company has been presented with the details of three potential investment projects. He has very little experience of project appraisal and has asked you for help.

The project details are given below:-

	Project A	Project B	Project C
Expected NPV	$150,000	$180,000	$180,000
Standard Deviation of Expected NPV	$10,000	$50,000	$30,000
IRR	12%	12%	10%

The three projects will require the same level of initial investment. The projects are mutually exclusive and therefore the Managing Director can only choose one of them.

Required:

Interpret the information for the Managing Director (your answer should include an explanation of the factors he should consider when deciding which project to undertake).   **(9 marks)**

(Total = 25 marks)

---

46 Section C: Projects One and Two (Specimen paper)   45 mins

The Board of Directors of a company are considering two mutually exclusive projects. Both projects necessitate buying new machinery and both projects are expected to have a life of five years.

Project One

This project has already been evaluated. Details of the project are:

Initial investment needed	£500,000
Net present value	£41,000
Accounting rate of return	31%

Project Two

Details of Project Two are:

Year	1	2	3	4	5
Revenue (£000)	370	500	510	515	475
Operating costs (£000)	300	350	380	390	400
Depreciation (£000)	90	90	90	90	90

The figures for revenue and operating costs in the table above are cash flow estimates, have been stated at current values and are assumed to occur at the year end. However differential inflation is expected: 8% per annum for revenue and 6% per annum for operating costs.

The machinery will cost £500,000 and will be sold for £50,000 cash at the end of year 5.

Additional information

The company pays tax at 30%. Tax is paid and / or received one year in arrears.

The machines qualify for tax depreciation at the rate of 25% per annum on a reducing balance basis.

The company's cost of capital is 12% per annum. The current rate of return on investments in the money market is 7%.

The project chosen will be funded by internal funds.

The target accounting rate of return is 30%. The company defines "Accounting rate of return" as the average profit before tax divided by the average investment.

Required

(a)   (i)   Calculate the Net Present Value and the Accounting Rate of Return of Project Two.   **(12 marks)**

      (ii)   Prepare a report for the Board of Directors which recommends which of the projects, if any, they should invest in;   identifies two non-financial factors that are relevant to the decision;   explains the strengths and weaknesses of net present value and accounting rate of return.   **(8 marks)**

(b)   A government organisation has a fixed interest ten-year loan. The interest rate on the loan is 8% per annum. The loan is being repaid in equal annual instalments at the end of each year. The amount borrowed was £250,000. The loan has just over 4 years to run.

     Ignore taxation.

     Required

     Calculate the present value of the amount outstanding on the loan.   **(5 marks)**

                              (Total = 25 marks)

47   Section C: Restaurant (MADM 11/08)   45 mins

A restaurant company is considering further investment in order to increase its seating capacity. The company prepares its accounts to 31 December each year and, if accepted, the proposed investment would be made on 1 January 20X9 and will become operational immediately.

Based on the actual results for the year to date, the latest forecast income statement for the company for the year to 31 December 20X8 is as follows:

	£'000	£'000
Food sales	180	
Drink sales	150	330
Food costs	125	
Drink costs	70	
Staff costs	55	
Other costs*	45	295
Profit		35

*These other costs include rent, light & heat, power and administration overheads. 30% of these costs vary in proportion to the value of sales and the remainder are fixed costs.

The proposed investment

At present the restaurant is not able to exploit the growing demand from customers because it does not have sufficient seating capacity. The restaurant is considering the investment of £40,000 on 1 January 20X9. It is expected that this will increase the seating capacity of the restaurant by 30% compared to the present level. The lease of the current business premises ends at the end of 20Y2.

At that time the £40,000 investment will have no residual value. Of this total investment, £30,000 will qualify for 100% tax depreciation in 20X9 and the remainder will qualify for 20% tax depreciation per year, commencing in 20X9, calculated on a reducing balance basis. Any balancing tax charge will be made or allowance will be available at the end of 20Y2.

Sales

It is expected that the additional sales of food and drink will be proportional to the seating capacity increase and that the mix of food sales and drink sales will not change.

Costs

It is expected that apart from the effects of inflation (see below):

- Food costs and drink costs will continue to be the same percentages of food sales and drink sales as they are in the forecast income statement shown above.

- Staff costs are step costs and are expected to increase by 20% from their forecast value for 20X8 if there is any capacity increase.

- The variable element of other costs is expected to increase in proportion to the capacity increase; the fixed cost element is expected to increase by £10,000 if there is any capacity increase.

Inflation

Cost inflation is predicted to be 4% per annum for each of the years 20X9 to 20Y2 whereas selling prices are only expected to increase by 3% per annum during the same period.

Taxation

The company pays tax on its profits at 20%. This is payable one year after the profit is earned.

Cost of capital

The company's post tax money cost of capital for evaluating this investment is 8% per annum.

Required

(a) Prepare calculations to show whether the investment is worthwhile assuming that the 30% increase in seating capacity is fully utilised and recommend whether the investment should proceed. **(14 marks)**

(b) Calculate and interpret the Internal Rate of Return (IRR) of the proposed investment. **(6 marks)**

(c) Calculate the sensitivity of your recommendation to changes in the percentage capacity utilisation.
(5 marks)

(Total = 25 marks)

48 Section C: H plc | 45 mins

H plc is considering purchasing a new machine to alleviate a bottleneck in its production facilities. At present it uses an old machine which can process 200 units of product P per hour. H plc could replace it with machine AB, which is product-specific and can product 500 units an hour. Machine AB costs £500,000. If it is installed, two members of staff will have to attend a short training course, which will cost the company a total of £5,000. removing the old machine and preparing the area for machine AB will cost £20,000.

The company expects demand for P to be 12,000 units per week for another three years. After this period, during year 4, the new machine would be scrapped and sold for £50,000. The existing machine will have no scrap value. Each P earns a contribution of £1.40. The company works a 40 hour week for 48 weeks in the year. H plc normally expects a payback within two years, and its after-tax cost of capital is 10 per cent per annum. The company receives writing-down allowances of 25 per cent, reducing balance. Corporation tax is payable at 30 per cent. Half of this is payable in the year in which the profit is earned and the remainder is payable in the following year.

Required

(a) Calculate the net present value (NPV) of the project. **(15 marks)**

(b)   A director of H plc has heard the terms *throughput accounting (TA)* and the *TA ratio* as methods of assessing performance. You are required to explain the terms.   **(3 marks)**

(c)   A company is thinking of investing in a new project. The details are as follows:

Investment	$15,000
Time span	3 years
Annual cash inflows	$30,000
Annual cash outflows	$22,500
Cost of capital	10%
NPV @ 10%	$3,652·50

The project does not have a residual value. Ignore taxation.

(i)   Calculate the Internal Rate of Return (IRR) of the investment proposal.   **(3 marks)**
(ii)   Calculate the sensitivity of the investment to changes in the annual cash inflows.   **(4 marks)**

(Total = 25 marks)

49   Section C: Print Co (MADM 5/05)   45 mins

A printing company is considering investing in new equipment which has a capital cost of £3 million. The machine qualifies for tax depreciation at the rate of 25% per year on a reducing balance basis and has an expected life of five years. The residual value of the machine is expected to be £300,000 at the end of five years.

An existing machine would be sold immediately for £400,000 if the new machine were to be bought. This existing machine has a tax written down value of £250,000.

The existing machine generates annual revenues of £4 million and earns a contribution of 40% of sales. The new machine would reduce unit variable costs to 80% of their former value and increase output capacity by 20%. There is sufficient sales demand at the existing prices to make full use of this additional capacity.

The printing company pays corporation tax on its profits at the rate of 30%, with half of the tax being payable in the year that the profit is earned and half in the following year.

The company's after tax cost of capital is 14% per year.

Required

(a)   Evaluate the proposed purchase of the new printing machine from a financial perspective using appropriate calculations, and advise the company as to whether the investment is worthwhile.

(15 marks)

(b)   Explain sensitivity analysis and prepare calculations to show the sensitivity of the decision to independent changes in each of the following:

(i)   Annual contribution
(ii)   Rate of corporation tax on profit.   **(10 marks)**

(Total = 25 marks)

50 Section C: CH Ltd   45 mins

CH Ltd is a swimming club. Potential exists to expand the business by providing a gymnasium as part of the facilities at the club. The directors believe that this will stimulate additional membership of the club.

The expansion project would require an initial expenditure of £550,000. The project is expected to have a disposal value at the end of five years which is equal to 10% of the initial expenditure.

The following schedule reflects a recent market research survey regarding the estimated annual sales revenue from additional memberships over the project's five-year life:

Level of demand	£'000	Probability
High	800	0.25
Medium	560	0.50
Low	448	0.25

It is expected that the contribution to sales ratio will be 55%. Additional expenditure on fixed overheads is expected to be £90,000 per annum.

CH Ltd incurs a 30% tax rate on corporate profits. Corporation tax is to be paid in two equal instalments: one in the year that profits are earned and the other in the following year.

CH Ltd's after-tax nominal (money) discount rate is 15.5% per annum. A uniform inflation rate of 5% per annum will apply to all costs and revenues during the life of the project.

All of the values above have been expressed in terms of current prices. You can assume that all cash flows occur at the end of each year and that the initial investment does not qualify for capital allowances.

Required

(a) Evaluate the proposed expansion from a financial perspective.   **(13 marks)**

(b) Calculate and then demonstrate the sensitivity of the project to changes in the expected annual contribution.

                                                                                    (5 marks)

(c) You have now been advised that the capital cost of the expansion will qualify for writing down allowances at the rate of 25% per annum on a reducing balance basis. Also, at the end of the project's life, a balancing charge or allowance will arise equal to the difference between the scrap proceeds and the tax written down value.

   Required

   Calculate the financial impact of these allowances.   **(7 marks)**

                                                                    (Total = 25 marks)

51 Section C: A Company (MADM 5/05, 5/06 and 5/09 - adapted)
45 mins

A company is considering the replacement of its delivery vehicle. It has chosen the vehicle that it will acquire but it now needs to decide whether the vehicle should be purchased or leased.

The cost of the vehicle is £15,000. If the company purchases the vehicle it will be entitled to claim tax depreciation at the rate of 25% per year on a reducing balance basis. The vehicle is expected to have a trade-in value of £5,000 at the end of three years.

If the company leases the vehicle, it will make an initial payment of £1,250 plus annual payments of £4,992 at the end of each of three years. The full value of each lease payment will be an allowable cost in the computation of the company's taxable profits of the year in which the payments are made.

The company pays corporation tax at the rate of 30% of its profits.

50% of the company's corporation tax is payable in the year in which profits are made and 50% in the following year. Assume that the company has sufficient profits to obtain tax relief on its acquisition of the vehicle in accordance with the information provided above.

The company's after tax cost of capital is 15% per year.

Note. Tax depreciation is not a cash cost but is allowed as a deduction in the calculation of taxable profits.

Required

(a)   Calculate whether the company should purchase or lease the vehicle and clearly state your recommendation to the company.   **(10 marks)**

The company is also considering when to replace its ovens. Each oven has a purchase cost of $14,000. It needs to decide whether to replace its ovens after one year, after two years or after three years.

The following forecast data have been collected for a single oven:

Year of ownership	1	2	3
	$	$	$
Operating costs	5,000	6,000	6,500
Maintenance costs	1,000	2,000	3,000
Trade-in value at the end of the year	10,000	7,000	5,000

The company's cost of capital for this type of decision is 12% per annum.

Ignore taxation.

Required

(b)   Prepare calculations to show the optimum replacement cycle for the company's ovens and state your recommendation.   **(7 marks)**

(c)   Explain two limitations of your solution to (b) above.   **(3 marks)**

A manager in the sister company is evaluating a three year project which has the following relevant pre-tax operating cashflows:

Year	1	2	3
	$000	$000	$000
Sales	4,200	4,900	5,300
Costs	2,850	3,100	4,150

The project requires an investment of $2m at the start of year 1 and has no residual value.

The company pays corporation tax on its net relevant operating cashflows at the rate of 20%. Corporation tax is payable in the same year as the net relevant pre-tax operating cashflows arise. There is no tax depreciation available on the investment.

The manager has discounted the net relevant post-tax operating cashflows using the company's post-tax cost of capital of 7% and this results in a post-tax net present value of the project of $1.018m.

Required

(d)   Calculate the sensitivity of the project to independent changes in

     (i)   the selling price;

     (ii)   the cost of capital.   **(5 marks)**

                 (Total = 25 marks)

52   Section C: SS Ltd   45 mins

SS Ltd is an Internet service provider and also stores and transmits client data over the Internet via its server infrastructure. SS Ltd generates approximately £100,000 in contribution each year from these services to clients.

Because of technical advances in information technology, the existing server infrastructure will shortly become obsolete, and the company is considering what to do. The maintenance of this server infrastructure costs £24,000 per annum and is paid in advance at the beginning of each year. The service infrastructure has been fully written off but has a scrap value of £3,000. A technical consultant, hired at a cost of £5,000, prepared a report outlining that two possible replacement server infrastructures are available on the market. The details of each alternative are as follows.

	Alternative 1	Alternative 2
Initial cost	£100,000	£100,000
Estimated useful life	3 year	5 years
Scrap value	£5,000	£3,000
Annual maintenance costs (in advance)	£24,000	£30,000
Annual contributions	£100,000	£105,000

SS Ltd incurs 30% tax on corporate profits. Writing down allowances are allowed at 25% each year on a reducing balance basis. At the end of the service infrastructure's life, a balancing charge or allowance will arise equal to the difference between the scrap proceeds and the tax written down value. Corporation tax is to be paid in two equal instalments: one in the year that profits are earned and the other in the following year.

SS Ltd's after tax nominal (money) discount rate is 12%.

You can assume that all cash flows occur at the end of each year unless otherwise stated.

Required

(a)   Calculate for each alternative the net present value and annual equivalent cost. Advise senior management which server infrastructure to purchase, stating any assumptions you have made.

(15 marks)

(b)   Briefly explain the purpose and limitations of sensitivity analysis in relation to investment appraisal.

(4 marks)

(c)   Calculate the sensitivity of your recommendation to changes in the contribution generated by Alternative 1, and discuss its relevance to the decision.   **(6 marks)**

(Total = 25 marks)

DEALING WITH UNCERTAINTY IN ANALYSIS

Questions 53 to 60 cover the treatment of uncertainty in decision making, the subject of Part E (Chapter 19) of the BPP Study Text for Paper P1.

53 Section A: Dealing with uncertainty in analysis · 36 mins

1 Daily sales of product X by Y Ltd are likely to be 400 units, 500 units or 600 units. The probability of sales of 500 units is 0.5, while the probability of sales of 600 units is 0.1.

   Required

   Calculate the expected value of the daily sales volume. **(2 marks)**

2 Explain (in less than fifty words) how the value of perfect information is calculated.

   ....

   ....

   (3 marks)

3 Which of the following is a drawback of the decision rule to choose the option with the highest expected value.

   A   The method is too concerned with the need to avoid losses.
   B   The method is concerned only with making the greatest possible profit.
   C   The method ignores less likely outcomes.
   D   The method takes no account of risk aversion. **(2 marks)**

4 The probability of an expected profit of £2,000 is 0.34, the probability of an expected profit of £1,850 is 0.15, the probability of an expected profit of £1,000 is 0.3 and the probability of an expected loss of £3,000 is 0.21. What is the probability of a profit of £1,000 or less?

   A   0.3
   B   0.49
   C   0.51
   D   0.21 **(2 marks)**

5 The decision tree below relates to the cost of sales options for a company.

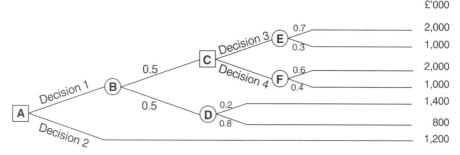

Which of the following statements about the above diagram is false?

   A   At decision point C, decision 4 would be chosen.
   B   The expected value at outcome point B is £680,000.
   C   Decision 2 would be chosen over decision 1.
   D   The expected value at outcome point D is £920,000. **(2 marks)**

The following data relates to questions 6 and 7

X Ltd can choose from five mutually exclusive projects. The projects will each last for one year only and their net cash inflows will be determined by the prevailing market conditions. The forecast annual cash inflows and their associated probabilities are shown below.

Market Conditions	Poor	Good	Excellent
Probability	0·20	0·50	0·30
	£'000	£'000	£'000
Project L	500	470	550
Project M	400	550	570
Project N	450	400	475
Project O	360	400	420
Project P	600	500	425

6   Determine, based on the expected value of the net cash inflows, which project should be undertaken.

(2 marks)

7   Calculate the value of perfect information about the state of the market.   **(3 marks)**

8   BG plc has recently developed a new product. The nature of BG plc's work is repetitive, and it is usual for there to be an 80% learning effect when a new product is developed. The time taken for the first unit was 22 minutes. Assume that an 80% learning effect applies.

Required

Calculate the time taken for the fourth unit.   **(2 marks)**

9   PT has discovered that when it employs a new test engineer there is a learning curve with a 75% rate of learning that exists for the first 12 customer assignments. A new test engineer completed her first customer assignment in 6 hours.

Calculate the time that she should take for her seventh assignment to the nearest 0.01 hours.

Note: The index for a 75% learning curve is –0.415.   **(2 marks)**

(Total = 20 marks)

> If you struggled with these objective test questions, go back to your BPP Study Text for Paper P1 and revise Chapter 19 before you tackle the Section B and Section C type questions on dealing with uncertainty in analysis.

54   Section B: Dealing with uncertainty in analysis   54 mins

(a)   A company has determined its activity level and is now predicting its costs for the forthcoming quarter. It has made the following predictions:

Variable costs	Probability	Fixed costs	Probability
$560,000	0·3	$440,000	0·15
$780,000	0·5	$640,000	0·55
$950,000	0·2	$760,000	0·30

Calculate the expected value of total cost and its standard deviation.

Note: $SD = \sqrt{\dfrac{\Sigma\left(x - \bar{x}\right)^2}{n}}$ **(5 marks)**

(b)   A company is considering investing in one of three marketing campaigns to increase its profitability. All three marketing campaigns have a life of five years, require the same initial investment and have no residual value. The company has already evaluated the marketing campaigns taking into consideration the range of possible outcomes that could result from the investment. A summary of the calculations is shown below:

Marketing campaign

	J	K	L
	$	$	$
Expected net present value	400,000	800,000	400,000
Standard deviation of net present value	35,000	105,000	105,000

Required

(i)   Explain the meaning of the data shown above; and

(ii)   Briefly explain how the data may be used by the company when choosing between alternative investments.   **(5 marks)**

(c)   A baker is trying to decide the number of batches of a particular type of bread that he should bake each day. Daily demand ranges from 10 batches to 12 batches. Each batch of bread that is baked and sold yields a positive contribution of £50, but each batch of bread baked that is not sold yields a negative contribution of £20.

Assuming the baker adopts the minimax regret decision rule, calculate the number of batches of bread that he should bake each day. You must justify your answer.   **(5 marks)**

(d)   (i)   Explain why the use of expected values might not be a satisfactory way of dealing with uncertainty in a once-only decision.

(ii)   Explain why a risk averse decision maker might use the maximin basis to make a choice between options where the outcome is uncertain.   **(5 marks)**

The following data relates to questions 54(e) and 54(f)

P Ltd currently sells 90,000 units of product Y per annum. At this level of sales and output, the selling price and variable cost per unit are £50 and £21 respectively. The annual fixed costs are £1,200,000. The management team is considering lowering the selling price per unit to £45.

The estimated levels of demand at the new price, and the probabilities of them occurring, are:

Selling price of £45

Demand	Probability
100,000 units	0.45
120,000 units	0.55

It is thought that at either of the higher sales and production levels, the variable cost per unit, and the probability of it occurring, will be as follows:

Variable cost (per unit)	Probability
£20	0.40
£18	0.60

(e)   Calculate the probability that lowering the selling price to £45 per unit would increase profit.   **(5 marks)**

(f)   Calculate the expected value of the company profit if the selling price is reduced to £45 per unit.

(5 marks)

(Total = 30 marks)

55   Section C: Theatre (MADM 11/06)   45 mins

A theatre has a seating capacity of 500 people and is considering engaging MS and her orchestra for a concert for one night only. The fee that would be charged by MS would be $10,000. If the theatre engages MS, then this sum is payable regardless of the size of the theatre audience.

Based on past experience of events of this type, the price of the theatre ticket would be $25 per person. The size of the audience for this event is uncertain, but based on past experience it is expected to be as follows.

	Probability
300 people	50%
400 people	30%
500 people	20%

In addition to the sale of the theatre tickets, it can be expected that members of the audience will also purchase confectionery both prior to the performance and during the interval. The contribution that this would yield to the theatre is unclear, but has been estimated as follows.

Contribution from confectionery sales	Probability
Contribution of $3 per person	30%
Contribution of $5 per person	50%
Contribution of $10 per person	20%

Required

(a)   Using expected values as the basis of your decision, advise the theatre management whether it is financially worthwhile to engage MS for the concert.   **(5 marks)**

(b)   Prepare a two-way data table to show the profit values that could occur from deciding to engage MS for the concert.   **(5 marks)**

(c)   Explain, using the probabilities provided and your answer to *(b)* above, how the two-way data table can be used by the theatre management to evaluate the financial risks of the concert, including the probability of making a profit.   **(9 marks)**

(d)   Calculate the maximum price that the theatre management should agree to pay for perfect information relating to the size of the audience and the level of contribution from confectionery sales.   **(6 marks)**

(Total = 25 marks)

56 Section C: Health clinic (MADM 5/06)   45 mins

A health clinic is reviewing its plans for the next three years. It is a not for profit organisation but it has a financial responsibility to manage its costs and to ensure that it provides a value for money service to its clients. The health clinic uses the net present value technique to appraise the financial viability of delivering the service, but it also considers other non-financial factors before making any final decisions.

The present facilities, which incur an annual total cost of £300,000, are only sufficient to meet a low level of service provision so the manager is considering investing in facilities to meet potential higher levels of demand. For the purpose of evaluating this decision the possible levels of demand for the health clinic's services have been simplified to high, medium or low.

The possible demand for the services in the first year and the level of demand that could follow that specific level in the next years, and their expected probabilities, are as follows

Year 1	Probability	Years 2 and 3	Probability
Low	30%	Low	40%
		Medium	60%
		High	0%
Medium	50%	Low	30%
		Medium	40%
		High	30%
High	20%	Low	0%
		Medium	30%
		High	70%

The level of demand will be the same in years 2 and 3.

The manager is considering two alternative investments in facilities:

Facility A has the capacity to meet the low and medium levels of demand and requires an investment at the start of year 1 of £500,000. Thereafter it incurs annual fixed costs of £100,000 and annual variable costs depending on the level of operation. These annual variable costs are expected to be £150,000 at the low level of operation and £250,000 at the medium level of operation.

Facility B has the capacity to meet all levels of demand and requires an investment at the start of year 1 of £800,000. Thereafter it incurs annual fixed costs of £200,000 and annual variable costs depending on the level of operation. These annual variable costs are expected to be £100,000 at the low level of operation, £150,000 at the medium level of operation and £200,000 at the high level of operation.

Neither of these alternative investments has any residual value at the end of year 3.

If the facilities of the health clinic are insufficient to meet the level of service demand that occurs, the clinic must obtain additional facilities on a yearly contract basis at the following annual costs:

Level of service provision available internally	Level of service provision demanded	Annual cost of additional facilities
Low	Medium	£100,000
Low	High	£250,000
Medium	High	£150,000

These additional facilities are not under the direct control of the health clinic manager.

Note. All monetary values used throughout the question have been stated in terms of their present value. No further discounting is required.

Required

(a)   Prepare a decision tree to illustrate the investment decision that needs to be made by the manager of the health clinic. (Numerical values are NOT required.)   **(6 marks)**

(b)   Advise the manager of the health clinic which investment decision should be undertaken on financial grounds.   **(15 marks)**

(c)   Briefly discuss any non-financial factors that the manager should consider before making her final investment decision.   **(4 marks)**

                    (Total = 25 marks)

57 Section C: MP Organisation (MADM 11/05) — 45 mins

The MP Organisation is an independent film production company. It has a number of potential films that it is considering producing, one of which is the subject of a management meeting next week. The film which has been code named CA45 is a thriller based on a novel by a well respected author.

The following additional costs have been estimated in order to produce the film:

	$'000
Production director's fee	100
Set design	10
Costumes and wardrobe	20
Actors' fees	50
Musician/songwriter for soundtrack	5
Camera and equipment hire	20
Actors' travel and accommodation costs	10
Other production costs	5

Production of the film is estimated to take 16 weeks, and all of the above costs would be incurred during this period, though there is some uncertainty about the accuracy of these cost estimates. These cost values are those most likely to be incurred. With the exception of the payment to the production director which is a fixed fee, the other costs could be up to 10% higher or lower than the values estimated.

In addition there will be advertising, promotion and marketing costs of $15,000 immediately, $10,000 in each of years 1 and 2, and then $5,000 during each of the next three years. These figures are not subject to any uncertainty.

The film is expected to have a life of five years. During the first three years the film will be sold to cinemas through distributors and MP will receive 25% of the gross revenues. The film will be sold as a DVD for the remaining two years and MP will receive 100% of these revenues. The expected gross revenues are as follows:

Year	Source	Gross revenue $	MP's share %
1	Cinema	400,000	25
2	Cinema	600,000	25
3	Cinema	450,000	25
4	DVD	50,000	100
5	DVD	30,000	100

However, it is thought that the gross revenues could vary by as much as 20% higher or lower than those stated, depending on the popularity of the film. The initial level of popularity will continue for all five years.

The MP Organisation evaluates new films using a cost of capital of 15% per year.

Required

(a) Prepare calculations for each combination of the most likely, optimistic and pessimistic cost and revenue values to revalue whether or not the MP Organisation should continue with the production of the film. Discuss your analysis and make a recommendation to MP. **(15 marks)**

(b) Prepare notes for the management meeting that explain how probabilities can be used:

    (i)   to calculate the expected NPV; and

    (ii)   in a simulation model to evaluate the risk of a long term decision. **(10 marks)**

(Total = 25 marks)

58 Section C: RY Ltd — 45 mins

RY Ltd, a transatlantic airline company, has recently launched a low-cost airline company providing flights within Europe. The market is highly competitive and two other low-cost airlines, B Ltd and G Ltd, together hold 98% of the market.

RY Ltd commissioned some market research to help with the pricing decision for one route, London to Paris, which it is thinking of offering. The research identified three possible market states and the likely number of passengers that would be attracted at three price levels on this route.

Ticket price		£80	£90	£100
		Passenger	Passenger	Passenger
Market	Probability	seats	seats	seats
Pessimistic	0.2	80	60	30
Most likely	0.6	100	90	80
Optimistic	0.2	150	150	120

Airport charges are incurred for each customer and these are expected to be either £5 or £6 per customer depending on the negotiations with the airports involved. The probabilities for the airport charges are 0.6 for an airport charge of £5 per passenger and 0.4 for an airport charge of £6 per passenger.

The fixed costs of a flight from London to Paris are £4,422.

Required

(a) Use decision tree analysis to advise RY Ltd on the optimum selling price to set. **(10 marks)**

(b) (i) Assuming RY Ltd knew that there would be a pessimistic market, determine the price that it should charge in order to maximise profit. **(3 marks)**

    (ii) The market research company has now stated that by performing further analysis, it will be able to accurately predict the state of the market. Calculate the maximum price that RY Ltd should pay for this further analysis. **(7 marks)**

(c) Discuss the limitations of basing this decision on expected value calculations. **(5 marks)**

(Total = 25 marks)

59   Section C: Purchase options   45 mins

Z Ltd is considering various product pricing and material purchasing options with regard to a new product it has developed. Estimates of demand and costs are as follows.

		Selling price of £15 per unit	Selling price of £20 per unit
		Sales volume ('000 units)	Sales volume ('000 units)
Forecasts	Probability		
Optimistic	0.3	36	28
Most likely	0.5	28	23
Pessimistic	0.2	18	13
Variable manufacturing costs (excluding materials) per unit		£3	£3
Advertising and selling costs		£25,000	£96,000
General fixed costs		£40,000	£40,000

Each unit requires 3 kg of material and because of storage problems any unused material must be sold at £1 per kg. The sole suppliers of the material offer three purchase options, which must be decided at the outset, as follows.

• Any quantity at £3 per kg
• A price of £2.75 per kg for a minimum quantity of 50,000 kg
• A price of £2.50 per kg for a minimum quantity of 70,000 kg

Required

Assume that the company is risk neutral.

(a) Prepare calculations to show what pricing and purchasing decisions the company should make, clearly indicating the recommended decisions. **(18 marks)**

(b) Calculate the maximum price you would pay for perfect information as to whether demand would be optimistic or most likely or pessimistic. **(7 marks)**

(Total = 25 marks)

60 Section C: Tourist hotel (MADM 11/07 & 5/05 – adapted) 45 mins

The owner of a tourist hotel is facing a difficult decision. It is low season and because the weather is unpredictable at this time of the year it is difficult to predict the demand for the hotel's facilities. If the weather is poor then there will be 200 room nights demanded for the hotel's facilities. There is a 70% likelihood of the weather being poor. If the weather is good then there will be 600 room nights demanded for the hotel's facilities, but there is only a 30% chance that the weather will be good.

The owner of the hotel is considering advertising some reduced prices locally or nationally in order to improve the demand during this period.

If the reduced prices are advertised locally and if the weather is poor, then there is a 60% chance that the lower prices would affect demand and would cause there to be 300 room nights demanded, but if the weather is good, then there is a 40% chance that the lower prices would affect demand and would cause there to be 800 room nights demanded.

If these lower prices were advertised nationally there is a 50% chance that these demand levels would increase to 400 room nights and 900 room nights respectively.

The earnings expected, (before deducting the costs of any local or national advertising), at different levels of demand are as follows:

Room nights demanded	Earnings ($)
200	(35,000)
300	(15,000)
400	(5,000)
500	20,000
600	30,000
700	45,000
800	65,000
900	90,000

The costs of advertising locally and nationally are $10,000 and $25,000 respectively.

Required

(a) Prepare a decision tree to illustrate the above problem and use this to recommend, with reasons, the best course of action for the owner of the hotel. **(7 marks)**

(b) Briefly discuss the limitations of using a decision tree to solve this problem. **(3 marks)**

(c) The CS group is planning its annual marketing conference for its sales executives and has approached the VBJ Holiday company (VBJ) to obtain a quotation. The relevant cost was calculated as $10,860.

Now that the quotation has been prepared, it is realised that there is some uncertainty concerning the hotel cost and the fuel cost. Further investigation has shown that these costs may be higher or lower than the original estimates. Estimated costs with their associated probabilities are as follows:

Estimated hotel cost $	Probability %	Estimated fuel cost $	Probability %
4,000	20	1,200	10
5,000	50	1,500	50
6,000	30	2,000	40

The following two-way data table shows the effect on the total relevant cost of these alternative values. All figures are in $:

		Hotel		
		$4,000	$5,000	$6,000
	$1,200	−1,300	−300	+700
Fuel	$1,500	−1,000	0	+1,000
	$2,000	−500	+500	+1,500

Required

(i)   Explain the meaning of the above two-way data table.

(ii)   Produce and interpret a table that shows how the two-way data table may be used in conjunction with the probabilities to improve the information available to the manager of VBJ.   **(15 marks)**

(Total = 25 marks)

61   Section A: Mixed objective test question bank 1   36 mins

1   What is the name given to a budget that has been prepared by re-evaluating activities and comparing the incremental costs of those activities with their incremental benefits?

A   Incremental budget
B   Functional budget
C   Zero base budget
D   Cash budget   **(2 marks)**

MAPE 11/08

2   The following table shows the number of patients treated and the total costs for a hospital for each of the past four months:

Month	Patients	Total Cost $
1	5,000	37,500
2	8,400	45,660
3	8,300	45,050
4	5,900	39,420

Applying the high low method to the above information, an equation that could be used to forecast total cost ($) from the number of patients to be treated (where x = number of patients to be treated) is:

A   22,900 + 2·40x
B   24,300 + 2·50x
C   25,000 + 2·50x
D   25,500 + 2·40x   **(2 marks)**

MAPE 11/08

3   The sales volume profit variance is defined as the difference between the

A   Actual and budgeted sales volumes valued at the actual profit per unit.

B   Actual and budgeted sales volumes valued at the standard profit per unit.

C   Actual and budgeted sales volumes valued at the difference between the actual and standard profit margins.

D   Actual and standard profit per unit multiplied by the budgeted sales volume.   **(2 marks)**

MAPE 11/08

The following data relate to questions 4 and 5 below

A company manufactures a fruit flavoured drink concentrate by mixing two liquids (X and Y). The standard cost card for ten litres of the drink concentrate is:

		$
Liquid X	5 litres @ $16 per litre	80
Liquid Y	6 litres @ $25 per litre	150
	11 litres	230

The company does not hold any inventory. During the last period the company produced 4,800 litres of the drink concentrate. This was 200 litres below the budgeted output. The company purchased 2,200 litres of X for $18 per litre and 2,750 litres of Y for $21 per litre.

---

4   The materials mix variance for the period was:

    A $150 adverse
    B $450 adverse
    C $6,480 favourable
    D $6,900 favourable   **(2 marks)**

MAPE 11/08

---

5   The materials yield variance for the period was:

    A $150 adverse
    B $450 adverse
    C $6,480 favourable
    D $6,900 favourable   **(2 marks)**

MAPE 11/08

---

6   A company is considering investing $100,000 in a new machine that will reduce its annual cash operating costs as follows:

Year	Operating cash costs saved
	$'000
1	35
2	45
3	55
4	30

Calculate the payback period to the nearest 0.1 years.   **(2 marks)**

MADM 11/08

---

7   A company has only $700,000 available for investment during the coming year. It has identified the following four investment opportunities, all of which are divisible, and have the same life.

Investment	Capital required	Net Present Value
	$	$
J	400,000	650,000
K	250,000	450,000
L	300,000	480,000
M	350,000	550,000

Calculate the correct rank order for these investments (best first).   **(2 marks)**

MADM 11/08

---

8   Which ONE of the following would **not** have the effect of shortening the working capital cycle?

    A   Reducing raw material inventory holding.
    B   Increasing credit given to customers.
    C   Delaying payments to suppliers.
    D   Increasing the turnover of finished goods inventory.   **(2 marks)**

FATP 11/08

9   State **four** factors that should be considered before the cause of a variance is investigated.   **(4 marks)**

MAPE 11/08

(Total = 20 marks)

62   Section A: Mixed objective test question bank 2   36 mins

1   If inventory levels have increased during the period, the profit calculated using marginal costing when compared with that calculated using absorption costing will be:

    A   Higher
    B   Lower
    C   Equal
    D   Impossible to answer without further information   **(2 marks)**

MAPE 5/08

2   Fixed production overheads will always be under-absorbed when:

    A   Actual output is lower than budgeted output
    B   Actual overheads incurred are lower than budgeted overheads
    C   Overheads absorbed are lower than those budgeted
    D   Overheads absorbed are lower than those incurred   **(2 marks)**

MAPE 5/08

The following scenario is to be used for questions 3 and 4

A company manufactures three products: W, X and Y. The products use a series of different machines, but there is a common machine that is a bottleneck.

The standard selling price and standard cost per unit for each product for the next period are as follows.

	W £	X £	Y £
Selling price	180	150	150
Cost:			
Direct material	41	20	30
Direct labour	30	20	50
Variable production overheads	24	16	20
Fixed production overheads	36	24	30
Profit	49	70	20
Time (minutes) on bottleneck machine	7	10	7

The company is trying to plan the best use of its resources.

3   Using a traditional limiting factor approach, the rank order (best first) of the products would be:

A   W, X, Y
B   W, Y, X
C   X, W, Y
D   Y, X, W

(2 marks)

MAPE 5/08

4   Using a throughput accounting approach, the rank order (best first) of the products would be:

A   W, X, Y
B   W, Y, X
C   X, W, Y
D   Y, X, W

(2 marks)

MAPE 5/08

5   Which of the following statements are true?

(i)   Enterprise Resource Planning (ERP) systems are accounting oriented information systems which aid in identifying and planning the enterprise wide resources needed to resource, make, account for and deliver customer orders.

(ii)   Flexible Manufacturing Systems (FMS) are integrated, computer-controlled production systems, capable of producing any of a range of parts and of switching quickly and economically between them.

(iii)   Just-In-Time (JIT) is a system whose objective is to produce, or to procure, products or components as they are required.

A   (i) and (ii) only
B   (i) and (iii) only
C   (ii) and (iii) only
D   (i), (ii) and (iii)

(2 marks)

MAPE 5/08

6   A company is considering the following investments for the year ending 30 June 20X9.

Investment	Capital required	NPV
	$	$
W	100,000	56,000
X	150,000	75,000
Y	140,000	68,000
Z	190,000	91,000

None of the investments are divisible. They cannot be undertaken more than once within each year. The company has only $350,000 available to invest in the year to 30 June 20X9. There are no other investments available at this time.

Which investment (if any) should the company undertake?

(2 marks)

MADM 5/08

7   A company will forecast its quarterly sales units for a new product by using a formula to predict the base sales units and then adjusting the figure by a seasonal index.

The formula is BU = 4,000 + 80Q

Where BU = Base sales units and Q is the quarterly period number

The seasonal index value are:

Quarter 1   105%
Quarter 2   80%
Quarter 3   95%
Quarter 4   120%

The forecast increase in sales units from Quarter 3 to Quarter 4 is:

A   25%
B   80 units
C   100 units
D   1,156 units   (2 marks)

MAPE 5/08

8   Which one of the following is correct?

A cash budget prepared on a monthly basis is done to calculate:

A   The amount of inventory to purchase in the following month
B   When to pay workers' wages
C   Next month's sales volumes
D   Whether there will be sufficient cash in the bank to meet requirements   (2 marks)

FATP 5/08

9   A company uses the economic order quantity model (EOQ model). Demand for the company's product is 36,000 units each year and is evenly distributed each day. The cost of placing an order is $10 and the cost of holding a unit of stock for a year is $2.

How many orders should the company make in a year?

A   60
B   120
C   300
D   600   (2 marks)

10   A project has an initial investment of $140,000 and a net present value of $42,500. The present value of the sales revenue generated by the project is $385,000.

The sensitivity of the investment to changes in the value of sales revenue is closest to:

A   36%
B $342,500
C   89%
D   11%   (2 marks)

MADM 5/08

(Total = 20 marks)

63   Section A: Mixed objective test question bank 3   36 mins

1   T Ltd uses a standard labour hour rate to charge its overheads to its clients' work. During the last annual reporting period production overheads were under-absorbed by £19,250. The anticipated standard labour hours for the period were 38,000 hours while the standard hours actually charged to clients were 38,500. The actual production overheads incurred in the period were £481,250.

The budgeted production overheads for the period were

A   £456,000
B   £462,000
C   £475,000
D   None of the above.   (2 marks)

MAPE 11/07

2   Operation B, in a factory, has a standard time of 15 minutes. The standard rate of pay for operatives is £10 per hour. The budget for a period was based on carrying out the operation 350 times. It was subsequently realised that the standard time for Operation B included in the budget did not incorporate expected time savings from the use of new machinery from the start of the period. The standard time should have been reduced to 12 minutes.

Operation B was actually carried out 370 times in the period in a total of 80 hours. The operatives were paid £850.

The operational labour efficiency variance was.

A   £60 adverse
B   £75 favourable
C   £100 adverse
D   £125 adverse   **(2 marks)**

MAPE 11/07

3   Two CIMA definitions follow:

1.   A system that converts a production schedule into a listing of the materials and components required to meet that schedule so that adequate stock levels are maintained and items are available when needed.

2.   An accounting oriented information system, generally software driven, which aids in identifying and planning the enterprise-wide resources needed to resource, make, account for and deliver customer orders.

Which of the following pairs of terms matches the definitions?

	Definition 1	*Definition 2*
A	Material requirements planning	Enterprise resource planning
B	Manufacturing resource planning	Material requirements planning
C	Material requirements planning	Manufacturing resource planning
D	Manufacturing resource planning	Enterprise resource planning

(2 marks)

MAPE 11/07

4   The fixed overhead volume variance is defined as

A   the difference between the budgeted value of the fixed overheads and the standard fixed overheads absorbed by actual production.

B   the difference between the standard fixed overhead cost specified for the production achieved, and the actual fixed overhead cost incurred.

C   the difference between budgeted and actual fixed overhead expenditure.

D   the difference between the standard fixed overhead cost specified in the original budget and the same volume of fixed overheads, but at the actual prices incurred.   **(2 marks)**

MAPE 11/07

5   Overheads will always be over-absorbed when

A   actual output is higher than budgeted output.
B   actual overheads incurred are higher than the amount absorbed.
C   actual overheads incurred are lower than the amount absorbed.
D   budgeted overheads are lower than the overheads absorbed.   **(2 marks)**

MAPE 11/07

6   A company has a real cost of capital of 6.00% per annum and inflation is currently 4.00% per annum.

The company's annual money cost of capital is closest to:

A   10.24%
B   10.00%
C   2.00%
D   1.92%   **(2 marks)**

`MADM 5/08`

The following data is to be used when answering questions 7 and 8

A company is considering investing in a new machine. The machine will cost $15,000 and has an expected life of five years with a residual value of $3,000. The machine will increase the operating cashflows of the company as follows.

Year	Increase in Operating cashflow
	$
1	2,500
2	3,000
3	5,500
4	4,000
5	3,000

7   Calculate the payback period of the new machine to the nearest 0.1 years.   **(2 marks)**

`MADM 5/08`

8   Calculate the average Annual Accounting Rate of Return over the lifetime of the investment in the new machine.   **(2 marks)**

`MADM 5/08`

9   A company is considering its costs in respect of a new product. The following tables show the predictions made by the company, together with their associated probabilities.

Fixed costs	Probability
$	
100,000	0.35
130,000	0.45
160,000	0.20

Variable costs	Probability
$	
70,000	0.40
90,000	0.35
110,000	0.25

Calculate the expected value of total costs.   **(2 marks)**

`MADM 5/08`

10   GS forecast its need for financing to be $220,000, comprising:

	$
Non-current assets	100,000
Permanent portion of current assets	70,000
Fluctuating portion of current assets	50,000
	220,000

GS plans to fund this requirement as follows:

	$
Equity share capital	125,000
Seven year bank loan	65,000
Bank overdraft and funding from trade payables	30,000
	220,000

Gs could be said to have a financing of working capital policy that is

A   aggressive.
B   conservative.
C   tactical.
D   strategic.   (2 marks)

FATP 11/08

(Total = 20 marks)

64 Section A: Mixed objective test question bank 4   36 mins

1   A company uses a standard absorption costing system. The fixed overhead absorption rate is based on labour hours.

Extracts from the company's records for last year were as follows.

	Budget	Actual
Fixed production overhead	$450,000	$475,000
Output	50,000 units	60,000 units
Labour hours	900,000	930,000

The under- or over-absorbed fixed production overheads for the year were:

A $10,000 under-absorbed
B $10,000 over-absorbed
C $15,000 over-absorbed
D $65,000 over-absorbed   (2 marks)

MAPE 5/08

2   Product XYZ is made by mixing three materials (X, Y and Z). There is an expected loss of 20% of the total input.

The budgeted and actual results for Period 1 are shown below. There were no opening or closing inventories of any materials or of the finished product.

	Budget		Actual	
Output of XYZ	800 kg		960 kg	
Material				
X	500 kg	@ $5.00 per kg	600 kg	@ $4.70 per kg
Y	300 kg	@ $6.00 per kg	380 kg	@ $6.50 per kg
Z	200 kg	@ $7.00 per kg	300 kg	@ $7.10 per kg
Total input	1,000 kg		1,280 kg	

Calculate for Period 1:

(i)   The total materials mix variance   (2 marks)
(ii)   The total materials yield variance   (2 marks)

MAPE 5/08

3   GL's trade payables days outstanding at 30 September 20X8 were 45 days. Purchases for the year to 30 September 20X8 were $324,444 accruing evenly throughout the year.

GL is budgeting for an increase in annual purchases to $356,900 for the 12 months to 30 September 20X9.

Assume that the accounts payable outstanding balance at 30 September 20X9 will be the same amount as at 30 September 20X8.

Calculate the budgeted trade payables days outstanding at 30 September 20X9.   (3 marks)

FATP 11/08

4   GF wants to sell an unquoted bond. The bond has a coupon rate of 5% and will repay its face value of $1,000 at the end of four years.

GF estimates that the market requires a yield to maturity of 11% from this type of bond. GF has asked you to recommend a selling price for the bond.

Calculate a selling price for the bond.   **(4 marks)**

FATP 11/08

5   A company has an annual post tax money cost of capital of 18%.

If inflation is 5% per annum the company's annual post tax real cost of capital is closest to

A   12%
B   13%
C   23%
D   24%   **(2 marks)**

MADM 11/08

6   A project has a net present value of $683,000. The present value of the direct material cost is $825,000. Calculate the sensitivity of the project to changes in the direct material cost to 2 decimal places.   **(2 marks)**

MADM 11/07

7   RDE plc uses an activity based costing system to attribute overhead costs to its three products. The following budgeted data relates to the year to 31 December 20X8:

Product	X	Y	Z
Production units (000)	15	25	20
Batch size (000 units)	2·5	5	4

Machine set up costs are caused by the number of batches of each product and have been estimated to be £600,000 for the year.

Calculate the machine set up costs that would be attributed to each unit of product Y.   **(3 marks)**

MADM 11/07

(Total = 20 marks)

65   Section A: Mixed objective test question bank 5   36 mins

The following data relate to questions 1 and 2 below

A manufacturing company recorded the following costs in October for Product X:

	$
Direct materials	20,000
Direct labour	6,300
Variable production overhead	4,700
Fixed production overhead	19,750
Variable selling costs	4,500
Fixed distribution costs	16,800
Total costs incurred for Product X	72,050

During October 4,000 units of Product X were produced but only 3,600 units were sold. At the beginning of October there was no inventory.

1   The value of the inventory of Product X at the end of October using marginal costing was:

    A $3,080
    B $3,100
    C $3,550
    D $5,075   **(2 marks)**

MAPE 11/07

2   The value of the inventory of Product X at the end of October using throughput accounting was

    A $630
    B $1,080
    C $1,100
    D $2,000   **(2 marks)**

MAPE 11/07

3   If an entity regularly fails to pay its suppliers by the normal due dates, it may lead to a number of problems:

    1   Having insufficient cash to settle trade payables;
    2   Difficulty in obtaining credit from new suppliers;
    3   Reduction in credit rating;
    4   Settlement of trade receivables may be delayed.

Which TWO of the above could arise as a result of exceeding suppliers' trade credit terms?

    A   1 and 2
    B   1 and 3
    C   2 and 3
    D   3 and 4   **(2 marks)**

FATP 5/06

4   PP Ltd is preparing the production and material purchases budgets for one of their products, the SUPERX, for the forthcoming year.

The following information is available:

SUPERX

Sales demand (units)	30,000
Material usage per unit	7 kgs
Estimated opening inventory	3,500 units
Required closing inventory	35% higher than opening inventory

How many units of the SUPERX will need to be produced?

    A   28,775
    B   30,000
    C   31,225
    D   38,225   **(2 marks)**

MAPE 5/07

The following data are given for sub-questions 5 and 6 below

X Ltd operates a standard costing system and absorbs fixed overheads on the basis of machine hours. Details of budgeted and actual figures are as follows:

	Budget	Actual
Fixed overheads	£2,500,000	£2,010,000
Output	500,000 units	440,000 units
Machine hours	1,000,000 hours	900,000 hours

5   The fixed overhead expenditure variance is

   A   £190,000 favourable
   B   £250,000 adverse
   C   £300,000 adverse
   D   £490,000 favourable   **(2 marks)**

                                                                               MAPE 5/07

---

6   The fixed overhead volume variance is

   A   £190,000 favorable
   B   £250,000 adverse
   C   £300,000 adverse
   D   £490,000 favorable   **(2 marks)**

                                                                               MAPE 5/07

---

7   A company is considering an investment of $400,000 in new machinery. The machinery is expected to yield incremental profits over the next five years as follows:

Year	Profit ($)
1	175,000
2	225,000
3	340,000
4	165,000
5	125,000

   Thereafter, no incremental profits are expected and the machinery will be sold. It is company policy to depreciate machinery on a straight line basis over the life of the asset. The machinery is expected to have a value of $50,000 at the end of year 5.

   Calculate the payback period of the investment in this machinery to the nearest 0·1 years.   **(3 marks)**

                                                                               MADM 11/07

---

8   A company has an annual money cost of capital of 20% and inflation is 8% per annum. Calculate the company's annual real percentage cost of capital to 2 decimal places   **(2 marks)**

                                                                               MADM 11/07

---

9   A company can produce many types of product but is currently restricted by the number of labour hours available on a particular machine. At present this limitation is set at 12,000 hours per annum. One type of product requires materials costing $5 which are then converted to a final product which sells for $12. Each unit of this product takes 45 minutes to produce on the machine. The conversion costs for the factory are estimated to be $144,000 per annum.

   Calculate the throughput accounting ratio for this product and state the significance of the result.
                                                                               (3 marks)

                                                                               MAPE 11/07

                                                                               (Total = 20 marks)

---

66 Section A: Mixed objective test question bank 6   36 mins

1   An investor buys $11,000 (nominal value) of a bond with a coupon rate of 10%, for the current market value of $10,000. Average market returns are 12%. What is the interest yield to the nearest one percent?

    A   9%
    B   10%
    C   11%
    D   12%   **(2 marks)**

2   A company operates a standard absorption costing system. The budgeted fixed production overheads for the company for the latest year were £330,000 and budgeted output was 220,000 units. At the end of the company's financial year the total of the fixed production overheads debited to the Fixed Production Overhead Control Account was £260,000 and the actual output achieved was 200,000 units.

    The under/over absorption of overheads was

    A   £40,000 over absorbed
    B   £40,000 under absorbed
    C   £70,000 over absorbed
    D   £70,000 under absorbed   **(2 marks)**

    `MAPE 5/07`

3   A company operates a standard absorption costing system. The following fixed production overhead data are available for the latest period:

    Budgeted Output   300,000 units
    Budgeted Fixed Production Overhead   £1,500,000
    Actual Fixed Production Overhead   £1,950,000
    Fixed Production Overhead Total Variance £150,000 adverse

    The actual level of production for the period was nearest to

    A   277,000 units
    B   324,000 units
    C   360,000 units
    D   420,000 units   **(2 marks)**

    `MAPE 5/07`

4   Which of the following best describes a basic standard?

    A   A standard set at an ideal level, which makes no allowance for normal losses, waste and machine downtime.
    B   A standard which assumes an efficient level of operation, but which includes allowances for factors such as normal loss, waste and machine downtime.
    C   A standard which is kept unchanged over a period of time.
    D   A standard which is based on current price levels.   **(2 marks)**

    `MAPE 5/07`

5   XYZ Ltd is preparing the production budget for the next period. The total costs of production are a semi-variable cost. The following cost information has been collected in connection with production:

            Volume (units)   *Cost*
               4,500   £29,000
               6,500   £33,000

The estimated total production costs for a production volume of 5,750 units is nearest to

A	£29,200
B	£30,000
C	£31,500
D	£32,500

(2 marks)

MAPE 5/07

6   AL's customers all pay their accounts at the end of 30 days. To try and improve its cash flow, AL is considering offering all customers a 1.5% discount for payment within 14 days.

Calculate the implied annual (interest) cost to AL of offering the discount, using compound interest methodology and assuming a 365 day year.   **(3 marks)**

FATP 5/05

The following data are to be used when answering questions 7 and 8

JKL plc has $1 million available for investment. It has identified three possible investments, J K and L, which each have a life of three years. The three-year period coincides with JKL plc's investment plans. JKL plc uses a 15% cost of capital when appraising investments of this type. Details of these investments are set out below

	J	K	L
	$'000	$'000	$'000
Initial investment	400	500	300
Net positive cashflows			
Year 1	40	70	50
Year 2	80	90	50
Year 3	510	630	380
Net present value	31	43	31

7   Assuming that each of the investments is divisible, they are not mutually exclusive and cannot be invested in more than once, state the optimum investment plan for JKL plc.   **(2 marks)**

MADM 11/05

8   Calculate the Internal Rate of Return of an investment in project K to the nearest 0.01%.   **(3 marks)**

MADM 11/05

9   A hospital is considering investing $80,000 in a new computer system that will reduce the amount of time taken to process a patient's records when making an appointment. It is estimated that the cash benefit of the time saved will be $20,000 in the first year, $30,000 in the second year and $50,000 in each of the next three years. At the end of five years the computer system will be obsolete and will need to be replaced. It is not expected to have any residual value.

Calculate the payback period to one decimal place of one year.   **(2 marks)**

MADM 11/06

(Total = 20 marks)

67   Section A: Mixed objective test question bank 7   36 mins

The following data are to be used when answering questions 1 and 2

A company expects to sell 1,000 units per month of a new product but there is uncertainty as to both the unit selling price and the unit variable cost of the product. The following estimates of selling price, variable costs and their related probabilities have been made:

Selling price £ per unit	Unit variable cost probability %	£ per unit	Probability %
20	25	8	20
25	40	10	50
30	35	12	30

There are specific fixed costs of £5,000 per month expected for the new product.

1   The expected value of monthly contribution is

A   £5,890
B   £10,300
C   £10,890
D   £15,300   **(2 marks)**

MADM 11/05

2   The probability of monthly contribution from this new product exceeding £13,500 is

A   24.5%
B   30.5%
C   63.0%
D   92.5%   **(2 marks)**

MADM 11/05

3   An investment project that requires an initial investment of $500,000 has a residual value of $130,000 at the end of five years. The project's cash flows have been discounted at the company's cost of capital of 12% and the resulting net present value is $140,500. The profitability index of the project is closest to:

A   0·02
B   0·54
C   0·28
D   0·26   **(2 marks)**

MADM 5/07

4   A project has a net present value of $320,000.

The sales revenues for the project have a total pre-discounted value of $900,000 and a total present value of $630,000 after tax.

The sensitivity of the investment to changes in the value of sales is closest to:

A $310,000
B $580,000
C   51%
D   36%   **(2 marks)**

MADM 5/07

5   A bond with a coupon rate of 7% is redeemable in 8 year's time for $100. Its current purchase price is $82. What is the percentage yield to maturity?   **(2 marks)**

FATP 5/05

6   Which ONE of the following transactions is most likely to affect the overall amount of working capital?

A   Receipt of full amount of cash from a customer to settle their trade receivable account.
B   Payment of a trade payable account in full.
C   Sale of a non-current asset on credit at its net book value.
D   Purchase of inventory on credit.   **(2 marks)**

7   RF Ltd is about to launch a new product in June 20X7. The company has commissioned some market research to assist in sales forecasting. The resulting research and analysis established the following equation:

$(Y = Ax^{0.6})$

Where Y is the cumulative sales units, A is the sales units in month 1, x is the month number.

June 20X7 is Month 1.

Sales in June 20X7 will be 1,500 units.

Calculate the forecast sales volume for each of the months June, July and August 20X7 and for that three month period in total.   **(4 marks)**

MAPE 5/07

8   S Ltd manufactures three products, A, B and C. The products use a series of different machines but there is a common machine, P, that is a bottleneck.

The selling price and standard cost for each product for the forthcoming year is as follows:

	A	B	C
	$	$	$
Selling price	200	150	150
Direct materials	41	20	30
Conversion costs	55	40	66
Machine P – minutes	12	10	7

Calculate the return per hour for each of the products.   **(4 marks)**

MAPE 5/07

(Total = 20 marks)

68 Section A: Mixed objective test question bank 8   36 mins

1   A manufacturer of china commemorating the Olympic Games is facing a short-term liquidity shortage. Which of the following assets could it sell in order to make good the cash shortfall while doing the minimum damage to its core activities?

A   10% of its fleet of delivery vehicles
B   The pigment blending plant
C   The patent on a new design of china pouring device intended to commemorate the Olympic Games
D   Its 60% equity stake in the company that supplies its gold leaf   **(2 marks)**

2   X is considering the following five investments:

Investment	J	K	L	M	N
	$000	$000	$000	$000	$000
Initial investment	400	350	450	500	600
Net Present Value	125	105	140	160	190

Investments J and L are mutually exclusive, all of the investments are divisible and none of them may be invested in more than once. The optimum investment plan for X assuming that the funding available is limited to $1m is

A $400,000 in J plus $600,000 in N.
B $400,000 in M plus $600,000 in N.
C $500,000 in M plus $500,000 in N.
D $350,000 in K plus $600,000 in N plus $50,000 in M.   **(2 marks)**

MADM 11/06

3　Which of the following definitions are correct?

　　I　Just-in-time (JIT) systems are designed to produce or procure products or components as they are required for a customer or for use, rather than for inventory.

　　II　Flexible manufacturing systems (FMS) are integrated, computer-controlled production systems, capable of producing any of a range of parts and of switching quickly and economically between them.

　　III　Material requirements planning (MRP) systems are computer based systems that integrate all aspects of a business so that the planning and scheduling of production ensures components are available when needed.

　　A　I only
　　B　I and II only
　　C　I and III only
　　D　II and III only　　　　　　　　　　　　　　　　　　　　　　　**(2 marks)**

MAPE 11/06

4　A five-year project has a net present value of $160,000 when it is discounted at 12%. The project includes an annual cash outflow of $50,000 for each of the five years. No tax is payable on projects of this type.

The percentage increase in the value of this annual cash outflow that would make the project no longer financially viable is closest to:

　　A　64%
　　B　89%
　　C　113%
　　D　156%　　　　　　　　　　　　　　　　　　　　　　　　　　　**(2 marks)**

MADM 11/05

5　DR has the following balances under current assets and current liabilities.

Current assets

	$
Inventory	50,000
Trade receivables	70,000
Bank	10,000

Current liabilities

	$
Trade payables	88,000
Interest payable	7,000

DR's quick ratio is

　　A　0.80:1
　　B　0.84:1
　　C　0.91:1
　　D　1.37:1　　　　　　　　　　　　　　　　　　　　　　　　　　**(2 marks)**

FATP 5/07

6　PQR Ltd operates a standard absorption costing system. Details of budgeted and actual figures are as follows:

	Budget	Actual
Sales volume (units)	100,000	110,000
Selling price per unit	£10	£9.50
Variable cost per unit	£5	£5.25
Total cost per unit	£8	£8.30

　　(i)　Calculate the sales price variance.　　　　　　　　　　　　　**(2 marks)**
　　(ii)　Calculate the sales volume profit variance.　　　　　　　　　**(2 marks)**

MAPE 5/07

7   SS Ltd operates a standard marginal costing system. An extract from the standard cost card for the labour costs of one of its products is as follows.

Labour Cost

5 hours × £12   £60

Actual results for the period were as follows:

Production	11,500 units
Labour rate variance	£45,000 adverse
Labour efficiency variance	£30,000 adverse

Calculate the actual rate paid per direct labour hour.   **(2 marks)**

MAPE 11/06

---

8   A company has the following budgeted sales figures:

Month 1	£90,000
Month 2	£105,000
Month 3	£120,000
Month 4	£108,000

80% of sales are on credit and the remainder are paid in cash. Credit customers paying within one month are given a discount of 1·5%. Credit customers normally pay within the following time frame:

Within 1 month	40% of credit sales
Within 2 months	70% of credit sales
Within 3 months	98% of credit sales

There is an expectation that 2% of credit sales will become bad debts.

Outstanding receivables at the beginning of month 1 includes £6,000 expected to be received in month 4.

Calculate the total receipts expected in month 4.   **(4 marks)**

MAPE 11/07

(Total = 20 marks)

---

69   Section A: Mixed objective test question bank 9   36 mins

The following data are given for sub-questions 1 to 3 below

A company uses standard absorption costing. The following information was recorded by the company for October:

	Budget	Actual
Output and sales (units)	8,700	8,200
Selling price per unit	£26	£31
Variable cost per unit	£10	£10
Total fixed overheads	£34,800	£37,000

---

1   The sales price variance for October was:

A   £38,500 favourable
B   £41,000 favourable
C   £41,000 adverse
D   £65,600 adverse
                                                                                   (2 marks)

MAPE 11/06

2   The sales volume profit variance for October was:

    A   £6,000 adverse
    B   £6,000 favourable
    C   £8,000 adverse
    D   £8,000 favourable   **(2 marks)**

MAPE 11/06

3   The fixed overhead volume variance for October was:

    A   £2,000 adverse
    B   £2,200 adverse
    C   £2,200 favourable
    D   £4,200 adverse   **(2 marks)**

MAPE 11/06

4   When receivables are sold to a debt factoring company, which of the following is LEAST likely?

    A   Cash will be received sooner than if debts were not sold.
    B   The receivables will be sold at a profit to the selling company.
    C   The debt factoring company will make a profit on the service provided.
    D   Working capital will decrease.   **(2 marks)**

5   PP Ltd operates a standard absorption costing system. The following information has been extracted from the standard cost card for one of its products:

Budgeted production	1,500 units
Direct material cost: 7 kg × £4.10	£28.70 per unit

Actual results for the period were as follows:

Production	1,600 units
Direct material (purchased and used): 12,000 kgs	£52,200

It has subsequently been noted that due to a change in economic conditions the best price that the material could have been purchased for was £4.50 per kg during the period.

    (i)   Calculate the material price planning variance.
    (ii)   Calculate the operational material usage variance.   **(3 marks)**

MAPE 11/06

The following data relates to both questions 6 and 7

TX Ltd can choose from five mutually exclusive projects. The projects will each last for one year only and their net cash inflows will be determined by the prevailing market conditions. The forecast net cash inflows and their associated probabilities are shown below.

	Market conditions		
	Poor	Good	Excellent
Probability	0.20	0.50	0.30
	$'000	$'000	$'000
Project L	500	470	550
Project M	400	550	570
Project N	450	400	475
Project O	360	400	420
Project P	600	500	425

6   Based on the expected value of the net cash inflows, which project should be undertaken?   **(2 marks)**

7   The value of perfect information about the state of the market is calculated as: **(3 marks)**

8   JJ Ltd manufactures three products: W, X and Y. The products use a series of different machines but there is a common machine that is a bottleneck.

The standard selling price and standard cost per unit for each product for the forthcoming period are as follows:

	W £	X £	Y £
Selling price	200	150	150
Cost			
Direct materials	41	20	30
Labour	30	20	36
Overheads	60	40	50
Profit	69	70	34
Bottleneck machine – minutes per unit	9	10	7

40% of the overhead cost is classified as variable

Using a throughput accounting approach, what would be the ranking of the products for best use of the bottleneck? **(2 marks)**

MAPE 11/06

9   An investment company is considering the purchase of a commercial building at a cost of £0·85m. The property would be rented immediately to tenants at an annual rent of £80,000 payable in arrears in perpetuity.

Calculate the net present value of the investment assuming that the investment company's cost of capital is 8% per annum.

Ignore taxation and inflation. **(2 marks)**

MADM 11/06

(Total = 20 marks)

70   Section A: Mixed objective test question bank 10   36 mins

The following data are given for sub-questions 1 to 3 below

The following data relate to product Z and its raw material content for September.

Budget
Output   11,000 units of Z
Standard materials content   3 kg per unit at $4.00 per kg

Actual
Output   10,000 units of Z
Materials purchased and used   32,000 kg at $4.80 per kg

It has now been agreed that the standard price for the raw material purchased in September should have been $5 per kg.

1   The materials planning price variance for September was:

A $6,000 Adverse
B $30,000 Adverse
C $32,000 Adverse
D $33,000 Adverse   **(2 marks)**

MAPE 11/05

2   The materials operational usage variance for September was:

   A $8,000 Adverse
   B $9,600 Adverse
   C $9,600 Favourable
   D $10,000 Adverse   **(2 marks)**

                                                              MAPE 11/05

3   The materials operational price variance for September was:

   A $6,000 Adverse
   B $6,400 Favourable
   C $30,000 Adverse
   D $32,000 Adverse   **(2 marks)**

                                                              MAPE 11/05

4   A company operates a just-in-time purchasing and production system and uses a backflush accounting
    system with a single trigger point at the point of sale. A summary of the transactions that took place in
    June (valued at cost) is:

                                                                    £
    Conversion costs incurred   890,000
    Finished goods produced   1,795,000
    Finished goods sold   1,700,000
    Conversion costs allocated   840,000

    The two items debited to the cost of goods sold account in June would be:

              £   £
    A   890,000   and   95,000
    B   1,700,000   and   50,000
    C   1,700,000   and   95,000
    D   1,795,000   and   50,000   **(2 marks)**

                                                              MAPE 11/05

5   A company uses time series and regression techniques to forecast future sales. It has derived a seasonal
    variation index to use with the multiplicative (proportional) seasonal variation model. The index values for
    the first three quarters are as follows:

    Quarter   *Index value*
       Q1   80
       Q2   80
       Q3   110

    The index value for the fourth quarter (Q4) is:

    A   −270
    B   −269
    C   110
    D   130   **(2 marks)**

                                                              MAPE 5/06

6   A company has estimated the selling prices and variable costs of one of its products as follows:

Selling price per unit		*Variable cost per unit*	
$	Probability	$	Probability
40	0.30	20	0.55
50	0.45	30	0.25
60	0.25	40	0.20

Given that the company will be able to supply 1,000 units of its product each week irrespective of the selling price, and variable costs per unit are independent of each other, calculate the probability that the weekly contribution will exceed $20,000.   **(3 marks)**

MADM 5/05

7   CJD Ltd manufactures plastic components for the car industry. The following budgeted information is available for three of their key plastic components:

	W	X	Y
	£ per unit	£ per unit	£ per unit
Selling price	200	183	175
Direct material	50	40	35
Direct labour	30	35	30
Units produced and sold	10,000	15,000	18,000

The total number of activities for each of the three products for the period is as follows:

Number of purchase requisitions	1,200	1,800	2,000
Number of set ups	240	260	300

Overhead costs have been analysed as follows:

Receiving/inspecting quality assurance	£1,400,000
Production scheduling/machine set up	£1,200,000

Calculate the budgeted profit per unit for each of the three products using activity based budgeting.

(3 marks)

MAPE 11/06

8   A supermarket is trying to determine the optimal replacement policy for its fleet of delivery vehicles. The total purchase price of the fleet is £220,000.

The running costs and scrap values of the fleet at the end of each year are:

	Year 1	Year 2	Year 3	Year 4
	£	£	£	£
Running costs	110,000	132,000	154,000	165,000
Scrap value	121,000	88,000	66,000	55,000

The supermarket's cost of capital is 12% per annum.

Ignore taxation and inflation.

Indicate when the supermarket should replace its fleet of delivery vehicles.   **(4 marks)**

(Total = 20 marks)

71   Section A: Mixed objective test question bank 11   36 mins

1   The fixed overhead volume variance is defined as the difference between

A   The budgeted value of the fixed overheads and the standard fixed overheads absorbed by actual production.

B   The standard fixed overhead cost specified for the production achieved, and the actual fixed overhead cost incurred.

C   Budgeted and actual fixed overhead expenditure.

D   The standard fixed overhead cost specified in the original budget and the same volume of fixed overheads, but at the actual prices incurred.   **(2 marks)**

The following data are given for sub-questions 2 and 3 below

The following data relate to a manufacturing company. At the beginning of April there was no inventory. During April, 2,000 units of Product X were produced, but only 1,750 units were sold. The financial data for Product X for April were as follows:

	£
Materials	32,000
Labour	12,600
Variable production overheads	9,400
Fixed production overheads	22,500
Variable selling costs	6,000
Fixed selling costs	19,300
Total costs for Product X	101,800

2   The value of inventory of Product X at the end of April using a marginal costing approach was:

    A   £5,575
    B   £6,750
    C   £7,500
    D   £9,563   **(2 marks)**

3   The value of inventory of Product X at the end of April using a throughput accounting approach was:

    A   £1,575
    B   £4,000
    C   £5,175
    D   £5,575   **(2 marks)**

4   A retailer uses the formula shown below when forecasting standard operating costs for its delivery vehicles. Analysis has shown that the relationship between miles driven and total monthly vehicle operating costs is given by the following formula:

$$y = £2,000 + £0·0003x^2$$
where
y is the total standard monthly vehicle operating cost
x is the number of miles driven in the month

The forecast then needs to be adjusted for inflation in vehicle operating costs, which for April was 2%.

Records for April show that the delivery mileage was 3,900 miles, and that the total actual vehicle operating costs for April were £5,500.

The total vehicle operating cost variance for April was closest to

    A   £4,459 adverse
    B   £1,194 adverse
    C   £1,194 favourable
    D   £4,459 favourable   **(2 marks)**

5   The budgeted profit statement for a company, with all figures expressed as percentages of revenue, is as follows:

	%
Revenue	100
Variable costs	80
Fixed costs	12
Profit	8

After the formulation of the above budget it has now been realised that the sales volume will be only 80% of that originally forecast.

The revised profit, expressed as a percentage of the revised revenue, will be:

A   5·0%
B   6·4%
C   8·0%
D   20·0%   **(2 marks)**

6   Overheads will always be over-absorbed when

A   Actual overheads incurred are higher than the overheads absorbed.
B   Actual overheads incurred are lower than the overheads absorbed.
C   Budgeted output is lower than actual output.
D   Budgeted overheads are lower than the overheads absorbed.   **(2 marks)**

7   A company makes many products, one of which is Product P. Extracts from the budget for the whole
     company for June are set out below:

Budget category	£	Cost driver details
Direct labour cost	64,000	8,000 direct labour hours
Set-up costs	22,000	44 set-ups
Quality testing costs	6,800	160 tests
General overheads	18,800	Absorbed using direct labour hours.

Budgeted data for the manufacture of Product P in June are as follows:

Budgeted output	200 units
Direct materials	£18.00 per unit
Direct labour	0·4 hours per unit
Batch size	100 units
Set-ups	1 set-up per batch
Quality tests	2 tests per batch

Calculate, using an activity-based costing approach, the budgeted cost per unit of Product P for June.
                                                                              (4 marks)

8   A manufacturing company produces only one type of product. The company has two production
     departments, Assembly and Finishing, and two service departments, Maintenance and Stores.

     Maintenance provides the following service to the production and service departments: 40% to Assembly,
     40% to Finishing and 20% to Stores.

     Stores provides the following service to the production departments: 55% to Assembly and 45% to
     Finishing.

     The budgeted information for the year was as follows:

     Budgeted fixed production overheads

Assembly	£200,000
Finishing	£160,000
Maintenance	£60,000
Stores	£80,000
Budgeted output	10,000 units

     At the end of the year after apportioning the service department overheads, the actual total fixed
     production overheads attributed to the Assembly department were £298,790.

     The actual output achieved was 10,800 units.

     Calculate the under/over absorption of fixed production overheads for the Assembly department.
                                                                              (4 marks)

                                                                     (Total = 20 marks)

72 Section A: Mixed objective test question bank 12 — 36 mins

1   A basic standard is:

A   A standard set at an ideal level, which makes no allowance for normal losses, waste and machine downtime.

B   A standard which assumes an efficient level of operation, but which includes allowances for factors such as normal loss, waste and machine downtime.

C   A standard which is kept unchanged over a period of time.

D   A standard which is based on current price levels.   **(2 marks)**

The following data are given for sub-questions 2, 3, and 4 below

A company uses a standard absorption costing system and adjusts for any under or over absorbed overheads at the end of each period. The company produces only one type of product. The unit standard costs were the same in both March and April.

Data for April included:

	Budget	Actual
Sales volume	90,000 units	85,000 units
Production volume	80,000 units	78,000 units
Total fixed production overheads	$400,000	$395,000
Selling price per unit	$11	$14
Variable production costs per unit	$4	$4

2   The sales price variance for April was

A $108,000 favourable
B $170,000 favourable
C $255,000 favourable
D $270,000 favourable   **(2 marks)**

3   The sales volume profit variance for April was

A $10,000 adverse
B $14,000 adverse
C $35,000 adverse
D $50,000 adverse   **(2 marks)**

4   If the company had used standard marginal costing to calculate the profit for April that profit, compared to what would have been calculated by standard absorption costing, would be:

A $10,000 higher
B $35,000 higher
C $49,000 higher
D $50,000 higher   **(2 marks)**

5   A company can produce a wide variety of products but its production plans are limited by the time available on Machine M. The budgeted time available for the next period for Machine M is 12,000 hours. The overheads for the next period are budgeted to be $216,000.

The company is reviewing the production plans for Product X. The product sells for $8 per unit and incurs material costs of $2 per unit and labour costs of $4 per unit. Each unit of Product X is worked on by Machine M for 10 minutes.

(i)   Calculate the throughput accounting ratio for Product X.

(ii)   State the significance of the figure you have calculated.   **(4 marks)**

6   An investment project, with an initial outlay of $150,000, has a net present value of $28,000 when it is discounted at 5%. The present value of the sales revenue of the investment project is $262,500. The sensitivity of the investment to changes in the sales revenue is closest to:

    A $112,500
    B $234,500
    C   10%
    D   11%   **(2 marks)**

7   The following incremental cash inflows relate to a new machine which has an initial purchase cost of $45,000:

Year	Incremental cash flow
1	$14,000
2	$22,000
3	$19,000
4	$11,000

Calculate the payback period to the nearest 0·1 years.   **(2 marks)**

8   A trainee management accountant is preparing HY's cash budget for the next financial period. She has obtained the following information:

Balances	Actual 30 April 20X9 $000	Forecast 31 October 20X9 $000
Trade receivables	75	80
Trade payables	47	40
Closing inventory	29	31

The production budget includes $331,000 for cost of raw materials to be used during the six month period to 31 October 20X9.

Calculate the forecast cash required to pay suppliers for the six month period ending 31 October 20X9.

        (4 marks)

        (Total = 20 marks)

73   Section A: Mixed objective test question bank 13   36 mins

1   The following facts are taken from the budget of a company:

- Profit is 30% of revenue
- The C/S (Contribution/Sales) ratio is 55%
- Fixed costs are £50,000

Given the above facts, the budgeted revenue is:

    A   £150,000
    B   £166,667
    C   £200,000
    D   £275,000   **(2 marks)**

The following data are given for sub-questions 2 and 3 below

A company uses standard absorption costing. Details from the previous period were:

	Budget	Actual
Selling price per unit	$25.00	$24.00
Variable costs per unit	$14.00	$13.00
Output and sales	50,000 units	52,000 units
Total fixed costs	$250,000	$286,000

2   The sales price variance was

    A $52,000 adverse
    B $50,000 adverse
    C $50,000 favourable
    D $52,000 favourable   **(2 marks)**

3   The sales volume profit variance was

    A $26,000 adverse
    B $12,000 favourable
    C $22,000 favourable
    D $26,000 favourable   **(2 marks)**

4   A company used marginal costing to calculate the profit for the previous period as $435,000.

    The opening and closing inventories for that period were 15,000 units and 10,000 units respectively.

    If the company had used absorption costing for that period the fixed production overhead absorption rate would have been $8 per unit.

    The profit using absorption costing would have been

    A $475,000
    B $435,000
    C $355,000
    D $395,000   **(2 marks)**

5   Which of the following statements about just-in-time (JIT) are true?

    (i)   Machines should be grouped by product or component instead of by type of work performed
    (ii)   JIT is a 'push' system
    (iii)   Employees must be highly proficient at one task to ensure evenness of the production flow
    (iv)   JIT purchasing should be based on large frequent deliveries against bulk contracts
    (v)   Preventative maintenance is an important aspect of production.

    A   (i) and (v)
    B   (ii), (iii) and (v)
    C   (i) and (iv)
    D   (ii), (iii) and (iv)   **(2 marks)**

6   Records from previous periods show the following relationship between machine hours and maintenance costs:

Machine hours	Maintenance costs
14,000	$26,800
9,800	$21,760
8,000	$19,600
15,400	$28,480

    The estimated maintenance costs for 12,000 machine hours are:

    A $22,200
    B $23,000
    C $24,400
    D $26,600   **(2 marks)**

7   A company uses activity based costing. Details of the budgeted production overheads for next year for the whole company are given in the table below.

Activity cost pool	Cost	Cost driver	Number of cost drivers
Inventory acquisition	£1,200,000	Purchase requisitions	4,000 requisitions
Production	£2,500,000	Production run set ups	10,000 set ups

The company manufactures many types of product. Information for two of the products, X and Y, is as follows:

	X	Y
Prime cost per unit	£5.00	£7.50
Budgeted output	2,400 units	3,000 units
Total purchase requisitions	4 requisitions	8 requisitions
Units per production run	400 units	1,000 units

Calculate, for X and for Y, the total production cost per unit.   **(4 marks)**

8   HA, a retailing entity, has annual sales of $48 million. HA earns a constant margin of 25% on sales. All sales and purchases are on credit and are evenly distributed throughout the year.

The following values are kept at a constant level throughout the year:

- Trade receivables $12 million
- Trade payables $8 million

If HA's working capital cycle is 57 days, what is its inventory turnover, to the nearest number of days?

(4 marks)

(Total = 20 marks)

74   Section A: Mixed objective test question bank (Specimen paper)
36 mins

1   The original budgeted profit statement for a product is as follows:

	$
Revenue	200,000
Variable costs	100,000
Fixed costs	36,000
Profit	64,000

It has now been realised that sales volume will be 10% higher than budgeted volume with no change in selling price. The product has also been redesigned to lower variable costs by 20% per unit.

The percentage increase in the budgeted profit as a result of the two changes will be:

A   2%
B   30%
C   50%
D   62.5%   **(2 marks)**

2   A project has the following present values when discounted at the company's cost of capital of 8% per annum:

	$
Initial investment	250,000
Cash inflows	500,000
Cash outflows	200,000

The sensitivity of the project to changes in the cash inflows is:

A   8%
B   10%
C   20%
D   50%   **(2 marks)**

The following data is for questions 3 and 4

D provides a motorist rescue service to its members. It has been proposed to change the annual membership fee to $120 for the next year. The impact of this on the number of members is uncertain but the following estimates have been made:

Number of members	Probability
20,000	0.1
30,000	0.6
40,000	0.3

It is thought that the variable operating costs vary in relation to the number of members but the cost per member is uncertain. The following estimates have been made:

Variable cost per member	Probability
$70	0.3
$60	0.5
$40	0.2

D expects to incur annual fixed costs of $1,100,000.

---

3   Calculate, based on expected values, the profit for the next year   **(2 marks)**

---

4   The Management Accountant of D has produced a two-way data table.

  (i)   Calculate the value that would be shown in that table in the cell for the profit from 40,000 members with a variable cost per member of $40   **(2 marks)**

  (ii)   Calculate the joint probability of having 20,000 members and a variable cost per member of $40.   **(2 marks)**

---

5   GF wants to sell an unquoted bond. The bond has a coupon rate of 5% and will repay its face value of $1,000 at the end of four years.

  GF estimates that the market requires a yield to maturity of 11% from this type of bond. GF has asked you to recommend a selling price for the bond.

  Calculate the selling price for the bond.   **(4 marks)**

---

6   A company has the following information:

Balances	Actual 31 December 2009 $'000	Forecast 30 June 2010 $'000
Trade receivables	75	80
Trade payables	47	40
Inventory of raw materials	29	31

  The production budget for the six month period to 30 June 2010 shows that the cost of raw materials to be used in that period will be $331,000.

  Calculate the cash that will be paid to suppliers during the six month period to 30 June 2010.   **(3 marks)**

---

7   A company's trade payables days outstanding at 30 September 2009 were 45 days. Purchases for the year to 30 September 2009 were $324,444 occurring evenly throughout the year.

  The company's budgeted purchases for the year ending 30 September 2010 are $356,900 occurring evenly throughout the year.

Calculate the budgeted trade payables days outstanding at 30 September 2010.

(Assume that the trade payables outstanding balance at 30 September 2010 will be the same amount as at 30 September 2009.) **(3 marks)**

(Total = 20 marks)

75 Section A: Mixed objective test question bank (5/10)   36 mins

1   Which of the following is not a symptom of overtrading?

    A   Increasing levels of inventory
    B   Increasing levels of trade receivables
    C   Increasing levels of current liabilities
    D   Increasing levels of long term borrowings   **(2 marks)**

2   The following information has been calculated for a business:

Trade receivable collection period	54 days
Raw material inventory turnover period	46 days
Work in progress inventory turnover period	32 days
Trade payables payment period	67 days
Finished goods inventory turnover period	43 days

The length of the working capital cycle is:

    A   134 days
    B   156 days
    C   108 days
    D   150 days   **(2 marks)**

3   A project with an initial outlay of $250,000 has a net present value of $46,000 when discounted at the cost of capital of 8%. The present value of the receipts from sales is $520,000.

The sensitivity of the investment decision to changes in the initial outlay is:

    A   18·4%
    B $204,000
    C $270,000
    D   8·8%   **(2 marks)**

The following data are given for sub-questions 4 and 5 below

The owner of a van selling hot take-away food has to decide how many burgers to purchase for sale at a forthcoming outdoor concert. The number of burgers sold will depend on the weather conditions and any unsold burgers will be thrown away at the end of the day.

The table below details the profit that would be earned for each possible outcome:

Weather	Number of burgers purchased			
	1,000	2,000	3,000	4,000
Bad	$1,000	$0	($1,000)	($3,000)
Average	$3,000	$6,000	$7,000	$6,000
Good	$3,000	$6,000	$9,000	$12,000

4   If the van owner applies the maximin rule he will purchase:

    A   1,000 burgers
    B   2,000 burgers
    C   3,000 burgers
    D   4,000 burgers   **(2 marks)**

5   If the van owner applies the minimax regret rule he will purchase:

    A   1,000 burgers
    B   2,000 burgers
    C   3,000 burgers
    D   4,000 burgers   **(2 marks)**

6   JB is concerned about the increasing level of trade receivables and is considering various options to encourage customers to pay earlier. The company offers a 30 day payment term but customers are taking on average 65 days to pay.

One option being considered is to offer an early settlement discount of 2·5% for customers paying within 15 days.

Calculate, to the nearest 0·1%, the effective annual interest rate to JB of offering this discount if all customers pay within 15 days. You should assume a 365 day year and use compound interest methodology.   **(3 marks)**

7   A company is considering investing in a new project. The following table shows the project's estimated cash inflows and cash outflows, together with their associated probabilities. The cash inflows and cash outflows are totally independent.

Cash Inflows		Cash Outflows	
$	Probability	$	Probability
120,000	0·30	50,000	0·25
140,000	0·45	60,000	0·35
160,000	0·25	70,000	0·40

Calculate the probability of net cash flows being $90,000 or greater.   **(3 marks)**

8   A $1,000 bond has a coupon rate of 8% and will repay its nominal value when it matures in four years' time.

The bond will be purchased today for $900 ex interest and held until maturity.

Calculate, to the nearest 0·01%, the yield to maturity for the bond based on today's purchase price.

                                                                 (4 marks)

                                                        (Total = 20 marks)

76 Section B: Mixed question bank 1   54 mins

(a)   The following information relates to the budget for the year ahead.

Production overhead cost budget

	£
Machinery costs	285,000
Set-up costs	235,000
Purchasing costs	300,000
Total production overheads	820,000

The following table shows the total budgeted activities of the company (it manufactures many different types of products) and the details relating to the manufacture of two product lines: S and T.

Data	Total	Product S	Product T
Machine hours	95,000	2 per unit	1 per unit
Number of production runs	235	20	5
Purchase orders	5,000	100	100
Production quantities of S & T		5,000 units	20,000 units

Calculate, using activity based costing, the production overhead costs that would be attributed to one unit of Product S and one unit of Product T. **(5 marks)**

MAPE 11/08

(b)   Explain how 'backflush accounting' differs from a traditional absorption costing system.   **(5 marks)**

MAPE 11/08

The following information is for sub-questions (c) and (d)

Two of the products that are manufactured by a company use the same machines. The products (P1 and P2) are manufactured using two machines (M1 and M2). During the next period the time available on the machines are 126 hours for M1 and 195 hours for M2.

The company uses throughput accounting.

Unit details of the two products are:

	P1	P2
	$	$
Selling price	36·00	39·00
Materials	14·20	16·75
Labour	6·00	7·50
Variable production overheads	1·00	1·25
Fixed production overheads	2·00	2·50
Profit	12·80	11·00

Any mix of output can be sold at the above prices and there is unlimited demand for each of the products.

The machine time needed to make one unit of the products is:

	P1	P2
M1	0·35 hours	0·40 hours
M2	0·60 hours	0·65 hours

(c)   (i)   Calculate the maximum production that is possible from each machine for each of the two products and state the bottleneck.

        (ii)   Calculate the throughput accounting ratio for each product.   **(5 marks)**

MAPE 11/08

(d)   Identify, using a throughput approach, the production plan for the next period that would result in the most profitable use of the machines. (All workings must be shown).   **(5 marks)**

MAPE 11/08

(e)   Your managing director has recently attended a conference about investment appraisal techniques. The presenter used an example that compared three investments that were evaluated using incremental profit, accounting rate of return, payback and net present value. The presenter argued that net present value is theoretically superior to the other methods.

        (i)   Explain why net present value is superior to the three other investment appraisal techniques stated above.

        (ii)   Explain what is meant by the internal rate of return (IRR) of a project.   **(5 marks)**

MADM 11/08 – adapted

(f)   GC manufactures a range of bicycles and holds an inventory of certain bicycle parts.

        Part number 1258 costs GC $8.00 per unit. GC expects to use 8,000 units of part 1258 per year.

        Ordering costs have been calculated at $150 per order and inventory holding costs have been estimated at $2.75 per unit per year.

        The supplier of part number 1258 has offered a 2% discount off the purchase price if each order is for 2,000 units or more.

Required

(i)   Calculate the economic order quantity for part 1258, assuming no discount is given.

(ii)   State whether GC should accept the discount offered.   **(5 marks)**

FATP 11/08

(Total = 30 marks)

77 Section B: Mixed question bank 2   54 mins

(a)   Describe **three** key features that are present in any organisation that is successfully focused on Total Quality Management (TQM).   **(5 marks)**

MAPE 5/08

(b)   GN is a retailer, selling directly to the public for cash payment and to other entities on credit. GN is preparing a cash forecast for the first three months of 20X9. Credit customers are given 30 days to pay. Credit sales are expected to be six times the value of direct sales to the public.

GN's estimate of sales for the first three months of 20X9 is as follows:

Month	January	February	March
	$'000	$'000	$'000
Sales value	400	400	500

Actual and estimated sales for the last three months of 20X8 are:

Month	October (actual)	November (estimate)	December (estimate)
	$'000	$'000	$'000
Sales value	396	428	550

From past experience, GN expects 10% of credit customers to pay in the same month as the sale is made, a further 25% to pay in the month after the sale, and 63% in the month after that. The outstanding balance is expected to be written off.

Required

Prepare a monthly cash forecast of GN's total receipts for January to March 20X9. (Work to the nearest $'000.)   **(5 marks)**

FATP 11/08

(c)   DN currently has an overdraft on which it pays interest at 10% per year. DN has been offered credit terms from one of its suppliers, whereby it can either claim a cash discount of 2% if payment is made within 10 days of the date of the invoice or pay on normal credit terms, within 40 days of the date of the invoice.

Assume a 365 day year and an invoice value of $100.

Required

Explain to DN, with reasons and supporting calculations, whether it should pay the supplier early and take advantage of the discount offered.   **(5 marks)**

FATP 5/07

(d)   Briefly explain Just-in-Time (JIT) and **two** major requirements for the successful operation of a JIT system.   **(5 marks)**

MAPE 11/07

(e)   (i)   Explain how a post-completion audit would be undertaken for a major investment project.

       (ii)   State **three** possible drawbacks of undertaking a post-completion audit.   **(5 marks)**

(f)   The following data relates to production of A Ltd's three products in period 6.

	Product X	Product Y	Product Z
Production and sales (units)	300	200	150
Machine hours per unit	30	10	10
No of production runs	7	2	1
No of deliveries to customers	5	5	5
No of deliveries of material into store	20	19	1

Production overhead costs	£
Machining	35,750
Set-up costs	5,250
Materials handling (receiving)	17,500
Packing costs (despatch)	22,500

What is the overhead cost per unit of product Y using activity based costing?   **(5 marks)**

(Total = 30 marks)

78 Section B: Mixed question bank 3   54 mins

The following data are given for sub-questions 3(a) and 3(b) below

QBQ produces one type of product. Details of the budgeted sales and production are given below.

Selling Price and Costs per unit

	£
Selling price	40
Material FX: 1·5kg @ £6 per kg	9
Conversion costs (variable)	8
Fixed production overheads	15

The fixed production overhead absorption rate is based on annual production overheads of £720,000 and budgeted annual output of 48,000 units. The fixed overheads will be incurred evenly throughout the year.

The company also incurs fixed costs for administration of £200,000 per year.

Budgeted Sales

Quarter	Units
1	10,000
2	12,000
3	14,000
4	12,000

Inventory

It has been decided that inventory levels are to be reduced. Details are as follows:

Finished goods: 5,500 units are currently held but it has been decided that the closing inventories for Quarters 1, 2 and 3 will be 45%, 40% and 35% of the following quarter's sales respectively.

Raw materials: 4,500 kg are currently held but it has been decided that the closing inventories for Quarters 1 and 2 will be 25% and 20% of the following quarter's production requirements respectively.

(a)   Prepare a materials purchase budget for Quarter 1.   **(5 marks)**

MAPE 11/07

(b)   In Quarter 3 the opening and closing inventories of finished goods will be 5,600 units and 4,200 units respectively. QBQ adjusts for any under- or over-absorption of overheads at the end of each quarter.

Assume that production and sales volumes were as budgeted and that inventory levels were as planned. Also assume that all costs and revenues were as budgeted.

(i)   Calculate using marginal costing the profit for Quarter 3;
(ii)   Calculate using absorption costing the profit for Quarter 3;
(iii)   Explain the difference, if any, in the profits you have calculated

(5 marks)

MAPE 11/07

(c)   Your company uses discounted cash flow techniques and the net present value approach in particular to appraise investment project. The production manager has commented, 'Since cash flow and profit are the same in the long run, we should always adopt courses of action which maximise accounting profit. I do not understand the logic behind our investment policy.'

Prepare a memorandum to the production director in response to his comments.   **(5 marks)**

(d)   A company is currently developing a system of environmental costing.

Explain the difference between internalised environmental costs and externalised environmental impacts and state **two** examples of each.   **(5 marks)**

(e)   Explain the main uses of overdraft facilities as part of a company's working capital management policy.
(5 marks)

(f)   Tree Cole Tarts plc is appraising an investment of £700,000 in plant, which will last four years and have no residual value. Fixed operating costs (excluding depreciation) will be £200,000 in the first year, increasing by 5% per annum because of inflation. The contribution in the first year is forecast at £620,000, increasing by 7% per annum due to inflation. The company's money cost of capital is 14%.

Required

Calculate the net present value of the investment, to the nearest £'000.   **(5 marks)**

(Total = 30 marks)

79   Section B: Mixed question bank 4 (MAPE 5/06)   54 mins

(a)   A manufacturing company uses a standard costing system. Extracts from the budget for April are shown below:

Sales	1,400 units
Production	2,000 units

	$	
Direct costs	15	per unit
Variable overhead	4	per unit

The budgeted fixed production overhead costs for April were $12,800.

The budgeted profit using marginal costing for April was $5,700.

(i)   Calculate the budgeted profit for April using absorption costing.   **(3 marks)**
(ii)   Briefly explain two situations where marginal costing is more useful to management than absorption costing.   **(2 marks)**

(b)   The standard cost schedule for hospital care for a minor surgical procedure is shown below.

Standard Cost of hospital care for a minor surgical procedure

Staff: patient ratio is 0.75:1

	£
Nursing costs: 2 days × 0.75 × £320 per day	480
Space and food costs: 2 days × £175 per day	350
Drugs and specific materials	115
Hospital overheads: 2 days × £110 per day	220
Total standard cost	1,165

The actual data for the hospital care for one patient having the minor surgical procedure showed that the patient stayed in hospital for three days. The cost of the drugs and specific materials for this patient was £320. There were 0·9 nurses per patient on duty during the time that the patient was in hospital. The daily rates for nursing pay, space and food, and hospital overheads were as expected.

Prepare a statement that reconciles the standard cost with the actual costs of hospital care for this patient. The statement should contain five variances that will give useful information to the manager who is reviewing the cost of hospital care for minor surgical procedures. **(5 marks)**

(c)   C plc uses a just–in–time (JIT) purchasing and production process to manufacture Product P. Data for the output of Product P, and the material usage and material price variances for February, March and April are shown below:

Month	Output (units)	Material usage variance £	Material price variance £
February	11,000	£15,970 (A)	£12,300 (F)
March	5,100	£5,950 (A)	£4,500 (F)
April	9,100	£8,400 (A)	£6,200 (F)

The standard material cost per unit of Product P is £12.

Prepare a sketch (not on graph paper) of a percentage variance chart for material usage and for material price for Product P for the three month period. (Note: your workings must show the coordinates of the points that would be plotted if the chart was drawn accurately.) **(5 marks)**

(d)   Briefly discuss three reasons why standard costing may not be appropriate in a modern business environment. **(5 marks)**

(e)   Compare and contrast marginal costing and throughput accounting. **(5 marks)**

(f)   T plc is a large insurance company. The Claims Department deals with claims from policy holders who have suffered a loss that is covered by their insurance policy. Policy holders could claim, for example, for damage to property, or for household items stolen in a burglary. The Claims Department staff investigate each claim and determine what, if any, payment should be made to the claimant.

The manager of the Claims Department has decided to benchmark the performance of the department and has chosen two areas to benchmark:

*   the detection of false claims
*   the speed of processing claims

For each of the above two areas:

(i)   State and justify a performance measure
(ii)   Explain how relevant benchmarking data could be gathered. **(5 marks)**

(Total = 30 marks)

---

80   Section B: Mixed question bank 5   54 mins

(a)   J Limited has recently been taken over by a much larger company. For many years the budgets have been set by adding an inflation adjustment to the previous year's budget. The new owners of J are insisting on a 'zero-base' approach when the next budget is set, as they believe many of the indirect costs in J are much higher than in other companies under their control.

(i)   Explain the main features of 'zero-based budgeting'. **(2 marks)**
(ii)   Discuss the problems that might arise when implementing this approach in J Limited.   **(3 marks)**

MAPE 11/05

(b)   UV Limited is a catering company that provides meals for large events. It has a range of standard meals at fixed prices. It also provides meals to meet the exact requirements of a customer and prices for this service are negotiated individually with each customer.

Discuss how a 'McDonaldisation' approach to service delivery would impact on budget preparation and cost control within UV Limited. **(5 marks)**

MAPE 11/05

(c)   A management consulting company had budgeted the staff requirements for a particular job as follows.

	£
40 hours of senior consultant at £100 per hour	4,000
60 hours of junior consultant at £60 per hour	3,600
Budgeted staff cost for job	7,600

The actual hours recorded were:

	£
50 hours of senior consultant at £100 per hour	5,000
55 hours of junior consultant at £60 per hour	3,300
Actual staff cost for job	8,300

The junior consultant reported that for 10 hours of the 55 hours there was no work that she could do.

Calculate the following variances:

- Idle time variance
- Labour mix variance
- Labour efficiency variance   **(5 marks)**

MAPE 11/05

(d)   (i)   Your colleague has commented, 'When we are performing investment appraisals, since we pay tax at a rate of 30% on all our profits, why is it not possible to calculate the net present value before tax and then simply deduct 30% from this to derive the post-tax net present value?'.

Explain briefly to your colleague why his suggested method of dealing with the impact of taxation in investment appraisal is not acceptable.

(ii)   LEFM Ltd is considering the purchase of a machine for £1,200,000. It would be sold after five years for an estimated realisable value of £450,000. By this time capital allowances of £950,000 would have been claimed. The rate of corporation tax is 30%.

Required

Calculate the cash flow arising as a result of the tax implications on the sale of the machine at the end of the five years.   **(5 marks)**

(e)   An education authority is considering the implementation of a CCTV (closed circuit television) security system in one of its schools. Details of the proposed project are as follows.

Life of project	5 years
Initial cost	£75,000

Annual savings:

Labour costs	£20,000
Other costs	£5,000
Cost of capital	15% per annum

(i)   Calculate the internal rate of return for this project.

(ii)   Calculate the percentage change in the annual labour cost savings that could occur before the project ceased to be viable.   **(5 marks)**

(f)   BF manufactures a range of domestic appliances. Due to past delays in suppliers providing goods, BF has had to hold an inventory of raw materials, in order that the production could continue to operate smoothly. Due to recent improvements in supplier reliability, BF is re-examining its inventory holding policies and recalculating economic order quantities (EOQ).

- Item 'Z' costs BF $10.00 per unit
- Expected annual production usage is   65,000 units
- Procurement costs (cost of placing and processing one order) are $25.00
- The cost of holding one unit for one year has been calculated as $3.00

The supplier of item 'Z' has informed BF that if the order was 2,000 units or more at one time, a 2% discount would be given on the price of the goods.

Required

    (i)   Calculate the EOQ for item 'Z' before the quantity discount.   **(2 marks)**

    (ii)   Advise BF if it should increase the order size of item 'Z' so as to qualify for the 2% discount.

    (3 marks)

FATP 11/05

(Total = 30 marks)

81 Section B: Mixed question bank 6   54 mins

(a)   Explain the concept and objectives of throughput accounting, and discuss its limitations.   **(5 marks)**

(b)   Briefly explain MRP, MRPII, ERP, OPT and JIT.   **(5 marks)**

(c)   Explain the changes in the modern business environment that have led to the need for the introduction of ABC to replace traditional absorption costing.   **(5 marks)**

(d)   (i)   State five factors that should be considered before management can decide whether or not to investigate a variance.   **(3 marks)**

    (ii)   Data collected for a transport company show that average transport costs are £20,000 per month. These are thought to conform to a normal distribution with a standard deviation of £2,000. The company investigates variances that fall outside the range that includes 95% of the outcomes.

            Actual travel expenses for October were £26,800. Should the resulting variance be investigated?

            (2 marks)

(e)   Discuss whether standard costing can be used in a TQM environment.   **(5 marks)**

(f)   A company is considering investing in a project that requires an initial outflow of £500,000 and will generate expected cash inflows in terms of today's £ of £130,000 over each of the next four years. The company's money cost of capital is 7 per cent and inflation is predicted to be 4 per cent over the next four years.

    (i)   Calculate the company's real cost of capital.

    (ii)   Calculate the company's present value of the cash inflow in year 3.   **(5 marks)**

(Total = 30 marks)

82 Section B: Mixed question bank 7   54 mins

(a)   Explain how a budget can cause conflict between "motivation" and "control".   **(5 marks)**

MAPE 5/09

(b)   Explain how "zero based budgeting" can overcome the problems that are associated with "incremental budgeting".   **(5 marks)**

MAPE 5/09

(c)

    A management consulting company had set the budget for the staff requirements for a particular job as follows:

	£
50 hours of senior consultant at £120 per hour	6,000
90 hours of junior consultant at £80 per hour	7,200
Budgeted staff cost for job	13,200

The actual hours recorded were:

	£
60 hours of senior consultant at £130 per hour	7,800
90 hours of junior consultant at £75 per hour	6,750
Actual staff cost for job	14,550

The junior consultant reported that for 10 hours of the 90 hours he recorded there was no work that he could do.

(i) Calculate the following variances:

- Idle time variance
- Labour mix variance **(3 marks)**

(ii) Explain the worth, or otherwise, of this company calculating the labour mix variance in this situation. **(2 marks)**

(Total for sub-question (c) = 5 marks)

`MAPE 5/09`

(d) A company budgeted to produce 400 units of a product in a period. The standard cost card of the product showed that the standard cost of the material used to manufacture each unit of the product was 6 kg costing £12 per kg.

The actual results for the period were that 380 units were produced from 2,500 kg of material which had cost £29,000.

It has now been realised that the standard material content per unit should have been 6·75 kg.

Calculate

(i) The materials usage planning variance
(ii) The operational materials price variance
(iii) The operational materials usage variance. **(5 marks)**

`MAPE 5/09`

(e) A new company, which manufactures only one type of product, had the following budget for its first year of business:

Production and sales 2,000 units

	$
Revenue	100,000
Variable production costs	30,000
Variable selling and administration costs	6,000
Fixed production overheads	40,000
Fixed selling and administration costs	10,000
Profit	14,000

The actual results for the year showed that 1,800 units were produced but only 1,700 units were sold. These were sold at the budgeted selling price. The fixed production overheads were $39,000. All of the other costs behaved as expected.

Calculate

(i) The under or over absorbed fixed production overheads
(ii) The actual profit for the year using absorption costing
(iii) The actual profit for the year using marginal costing **(5 marks)**

`MAPE 11/09`

(f) HW puts $50,000 into a bank deposit account on 31 October 20X6. The account pays interest every six months, at a rate of 2% for every six month period. Assume that HW reinvests all interest.

Calculate how much HW will have in its bank deposit account at 30 April 20X9 (to the nearest $) (ignore tax): **(5 marks)**

`FATP 5/09`

(Total = 30 marks)

83 Section B: Mixed question bank 8 (Specimen paper)   54 mins

(a)   A company manufactures office equipment in England but sells it in the UK and to overseas customers.

Current situation

UK customers (£2·1m annual revenue)

The company offers a cash discount of 3% for payment within 10 days to UK customers. Approximately 40% of customers take advantage of the early payment discount whilst the remainder pay in 30 days.

Overseas customers (£0·9m annual revenue)

All sales are on credit but customers are required to pay a 20% deposit when they place their orders and the balance in 60 days.

Debt factoring

The company is thinking about debt factoring. Investigations have revealed that a non-recourse factor will accept 85% of the company's UK customers. It is assumed that the remaining 15% will not take advantage of the early settlement discount.

Required

Calculate, based on a 365-day year, the total debtors' days if:

(i)   the current situation continues

(ii)   debt factoring is introduced   **(5 marks)**

(b)   Discuss the non-financial factors that a company would need to consider before making a decision to factor its debts.   **(5 marks)**

(c)   The manager of a hotel is deciding if he should carry out repairs to the hotel immediately or postpone them for a year. He has made the following estimates for the coming year:

The cost of the repairs would be £90,000.

If the repairs are started immediately there is only a two-in-three chance of them being completed in time. If the repairs are completed in time the contribution for the hotel could be any one of the three levels below with equally probability. If the repairs are not completed on time some rooms will be unavailable and consequently demand could be either medium or low, with equal probability.

Contribution for the coming year if the repairs are undertaken could be:

£200,000 if there is high demand

£150,000 if there is medium demand

£100,000 if demand is low

If the repairs are not undertaken the contribution for the coming year is estimated to be £37,500.

Required

Demonstrate, using a decision tree, if the repairs should be started immediately or postponed for a year.
                                                                              (5 marks)

(d)   A fast food outlet served the following number of burgers in the past 13 quarters:

		2007				2008				2009			2010
	Q1	Q2	Q3	Q4	Q1	Q2	Q3	Q4	Q1	Q2	Q3	Q4	Q1
Burgers '000	75	80	110	175	92	96	122	210	111	116	164	259	135

Regression analysis was used to determine the following equation for the trend of sales:

S = 134·23 + 7·945Q where

S = quarterly sales ('000)

Q = quarter number. (The 13 quarters in the period Q1 2007 to Q1 2010 were coded from −6 through to +6).

Previous research has established that the sales follow a seasonal pattern:

Quarter	1	2	3	4
Seasonality	–25%	–25%	0	+50%

Required

Calculate the number of burgers that are forecast to be sold in quarters 2, 3 and 4 of 2010.   **(5 marks)**

(e)   Explain how a budget can cause conflict between "motivation" and "control".   **(5 marks)**

(f)   Two classifications of environmental costs are "environmental internal failure costs" and "environmental external failure costs".   Explain each one of the two classifications of environmental costs mentioned above. Your answer should include, for each classification, an example of an activity that would cause such costs.   **(5 marks)**

(Total = 30 marks)

84   Section B: Mixed question bank 9 (05/10)   54 mins

(a)   The trade receivable ledger account for customer J from 1 January to 30 April 2010 shows the following:

	Debit	Credit	Balance
	$	$	$
01-Jan-2010 Balance b/fwd			125
10-Jan-2010 Invoice No. 234	181		306
12-Jan-2010 Invoice No. 263	92		398
18-Jan-2010 Invoice No. 297	287		685
23-Jan-2010 Receipt No. 85		217	468
(Balance b/fwd+ Inv No. 263)			
09-Feb-2010 Invoice No. 328	294		762
13-Feb-2010 Credit Note No.167 (Inv No. 234)		63	699
05-Mar-2010 Invoice No. 365	135		834
15-Mar-2010 Invoice No. 379	232		1066
18-Mar-2010 Receipt No. 102 (Inv No. 297)		287	779
25-Mar-2010 Invoice No. 391	71		850
01-Apr-2010 Receipt No. 126 (Inv No. 328)		294	556
24-Apr-2010 Invoice No. 438	145		701

(i)   Prepare an age analysis of trade receivables, for customer J, at 30 April 2010 showing the outstanding balance analysed by month   **(3 marks)**

(ii)   State two benefits of preparing an age analysis of trade receivables.   **(2 marks)**

(Total for sub-question (a) = 5 marks)

(b)   A company, which uses the EOQ inventory management model, purchases 64,000 units of raw materials per year. The purchase price of the raw material is $10 per unit. The cost of holding one unit in inventory is $1·20 per year. The cost of reordering and taking delivery is $150 per order regardless of the size of the order.

Assuming that usage is predictable and spread evenly throughout the year and that ordering and delivery are simultaneous, calculate for the raw material:

(i)   The total annual cost of holding and ordering inventory.   **(3 marks)**

Past experience has shown that the supplier of the raw material can be unreliable and that the delivery period can be between one week and three weeks. If the company wants to hold enough raw material to ensure that it never runs out, calculate for the raw material:

(ii)   The lowest inventory level at which raw material should be reordered.   **(2 marks)**

(Total for sub-question (b) = 5 marks)

The following scenario is given for sub-questions (c) and (d)

A medium-sized manufacturing company, which operates in the electronics industry, has employed a firm of consultants to carry out a review of the company's planning and control systems. The company presently uses a traditional incremental budgeting system and the inventory management system is based on economic order quantities (EOQ) and reorder levels. The company's normal production patterns have changed significantly over the previous few years as a result of increasing demand for customised products. This has resulted in shorter production runs and difficulties with production and resource planning.

The consultants have recommended the implementation of activity based budgeting and a manufacturing resource planning system to improve planning and resource management.

(c)   Explain how a manufacturing resource planning system would improve the planning of purchases and production for the company.   **(5 marks)**

(d)   Explain the benefits for the company that could occur following the introduction of an activity based budgeting system.   **(5 marks)**

(e)   The production budgets for quarters 1 and 2 for a manufacturing company are as follows:

	Quarter 1	Quarter 2
Production (Units)	15,000	20,000
Budgeted production costs	$	$
Direct materials	180,000	240,000
Production labour	155,000	195,000
Production overheads	210,000	240,000

The cost structure, which is expected to continue unchanged in quarter 3, is as follows:

(ii)   The variable cost elements are linear and vary in direct proportion to volume.

(iii)   There is a bulk purchase discount of 5% on materials if orders exceed $250,000 per quarter. The discount will apply to the purchase of all materials in that quarter.

(iv)   The company operates a JIT system for material purchases.

(v)   Fixed production overheads will increase by $20,000 per quarter at production output levels in excess of 22,000 units in a quarter.

The budgeted production volume for quarter 3 is 23,000 units.

Prepare the production cost budget for quarter 3.   **(5 marks)**

(f)   An events management company is trying to decide whether or not to advertise an outdoor concert. The sale of tickets is dependent on the weather. If the weather is poor it is expected that 5,000 tickets will be sold without advertising. There is a 70% chance that the weather will be poor. If the weather is good it is expected that 10,000 tickets will be sold without advertising. There is a 30% chance that the weather will be good.

If the concert is advertised and the weather is poor, there is a 60% chance that the advertising will stimulate further demand and ticket sales will increase to 7,000. If the weather is good there is a 25% chance the advertising will stimulate demand and ticket sales will increase to 13,000.

The profit expected, before deducting the cost of advertising, at different levels of ticket sales are as follows:

Number of tickets sold	Profit
	$
5,000	(20,000)
6,000	(5,000)
7,000	35,000
8,000	55,000
9,000	70,000
10,000	90,000
11,000	115,000
12,000	130,000
13,000	150,000

The cost of advertising the concert will be $15,000.

Required

Demonstrate, using a decision tree, whether the concert should be advertised.   **(5 marks)**

(Total = 30 marks)

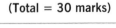

ANSWERS

114

1 Section A: Working capital and cash management I

1 A This is an example of an aggressive working capital policy.

2 A Short-term finance is matched to fluctuating current assets. B is a conservative policy, while C and D are aggressive policies.

3 D Current assets excluding inventories (in \$'000) = 600 + 200

               = 800

     Quick ratio = 800/800 payables   = 1.00

     Option C is incorrect because the loan stock would normally be included with non-current liabilities, since it is due in three years. Option B is the current ratio.

4 A $\dfrac{25,000}{180,000} \times 365 = 50.7$ days

5 A As the current ratio is 2:1 the reduction of cash and payables by the same amount will increase the ratio. Payable days reduce the cash operating cycle, so if these are reduced, the cycle increases.

6 B Receivables at 31.3.X7 = 290,510/365 × 49 = 39,000

	$
Cash received is therefore:	
Opening receivables	22,000
Credit sales	290,510
Closing receivables	(39,000)
Cash received	273,510

7 88 days

	Days
Inventory days ((360/1,400) × 365)	94
Receivables days ((290/2,400) × 365)	44
Payables days ((190/1,400) × 365)	(50)
	88

8 44 days

RECEIVABLES CONTROL ACCOUNT

	$			$
Opening balance	68,000	Returns		2,500
Sales	250,000	Cash received		252,100
		Write off*		3,400
	–	Balance		60,000
	318,000			318,000

* (68,000 × 5%)

Receivables days: 60/(500 – 5) × 365 = 44.2
(Or you could use 60/(250 – 2.5) × 182.5)

2 Section A: Working capital and cash management II

1 D A conservative policy makes the greatest use of long-term finance.

2 D Say current assets are \$75,000

     Current liabilities are \$50,000

     30% decrease in both will be \$15,000. Current assets will then be \$60,000, current liabilities \$35,000, and current ratio will be 60:35 = 1.71. This is an increase of less than 30%.

3 D No cash movements have taken place, and inventory levels are the same.

4   C   Cash cycle = Inventory turnover + Receivables turnover – Payables turnover

$$= \left(\left(\frac{6}{36\times0.8}\right)\times365\right)+\left(\left(\frac{8}{36}\right)\times365\right)-\left(\left(\frac{3}{36\times0.8}\right)\times365\right)$$

= 119 days

5   C   Non-current assets are sold. The other events may have limited or no effect on working capital.

6   A   EX will take into account the **cash received** on the disposal. The gain is not relevant.

7   $345,379

At 31 October 20X7:

Cost of goods sold = $350,000

Inventory = $350,000 × 60/365 = $57,534

	$
Inventory b/f 1/11/X6	56,000 ✓
Purchases (balancing figure)	351,534
	407,534
Inventory c/f 31/10/X7	57,534 ✓
	350,000 ✓

Closing trade payables = $351,534 × 50/365 = $48,155

Trade payables b/f 1/11/X6	42,000
Purchases	351,534
	393,534
Trade payables c/f 31/10/X7	48,155
Paid	345,379

8   172.7 days

	Days
Inventory days ((79 /139) × 365)	207.4
Receivables days ((52/270) × 365)	70.3
Payables days ((40/139) × 365)	(105.0)
	172.7

3   Section B: Working capital and cash management

Text references. Working capital, the operating cycle and cash management are covered in Chapters 1 and 2. Expected values are covered in Chapter 19.

Top tips. Part (d) of this question is a good reminder that the examiner can choose to select from different parts of the syllabus for the content of an individual question. Do not expect each question to be self contained within a single part of the syllabus.

Easy marks. Several of the answers require tabulated calculations. Set up your pro formas first and you can then slot in the known figures to earn the first easy mark or two.

(a)   **Length of operating cycle** $= 365\left(\dfrac{\text{Average raw materials}}{\text{Purchases}} + \dfrac{\text{Average finished goods}}{\text{Cost of sales}} + \dfrac{\text{Average receivables}}{\text{Sales}} + \dfrac{\text{Average payables}}{\text{Purchases}}\right)$

$$= 365\left(\frac{0.5(55+80)}{850} + \frac{185}{1,830} + \frac{0.5(114+200)}{1,996} - \frac{0.5(50+70)}{850}\right)$$

= 29.0 days + 36.9 days + 28.7 days – 25.8 days

= 68.8 days

(b)

> **Top tips.** Make sure that you always read the question carefully. Note that sales are invoiced at the **end** of the month. ✓

	October $'000	November $'000	December $'000	January $'000	Total $'000
Class A customers (W1)					
October sales			50 ✓	30	80
November sales				75	75
			50	105	155
Class B customers (W2)					
October sales		36	15	6	57
November sales			48	20	68
December sales				24	24
		36	63	50	149
Total cash received		36	113	155	304

Workings

1   Class A customers

October sales
50% received December $100,000 × 50% = $50,000 ✓
30% received January $100,000 × 30% = 30,000 ✓

November sales
50% received January $150,000 × 50% = $75,000 ✓

2   Class B customers

October sales
60% received November $60,000 × 60% = $36,000 ✓
25% received December $60,000 × 25% = $15,000 ✓
10% received January $60,000 × 10% = $6,000 ✓

November sales
60% received December $80,000 × 60% = $48,000 ✓
25% received January $80,000 × 25% = $20,000 ✓

December sales
60% received January $40,000 × 60% = $24,000 ✓

(c)

> **Examiner's comments.** Most candidates did well on this question. The most common error was not separately identifying the different categories of inventory, and including each in the correct calculation. A few candidates failed to deduct payables days.

154.5 days

		Days
Inventory days – raw materials = 111/641 × 365	— Purchase in year	63.2 ✓
Inventory days – WIP and finished goods = 165/898 × 365	Cost of sales.	67.0
Receivables days = 216/992 × 365		79.5 ✓
Payables days = 97/641 × 365		(55.2)
		154.5

(d)   Expected cash balance/overdraft

	$'000
Balance at 1 December	+ 175
December cash flow ((+700 × 0.7) + (-300 × 0.3))	+ 400
	+ 575
January	– 900
Expected overdraft	– 325

Using expected values and probabilities the expected value of the overdraft at the end of January is $325,000.

However this outcome will never actually occur. Given the two possibilities for the cash flow in December the reality is that there will be either an overdraft of $25,000 (+ 175 + 700 – 900) or an overdraft of $1,025 (+ 175 – 300 – 900).

The expected value of $325,000 is only of relevance for a situation that is happening time after time. For a one-off situation such as this there is therefore little point in basing any decision-making on the expected value. Instead the short-term cash planning should be based upon both possible overdraft requirements rather than the expected value.

(e)

> **Examiner's comments.** Some candidates took 30 days credit to mean that customers paid within the month of sale instead of in the following month and made the same error in relation to purchases.
>
> Some failed to give any conclusion regarding the likelihood of AM being able to pay for the equipment

		May $'000	June $'000	July $'000
Receipts				
Cash sales		35	40	40
Credit sales:	30 days	66 –	66	72
	60 days	30 –	33	33
	90 days	5 –	5	6
Total receipts		136	144	151
Payments				
Purchases:	70%	35	39	39
	30%	15	15	16
Expenses		50	50	50
Equipment purchase		–	–	250
Total payments		100	104	355
Net movement		36	40	(204)
Cash balance b/f		96	132	172
Cash balance c/f		132	172	(32)

It is clear that AM will not have sufficient funds to pay for the equipment when the payment falls due.

(f)

	$
April credit sales (60,000 × 50% × 20%)	6,000
May credit sales (60,000 × 102% × 50% × 75%)	22,950
June cash sales (60,000 × 102% × 102% × 50%)	31,212
	60,162

4 Section C: BB

> **Text references.** Working capital ratios are covered in Chapter 1 and cash budgeting and cash management are covered in Chapter 2.
>
> **Top tips.** This question required little specialised knowledge, but you do have to be methodical and well-organised in your approach. You are given a lot of information so make sure you remember to underline or highlight key points as you read through.
>
> **Easy marks.** The proforma for (b) is very simple here. In order to keep it simple, you should do separate workings, as we have. But show all the workings in full. The marker must be able to understand what you are doing. You can get the full 10 marks here and you should be able to get at least 3 marks on (c). So don't get bogged down in (a).
>
> **Examiner's comments.** Part (a) was well done, but few candidates were able to calculate the forecast balance at 30 June. Part (b) was very well done. The main problem was with short course income calculation and remembering to include the cash balance brought forward. In Part (c) many students did not identify enough options for five marks or give sufficient detail for each option.

Marking scheme

			Marks
(a)	(i)	Receivables days 31 December 20X5	1 ✓
	(ii)	Forecast receivables balance 30 June 20X6	3 ×
		Receivables days 30 June 20X6	1 ×
			$\overline{5}$
(b)		Layout of cash budget	1 ✓
		Short training course receipts	3 ✓
		In house course receipts	1 ✗
		Short course expenses	1 ✓
		Other costs and monthly balances	4 ✓
			$\overline{10}$
(c)		1 mark for each appropriate action, to a max of	5
(d)		1 to 2 marks for each point made	5

(a) (i) Trade receivables days outstanding $= \dfrac{34,100}{125,000} \times 365$

$= 100$ days ✓

(ii) Trade receivables budgeted for 30 June 20X6

	$
Receivables at 31 December 20X5	34,100 ✓
6 months income (130,000/2)	65,000 ✓
Less: receipts (5 + 8 + 10 + 11 + 12 + 6)	(52,000) ✓
Trade receivables at 30 June 20X6	47,100

Trade receivables days outstanding $= \dfrac{47,100}{65,000} \times 183$

$= 133$ days

(b) Cash budget for January to June 20X6

	Jan $	Feb $	Mar $	Apr $	May $	June $	Total $
Receipts							
Short training courses (W1)	667	2,533	3,600	4,267	5,466	5,467	22,000
In house courses	5,000	8,000	10,000	11,000	12,000	6,000	52,000
	5,667	10,533	13,600	15,267	17,466	11,467	74,000

	Jan $	Feb $	Mar $	Apr $	May $	June $	Total $
Expenditure							
Part time wages	0	2,500	4,000	4,000	5,000	6,000	21,500
Full time salaries	4,000	4,000	4,200	4,200	4,200	4,200	24,800
Rent	625			625			1,250
Short course expenses (W2)	0	300	450	450	600	600	2,400
In house course expenses	100	100	100	100	100	100	600
Overheads	1,500	600	600	1,500	600	600	5,400
Furniture				5,000			5,000
Computers					40,000		40,000
	6,225	7,500	9,350	15,875	50,500	11,500	100,950
Bank balance b/f	12,460	1,902	14,935	19,185	18,577	(14,457)	12,460
Net income/(expenditure)	(558)	3,033	4,250	(608)	(33,034)	(33)	(26,950)
Bank balance c/f	11,902	14,935	19,185	18,577	(14,457)	(14,490)	(14,490)

Workings

1   Short training course receipts

	Jan	Feb	Mar	Apr	May	June
Number of courses	0	2	3	3	4	4
Number of students per Course	0	10	12	12	14	13
Total number of students	0	20	36	36	56	52
	$	$	$	$	$	$
Income	0	2,000	3,600	3,600	5,600	5,200
Receipts – month in advance	667	1,200	1,200	1,867	1,733	2,000
Receipts – in month	–	1,333	2,400	2,400	3,733	3,467
	667	2,533	3,600	4,267	5,466	5,467

2   Short course expenses

	Jan	Feb	Mar	Apr	May	June	July
Number of courses	0	2	3	3	4	4	4
	$	$	$	$	$	$	$
Cost $150 per course	0	300	450	450	600	600	0

(c)   The cash budget currently indicates that if the new technology is purchased in April and paid for in May as planned BB will exceed its agreed overdraft limit by $9,490. There are a variety of possible actions that BB could take in order make sufficient funds available for this purchase.

(i)   An **increase in the overdraft facility** could be negotiated with the bank.

(ii)   Negotiations could take place with the computer supplier to **spread the $40,000 payment** over a number of instalments.

(iii)   BB could consider **leasing the computer equipment** rather than purchasing it

(iv)   BB could take out a **short term loan** for the purchase of the computer equipment

(v)   Purchase of the managing director's furniture could be **delayed** to free up $5,000 more funds

(vi)   A **strict policy of payment for short courses in the month before** the course could be introduced in order to speed up cash receipts

(vii)   Clearly slow paying receivables for in-house courses are a problem and a **cash discount** for payment within say one month compared to the budgeted position of 100 days in December and 133 days in June could be introduced.

(d)   Loans and overdrafts

Companies often have a greater proportion of their debt in the form of overdraft due to the problems of providing sufficient security to lenders. However, a term loan will often be more attractive than an overdraft for the following reasons.

1   Overdraft finance is generally repayable on demand. It therefore carries a higher level of financial risk than does a term loan.

2   The bank may become uncomfortable with a growing overdraft and seek to secure scheduled repayment or other conditions from the company. This can present a growing firm with cash flow problems.

3   Overdraft finance is generally floating rate, thus exposing the company to interest rate risk. Term loans can often be negotiated at a fixed rate thus reducing this element of risk and assisting with cash flow forecasting.

4   Term loans can be negotiated over a timescale that can be related to the company's forecast need for financing, and with a repayment schedule that can be tailored to the company's requirements. For example, capital may be repaid in stages or at the end of the period.

5   If the company has a good trading record and/or a good asset base and can therefore offer reasonable security, it may be able to negotiate a lower interest rate than would be payable on an overdraft.

5 Section A: Short-term finance I

1   7.8%

We will take 7% and 9% as the rates.*

7%:	6 × 7.024	42.14
	100 × 0.508	50.80
		92.94

9%:	6 × 6.418	38.51
	100 × 0.422	42.20
		80.71

Extrapolating:

$$7\% + \frac{92.94 - 88.00}{92.94 - 80.71} \times 2 = 7\% + \frac{4.94}{12.23} \times 2 = 7.8\%$$

* You can choose different rates – you should still get the same answer. We would expect the yield to maturity to be slightly above the coupon rate.

2   D   A property mortgage is generally for a term longer than five years, and this is therefore a long-term source of finance.

3   D   Interest is only paid on the amount borrowed, not on the full facility.

4   D   This is also known as a documentary credit.

5   B   Although the level of return is a factor in the decision, it is more important to minimise the risk to the original capital invested.

6   C   Deciding what credit limits customers should be given.

7   A   Short-term cash surpluses will not normally be invested in equities owing to the risks associated with achieving a return over a short period.

8   Effective annual interest rate = 14.78%

$$\text{Annual cost} = \left(\frac{100}{98.5}\right)^{\frac{365}{40}} - 1$$

$$= \left(\frac{100}{98.5}\right)^{9.125} - 1 = 14.78\%$$

6 Section A: Short-term finance II

1   B   Treasury bills are issued by the Central Bank on behalf of the government, to raise short-term cash (mostly for 90 days). They are traded 'second hand' on the discount market, and carry a low rate of interest because they are risk free. Other money market instruments carry slightly higher rates of interest.

2   Any four of:

- Bank loan
- Bank overdraft
- Factoring
- Invoice discounting
- Use of trade credit

3   A   It is a method of providing medium-term export finance.

4   C   Certificates of deposit are negotiable instruments.

5   D   Preference shares. Shares are generally higher risk than loan stock.

6   A   The date of payment will be specified on the bill of exchange.

7       $10,000 \times \left(1 - \dfrac{0.06 \times 40}{365}\right) = \$9,934.25$

8   9.21%

Using rates of 9% and 11% from the tables:

$(1,000 \times 0.708) + (120 \times 3.240) = 1,097$
$(1,000 \times 0.659) + (120 \times 3.102) = 1,031$

$9 + \left(\dfrac{1,097 - 1,090}{1,097 - 1,031} \times 2\right) = 9 + \left(\dfrac{7}{66} \times 2\right) = 9.21\%$

7   Section A: Short-term finance III

1   B   Treasury shares have been repurchased but not cancelled.

2   Forfaiting has the following advantages for the exporter:

     (i)   He obtains immediate cash payment
     (ii)   The forfaiting bank has no recourse to the exporter, so the exporter carries no liability
     (iii)   The exporter has transferred all risks to the forfaiting bank
     (iv)   Forfaiting enables transactions to be entered into which may not otherwise be possible.

3   A   The credit cycle begins with the receipt of the customer's order. Price negotiations take place prior to this point.

4   D   (Total sales × 2%) + $5,000. 'Without recourse' means that the factor carries the risk of the bad debts.

5   A   C ignores the effect of the changes on the level of inventories and payables. B and D are wrong because they assume that the financing cost will increase not decrease.

Current level of receivables = $\$2m \times {}^{90}/_{365} = \$493,151$
New level of receivables = $\$2m \times 80\% \times {}^{30}/_{365} = \$131,507$ ✓

Current financing requirement = $500,000 + $493,150 – $30,000 = $963,150 ✓
New financing requirement = $400,000 + $131,507 – $24,000 = $507,507 ✓

Reduction in financing requirement = $963,150 – $507,507 = $455,643 ✓
Reduction in financing cost = $455,643 × 10% = $45,564 (round to $46,000) ✓

6   B   Return on discount $= \left(\dfrac{100}{100-d}\right)^{\frac{12}{m}}$

where   d   = % size of the discount
         m   = reduction in payment period in months necessary to achieve discount

Return on X's discount $= \left(\dfrac{100}{97}\right)^{4} - 1 = 12.96\%$

Return on Y's discount $= \left(\dfrac{100}{96}\right)^{3} - 1 = 13.02\%$

(Note that the formula here uses months rather than days. In this case, months is more accurate.)

7

	$
90 days (345 + 150 – 200)	295
60 days	–
30 days (Invoice 420)	231
Current (Invoice 556)	319
Total	845

8   D   A banker's draft cannot be stopped or cancelled once it is issued, and is effectively a cheque drawn on the bank. It is accepted by most people as being as good as cash, but has none of the inconvenience that cash would involve in a payment of this size.

8   Section A: Short-term finance IV

1   A   Administrative costs, postage and quality control cost.

2   Optimal order size = 500 units

$$EOQ = \sqrt{\frac{2 \times \text{order cost} \times \text{demand}}{\text{holding cost}}}$$

$$EOQ = \sqrt{\frac{2 \times 200 \times 10{,}000}{\$4 + (3\% \times \$400)}}$$

$$EOQ = 500$$

3       $\sqrt{\dfrac{2 \times 15 \times 95{,}000}{3}} = \sqrt{950{,}000} = 975$

No. of orders = 95,000/975 = 98 orders

4   D   The EOQ model can be used:

$$EOQ = \sqrt{\frac{(2C_o D)}{C_h}}$$

where   EOQ = the reorder quantity
         C_o = cost of making one order
         C_h = holding cost per unit of inventory per year
         D = usage in units per year

In this case:

$$EOQ = \sqrt{\frac{(2 \times 25 \times 10{,}000)}{0.50}}$$

$$= 1{,}000$$

5   D $EOQ = \sqrt{\dfrac{(2 \times 100 \times 40{,}000)}{2}}$

$$= 2{,}000$$

Since 40,000 wheels are required each year, 20 orders will be placed.

6   A $EOQ = \sqrt{\dfrac{(2 \times 400 \times 160{,}000)}{8}}$

$$= 4{,}000$$

Since 160,000 wheels are required each year, 40 orders will be placed.

Orders will therefore be placed every 52 ÷ 40 = 1.3 weeks.

7   D   Although the purchasing manager may sanction payments to suppliers, the payment will normally be raised by the finance department.

8   D   Higher levels of inventory reduce the risk of running out of inventory.

9   B   Inventory shortages are the most likely problem with a JIT inventory ordering system.

9   Section B: Short-term finance

> **Text references.** Borrowing, investing, receivables, payables and managing inventory are covered in Chapters 3 to 5.
>
> **Top tips.** Remember that only five marks are available for each part of Section B questions. So don't be tempted to write everything you know about a subject. Only make and explain sufficient points to earn the five marks available. You will see in our answers to parts (e) and (f) that we could have made several more points, but we have selected only the most important points to write about in the time available.
>
> **Easy marks.** There were some easy marks to be earned in part (b), simple by **applying** general knowledge and commenting on the risk of investing in the stock market. Make sure that you use the data or scenario provided in the question. Picking up and **applying** information that you are given in part (c) is a quick way to earn easy marks.

(a)

> **Examiner's comments.** Many candidates were unable to explain the terms 'coupon rate' and 'yield to maturity' satisfactorily. The vast majority of candidates were unable to calculate the yield to maturity. Very few candidates even got the formula correct.

(i)   The coupon rate of a security is the actual amount of interest that is paid on the security based upon its face value. In the case of the bond illustrated this is $70 ($1,000 × 7%).

The yield to maturity however is the overall return that the security holder achieves over the period of holding the security to maturity. This is the interest receivable on the security together with the repayment at maturity compared to the original cost of the bond.

(ii)   Yield to maturity = internal rate of return

Year	Cash flow	Discount factor @ 8%	Present value $	Discount factor @ 12%	Present value $
0	(850)	1.00	(850.00)	1.00	(850.00)
1-5	70	3.993	279.51	3.605	252.35
5	1,000	0.681	681.00	0.567	567.00
			$\overline{110.51}$		$\overline{(30.65)}$

$$\text{Internal rate of return} = 8\% + \frac{110.51}{110.51+30.65}(12\%-8\%)$$

$$= 8\% + \left(\frac{110.51}{141.16} \times 4\right)\%$$

$$= 8\% + 3.13\%$$

Yield to maturity = 11.13%

(b)   **To:**   Management Accountant
From: Assistant Management Accountant
Re: Investment of cash surplus

In the case of this cash surplus the issues are as follows:

1   This cash is needed to **pay for the factory**. Therefore the risk of loss must be minimised, even at the cost of lower returns during the period of investment.

2   The cash will be needed in **3-4 months**. Therefore it cannot be tied up for a longer period.

I have looked at the three possible investment opportunities and found the following:

(i)   **Treasury bills.** These are virtually risk free and have an annual yield of 4% (1% over 3 months × 4). Purchased now and held for 91 days, they will give us a return of 1% over the three months.

(ii) **Equities** are higher yield (10%) but with a far higher level of risk. We have no way of knowing how the share index will perform over three months and we may end up selling at a loss in order to release the cash. If the shares are sold before the dividend is declared we will lose the dividend.

(iii) **A bank deposit account** will pay 3.5% per annum. This is slightly less than Treasury bills but is also virtually risk-free and only requires 30 days notice. If notice is not given, a month's interest will be lost.

The best option would appear to be the Treasury bills for 91 days. If at the end of that time the cash is not needed for another month it could be put into a bank deposit account.

(c)

> **Examiner's comments.** Most candidates were able to identify possible sources of funding but most gave only superficial explanations. Very few candidates used the information provided to calculate trade payable/receivable days outstanding. A large proportion of the answers did not give realistic solutions and ignored the data provided in the question.

DF has the following sources available:

(i) **Short-term loan**. This would be easy to arrange and DF will probably be able to repay it in 6 months.

(ii) **Overdraft**. This will be more expensive but more flexible. With a turnover of $240m an additional $2m on the overdraft should not be a problem.

(iii) **Delaying payment to suppliers**. DF has a gross margin of 50% on $240m, so its cost of sales is $120m. With $16m trade payables outstanding, DF is taking 49 days ($16/120 \times 365$) to pay suppliers. Increasing the amount outstanding by $2m will mean that suppliers are being paid after 55 days ($18/120 \times 365$). This is still less than 60 days, so DF may not get too much protest from suppliers as the change may not be apparent from looking at their receivables ageing reports. However, for those suppliers who do become aware of it, DF's trading relationship may be adversely affected.

(iv) **Accelerating collection from customers**. DF's customers are currently paying after 30 days ($20/240 \times 365$). These are normal trade terms and it is unreasonable to think that this period can be reduced without offering customers some incentive, such as a discount.

(d) (i) Working capital management

The **net working capital** of a business can be defined as its **current assets less** its **current liabilities**. The management of working capital is concerned with ensuring that **sufficient liquid resources** are **maintained** within the business. For the majority of businesses, particularly manufacturing businesses, trade payables will form the major part of the current liabilities figure.

Trade credit period

It follows that the **trade credit period** taken will be a major determinant of the working capital requirement of the company. This is calculated (in days) as the total value of **trade payables divided** by the level of **credit purchases** $\times$ 365.

Cash conversion cycle

A link can be made between working capital and liquidity by means of the **cash conversion cycle**. This measures the length of time that elapses between a firm **paying** for its **various purchases** and **receiving payment** for its **sales**. It can be calculated as the receivable days plus the inventory period less the trade credit period, and it measures the length of time for which net current assets must be financed.

(ii) Use of trade credit

For many firms, trade payables provide a very **important source** of **short-term credit**. Since very few companies currently impose interest charges on overdue accounts, taking extended credit can appear to be a very cheap form of short-term finance. However, such a policy entails some risks and costs that are not immediately apparent, as follows.

(1) If discounts are being forgone, the **effective cost** of this should be evaluated – it may be more beneficial to shorten the credit period and take the discounts.

(2) If the company gains a reputation for slow payment this will **damage its credit standing** and it may find it difficult to obtain credit from new suppliers in the future.

(3) Suppliers who are having to wait for their money may seek recompense in other ways, for example by raising prices or by placing a lower priority on new orders. Such actions could do **damage** to both the **efficiency and profitability** of the company.

(4) Suppliers may place the company **'on stop'** until the account is paid. This can jeopardise supplies of essential raw materials which in turn could cause production to stop: this will obviously provide the company with a high level of unwanted costs.

(e)

> **Examiner's comments.** Many candidates spent too long on the question, writing far more than required for five marks.

Benefits

Possible benefits of a JIT purchasing system are as follows.

(i) Reduction of inventory holding costs.

(ii) Reduced manufacturing lead times.

Limitations

A JIT purchasing system has the following limitations.

(i) Not always appropriate. For example, running out of inventory in a hospital could prove fatal.

(ii) Large up-front costs of a full study of production methods.

(iii) Access to sizeable funds is required to run a JIT purchasing system.

Note. The examiner has stated that any other valid benefits or limitations would be given credit.

> Alternative Answers
>
> We have given five points here as the question is for five marks. You would also have scored marks for the following.
>
> Benefits
>
> - Improved labour productivity.
>
> - Reduced scrap/rework/warrant costs.
>
> - Elimination of poor quality production as scrapping work in progress and producing additional units can lead to time delays. Higher quality products will result in improved customer satisfaction.
>
> - Increased flexibility to supply small batches as production matches ultimate demand.
>
> - May help with the identification of weaknesses such as unreliable suppliers.
>
> Limitations
>
> - A JIT purchasing system requires long-term commitment to suppliers and so reduces flexibility in supplier choice.
>
> - For JIT to work, suppliers must be able to regularly deliver materials of appropriate quality on time and at short notice.

(f)

> **Examiner's comments.** Most candidates did not seem to know what an age analysis was or how to prepare one.

(i) Customer X – age analysis

	Current $	30 days $	60 days $	90 days $	Total $
Invoice AC913	233				233
Invoice AC690		204			204
Invoice AC112				160	160 ✓
	233	204	–	160	597

(ii) • It highlights overdue amounts which the credit controller needs to chase up

- It highlights particular customers who may have a large outstanding balance and to whom no further goods should be delivered until the account is settled. If there is a possibility of a debt becoming irrecoverable, the credit controller will seek to minimise the size of the debt.

Alternative answers.

You would also have been given credit for the following.

- It draws attention to items which may be in dispute. For instance customer X above has only part paid invoice AC112 and the balance is now 90 days. This suggests that the balance of the invoice may be in dispute.

- It provides useful information for management accounting. For instance, if the cash flow forecast has been prepared on the basis of goods being paid for in the month following the month of sale and the age analysis shows that 70% of sales are paid after 60 days, the cash flow forecast will need to be revised.

---

10 Section C: CK

Text references. Working capital ratios are covered in Chapter 1, cash budgeting and cash management are covered in Chapter 2, receivables and payables are covered in Chapter 4 and managing inventory is covered in Chapter 5.

Top tips. There is a lot of information provided in this question. Make sure you read through carefully, highlighting key or unusual items. Always be careful you answer the requirements in the narrative parts of the question.

Easy marks. Once again a clear layout for your budget pro forma, with all the appropriate cost and revenue categories, will earn you easy marks.

Examiner's comments. Part (a) was generally well done as was part (d). Part (b) was not done at all well. Most candidates were not aware of the adjustments required to the cash flows as a result of the changes in the working capital policies.

(a) Trade receivables days = 1,083/6,192 × 365 = 64 days
Trade payables days = 344/4,128 × 365 = 30 days
Inventory days = 1,020/4,128 × 365 = 90 days

(b) CK – CASH BUDGET FOR YEAR TO 31 MARCH 20X7

	$'000	$'000
Receipts		
Revenue (6,192 × 97% × 110%)	6,607	
Additional receivables collection (1,083 – 815(W1))	268	
Total receipts		6,875
Payments		
Purchases (4,128/6,192 × 6,607)	4,404	
Reduction in inventory (1,020 × 40%)	(408)	
Increase in payables (437(W2) – 344)	(93)	
Purchase payments		(3,903)
Salaries and wages		(620)
Other operating expenses		(432)
Capital expenditure		(2,500)
Net payments		(580)
Cash balance at 31 March 20X6		622
Cash balance at 31 March 20X7		42

Workings

1   New receivables = 6,607 ÷ 365 × 45 = 815
2   New payables = (4,404 – 408) ÷ 365 × 40 = 437

(c)   If CK decides to lease $1.5m of the non-current assets, there will be an immediate improvement in its cash budget for 20X7. As the payments are due prior to 1 April, it appears likely that it will have to pay two instalments in the year ending 31 March 20X7, but this will still be a saving of $700,000 (1,500 – 800). However, it will pay an additional $500,000 in financing over the term of the lease, which must be taken into consideration.

(d)   Customer relationships

We are not told how the efficiency changes are to be achieved. However we can assume that the reduction in receivables days will be achieved by more energetic credit control. Any new or additional discounts offered would impact on the amount collectable, so we presume this is not the case. CK is in a market where there are plenty of competitors, and its customers are retail stores, who will also be seeking to maximise their payables days. Depending on the relationship it has with its customers, CK will be able to push tighter credit control just so far. It does not want customers deserting it for another supplier who will allow more liberal payment terms.

Supplier relationships

At the same time, CK is seeking to increase its payables days, so it is dealing with the same situation in reverse. There is no mention of loss of discounts, so we have to assume that is not an issue. If CK's suppliers are *willing* to wait 40 days for payment, then its relationship with them will not be affected by the change. It is important that CK retains the goodwill of its suppliers, as lower inventory levels will make it more dependent on suppliers delivering quickly.

Stock out

An inventory reduction of 40% will need to be carefully managed. If CK's customers require parts that it does not have in inventory, they are likely to go elsewhere. Computer spare parts will usually be required on an immediate basis – people want their systems to keep running. CK will need to have close supplier relationships in order to deal with this. It does not seem likely that suppliers will be willing to give this sort of service *and* wait longer to get paid.

(e)   A factor normally manages the debts owed to a client on the client's behalf

Services provided by factoring organisations

(i)   **Administration** of the client's invoicing, sales accounting and debt collection service.

(ii)   **Credit protection** for the client's debts, whereby the factor takes over the risk of loss from bad debts and so 'insures' the client against such losses. The factor may purchase these debts 'without recourse' to the client, which means that if the client's customers do not pay what they owe, the factor will not ask for the money back from the client.

(iii) **'Factor finance'** may be provided, the factor advancing cash to the client against outstanding debts. The factor may advance up to 85% of approved debts from the date of invoice.

(iv)   A **confidentiality agreement** may be offered to conceal the existence of the arrangement from customers.

11 Section A: Costing systems

1   D   OAR for last year   = Budgeted overheads/Budgeted machine hours
                             = £660,000/44,000 hours
                             = £15 per hour

OAR per unit = £15 per hour × 0.2 hours/unit = £3

Overheads absorbed = 200,000 × £3
                   = £600,000

Actual overheads   = £590,000

∴ overheads were over absorbed by £590,000 – £600,000
                   = £10,000 over absorption

2   B   Closing inventory valuation under absorption costing will always be higher than under marginal costing because of the absorption of fixed overheads into closing inventory values.

The profit under absorption costing will be greater because the fixed overhead being carried forward in closing inventory is greater than the fixed overhead being written off in opening inventory.

3   A   Using marginal costing, the profit in March was:

	£'000	£'000
Sales revenue		820,000
Less: variable production costs [£300,000 − $\frac{150}{1,000}$ × £300,000]		(255,000)
		565,000
Less: fixed production costs	180,000	
variable selling costs	105,000	
Fixed selling costs	110,000	
		(395,000)
		170,000

4   A   If marginal costing is used to value inventory instead of absorption costing, the difference in profits will be equal to the change in inventory volume multiplied by the fixed production overhead absorption rate = 80 units × £34 = £2,720 ✓

Since closing inventory are higher than opening inventories, the marginal costing profit will be lower that the absorption costing profit (so **option B** is incorrect). This is because the marginal costing profit does not 'benefit' from the increase in the amount of fixed production overhead taken to inventory (rather than to the income statement).

If you selected **options C or D** you based the difference on 100 units of opening inventory.

5   B   An attainable standard is based on the expectation that a standard amount of work will be carried out efficiently, machines properly operated or materials properly used. **Allowance are included** for factors such as losses, waste and machine downtime.

Option A describes an **ideal standard**
Option C describes a **current standard**
Option D describes a **basic standard**

6   Using the high two method to determine the period fixed costs:

Production (units)	Production costs £
1,210	3,394
990	3,086
220	308

Variable cost per unit = £308/220 = £1.40

Fixed cost = £3,394 − (1,210 × £1.40) = £1,700

Overhead absorption rate = £1,700/1,000 units
                                         = £1.70 per unit

Difference in reported profit = change in inventory units × £1.70
                                            = (1,200 − 1,040) × £1.70
                                            = £272

The absorption costing profit will be lower than the marginal costing profit because the number of units in inventory reduced during the period.

Absorption costing profit = £8,160 − £272 = £7,888

7   (i)   Marginal costing:

	$'000	$'000
Sales (20,000 × $70)		1,400
Opening inventory		
Variable production overhead (W1)	1,210	
	1,210	
Less closing inventory (W2)	110	
Variable cost of sales		1,100
Contribution		300
Less fixed costs (W3)		193
Profit		107

Workings

(1)   22,000 units × $55 = $1,210,000

(2)   Production units + opening inventory – sales   = closing inventory

        = 22,000 + 0 – 20,000 = 2,000

        units

        Valued at marginal cost: 2,000 × $55   = $110,000

(3)   Fixed production overhead + fixed selling costs   = $118,000 + $75,000 = $193,000

Alternative approach

	$'000
Total contribution (20,000 × $15 (W1))	300
Less fixed production overhead	(118)
Less fixed selling costs	(75)
MC profit	107

Workings

1 contribution per unit = $70-$55 = $15

    (ii)   Absorption costing

OAR = Budgeted overhead / budgeted production = $130,000/25,000 = $5.2/unit

As inventory has increased, absorption costing will report a higher profit than marginal costing.

The difference in profit	=	change in inventory volume × fixed production overhead per unit
	=	2,000 × $5.2
	=	$10,400

Marginal profit	=	$107,000
∴ absorption profit	=	$107,000 + $10,400 = $117,400

8   Budgeted profit = £1 million

Therefore total contribution = £6.5 million and contribution from Z must be £3 million

	Product X	Product Y	Product Z	Total X, Y & Z
Revenue	£10 m	£20 m	£12 m	
Contribution/Sales ratio	15%	10%	25%	
Contribution (£m)	1.50	2.00	3.00	6.50
Fixed costs (£m)				5.50
Profit (£m)				1.10

12 Section B: Costing systems

(a)   The **advantages** of using **marginal costing** are as follows.

   (i)   Marginal costing is **based on cost behaviour patterns**, the key principle being that contribution will vary in proportion to the units sold. Hence marginal costing demonstrates clearly how **cash flows and profits** will be **affected** by **changes in sales volume**.

   (ii)   Using marginal costing means that **fixed costs** that relate to a period of time are **matched** against the period by being charged against the period's **revenues**.

   (iii)   Marginal costing situations can be shown easily and clearly on graphs.

   (iv)   Use of marginal costing will help in **short-term pricing decisions** concerning incremental profits. It will also help in **setting a buffer inventory level**. Buffer inventory must be valued at marginal cost, since fixed costs have not been incurred to produce a marginal quantity of finished goods that are unsold at the end of the period.

(b)   Absorption costing purpose

The **aim of absorption costing is to produce a product cost which ensures that overheads incurred during a period are recovered** via the inclusion of a share of overhead in each unit of output. Its principal aim is not, therefore, to produce accurate product costs.

Subjective judgement

The determination of absorption costing product costs **depends on a great deal of subjective judgement and hence, due to the requirement of accurate product costs for decision making, it is totally unsuitable for decision making.**

Due to the high degree of subjectivity involved in its operation, absorption costing can result in inaccurate and hence misleading information for decision making and should not therefore be used for that purpose.

Marginal spare capacity

It is not just the inaccuracy of the resulting product cost which makes absorption costing information unsuitable for decision making, however. Consider the following example.

Suppose that a sales manager has an item of product which he is having difficulty in selling. Its historical full cost is £80, made up of variable costs of £50 and fixed costs of £30. A customer offers £60 for it.

   (i)   **If there is no other customer** for the product, £60 would be better than nothing and the **product should be sold to improve income and profit** by this amount.

   (ii)   If the company has **spare production capacity** which would otherwise not be used, it would be **profitable to continue making more** of the same product, if customers are willing to pay £60 for each extra unit made. This is because the additional costs are only £50 so that the profit would be increased marginally by £10 per unit produced.

Thus, for **once-only decisions or decisions affecting the use of marginal spare capacity, absorption costing information about unit profits is *irrelevant***. On the other hand, since total contribution must be sufficient to cover the fixed costs of the business, **marginal costing would be unsuitable as a basis for establishing *long-term* prices for all output**.

(c)

	Assembly £	Painting £	Stores £	Maintenance £
Overheads	200,000	300,000	100,000	80,000
Apportionment				
Maintenance	32,000	36,000	12,000	(80,000)
Stores	67,200	44,800	(112,000)	–
	299,200	380,800	–	–

Standard overhead absorption rate $= \dfrac{£299{,}200}{100{,}000} = £2.992$ per unit

	£
Overheads absorbed 120,000 × £2.992	359,040
Actual overheads incurred by Assembly department	360,000
Under absorbed	960

(d) **Overhead allocation** is the **process of assigning a whole item of cost** to a single cost unit, centre, account or time period.

An example of a cost allocation would be assigning the salary of a catering manager to the works canteen.

Overhead apportionment is the **spreading of indirect revenues or costs** over two or more cost units, centres accounts or time periods. Apportionment may also be referred to as 'indirect allocation'.

(CIMA Official Terminology)

The overhead costs that have been allocated to cost centres will need to be apportioned to production departments.

An example of overhead apportionment would be the indirect allocation of the costs of the works canteen to the production department.

(e) An **overhead absorption rate** is a means of **attributing overhead to a product or service**, based for example on direct labour hours, direct labour cost or machine hours.   *(CIMA Official Terminology)*

An overhead absorption rate may be based on:
(i)   Direct labour cost percentage rate
(ii)   Direct labour hour rate
(iii) Machine hour rate
(iv)   Volume of production

The choice is made with the objective of obtaining accurate costs. It is a matter of judgement and common sense. There are no strict rules involved but what is required is an absorption basis which realistically **reflects the characteristics of a given cost centre** and which avoids undue anomalies.

(f) (i)   Over absorption = £2,400

Number of units produced in excess of normal/budget activity = £2,400/£8 = 300 units

This represents a margin of safety of 20%

Therefore 20% of actual sales volume = 300 units

Actual sales = 300/0.20 = 1,500 units

Budget/normal activity = 1,500 – 300 units = 1,200 units

Therefore fixed overheads each period = 1,200 x £8 = £9,600

Breakeven point = £9,600/£(27 – 15) = 800 units

(ii)   Units required to achieve target profit = £(9,600 + 6,600)/£(27 – 15)
= 1,350 units

13 Section B: Costing systems

(a)   <u>What is standard costing?</u>

The CIMA *Official Terminology* definition of standard costing is 'A control technique that reports variances by comparing actual costs to pre-set standards so facilitating action through management by exception.

<u>Setting standards for materials costs</u>

Direct material prices will be estimated by the purchasing department from their existing knowledge.
- Purchase contracts already agreed
- Pricing discussions with regular suppliers
- Quotations and estimates from potential suppliers
- The forecast movement of prices in the market
- The availability of bulk purchase discounts
- Material quality required

Price inflation can cause difficulties in setting realistic standard prices. Suppose that a material costs £10 per kilogram at the moment, and during the course of the next 12 months, it is expected to go up in price by 20% to £12 per kilogram. **What standard price should be selected?**

- The **current price** of £10 per kilogram
- The **expected price** for the year, say, £11 per kilogram

Either price above would be possible, but neither would be entirely satisfactory.

Standard costing for materials is therefore more **difficult in times of inflation but it is still worthwhile**.

(i)   Usage and efficiency variances will still be meaningful.

(ii)   Inflation is measurable: there is no reason why its effects cannot be removed from the variances reported.

(iii)   Standard costs can be revised, so long as this is not done too frequently.

(b)   Types of performance standard

The setting of standards raises the problem of how demanding the standard should be. Should the standard represent a perfect performance or an easily attainable performance? The type of performance standard used can have behavioural implications. There are four types of standard.

(i)   Ideal   These are based on **perfect operating conditions**: no wastage, no spoilage, no inefficiencies, no idle time, no breakdowns. Variances from ideal standards are useful for pinpointing areas where a close examination may result in large savings, but they are likely to have an **unfavourable motivational impact** because reported variances will always be adverse. Employees will often feel that the goals are **unattainable** and not work so hard.

(ii)   Attainable   These are based on the hope that a standard amount of work will be carried out **efficiently**, machines properly operated or materials properly used. Some **allowance** is made for **wastage** and **inefficiencies**. If well-set they provide a useful psychological **incentive** by giving employees a **realistic**, but **challenging** target of efficiency. The consent and co-operation of employees involved in improving the standard are required.

(iii)   Current   These are based on **current working conditions** (current wastage, current inefficiencies). The disadvantage of current standards is that they **do not attempt to improve** on **current** levels of **efficiency**.

(iv)   Basic   These are kept **unaltered** over a **long period of time**, and may be **out of date**. They are used to show changes in efficiency or performance over a long period of time. Basic standards are perhaps the **least useful** and least common type of standard in use.

Ideal standards, attainable standards and current standards each have their supporters and it is by no means clear which of them is preferable.

(c)   McDonaldisation is a term coined by George Ritzer in his 1996 book 'The McDonaldisation of Society'. Ritzer, analysing the American hamburger chain, noted that the principles of McDonalds' operations are now being applied to many sectors of society.

The application of McDonaldisation in service industries is assisting the use of standard costing for cost and planning control because it overcomes the potential lack of homogeneity in services.

Ritzer identified four dimensions of McDonaldisation.

(i)   **Calculability**. The content of every McDonalds meal is **identical** and **standardised**. Every burger should contain a **standard amount** of meat, every bun is of the **same size** and all fries are of the same thickness. The **human element** is **eliminated** as far as possible in the actual production process in order to make the food in a standard time using standard materials. Human initiative is eliminated in actually putting together the meal at the point of sale through the issuing of standard instructions concerning the content of each type of meal ordered. Thus each meal is a **measurable standard cost unit** for which a standard cost can be established and the actual cost can be measured for cost control purposes.

(ii) **Control**. Control over the service is achieved in particular by **reducing the human influence**, which can lead to **variation** in output and quality. **Machines** and **technology substitute** for **humans**: automatic drink dispensers which measure the exact quantity to be delivered and cash registers which require only one button to be pressed to record the sale of a complete meal are examples of improved control and the reduction of the possibility of human error in the delivery of the service.

(iii) **Efficiency**. Ritzer described efficiency as 'the optimum method of getting from one point to another'. Every McDonalds business is **organised** to ensure **maximum efficiency** so that the customer can get exactly what they want as quickly as possible. This increases **customer satisfaction** and also increases the company's **profitability**.

(iv) **Predictability**. The McDonalds service is the **same in every outlet** throughout the world, whether a meal is purchased in Shanghai or London. Again this helps with the **standardisation of the service** and the **setting of standard costs** throughout the organisation.

(d) A **budget** is a **quantified monetary plan** for a future period, which managers will try to achieve. Its major function lies in communicating plans and co-ordinating activities within an organisation.

On the other hand, a **standard** is a carefully **predetermined quantity target** which can be achieved in certain conditions.

Budgets and standards are similar in the following ways.

(i) They both **involve looking to the future** and forecasting what is likely to happen given a certain set of circumstances.

(ii) They are both **used for control purposes.** A budget aids control by setting financial targets or limits for a forthcoming period. Actual achievements or expenditures are then compared with the budgets and action is taken to correct any variances where necessary. A standard also achieves control by comparison of actual results against a predetermined target.

As well as being similar, budgets and standards are interrelated. For example, a standard unit production cost can act as the basis for a production cost budget. The unit cost is multiplied by the budgeted activity level to arrive at the budgeted expenditure on production costs.

There are, however, important differences between budgets and standards.

Budgets

- Gives planned total aggregate costs for a function or cost centre
- Can be prepared for all functions, even where output cannot be measured
- Expressed in money terms

Standards

- Shows the unit resource usage for a single task, for example the standard labour hours for a single unit of production

- Limited to situations where repetitive actions are performed and output can be measured

- Need not be expressed in money terms. For example, a standard rate of output does not need a financial value put on it

(e) Direct labour costs

Standard costing places **too much emphasis on direct labour costs**. Direct labour is only a small proportion of costs in the modern manufacturing environment and so this emphasis is not appropriate.

Dynamic business environment

Standard costing systems were **developed** when the **business environment** was more **stable** and **less prone to change**. The current business environment is more dynamic and it is not possible to assume stable conditions

Quality

Variance analysis concentrates on a **narrow range of costs** only and does not give sufficient attention to issues such as quality and customer satisfaction. Today's business environment is more focused on **continuous improvement** in a **total quality** environment.

(f) Diagnostic related groups

Diagnostic related groups (DRGs) are a system of classifying patients into one of a large number of groups according to their condition and treatment. This classification provides a basis to determine the **resources that will be required** to treat and care for the patient.

Applying the principles of standard costing

The principles of standard costing can only be applied where a **standard input of resources can be determined** for a given 'output'. Cost control can then be achieved through the comparison of the actual cost of resources used with the pre-determined standard cost.

The use of DRGs helps to **establish a standard cost** for each patient's treatment and care in order to provide the necessary basis of comparison for cost control. The use of a large number of DRGs helps to standardised the range of resources required for patient treatment and care.

The DRGs are used as the basis of payment to hospitals and other healthcare services by health insurance companies. The hospital would then need to **control its costs** to avoid exceeding the payment received.

14 Section C: Marginal and absorption reconciliation

Text references. Marginal and absorption costing are covered in Chapter 6b.

Top tips. Use of a columnar format in (a) would have saved time. The key information when splitting fixed and variable production overheads was the over and under absorption in each period. In (b) you should remember that it is the net effect of the change in inventory levels that is used when reconciling absorption and marginal costing profits. Note in (c) the change in distribution costs has to be taken into account separately when reconciling the absorption costing profits of two periods. Under marginal costing the change would be reflected by a change in total contribution.

Easy marks. Marks will be gained by setting out the appropriate columnar format with the right headings and putting in all the known numbers. Gradually work through the missing numbers, clearly marking your workings and gaining further marks along the way. You don't have to get everything right to pass.

(a)

	January – June		July – December	
	£'000	£'000	£'000	£'000
Sales		540		360
Opening inventory (£18 (W1) × 5,000/8,000 (W4))	90		144	
Production costs				
Direct materials	108		36	
Direct labour	162		54	
Variable overhead (£3 (W1) × 18,000/6,000)	54		18	
	414		252	
Closing inventory (£18 (W1) × 8,000/4,000 (W4))	(144)		(72)	
		270		180
		270		180
Variable distribution costs				
(£1 (W5) × 15,000/10,000)		15		10
Contribution		255		170
Fixed costs				
Production overhead (W2)	24		24	
Selling costs	50		50	
Distribution costs (W5)	30		30	
Administration costs	80		80	
		184		184
Budgeted profit/(loss) under marginal costing		71		(14)

Workings

1   Fixed and variable costs per unit

	£
Direct materials (£108,000 ÷ 18,000)	6
Direct labour (£162,000 ÷ 18,000)	9
Variable overhead (W2)	3
Variable costs per unit	18
Fixed cost per unit (W3)	2
Total cost per unit	20

2   Fixed and variable overheads

	January – June £'000	July – December £'000
Overhead absorbed	90	30
(Over)/under absorption	(12)	12
Actual overhead	78	42

Using the high-low method, we can determine the fixed and variable elements of the production overheads.

	Production Units	Production overheads £
High	18,000	78,000
Low	6,000	42,000
	12,000	36,000

$$\text{Variable production overhead cost per unit} = \frac{£36,000}{12,000} = £3 \text{ per unit}$$

∴ When 18,000 units are produced, total variable production overheads = 18,000 × £3 = £54,000.

Since total costs	= fixed costs + variable costs
£78,000	= fixed costs + £54,000
∴ Fixed costs	= £78,000 – £54,000
	= £24,000

3   Total overhead cost per unit

January – June, total overheads = £90,000

January – June, production units = 18,000

$$\therefore \text{Total overhead cost per unit} = \frac{£90,000}{18,000} = £5 \text{ per unit}$$

In (W2) we established that the variable overhead cost per unit = £3. Therefore the fixed overhead cost per unit = £5 – £3 = £2.

4   Opening and closing inventory levels

	January – June Units		July – December Units
Opening inventory (£100,000 ÷ £20 (W1))	5,000	(£160,000 ÷ £20 (W1))	8,000
Closing inventory (£160,000 ÷ £20 (W1))	8,000	(£80,000 ÷ £20 (W1))	4,000

5   Distribution costs

	Sales units	Distribution costs £
High	15,000	45,000
Low	10,000	40,000
	5,000	5,000

$$\text{Variable distribution cost per unit} = \frac{£5,000}{5,000} = £1 \text{ per unit}$$

Fixed costs	=	£45,000 – (15,000 × £1)
	=	£45,000 – £15,000
	=	£30,000

(b)   From (W1) in part (a), it can be seen that the cost of inventory under marginal costing = £18 per unit and the cost of inventory under absorption costing = £20 per unit.

	January – June £'000	July – December £'000
Absorption costing profit	77 ✔	(22)
Fixed overheads b/f in opening inventory (£2 (W3) × 5,000/8,000)	10	16
Fixed overhead c/f in closing inventory (£2 (W3) × 8,000/4,000)	(16)	(8)
Marginal costing profit (see (a))	71	(14)

(c)

	£'000
Profit January – June 20X7	77
Decrease in sales volume (5,000 × £16 (see below))	(80)
Difference in overhead recovery	(24)
Decrease in distribution costs	5
Loss July – December 20X7	(22)

Profit per unit under absorption costing = sales price per unit (£540,000 ÷ 15,000) – cost per unit
= £(36 – 20)
= £16

(d)   Fixed costs = £184,000 × 2
= £368,000

Contribution per unit = selling price – variable production costs – variable distribution costs

= £36 – £18 (W1) – £1 (W5)
= £17

$$\therefore \text{Breakeven point} = \frac{368,000}{17}$$
= 21,647 units

15 Section A: Variance analysis

1   The correct answer is A

> **Top tips.** Fixed overhead *volume* variance is a measure of the over or under absorption of fixed overhead cost caused by actual production volume differing from that budgeted. It is calculated as the difference between actual and budgeted production (volume) multiplied by the standard absorption rate per unit.
>
> Answer C is incorrect because it refers to fixed overhead expenditure variance which is calculated as the difference between the budgeted fixed overhead expenditure and the actual fixed overhead expenditure.

> Answer B is incorrect because it refers to the fixed overhead *total variance* which is the difference between *fixed overhead incurred* and *fixed overhead absorbed*.

2   D   The direct materials usage variance compares the standard material usage for the **actual** production with the **actual** material used. This means that the budgeted output volume is not relevant because it is not included in the calculation of the variance.

Options A and C are both likely to lead to a reduction in wastage rates which, like Option B, will lead to lower usage and a favourable materials usage variance.

3   D   The direct labour rate variance for April is calculated as:

The actual direct labour rate paid is calculated as:

$$\frac{\text{Direct labour cost}}{\text{Direct labour hours}} = \frac{£336,000}{24,000 \text{ hours}} = £14 \text{ per hour}$$

The direct labour rate variance is calculated as:

Actual hours worked × [standard rate per hour – actual rate per hour] = 24,000 hours × [£15 – £14] = £24,000 favourable.

The correct answer is D

4   A   The variable overhead efficiency variance for April is:

[Standard labour hours for production achieved – Actual labour hours] × standard variable overhead rate = [(11,000 units × 2 hours per unit) – 24,000 hours] × £6 = £12,000 adverse.

5   The sales volume variance in a marginal costing system is valued at standard contribution per unit, rather than standard profit per unit.

Contribution per unit of E = £15 – £8 = £7

$$\text{Sales volume variance in terms of contribution} = \frac{£9,000\text{(A)}}{£5} \times £7 = £12,600 \text{ (A)}$$

6   Product TRD100

	Actual mix	Standard mix	Difference	Price	Variance
	Litres	Litres	Litres	£	£
X	984	885.6	98.4 (A)	2·50	246.0 (A)
Y	1,230	1,328.4	98.4 (F)	3·00	295.2 (F)
Total	2,214	2,214.0	nil		49.2 (F)

7   Expected output of product TRD100 $\frac{2,214}{30}$ = 73.8 units

Actual output   = 72.0 units

Shortfall   = 1.8 units

1.8 units × £84/unit   = £151.2(A)

An alternative would be only 73 complete units of output were expected. With a shortfall of 1 unit, the variance would be 1.0 × £84 per unit = £84 adverse.

8   Selling price planning variance

Original plan   600 × £72 = £43,200
Revised plan   600 × £82 = £49,200
Actual   600 × £86 = £51,600

(i)   Selling price planning variance = Revised plan – original plan
                                      = £49,200 – £43,200
                                      = £6,000 (F)

(ii)   Selling price operating variance = Actual sales – revised plan
                                                             = £51,600 – £49,200
                                                             = £2,400 (F)

16 Section B: Variance analysis

(a)   Calculation of variances

	£
64,000 units should have sold for (× £10)	640,000
but did sell for (× £8.40)	537,600
Selling price variance	102,400 (A)

Budgeted sales volume	72,000 units
Actual sales volume	64,000 units
Sales volume variance in units	8,000 units (A)
× standard contribution per unit	× £4
Sales volume contribution variance	£32,000 (A)

	£
Variable cost of 64,000 units should have been (× £6)	384,000
but was (× £6.20)	396,800
Variable cost variance	12,800 (A)

Possible causes of variances

(i)   Stronger than anticipated **competition** forced prices down

(ii)   A **reduction** in the overall levels of **demand** resulted in a reduction in sales volume and a downward pressure on prices.

> Any cause of the variances that is consistent with whether the variance is adverse or favourable would earn marks. For five marks in total, including the marks available for the calculations, you would not be expected to provide more than two or three possible causes. Remember to stick to the time allowance for the question.
>
> Other causes that you might have thought of include:
>
> The **costs** of labour and raw materials (variable costs) **could have risen** more than anticipated, resulting in an adverse variable cost variance.
>
> The **actual mix** of labour and raw materials used could have resulted in the use of a **higher proportion of more skilled labour and/or more expensive materials** than those included in the standard, thereby increasing the actual variable cost per unit.
>
> **Assumptions** upon which the budgeted figures were based **could have changed** during the control period but the budget figures were not revised.

(b)   (i)   Labour rate planning variance

	£
Revised standard cost 680 units × 900/600 × £31.20	31,824
Original standard cost 680 units × 900/600 × £30	30,600
	1,224 (A)

Operational labour efficiency variance

680 units should have taken (× 900/600)	1,020
But did take	1,070
Operational efficiency variance in hours	50 (A)
× revised standard rate per hour	× £31.20
	1,560 (A)

(ii)   Planning and operational variances provide a **more detailed analysis** than the conventional approach. They help to classify variances into those caused by **planning errors** and those caused by **operational inefficiencies**. The major benefit of this analysis is that it helps to produce a revised, more realistic standard.

(c)

Factors to be considered before deciding to investigate a variance.

Materiality

Small variations in a single period are bound to occur and **are unlikely to be significant**. Obtaining an 'explanation' is likely to be time-consuming and irritating for the manager concerned. The explanation will often be 'chance', which is not, in any case, particularly helpful. For such variations further investigation is not worthwhile.

Cost

The likely cost of an investigation needs to be weighed against the cost to the organisation of allowing the variance to continue in future periods.

Controllability

Controllability must also influence the decision whether to investigate further. If there is a general worldwide price increase in the price of an important raw material there is **nothing that can be done internally** to control the effect of this. Uncontrollable variances call for a **change in the plan**, not an investigation into the past.

You only need to discuss three factors but your answer may also have included the following.

Variance trend

Caution should be exercised before investigating a 'snapshot' variance in too much detail. For example, an adverse materials usage variance in Month 1 could indicate that control action is needed, but in a large company with many processes to monitor, it may be advisable to postpone direct action until the variances for subsequent months have been analysed. If they show a favourable trend then intervention will not be necessary.

Interrelationship of variances

Quite possibly, individual variances should not be looked at in isolation. One variance might be inter-related with another, and much of it might have occurred only because the other, inter-related, variance occurred too. When two variances are **interdependent (interrelated) one** will usually be **adverse** and the other **one favourable**.

(d)

(i) $Z = \dfrac{X - \mu}{\sigma} = \dfrac{110 - 90}{10} = \dfrac{20}{10} = 2$

Using the normal distribution tables

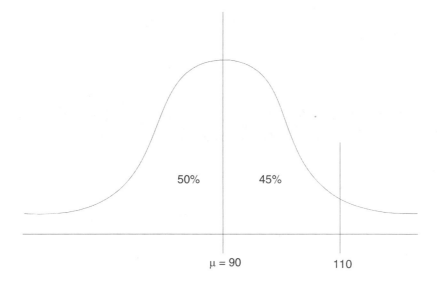

50%   45%

μ = 90   110

For Z = 2

From normal distribution tables

	0.4772
Add	0.5000
	0.9772

ie 97.72%

Therefore 110kgs is outside the range of 95%. The variance should be investigated.

(ii) Other factors to take into account when deciding whether to investigate a variance.

- Materiality of the variance
- Regular occurrence
- Anticipated costs of investigation compared to benefits of correcting it

(e) **Internal benchmarking** may provide information that is more **useful** to the manager than external benchmarking information for the following reasons.

(i) The manager should find it **easier** to persuade other internal managers to **share information**. This should mean that the quality of information is better. Persuading other organisations to share information can be difficult.

(ii) The practices which the company use should be **more readily transferable** from one division to another. Successful practices in one organisation may not transfer successfully to another.

(iii) Even if external organisations can be persuaded to share their results, this may not prove to be useful if the company doesn't know **how** the external organisation achieved that performance. Dealing with internal divisions means that **more details** can be obtained to help improve performance.

(f) <u>Standard mix of actual hours</u>

			Hrs
I	7/19 × (3,398 + 6,786)		3,752
II	12/19 × (3,398 + 6,786)		6,432
			10,184

<u>Mix</u>

Grade	Mix should have been	but was	Variance	× standard rate	Variance
	Hrs	Hrs	Hrs	£	£
I	3,752	3,398	354 (F)	12	4,248 (F)
II	6,432	6,786	354 (A)	15	5,310 (A)
	10,184	10,184	-		1,062 (A)

Yield

10,184 hours should have yielded (÷ 19)	536	units
but did yield	522	units
Variance in units	14	units (A)
× standard cost per unit of output	× £264	
Variance	£3,696	(A)

17 Section C: CP

Text references. Operating statements and mix and yield variances are covered in Chapter 8. Standard costing and new technology is covered in Chapter 7a in Section 6.2.

Top tips. For part (a) you need to organise your workings on a separate piece of paper. Don't waste too much time if your find that you reconciliation doesn't work. You will get marks for your workings and the layout of the reconciliation. For part (b) you need to discuss three reasons why standard costing is not always appropriate in an AMT environment. Don't waste time discussing any more than three reasons. Write three paragraphs and give each one a heading.

Easy marks. The easy marks in this question are for your variance calculations. If you have learnt the correct layout for variance calculations you should score well.

Examiner comments. The examiner commented that sometimes it was unclear which variance the student was calculating. Make sure you label your variances.

Marking scheme

		Marks
(a)	Budgeted gross profit	1
	Sales variances	4
	Material price variances	2
	Mix variances	3
	Yield variances	3
	Fixed overhead variances	3
	Actual gross profit	3
		19
(b)	Up to 2 marks for each reason	6
		25

(a) Reconciliation statement

	$	$	$
Budgeted profit (W1)			432,000
Sales volume profit variance (W2)		6,000	
Sales price variance (W3)	21,300		
Materials price variance ETH1 (W4)		2,210	
Materials price variance RXY2 (W5)	9,580		
Materials mix variance (W6)		13,200	
Materials yield variance (W7)	18,000		
Fixed overhead expenditure (W8)	2,000		
Fixed overhead volume (W9)		4,000	
	50,880	25,410	25,470
Actual profit (W10)			457,470

Workings

1

	$'000	$'000
Sales (72,000 kg × $20.00)		1,440
Less: cost of sales		
Opening inventory	28	
Materials (70,000 × $10.00)	700	(728)
Gross profit		712
Less: fixed production overheads		(280)
Budgeted profit		432

Alternatively
(Sales price per unit – total cost per unit) x budgeted sales units
($20.00 -$14.00) x 72,000 units   = $432,000 ✓

2   Sales volume profit variance

Should have sold	72,000 kg
But did sell	71,000 kg
Variance in kg	1,000 kg (A)
× profit ($20 – $14)	× $6
	$6,000 (A)

3   Sales price variance

	$
71,000 should have sold for (×$20.00)	1,420,000
But did sell for (× $20.30)	1,441,300
	21,300 (F)

4   Materials price variance ETH1

	$
22,100kg should have cost (× $18.00)	397,800
But did cost (22,100 × $18.10)	400,010
	2,210 (A)

5   Materials price variance RXY2

	$
47,900kg should have cost (× $6.00)	287,400
But did cost (47,900 × $5.80)	277,820
	9,580 (F)

6   Materials mix variance

Actual input = 22,100kg + 47,900kg = 70,000kg

Standard mix of actual input
ETH1	0.3 × 70,000 kg =	21,000 kg
RXY2	0.7 × 70,000 kg =	49,000 kg
		70,000 kg

	Should mix Actual qty Std mix	Did mix Actual qty Actual mix	Difference	Std price	Variance
ETH1	21,000 kg	22,100 kg	1,100 kg (A)	$18	$19,800 (A)
RXY2	49,000 kg	47,900 kg	1,100 kg (F)	$6	$6,600 (F)
	70,000 kg	70,000 kg	0		$13,200 (A)

7

Material yield variance

Each unit of output requires (0.3kg + 0.7kg)/96%
70,000 kg should have yielded (× 96%)	67,200 kg
But did yield	69,000 kg
Variance in kg	1,800 kg
× standard cost per kg of output	× $10
	$18,000 (F)

8   Fixed overhead expenditure variance

	$
Fixed overhead should have cost	280,000
But did cost	278,000
	2,000 (F)

9   Fixed overhead volume variance

	$
Budgeted production	70,000
Actual production	69,000
	1,000 (A)
x OAR per unit ($4.00)	
	4,000 (A)

10

	$	$
Sales (71,000 kg × $20.30)		1,441,300
Less: cost of sales		
Opening inventory	28,000	
Materials (22,100 × $18.10) + (47,900 × $5.80)	677,830	(705,830)
Gross profit		735,470
Less: fixed production overheads		(278,000)
Actual profit		457,470

(b) Use of variance analysis

Standard costing has traditionally been associated with **labour-intensive operations**. In an environment which includes AMT, where processes are more automated the cost of **labour** is a **small proportion** of total costs . In addition, in theory material usage variances should be virtually non-existent given the accuracy of machines as opposed to human operators. Therefore traditional variances for control purposes can be of little value.

Focus on cost control

Standard costing tends to focus on how to control costs whereas in a modern business environment the focus should be on quality and continuous improvement. Setting standards indicates to staff that merely achieving the standard is sufficient, however businesses should be focused on improving to increase competitive advantage.

Suited to stable business environments

Standards can quickly become out of date in the modern environment as technology and customer demands change rapidly. This would mean regular revision would be required of the standards which would be time consuming and expensive. Also the information provided would be of little use to management who need up-to-date, real time information in an AMT environment to make effective and responsive decisions.

18 Section C: Hospital

Text references. Operating statements and planning and operational variances are covered in Chapter 8. Budgets and standards are compared in Chapter 7a in Section 5.

Top tips. For part (a) you need to organise your workings on a separate piece of paper. Don't waste too much time if your find that you reconciliation doesn't work. You will get marks for your workings and the layout of the reconciliation. For part (b) you just need to plug the figures into your variance calculations. For part (c), explain budgeting control and standard costing and then explain how they can be used together.

Easy marks. The easy marks in this question are for your variance calculations. If you have learnt the correct layout for variance calculations (particularly for planning and operational variances) you should score well.

(a)   Reconciliation statement

	$	$	$
Budget (W1)			
Team fee			60,000
Variable overheads			39,000
Fixed overheads			48,000
Total cost			147,000
Flexed budget additional costs (W2)			9,900
			156,900

	$	$	$
Variances	F	A	
Team fee rate (W3)		4,900	
Team efficiency (W4)		4,500	
Variable overhead expenditure (W5)		2,175	
Variable overhead efficiency (W6)		2,925	
Fixed overhead expenditure (W7)	2,000		
	2,000	14,500	12,500
Actual cost (W8)			169,400

Workings

1   Budget for 20 procedures

Team fee ($3,000 × 20)   = $60,000

Variable overheads ($1,950 × 20) = $39,000

Fixed overheads (from question)   = $48,000 ✓

2   20 procedures were budgeted but 22 were performed.

Extra variable cost   = 2 procedures × ($3,000 + $1,950)

                  = $9,900

3   *Fee rate variance*

	$
47 hours should have cost (×$1,500)	70,500
But did cost	75,400
	4,900 (A)

4   *Fee efficiency variance*

22 procedures should have taken (×2hrs)	44 hrs
But did take	47 hrs
Variance in hours	3 hrs
× standard rate	× $1,500
	$4,500 (A)

5   65% of team fee per hour   = 65% × $1,500

                         = $975

Variable overhead expenditure variance

	$
47 hours should have cost (×$975) ✓	45,825
But did cost	48,000
	2,175 (A)

6   *Variable overhead efficiency variance*

22 procedures should have taken (×2hrs)	44 hrs
But did take	47 hrs
Variance in hours	3 hrs (A)
× standard rate	× $975
	$2,925 (A)

7   *Fixed overhead expenditure variance*

	$
Fixed overhead should have cost	48,000
But did cost	46,000
	2,000 (F)

8   Check:

$75,400 + $48,000 + $46,000 = $169,400

(b)   *Planning variance*

	$
Revised std cost for revised hrs for actual output ($1,625 × 2hrs × 22)	71,500
Original std cost for revised hrs for actual output ($1,500 × 2hrs × 22)	66,000
	5,500 (A)

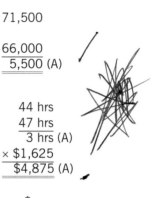

Operational variances

22 procedures should have taken (×2hrs)	44 hrs
But did take	47 hrs
Efficiency variance in hours	3 hrs (A)
× revised standard rate	× $1,625
Efficiency variance in $	$4,875 (A)

	$
Revised standard rate of actual hours ($1,625 × 47)	76,375
Actual price of actual hours paid	75,400
Rate variance	975 (F)

(c)   Budgetary control

A budget aids control by setting financial targets or limits for a forthcoming period. Actual expenditure is compared with the budget and action is taken to correct any variances where necessary.

Standard costing

A standard also achieves control by comparison of actual results against a predetermined target. A standard need not be expressed in monetary terms and measures performance at a low operation level.

Both methods are suitable for service industries.

Used together in service industries

Using budgetary control and standard costing together will be more effective than using one control system on its own.

Standard costing can be used at a lower level and budgetary control at a higher level, therefore controlling all levels of the business. It makes little sense to focus on one level of business and ignore the other.

19   Section C: X & Y

Text references. Variance analysis is covered in Chapters 7b to 8. ABC is covered in Chapter 11.

Top tips. Part (a) is about cost behaviour and is knowledge brought forward from your earlier studies. Parts (b) and (c) highlight that you must know how to calculate the various types of variance. Don't worry if you can't get your statement to reconcile. You will pick up marks for the variances that you have calculated correctly. It is important not to overrun on time on any part of the question.

Easy marks. The easy marks here are for understanding cost behaviour and for calculating variances. If you know the layout required for each type of variance you could score very well in this question

(a)   Average variable cost

In theory the variable cost per unit should stay constant for any volume of units. In this case the variable cost per unit begins to decrease as volume increases. This could be due to bulk discounts received. As the volume increases further the cost per unit increases again, which may be due to a shortage of supply and a price premium for the extra volume.

Total product specific fixed costs

In theory fixed costs are fixed and so should be the same for any volume of units produced. However, these costs appear to stepped-fixed costs as they increase when 15,000 units are produced and again when 25,000 units are produced. Stepped fixed costs could include, for example, extra premises needed after a certain number of units are reached. Additional machinery could also be required as the volume increases.

Head office costs

These costs look like traditional variable costs. For every 5,000 units produced there is a charge of $300,000. This equates to $60 per unit.

(b)   Standard cost per unit

	$
Direct materials (6kg × $2/kg)	12
Direct labour (2.5hrs × $8/hr)	20
Fixed overhead	8
	40

Reconciliation statement

	$(A)	$(F)	$
Standard cost of 76,000 units			3,040,000
Material price variance (W1)	64,500		
Material usage variance (W2)		52,000	
Labour rate variance (W3)	58,800		
Labour efficiency variance (W4)	48,000		
Fixed overhead expenditure (W5)		50,000	
Fixed overhead volume (W6)	32,000		
	203,300	102,000	101,300
Actual cost			3,141,300

Workings

1   Materials price variance

	$
430,000kg should have cost (× $2.00)	860,000
But did cost	924,500
	64,500 (A)

2   Materials usage variance

76,000 units should have used (× 6kg)	456,000 kg
But did use	430,000 kg
Variance in kg	26,000 kg (F)
× std cost per kg	× $2
	$52,000 (F)

3   Labour rate variance

196,000 hours should have cost (× $8)	1,568,000
But did cost	1,626,800
	58,800 (A)

4   Labour efficiency variance

76,000 units should have taken (× 2.5 hours)	190,000 hours
But did take	196,000 hours
Variance in hours	6,000 hours (A)
× std cost per hour	× $8
	$48,000 (A)

5   <u>Fixed overhead expenditure variance</u>

		$
Fixed overhead should have cost		640,000
But did cost		590,000
		50,000 (F)

6   <u>Fixed overhead volume variance</u>

Budgeted production	80,000
Actual production	76,000
x OAR per unit ($8.00)	4,000
	32,000 (A)

(c)   <u>Material price planning variance</u>

Original std cost for the revised std kgs for actual output (76,000 × $2 × 6kg)	912,000
Revised std cost for the revised std kgs for actual output (76,000 × $2.10 × 6kg)	957,600
	45,600 (A)

<u>Materials usage operational variance</u>

76,000 units should have used (× 6kg)	456,000 kg
But did use	430,000 kg
Variance in kg	26,000 kg (F)
× revised std cost per kg	× $2.10
	$54,600.00 (F)

<u>Material price operational variance</u>

Revised std cost for the revised std kg (430,000 × $2.10)	903,000
Actual price of actual kg	924,500
	21,500(A)

(d)   The traditional assumption is that products consume all resources in proportion to their production volumes, ie variable costs vary in relation to volume.
Activity based costing (ABC) identifies the activities or transactions (cost drivers) which cause the incidence of the activity, and hence the cost of the activity, to increase. This means that ABC gives management better information about cost behaviour, particularly about those costs which do not vary with production but with other activities. Thus ABC leads to better monitoring of those costs.

20   Section C: Chemical fertilisers

Text references. Variance analysis is covered in Chapters 7b to 8.

Top tips. You must make sure that you know how to calculate the various types of variance. This question demonstrates that you also need to be able to discuss variance analysis as well as perform the calculations. This is an important part of the syllabus.

Easy marks. The calculations in this question are fairly straightforward so make sure you earn all the marks available by showing clear, easy to follow workings with subtotals underlined as appropriate.

Examiner's comments. The examiner commented that part (c) was less well answered because little mention was made of a modern manufacturing environment. Remember **always** to relate your answer to the specific scenario in the question.

Further question practice. If you struggled with this question you should try Question 21 next.

Marking scheme

			Marks
(a)		1 mark for standard usage for each product	2
		Correct usage variance in monetary terms	2
		Correct treatment loss percentage	2
			$\overline{6}$
(b)	(i)	Correct planning variance	3
		2 marks for each operational variance	4
			$\overline{7}$
	(ii)	Up to 2 marks for each problem explained, to a max of	3
(c)		Up to 2 marks for each feature of a modern manufacturing environment and the impact on planning and control, to a max of	4
		Up to 2 marks for each aspect of variance analysis relevant to a modern manufacturing environment to a max of	5
			$\overline{9}$

(a) (i)

FA 38,000 units should have used (0.2kg/70%)	10,857.14
FB 25,000 units should have used (0.2kg/70%)	7,142.86
But did use	17,740.00
Variance in kg	260 00 (F)
× standard cost per kg	× $8
	$2,080 (F)

(ii) Content of output = (38,000+25,000) × 0.2kg of C1   =12,600 kg of C1

Materials input   =17,740 kg of C1

∴ actual losses   =5,140 kg of C1

∴ actual loss percentage =5,140kg/17,740kg   =29.0% ✓

(b) (i) Planning variance

	$
Revised standard cost (25,000 units × 0.25kg × $14.50)	90,625
Original standard cost (25,000 units × 0.25kg × $12)	75,000
	15,625 (A)

Operational price variance

	$
6,450 should have cost (× $14.50)	93,525
But did cost	94,000
	475 (A)

Operational usage variance

25,000 units should have used (× 0.25kg)	6,250
But did use	6,450
Variance in kg	200 (A)
× revised standard cost per kg	× $14.50
	$2,900 (A)

> **Top tip.** You are asked to explain two problems so don't waste time explaining more than two.

(ii) One of the problems of planning variances is that it is often **difficult even with hindsight to decide what the realistic standard should have been**. How is the revised standard set and is the information correct?

Another problem is that it may become **too easy to justify all of the variances as being due to bad planning**, so no operational variances will be highlighted. There must be a good reason why there was an error in the planning otherwise it could just be an excuse to shift the blame from operations to the planning manager.

(c) <u>The business environment</u>

Variance analysis (and standard costing systems) were **developed** when the **business environment** was more **stable** and **less prone to change.** The current business environment is more dynamic and it is not possible to assume stable conditions. This means that the use of variance analysis for planning and control purposes is not always ideal.

<u>Quality</u>

Modern businesses need to plan for and control quality. Variance analysis concentrates on a **narrow range of costs** only and does not give sufficient attention to issues such as quality and customer satisfaction. Today's business environment is more focused on **continuous improvement** in a **total quality** environment.

<u>Building in continual improvement</u>

Predetermined fixed standards are at odds with the philosophy of **continual improvement** inherent in a total quality management programme, as continual improvements are likely to alter methods of working, prices, quantities of inputs and so on.

<u>Responsibility for variances</u>

Standard costing systems make **individual managers responsible** for the variances relating to their part of the organisation's activities. A TQM programme, on the other hand, aims to make **all personnel** aware of, and responsible for, the importance of supplying the customer with a quality product.

<u>Standard costing – the wrong focus</u>

The use of standard costing in the modern manufacturing environment can make managers **focus their attention on the wrong issues.** For example, **adverse efficiency variances** are meant to be avoided, which means that managers need to prevent idle time and keep up production. In **a just-in-time environment**, however, action to **eliminate idle time** could result in the **manufacture of unwanted products** that would need to be held in store and might eventually be scrapped, which is totally at odds with the aims of JIT.

It could therefore be argued that standard costing and variance analysis are irrelevant in today's manufacturing world.

<u>Standard costing can be relevant</u>

Despite the arguments set out above, standard costing and variance analysis can be relevant in the modern manufacturing environment.

Standard costing and variance analysis can be usefully **employed by modern manufacturing organisations as follows.**

- **Planning**. Even in a TQM environment, budgets will still need to be quantified. For example, the planned level of prevention and appraisal costs needs to be determined. Standards, such as 'returns of a particular product should not exceed 1% of deliveries during a budget period', can be set.

- **Control**. Cost and mix changes from plan will still be relevant in many processing situations.

- **With ABC**. Standard costing can be used to control the costs of unit-level activities (which consume resources in proportion to the number of units produced) and to manage those overhead costs that are fixed in the short term, but variable in the longer term.

21 Section C: FX

Marking scheme

		Marks
(a)	Report format, summary and conclusions	3
	Up to 2 marks for explanation and interpretation of each variance to a max of	14
		17
(b)	2 marks each	8

(a) To: Managing director
     From: Management accountant
     Date: 11 May 20X8
     Subject: Month 6 variance report

This report has been written to explain and interpret the month 6 variance report, starting with the sales variances and moving onto cost variances and finally profit variances.

Sales variances

Selling price variance

The actual number of units sold in the month was 1,200 units. If they were sold at the standard selling price of £250 each, this would give sales income of 1,200 × £250 = £300,000. Unfortunately the variance report shows that there is an adverse selling price variance of £12,000. What this means is that we didn't sell the 1,200 units for £250 each. We actually sold the 1,200 units for an average of £240 each.

We should have received income of £300,000 but we only received £300,000 – £12,000 = £288,000. £288,000 ÷ 1,200 units gives a selling price of £240 each. So we sold them for £10 less per unit than we budgeted for, giving an adverse selling price variance of £12,000 (ie 1,200 × £10.)

Sales volume contribution variance

The budgeted contribution per unit was £90. (That is a selling price of £250 less material of £100, less labour of £40 less variable overheads of £20.) The budgeted sales volume was 1,000 units but we actually sold 1,200 units. At a budgeted contribution of £90 per unit, this gives us a favourable sales volume contribution variance of 200 extra units × £90 = £18,000. ✓

Reasons/interdependence

Note that the sales price variance and the sales volume variance may be interdependent. A reduction in the sales price (from £250 to £240) may have stimulated the greater demand in sales of 1,200 units.

Production variances

Materials

Each unit was budgeted to need 5 kg of material at a cost of £20 per kg. The variance report shows an adverse materials price variance of £6,300 and an adverse materials usage variance of £6,000. ✓

This means that each unit needed more than 5 kg of material and the cost per kg was more than the budgeted £20.

Usage variance

1,200 units should have used 1,200 × 5 kg = 6,000 kg. The adverse usage variance of £6,000 divided by the standard cost of £20 (= 300 kg) tells us that there was a usage variance in kg of 300 kg. This means that instead of using 6,000 kg, we used 6,300 kg. That is an average of 5.25 kg per unit instead of the budgeted 5 kg per unit.

Price variance

6,300 kg should have cost (x £20) £126,000 but the £6,300 adverse materials price variance means that it actually costs £126,000 + £6,300 = £132,300. That is an average of £21 per kg instead of the budgeted £20 per kg.

Reasons/interdependence

Adverse material usage variances could be due to defective material, excessive waste, theft, or even stricter quality control. Adverse material price variances could be due to price increases, careless purchasing or a change in material standard.

Note that the price and usage variance may be interrelated. For example, if material had been purchased and used and was subsequently found to be defective, then better quality material would have to be purchased (presumably at a price higher than the standard) and the units re-worked. This would lead to adverse price and usage variances.

Labour

Each unit was budgeted to need 4 hours of labour at a cost of £10 per hour. The variance report shows a favourable labour rate variance and an adverse labour efficiency variance.

This means that each unit needed more than 4 hours of labour but the cost per hour was less than the budgeted £10 per hour.

Efficiency variance

1,200 units should have taken 1,200 × 4 hours = 4,800 hours. The adverse efficiency variance of £2,400 divided by the standard cost of an hour of £10 (= 240) tells us that the efficiency variance in hours was 240. This means that instead of taking 4,800 hours to make 1,200 units, it actually took 4,800+240 = 5,040 hours. This is an average of 4.2 hours per unit instead of the budgeted 4 hours per unit.

Rate variance

5,040 hours should have cost (x £10) £50,400 but the £5,040 favourable labour rate variance means that it actually cost £50,400 – £5,040 = £45,360. That is an average of £9 per hour instead of the budgeted £10 per hour.

Reasons/interdependence

A favourable labour rate variance may be due to the use of apprentices or other workers at a rate of pay lower than standard. An adverse labour efficiency variance may be due to lack of staff training or experience, use of sub-standard material or errors in allocating time to jobs.

Note that inexperienced workers will probably be paid at a lower rate so the adverse efficiency and favourable rate variance may be interrelated.

Variable overheads

Each unit was budgeted to need 4 hours at a cost of £5 per hour. The variance report shows no expenditure variance but an adverse efficiency variance of £1,200. ✔

This means that each unit needed more than 4 hours but the budgeted cost of £5 per hour was the same as the actual cost per hour.

Efficiency

1,200 units should have taken 1,200 × 4 hours = 4,800 hours. The adverse efficiency variance of £1,200 divided by the standard cost of £5 (= 240) tells us that there was an efficiency variance in hours of 240. This means that instead of taking 4,800 hours, we actually took 4,800 + 240 = 5,040 hours. That is an average of 4.2 hours per unit instead of the budgeted 4 hours per unit. (Note the link to the labour efficiency variance above.)

Expenditure

5,040 hours should have cost (x £5) £25,200 and because the expenditure variance is nil, this must be what it actually cost.

Reasons/interdependence

The reasons for an adverse variable efficiency variance are the same as those of the adverse labour efficiency variance above (because the variance overhead absorption rate is based on direct labour hours.)

Fixed overheads

The budgeted fixed overhead amount was £70,000 per month. The £4,000 adverse variance on the variance report tells us that the actual cost was £74,000 for month 6 instead of the budgeted amount.

Profit variance

The budgeted profit on the variance report has been 'flexed' (adjusted) to account for the fact that 1,200 units were sold instead of 1,000. Using all the budgeted costs and income per unit, 1,200 units should have made a profit of £38,000. Because of the variances mentioned above, the actual profit was £11,140, ie £26,860 lower than it should have been.

(b)

> **Top tips.** Perform your own quick check on the results of your calculations by ensuring that the planning and operational variances sum to give your calculated total materials variance.

Variances

Total materials variance

	£
1,200 units should have cost (× 5 kg × £20)	120,000
But did cost (see report in (a)) (× 5.25 kg × £21)	132,300
	12,300 (A) ✓

Planning variance

	£
Revised standard cost (1,200 × £23 × 5 kg)	138,000
Original standard cost (1,200 × £20 × 5 kg)	120,000
	18,000 (A) ✓

Operational price variance

	£
Revised standard cost of actual materials (1,200× £23 × 5.25 kg)	144,900
Actual cost of actual materials (1,200× £21 × 5.25 kg)	132,300
	12,600 (F)

Operational usage variance

Actual usage should have been (1,200 × 5 kg)	6,000 kg
But was	6,300 kg
Operational usage variance in kg	300 kg (A)
× revised standard cost per kg	× £23
	£6,900 (A)

22 Section C: Product P

Text references. Variances and their interpretation are covered in Chapters 7b to 8.

Top tips. As X Ltd uses standard marginal costing, the operating statement will show no fixed overhead volume variance and the sales volume variance will be valued at standard contribution margin, not standard profit margin.

Easy marks. Draw up the operating statement proforma before you start on the calculations. An easy mark was also available for using a report format in part (b).

Examiner's comments. The examiner noted that many students calculated the sales volume variance using the sales value instead of using the contribution rate. Students also calculated the fixed overhead volume variance which does not arise in marginal costing. Remember these errors and don't make them in your exam.

Further question practice. If you struggled with this question you should try Question 24 next.

Marking scheme

		Marks
(a)	Layout of statement	1
	1 mark for each sales variance	2
	3 marks each for material price and mix variances	6
	Material yield variance	2
	Fixed production overhead expenditure variance	1
		12
(b)	Report format	1
	Interpretation of price variance and yield variance	2
	Interpretation of mix variance	2
	1 mark for each point about merits of mix and yield variances, to a max of	3
		8
(c)	Max of	5

(a)   Operating statement

			£	
Budgeted profit			586,000	
Sales volume contribution variance (W1)			84,240	(F)
			670,240	
Selling price variance (W2)			129,710	(F)
			799,950	

	(F)	(A)		
Variable cost variances	£	£	£	
Materials usage split into:				
Mix (W3)	18,000			
Yield (W4)	222,300			
Materials price (W5)		(30,375)		
	240,300	(30,375)	209,925	
Less: Fixed production overhead expenditure				
Variance			1,009,875	
Actual profit			(35,000)	
			974,875	

Workings

1 Selling price for product P

	£
Total standard marginal cost	234.00
80% mark-up	187.20
Selling price per unit	421.20

Sales volume contribution variance

Budgeted sales	5,000 units
Actual sales	5,450 units
Sales volume variance in units	450 units (F)
× standard contribution margin per unit × £187.20	
	84,240 (F)

2

	£
Selling price variance	
Revenue from 5,450 should be 5,450 × 421.20	2,295,540
but was	(2,425,250)
	129,710 (F)

or actual sales volume × (standard selling price − actual selling price)

3

> **Top tips**. You are specifically asked for the breakdown of the usage variance into the mix and yield variances. Remember that you have to work out the standard mix of the actual input. The mix variance in **kilograms** will therefore always be zero as this measures the change in relative proportion of the **actual** total input.

Mix variance

Actual input = 103,500 kgs

Standard mix of actual input

A $103,500 \times \dfrac{10}{23}$ = 45,000 kgs

B $103,500 \times \dfrac{8}{23}$ = 36,000 kgs

C $103,500 \times \dfrac{5}{23}$ = 22,500 kgs

	'Should' mix Actual quantity	'Did' mix Actual quantity	Difference	Standard price	Variance
	Standard mix	Actual mix			
A	45,000	43,000	2,000 (F)	£15	£30,000 (F)
B	36,000	37,000	1,000 (A)	£8	£8,000 (A)
C	22,500	23,500	1,000 (A)	£4	£4,000 (A)
	103,500	103,500	−		£18,000 (F)

4 Materials yield variance

Each output of P requires:

			£
10 kgs	A	costing	150
8 kgs	B	costing	64
5 kgs	C	costing	20
			234

$$103,500 \text{ actual input of kgs should have yielded } \frac{103,500}{23} = \quad 4,500 \text{ units of P}$$

but did yield

5,450 units of P

950 units of P

× standard cost per unit of output

× £234

Yield variance in £

£222,300 (F)

5　Direct materials price variance

			£
Materials should have cost			
A	43,000 kg × £15 per kilo =		645,000
B	37,000 kg × £8 per kilo =		296,000
C	23,500 kg × £4 per kilo =		94,000
			1,035,000
But did cost £688,000 + £277,500 + £99,875			(1,065,375)
			30,375 (A)

(b)　To:　　Production Manager

From:　Management Accountant

Date:　November 20X6

<u>Title: Materials price, mix and yield variances</u>

The purpose of this report is to interpret the materials price, mix and yield variances and discuss the advantages and disadvantages of calculating mix and yield variance.

(i)　**Materials price variance** is simply the difference between what the materials purchased actually cost and what they should have cost. The price variance is adverse because materials cost more to buy than budgeted.

The **mix variance** explains how much of the **usage** variance was caused by a change in the **relative** proportions of the materials used.

The **mix variance** is favourable as **overall** the mix of materials used were cheaper than budgeted (ie the standard mix), ie more of the cheaper materials were used in the mix.

The **yield variance** shows how much of the **usage variance** was caused by caused by **using more or les material** than standard.

The **yield variance** is favourable as overall the materials used were less than standard. The **output** from the **input** was more than standard.

Materials mix and yield variances are inter-related and, should not be interpreted in isolation. **Changing the standard mix** has led to a favourable mix variance. The mix was more efficient as the yield variance was also favourable.

(ii)　The total of the **material mix and yield variances is the material usage variance**. The usage variance alone does not consider how adjusting the mix of different materials can impact on the yield of a product. By subdividing the usage variance into mix and yield, we gain insight into aspects of the production process as we explained before, and help attain the best combination of materials. We should, however, note that mix and yield variances are not appropriate where inputs are not substitutes and the mix cannot be varied.

Please do not hesitate to contact me if you need further information.

(c)　<u>Advantages of calculating the price variances at the time of purchase</u>

(i)　The variance is **reported promptly**, and hence any necessary management action can be taken more quickly.

(ii)　The raw materials stock account is maintained at standard cost. This means that all **issues** can be made at a **standard price**. If the raw materials account is maintained at actual price, it will be necessary to calculate a separate variance on every issue.

(iii)　Prompt reporting means the **effect** of any purchase variance can be seen **immediately**, rather than being carried over the periods of usage.

(iv)　Reporting the price variance on usage requires decisions to be made concerning **issue pricing** (FIFO, LIFO etc) before the conversion to standard cost. The problem is avoided if the price variance is calculated on purchase.

23 Section C: RBF Transport Ltd

Text references. Standard costing and variances are covered in Chapters 7a, 7b and 7c.

Top tips. Part (a) really tests your understanding of variances. You need to take an algebraic approach. A common mistake often made by candidates is to think that the sales volume profit variance is calculated using the standard selling price per unit rather than the standard profit per unit. If you made the same mistake in part (a)(i) this would have had a direct effect on the answers that you calculated for parts (a)(iii) and (iv).

Easy marks. Set up the proformas for calculating the variances. This should help you to 'work backwards'. Remember to set out the report in a report format.

(a) (i) Standard profit per delivery mile $= \dfrac{\text{budgeted profit}}{\text{budgeted activity}}$

$$= \dfrac{£8,000}{200,000} = £0.04$$

<u>Sales volume profit variance</u>

Budgeted activity	200,000 delivery miles
Actual activity	x delivery miles
Sales volume variance in delivery miles	22,000* delivery miles (A)
× standard profit per delivery mile	× £0.04
Sales volume profit variance (given)	£880 (A)

* This figure is calculated by working backwards from the sales volume profit variance which is given in the question. £880 ÷ £0.04 = 22,000.

We can therefore deduce that the **actual number of delivery miles** was 22,000 less than expected (since the sales volume variance was adverse) ie (200,000 – 22,000) delivery miles = 178,000 delivery miles.

(ii) Let x = the cost of 3,620 direct labour hours.

	£
3,620 direct labour hours cost	x
but should have cost (× £4 *)	14,480
Direct labour rate variance (given)	1,086 (F)

* Standard direct labour rate per hour $= \dfrac{£0.08}{0.02\,\text{hrs}} = £4$

∴ x = £14,480 – £1,086 = £13,394

$$\dfrac{£13,394}{3,620\,\text{hrs}} = £3.70$$

∴ The **actual direct labour rate per hour** = £3.70.

(iii) Let x = the number of litres of fuel that 178,000 delivery miles actually used.

178,000 delivery miles did use	x L
but should have used (× 0.1 litres)	17,800 L
Fuel usage variance in litres	3,200 L* (A)
× standard rate per litre	× £0.4 **
Fuel usage variance (given)	£1,280 (A)

* This figure is calculated by working backwards (£1,280 ÷ £0.4 = 3,200 litres)
** £0.04 ÷ 0.1 litres = £0.4 per litre

∴ x = (17,800 + 3,200) litres = 21,000 litres

∴ **The actual number of litres of fuel consumed = 21,000**

(iv)

	£
Variable overhead cost of 178,000 delivery miles should have been (× £0.06)	10,680
but was	y
Variable overhead variance (£280 (F) + £180 (A))	100 (F)

∴ **Actual variable overhead cost** = £(10,680 – 100) = £10,580

(b)

REPORT

To: Transport operations manager
From: Management accountant
Date: 10 September 20X1
Subject: Operating standards

1   Introduction

1.1   This report explains the different types of standard that may be set and the importance of keeping standards meaningful and relevant.

2   Types of standard

2.1   When standards are set, it raises the problem of **how demanding** the standard should be. There are four types of standard.

2.2   Ideal standard

These standards are based on **perfect operating conditions** where there is no wastage, no spoilage, no inefficiencies, no idle time and no breakdowns. Such variances are likely to have an **unfavourable motivational impact** because reported variances will always be **adverse**. Employees will often feel that the goals are **unattainable** and not work so hard.

2.3   Attainable standard

These standards are based on the hope that a standard amount of work will be carried out **efficiently**, machines **properly operated** or materials **properly used**. Some **allowance** is made for **wastage** or **inefficiencies**. If such standards are well set, they provide a useful psychological incentive by giving employees a **realistic** but **challenging** target of efficiency.

2.4   Current standard

These standards are based on current working conditions (**current wastage, current inefficiencies**). The disadvantage of such standards is that they **do not attempt to improve on current levels of efficiency.**

2.5   Basic standard

These standards are kept **unaltered** over a long period of time and may therefore be **out-of-date**. They are used to show changes in efficiency or performance over time. Such standards are perhaps the **least useful** and **least common** type of standard in use.

3   The importance of keeping standards meaningful and relevant

3.1   Standards may be **used as a control device**. If irrelevant standards are used, they cannot be used for control – to be effective they **need to be relevant**.

3.2   Standards must be determined in a way that is understood by the **employees** whose actual **performance** will be compared with standards, ie they **must be meaningful**. If they are not meaningful, the employees who are being assessed will have no reason to have any faith in the system operating.

3.3   If **out-of-date** standards are in use, they are not relevant to conditions that are currently operating within a system. Such standards may **encourage slack** and **waste** to be built into the system.

3.4   **Motivation and morale of employees** is affected by the control system operating within the workplace. If such a system has been poorly implemented, employees may react adversely. For example, if standards are set which even the most conscientious employee fails to reach, he will be demotivated and may give up working as hard as he can as there 'doesn't seem to be any point'.

3.5   If standards are to be meaningful and relevant then they should set out to **focus on the controllability of costs.**

Signed: Management accountant

24 Section C: POC Ltd

(a)   (i)   Usage variance

Output of 15,408 kgs should have used input of 15,408/90% = 17,120 kgs.

∴Standard input should have been as follows.

		Kgs
S1	$^8/_{16}$ × 17,120	8,560
S2	$^5/_{16}$ × 17,120	5,350
S3	$^3/_{16}$ × 17,120	3,210
		17,120

	S1	S2	S3
Output 15,408 kgs should have used	8,560 kgs	5,350 kgs	3,210 kgs
but did use	8,284 kgs	7,535 kgs	3,334 kgs
Usage variance in kgs	276 kgs (F)	2,185 kgs (A)	124 kgs (A)
× standard cost per kg	× £0.30	× £0.50	× £0.40
Usage variance	£82.80 (F)	£1,092.50 (A)	£49.60 (A)

∴Total variance   =   £(82.80 (F) + 1,092.50 (A) + 49.60 (A))
                  =   £1,059.30 (A)

Mix variance

Actual usage   =   (8,284 + 7,535 + 3,334) kgs
               =   19,153 kgs

Standard mix of actual usage

		Kgs
S1	$^8/_{16}$ × 19,153	9,576.5
S2	$^5/_{16}$ × 19,153	5,985.3
S3	$^3/_{16}$ × 19,153	3,591.2
		19,153.0

	Actual input	Standard mix of actual input	Variance	× std cost per kg	Variance
	kgs	kgs	kgs	£	£
S1	8,284	9,576.5	1,292.5 (F)	0.30	387.75 (F)
S2	7,535	5,985.3	1,549.7 (A)	0.50	774.85 (A)
S3	3,334	3,591.2	257.2 (F)	0.40	102.88 (F)
	19,153	19,153.0	–		284.22 (A)

Yield variance

Each batch of S requires

kg		£
8	of S1, costing (× £0.30)	2.40
5	of S2, costing (× £0.50)	2.50
3	of S3, costing (× £0.40)	1.20
16		6.10

This will produce 16 × 90% = 14.4 kgs of output.

∴ Standard cost per kg of output = £6.10/14.4 = £0.4236

19,153 kg should have yielded (× 90%)	17,237.70 kgs
but did yield	15,408.00 kgs
Yield variance in kgs	1,829.70 kgs (A)
× standard cost per unit of output	× £0.4236
Yield variance	£775.06 (A)

(ii)

	£
1,235 hrs should have cost (× £5)	6,175
but did cost	6,916
Labour rate variance	741 (A)

Standard input per batch = (8 + 5 + 3) = 16 kgs

Standard output = 16 × 90% = 14.4 kgs

∴ 14.4 kgs of output are processed in 1 standard hour

15,408 kgs should have taken (÷ 14.4)	1,070 hrs
but did take	1,235 hrs
Efficiency variance in hrs	165 hrs (A)
× standard rate per hour	× £5
Labour efficiency variance	£825 (A)

(b)

REPORT

To: Management of POC Ltd
From: Management accountant
Date: 17 January 20X1
Subject: Analysis of material and labour variances, week number 2

1   Introduction

1.1   This report explains and interprets the variance analysis carried out on material and labour for week 2 (set out in the Appendix to this report). It will consider in detail the materials mix and yield variances and will suggest reasons for the results of the variance analysis.

2   Materials variances

2.1   The total materials variance (the difference between what week 2 output should have cost in terms of material, and what it did cost) can be divided into two variances, price and usage. Product S uses three types of material and so the usage can then be divided into mix and yield components.

2.2   Mix variance

2.2.1   Although there is a standard mix of the three input materials to produce a batch of product S, this standard mix is not always used as it is possible to use a range of different proportions of the input materials without affecting the quality of S too adversely. If the **proportions of the input materials used differ from the standard proportions** a mix variance will occur. The effect of a mix variance on profit will depend on whether the particular mix used is **cheaper than the standard mix** (if the proportion of the cheaper materials in the mix has increased) or **more expensive**.

2.2.2   The mix variance for week 2 was £284 adverse as S2, the **most expensive input material, comprised a greater proportion of the actual mix** than standard (the proportions of the two cheaper input materials being less than standard). There may have been a **shortage** of S1 and S3 so that S2 had to be used as a replacement.

2.3   Yield variance

2.3.1 By changing the proportions in the mix, the **efficiency of the combined material usage may change**. The yield variance shows the **effect** on profit of **any difference between the actual input materials used and the amounts that should have been used given the actual output** of S.

2.3.2 In week 2, more input material was required than expected given actual production of 15,408 kgs of S. It may be that the **actual mix** of input materials was **unstable** or **difficult to use** and so **wastage levels were higher**. This had an adverse effect on profit of £775.

3   Labour variance

3.1   The total labour variance (the difference between what week 2 output should have cost in terms of labour and what it did cost) can be split into a rate variance and an efficiency variance.

3.2   Rate variance

3.2.1 The **actual hours** worked during week 2 **cost more than anticipated** as the labour rate variance for the period was £741 adverse. The variance was caused by payment of a rate of £5.60 compared with a standard rate of £5. There are a number of possible **reasons** for this.

    (i)   Overtime working may have been required, resulting in the payment of an overtime premium.

    (ii)   The standard rate may not have been updated to reflect a pay increase.

    (iii) The mix of workers used may have differed from standard and incorporated a larger proportion of more skilled, and hence more expensive, workers.

3.3   Efficiency variance

3.3.1 The efficiency variance of £825 adverse reflects the fact that it **took longer to produce the given output than the standard time allowed**, at an additional cost of £825. This may be because the materials were difficult to work with (see comments on yield variance above), the introduction of new machinery or processes or possibly the use of new (and hence untrained) workers.

4   Conclusion

4.1   Management should carry out **investigative action** to determine the reasons for the occurrence of these variances. The standards used may no longer be appropriate and may need amending or additional control procedures may need adopting over, for example, wastage levels.

4.2   Analyses carried out over the last few weeks should also be reviewed to assess whether these poor results are part of a **trend** or simply a one-off occurrence.

4.3   If I can provide any further information please do not hesitate to contact me.

25   Section C: NFL Ltd

Text references. Variances are covered in Chapters 7b to 8.

Top tips. In this question, you are asked to calculate planning and operational variances (parts (a) and (c)) as well as to discuss their significance and usefulness (part (b)). Remember to link your discussion in (b) to the variances you have calculated in (a).

Easy marks. You can still gain marks from part (b), even if you have some incorrect answers to part (a).

(a)   Sales volume variance

	Model 1	Model 2	Model 3	Total
Budgeted sales (units)	30	14	10	
Actual sales (units)	40	12	15	
Volume variance in units	10 (F)	2 (A)	5 (F)	
× standard margin per unit	× £(4)	× £5	× £43	
Volume variance in £	£40 (A)	£10 (A)	£215 (F)	£165 (F)

Selling price variance

Only model 1 desks are sold at non-standard price.

	£
Sales revenue from 40 desks should have been (× £220)	8,800
but was (40 × £200)	8,000
Selling price variance	800 (A)

Labour efficiency - planning variance

Per the original standard, labour should have taken

Model 1 – 40 × 16 hrs =	640 hrs
Model 2 – 12 × 20 hrs =	240 hrs
Model 3 – 15 × 24 hrs =	360 hrs
	1,240 hrs
Per the revised budget, labour should have taken (1,240 × 0.95)	1,178 hrs
Variance in hours	62 hrs (F)
× standard rate per hour (£80 ÷ 16)	× £5
	£310 (F)

Labour efficiency – operational variance

Labour should have taken	1,178 hrs
but did take	1,180 hrs
Variance in hours	2 hrs (A)
× standard rate per hour	× £5
	£10 (A)

(b) The analysis of variances into planning and operational elements provides useful information to management about **controllable costs and revenues**. A planning variance represents the difference between the original standard and a more appropriate or realistic one. In the case of NFL Ltd the revised standard relates to an increase in productivity that needs to be incorporated following the negotiated agreement. If the labour efficiency variance had not been analysed into planning and operational, the total variance of £300F **would have given misleading information** to management.

The resulting 5% agreed improvement in efficiency is part of a negotiated agreement for which the company incurs a cost in the form of the job security package. It should be reflected in the revised standard so that management can focus on the total labour efficiency variance.

(c) Planning variance

	£
Revised standard cost (2,800 × 3 hrs × £6)	50,400
Original standard cost (2,800 × 3 hrs × £5)	42,000
	8,400 (A)

Operational variance

	£
Actual cost for 2,800 units	50,032
Revised standard cost, as above	50,400
	368 (F)

26 Section C: M plc

> **Text references**. Variances and operating statements are covered in Chapters 7b to 8.
>
> **Top tips**. Part (a) really is as straightforward as we have shown it. You did not need to think about closing inventory or under/over absorption of overhead.
>
> And part (b) is nearly as straightforward. It was vital that you noted that closing inventories of finished products and raw materials were valued at standard cost. By including actual fixed overheads you avoid the need to calculate under or over absorption of fixed overheads.
>
> Hopefully you noticed that three of the variances required in (c) had already been calculated for you and did not waste time trying to calculate them yourself. The variances required were not specified in the question: did you remember them all?
>
> Because two products were involved you needed to take extra care with your calculations and to show clear workings to ensure you earned marks even if you did make an arithmetical mistake.
>
> **Easy marks**. Don't become too disillusioned if your reconciliation doesn't work. Remember that the first 50% of the marks are the easiest and you only need 50% to pass.

(a) **Budgeted profit** for October = (7,600 × $30.90) + (11,000 × $33.50) = $603,340

(b)

	$	$
Sales revenue		
X	1,260,000	
Y	1,430,000	
		2,690,000
Full cost of production		
Material	1,150,400	
Labour	690,320	
Fixed production overhead	1,200,780	
	3,041,500	
Less: closing inventory		
Material (W1)	(27,500)	
Finished units (W2)	(149,500)	
Cost of sales		2,864,500
Actual loss for October		(174,500)

Workings

1 (180,000 – 174,500) kgs × standard cost of $5 per kg

2 Closing inventory = (sales – production) × standard total production cost

   = (700 units of X × $122.50) + (500 units of Y × $127.50)
   = $149,500

(c) <u>Sales price variance</u>

	$	$	
Revenue from 8,300X should have been			
(× $153.40)	1,273,220		
but was	1,260,000		
		13,220	(A)
Revenue from 9,000Y should have been			
(× $161)	1,449,000		
but was	1,430,000		
		19,000	(A)
Sales price variance		32,220	(A)

Sales volume variance

Budgeted sales volume of X	7,600	units		
Actual sales volume	8,300	units		
Variance in units	700	units (F)		
× standard profit per unit	× $30.90			
			$21,630	(F)
Budgeted sales volume of Y	11,000	units		
Actual sales volume of Y	9,000	units		
Variance in units	2,000	units (A)		
× standard profit per unit	× $33.50			
			$67,000	(A)
Sales volume variance			$45,370	(A)

Direct labour efficiency variance

9,000 units of X should have taken (× (24/8))	27,000	hrs
9,500 units of Y should have taken (× (40/8))	47,500	hrs
	74,500	hrs
but did take (82,500 – 2,670)	79,830	hrs
Variance in hours	5,330	hrs
× standard rate per hour	× $8	
Direct labour efficiency variance	$42,640	(A)

Idle time variance

Idle labour hours	2,670	hrs
× standard rate per hour	× $8	
Idle time variance	$21,360	(A)

Fixed production overhead expenditure variance

	$	$	
Budgeted fixed production overhead expenditure			
X: 8,500 × $36	306,000		
Y: 11,500 × $60	690,000		
		996,000	
Actual fixed production overhead expenditure		1,200,780	
Fixed production overhead expenditure variance		204,780	(A)

Fixed production overhead volume variance

	$	$	
Budgeted production at standard rate			
X: 8,500 × $36	306,000		
Y: 11,500 × $60	690,000		
		996,000	
Actual production at standard rate			
X: 9,000 × $36	324,000		
Y: 9,500 × $60	570,000		
		894,000	
Fixed production overhead volume variance		102,000	(A)

Reconciliation of budgeted and actual profit/loss
October 20X3

		$		$	
Budgeted profit				603,340	
Sales volume variances	X	21,630 (F)			
	Y	67,000 (A)			
				45,370	(A)
Budgeted profit from actual sales				557,970	
Sales price variances	X	13,220 (A)			
	Y	19,000 (A)			
				32,220	(A)
Actual sales minus standard cost of sales				525,750	
Cost variances			$		
Material price			250,400 (A)		
Material usage			48,750 (A)		
Labour rate			30,320 (A)		
Labour efficiency			42,640 (A)		
Idle time			21,360 (A)		
Fixed production overhead expenditure			204,780 (A)		
Fixed production overhead volume			102,000 (A)		
				700,250	(A)
Actual loss				(174,500)	

27 Section C: RJ

Text references. Activity based costing is covered in Chapter 11 and activity based budgeting is covered in Chapter 13.

Top tips. Make sure you don't fall into the trap of apportioning fixed production overheads to products on the basis of machine hours per car (200:300).

Easy marks. Remember to highlight the contribution in your marginal costing statement.

Examiner's comments. The examiner commented that Part (a) was not answered well by most candidates. Many candidates introduced inventory adjustments into their calculations which were not necessary and caused difficulty.

Marking scheme

		Marks
(a)	Calculation of fixed overhead cost per car	1
	Calculation of variable production cost of sales	2
	Calculation of gross contribution before marketing costs	1
	Calculation of net contribution after marketing costs	1
	Calculation of general fixed costs	1
	Calculation of profit	1
		7
(b)	Calculation of change in overhead value in inventory	2
	Correct identification of increase or decrease in profit for each change in inventory	2
	Final reconciliation	1
		5
(c)	1 mark for each cost driver rate	5
	Correct application of each cost driver rate (0.5 for each car x 5 rates)	5
	Correct figures for direct costs	1
	Correct unit cost figures	2
		13

(a) Budgeted marginal operating statement year ending 30 June 20X8

	Car X $'000	Car Y $'000	Total $'000
Sales	52,500	105,000	157,500
Variable production costs (W1)	30,000	56,000	86,000
Variable admin costs	6,300	12,600	18,900
Contribution	16,200	36,400	52,600
Specific fixed costs			
Marketing	2,000	4,000	6,000
	14,200	32,400	46,600
General fixed costs			
Production			35,000
Admin (W2)			10,000
Profit			1,600

Workings

1

		Car X $	Car Y $
Production cost of sales per car			
$\left(\dfrac{40,000,000}{1,000} \text{ and } \dfrac{82,250,000}{1,750}\right)$		40,000	47,000
Deduct fixed overhead absorbed			
$\dfrac{35,000,000}{(200\text{hrs} \times 1,100) + (300\text{hrs} \times 1,600)}$	$= \$50 \ (\times\ 200 \text{ and } \times$	(10,000)	(15,000)
300)			
Variable production costs per car		30,000	32,000
× number of cars		30,000,000	56,000,000

2

	$'000
Fixed admin cost	16,000
Less marketing campaigns	(6,000)
	10,000

(b) If inventory levels increase, absorption costing will report a higher profit than marginal costing. If inventory levels decrease, absorption costing will report the lower profit.

	Car X Units	Car Y Units
Opening inventory	200	250
Closing inventory	300	100
	100 (increase)	150 (decrease)
	So absorption profit will be higher	So absorption profit will be lower

	$'000
Marginal costing profit	1,600
Car X inventory increase × fixed production overhead (100 units × $10,000)	1,000
Car Y inventory decrease × fixed production overhead (150 units × $15,000)	(2,250)
Absorption costing profit	350

(c) Calculate cost per driver for each activity

Machining costs

Cost driver = machine hours = (200 hrs × 1,100 car X) + (300 hrs × 1,600 car Y) = 700,000 hrs

Machine cost per driver $= \dfrac{\$7,000,000}{700,000 \text{ hours}} = \$10$ per hour

Set up costs

Cost driver = number of production runs $\left(\dfrac{1,100}{10}\right) + \left(\dfrac{1,600}{40}\right)$ = 150 runs

Set up costs per driver = $\dfrac{\$12,000,000}{150}$ = \$80,000 per set up

Quality inspections

Cost driver = number of inspections = $\left(\dfrac{1,100}{10} \times 20\right) + \left(\dfrac{1,600}{40} \times 80\right)$ = 5,400 inspections

Inspection cost per driver = $\dfrac{\$7,020,000}{5,400}$ = \$1,300 per inspection

Stores receiving

Cost driver = number of deliveries = 492 + 900 = 1,392 deliveries

Stores receiving costs per driver = $\dfrac{\$3,480,000}{1,392}$ = \$2,500 per delivery

Stores issues

Cost driver = number of issues from store = 4,000 + 7,000 = 11,000

Stores issues cost per driver = $\dfrac{\$5,500,000}{11,000}$ = \$500 per issue

Budgeted cost

		Car X $'000		Car Y $'000
Machining costs	(1,100 × $10 × 200)	2,200	(1,600 × $10 × 300)	4,800
Set up costs	(1,100/10 × $80,000)	8,800	(1,600/40 × $80,000)	3,200
Quality inspections	(1,100/10 × 20 × $1,300)	2,860	(1,600/400 × 80 × $1,300)	4,160
Stores receiving	(492 × $2,500)	1,230	(900 × $2,500)	2,250
Stores issues	(4,000 $500)	2,000	(7,000 × $500)	3,500
Direct costs (from (a) (W1))	(1,000 × $30,000)	33,000	(1,600 × $32,000)	51,200
		50,090		69,110
Cost per car	(÷1,100)	$45,536	(÷1,600)	$43,194

28 Section A: Modern business environment and costing systems

1   C   The cost of sales for the 1,000 units will be debited at standard cost (1,000 × £100) = £100,000 to the cost of goods sold account.

The conversion cost allocated per unit is £55. (This is the standard cost of £100 per unit minus the material cost of £45). So for 1000 units the conversion cost credited to the conversion account should be £55,000.

The actual conversion cost incurred is £60,000 and this will be debited to the conversion account. The balancing figure in the conversion account of £5,000 is then transferred back to the cost of sales account, giving a total debit on the cost of goods sold account of £105,000.

2   D   *Optimised production technology* and *just-in-time* are the terms that correspond to the definitions given.

3   A   The only correct statement is (i), on CIM.

4

	Maximum number of Z1 units	Maximum number of Z2 units
Department 1	480/12 = 40	480/16 = 30
Department 2	840/20 = 42	840/15 = 56

The bottleneck or limiting factor is labour in Department 1 as Department 2 has capacity to produce more of both Z1 and Z2.

5   The question requires us to use traditional contribution analysis:

We need to calculate the contribution (sales less direct materials, labour and variable overheads) per unit of the bottleneck resource, which is time in Department 1. The contribution maximising output is found by dividing contribution per unit of product Z1 and Z2 by the time in minutes required by each product in department 1.

		Z1		Z2
	£	£	£	£
Sales price		50.00		65.00
Less variable costs				
Direct materials	10.00		15.00	
Direct labour	10.40		6.20	
Variable overheads	6.40		9.20	
		(26.80)		(30.40)
Contribution		23.20		34.60

£		£	
$\dfrac{23.20}{12}$ = £1.933		$\dfrac{34.60}{16}$ = £2.1625	

Contribution is maximised by making as many Z2 as possible, as all units made can be sold.

The maximum number of Z2 units that can be sold is 30:

Total contribution is £34.60 × 30 units = £1,038

6   The throughput approach is based on throughput maximisation. Throughput is defined as sales less direct materials.

	Z1	Z2
	£	£
Sales price	50	65
Less: direct materials	(10)	(15)
	40	50

Throughput per minute of bottleneck resource is:

	£		£
	40/12 = 3.333		50/16 = £3.125

Contribution is maximised by producing 40 units of Z1, the maximum number of Z1 that can be produced, given the bottleneck resource of labour in Department 1. The maximum throughput contribution is 40 × £40 = £1,600.

7   (a)   To find the annual number of batches, the budgeted annual production in units for each product is divided up by the batch size in units.

Budgeted number of batches

Product D (100,000/100)	1,000
Product R (100,000/50)	2,000
Product P (50,000/25)	2,000
	5,000

(b)   To find the annual budgeted number of machine setups, we multiply the annual number of batches for each product in (a) above by the machine set-ups per batch.

Budgeted machine set-ups:

Product D (1,000 × 3)	3,000
Product R (2,000 × 4)	8,000
Product P (2,000 × 6)	12,000
	23,000

(c)   To find the annual budgeted number of purchase orders we multiply the number of batches from (a) above with the purchase orders per batch.

Budgeted number of purchase orders:

Product D (1,000 × 2)	2,000
Product R (2,000 × 1)	2,000
Product P (2,000 × 1)	2,000
	6,000

(d)   The annual budgeted number of processing minutes is calculated by multiplying the budgeted annual production in units per product with the processing time per unit in minutes.

Budgeted processing minutes:

Product D (100,000 × 2)	200,000
Product R (100,000 × 3)	300,000
Product P (50,000 × 3)	150,000
	650,000

8   Budgeted cost/set-up for product R:

$$= \frac{£150,000}{23,000} = £6.52 \qquad \text{Budgeted unit cost of R:} = \frac{£6.52 \times 4}{50} = £0.52$$

Budgeted cost/purchase orders:

$$= \frac{£70,000}{6,000} = £11.67 \qquad \text{Budgeted unit cost of R:} = \frac{£11.67 \times 1}{50} = £0.23$$

Budgeted processing cost per minute:

$$= \frac{£80,000}{650,000} = £0.12 \qquad \text{Budgeted unit cost of R} = £0.12 \times 3 = £0.36$$

Total budgeted cost of R per unit is:

	£
Set-up costs	0.52
Purchasing costs	0.23
Processing costs	0.36
Total cost	1.11 per unit

29 Section B: Modern business environment and costing systems

(a)   JIT production systems will include the following features.

Multiskilled workers

In a JIT production environment, production processes must be shortened and simplified. **Each product family is made in a workcell based on flowline principles. Workers must therefore be more flexible and adaptable, the cellular approach enabling each operative to operate several machines.** Operatives are trained to operate all machines on the line and **undertake routine preventative maintenance**.

Close relationships with suppliers

For JIT purchasing to be successful this requires the organisation to have confidence that the supplier will deliver on time and that the supplier will deliver materials of 100% quality, that there will be no rejects, returns and hence no consequent production delays. The **reliability of suppliers is of utmost importance** and hence the company must **build up close relationships** with their suppliers.

Machine cells

With JIT production, factory layouts must change to reduce movement of workers and products. **Material movements between operations are minimised by eliminating space between work stations and grouping machines or workers by product or component** instead of by type of work performed. Products can flow from machine to machine without having to wait for the next stage of processing or returning to stores. **Lead times and work in progress are thus reduced.**

Quality

Quality reduces costs. Quality is assured by **designing products and processes with quality in mind, introducing quality awareness programmes** and **statistical checks on output quality**, providing **continual worker training** and implementing **vendor quality assurance programmes** to ensure that the correct product is made to the appropriate quality level on the first pass through production.

Set-up time reduction

If an organisation is able to **reduce manufacturing lead time** it is in a better position to **respond quickly to changes in customer demand**. Reducing set-up time is one way in which this can be done. Machinery set-ups are non-value-added activities which should be reduced or even eliminated.

(b)   JIT systems have a number of financial **benefits**.

> **Easy marks.** In the exam you would probably only need to provide five (relevant) financial benefits in part (b) to gain the full five marks.

- Reduction in costs of storing inventory
- Reduction in costs associated with scrap, defective units and reworking
- Reduction in the costs of setting up production runs
- Higher revenues as a result of faster response to customer demands
- Reduction in risk of inventory obsolescence

> Alternative financial benefits
>
> - Increase in labour productivity due to labour being multiskilled and carrying out preventative maintenance
> - Reduction of investment in plant space
> - Lower investment in inventory
> - Reduction in costs of handling inventory
> - Higher revenue as a result of reduction in lost sales following failure to meet delivery dates (because of improved quality)

(c)   TQM in a Just-in-time (JIT) systems environment:

- **JIT production** is a system driven by demand for finished products. Work in progress is only processed through a stage of production when it is needed by the next stage. The result is **minimal** (or in some cases non-existent) **inventories of work in progress and finished goods.**
- **JIT purchasing** seeks to match the usage of materials with the delivery of materials from external suppliers. This means that **material inventories** can be kept at **near-zero levels.**

Eliminating scrap and defective units

Production management within a JIT environment therefore needs to **eliminate scrap and defective units** during production and **avoid the need for reworking of units. Defects stop** the **production line**, creating **rework** and possibly resulting in a **failure to meet delivery dates** (as **buffer inventories** of work in progress and finished goods are **not held**). **TQM** should ensure that the **correct product** is made to the **appropriate level of quality** on the **first pass through production**.

Supplier quality assurance

For JIT purchasing to be successful, the organisation must have confidence that the **supplier** will **deliver on time** and will deliver **materials of 100% quality**, that there will be no rejects, returns and hence **no consequent production delays**. This confidence can be achieved by **adopting supplier quality assurance schemes** and stringent **procedures for acceptance and inspection of goods inwards**, which are integral parts of TQM.

(d)   The appropriateness of ABC in the modern manufacturing environment

Reasons for the inappropriateness of traditional methods

(1)   Nowadays with the **advent of advanced manufacturing technology, overhead costs** have become a **greater proportion of total production costs** and the **direct labour cost proportion has declined**, as a result of **automation, multiskilling and teamworking**.

(2)   The accessibility of **information technology** now allows for **more sophisticated overhead allocation methods** than in the past.

(3)   The **majority of the overhead costs** incurred within the modern manufacturing organisation are **fixed in the short term** rather than variable, **and so marginal costing is not a particularly appropriate costing convention to use**. Some method of absorption costing is therefore preferred by AMT organisations.

(4)   The **absorption of overhead costs on a direct labour hour basis does not recognise the cost relationships within the modern environment**.

It is against this background that ABC has emerged.

The ABC method of dealing with overhead costs

The ABC approach of identifying the activities or events that cause overhead costs to occur/increase/decrease and the use of a product's need for these activities/events as the basis for apportioning overheads to products is seen by the proponents of ABC to be more appropriate to a manufacturing environment in which the level of overhead costs has increased while the level of direct costs has decreased.

(e)   ABC as an aid to decision making

Many of **ABC's** supporters claim that it can **provide effective assistance with decision making** in a number of ways.

(i)   It provides **accurate and reliable cost information.**

(ii)   It **establishes a long-run product cost.**

(iii)   It **provides data which can be used to evaluate different possibilities of delivering business.**

It is therefore **particularly suited for pricing decisions, decisions about promoting or discontinuing products or parts of the business or decisions concerning the development and design of changed products, new products or new ways to do business**.

Limitations of ABC as an aid to decision making

The conventional **ABC model may not be appropriate for costing short-life products or minor volume changes** as these may have no discernible impact on many overhead costs. And an ABC cost is not a true cost, but simply an average cost because some costs such as depreciation are still arbitrarily allocated to products. An ABC cost is therefore **not a relevant cost for all decisions**.

The problem is that the **speed with which the manufacturing environment is changing** means that **even ABC product costs can no longer be considered reliable for decision making**. Many products have very short lives, whilst those products which have long lives often incur heavy long-term fixed costs as their manufacture may be almost entirely automated. Management therefore need to **use a mixture of ABC and marginal costing**, concentrating on the costs relevant to the decision.

Prime benefits of ABC

These are behavioural rather than related to an improvement in decision-making information. The key benefit of the technique is **better cost management** by both support service users and support service providers. Yet, ironically, this was not what ABC was developed for. Instead, it was designed to improve the accuracy of product costs and hence help managers to optimise the allocation of production capacity between products.

Summary

Managers of those organisations that have introduced ABC have gained a better understanding of cost behaviour. And this can lead to a more accurate identification of decision-relevant costs.

(f)

Environmental costs

There are two types of environmental cost: internal or internalised costs and external or externalised costs.

Internal costs are those environmental costs incurred within the organisation such as waste management costs and the costs of obtaining emissions permits.

External costs are those costs that arise due to the organisation's impact on the environment, such as its use of a finite natural resource.

The visibility of environmental costs

Traditional absorption costing systems **do not always trace environmental costs** to individual products or processes. Instead these costs are grouped together with general overhead costs and absorbed into product costs, usually using a time-based overhead absorption rate.

This **reduces the visibility of these costs** and consequently management are not aware of the impact of individual products and processes on the environment.

Using an activity based costing (ABC) system

An ABC system is capable of **separating environmental costs from general overhead costs** in order to facilitate their separate analysis. The resources and activities used to produce each product are identified to **enable the environmental costs to be traced** to individual products and processes.

For example a **cost driver** used to trace energy costs might be energy consumption. A product that uses a lot of energy in its production would generate a higher number of energy consumption cost drivers and hence would absorb a higher amount of energy costs from this particular cost pool.

The resulting product costs **would not be distorted by the grouping together of environmental costs** with general overhead costs and would enable management to make decisions that take account of a product's impact on the environment.

Even if it is not possible to trace environmental costs to individual products it will in many cases be **possible to trace such costs to processes**. For example waste disposal costs can be traced to individual processes. Products that are manufactured in these processes would then absorb a share of these costs through the **application of appropriate cost drivers** for the individual process.

Once the **visibility and traceability** of environmental costs have been improved through the use of more detailed analysis and relevant cost drivers in an ABC system, it will be possible for managers to monitor the impact of environmental costs on the total cost of a product or service.

Management will also be able to **monitor the effect on cost** of any measures put in place to minimise the organisation's impact on the environment.

30 Section C: F plc

Text references. Activity based costing is covered in Chapter 11.

Top tips. There is a lot of information to work through in this question and careful reading and a systematic approach is required. The most likely trap is not reading the question carefully enough and not following through the calculations for each of the cost drivers.

Easy marks. You could earn the first two easy marks on part (a)(i) by calculating the selling and distribution overhead per order under the current absorption system. This involved doing exactly what the question required and dividing budgeted overheads/budgeted total list price.

It is important to recognise that the number arrived at is the rate charged for overheads per £ of list price of the drugs ordered.

Examiner's comments. Part (a)(i) was, in general, correctly calculated although the examiner was surprised to come across a few miscalculations.

For part (a)(ii) candidates generated correctly only part of the answer with very few being able to follow all calculations through to a correct ABC charge for overheads.

The commonest errors were in the calculation of the cost drivers which then affected the calculation of the ABC charge.

Part (b)(i) on the strengths and weaknesses of ABC for F plc was reasonably well answered.

However, part (b)(ii) was not well answered with candidates showing a lack of ideas in recommending appropriate action to F plc.

Marking scheme

			Marks
(a)	(i)	Correct charge for s & d overheads	2
	(ii)	Calculation of cost driver rates	3½
		Correct application of calculated cost driver rates	4½
			10
(b)	(i)	Report headings	
		1 mark for each strength or weakness, to a max of	1
			4
			5
	(ii)	1 mark for each point made, to a max of	5
(c)		1 mark for each point made, to a max of	5

(a) (i) Budgeted annual total list price/total budgeted overheads $\dfrac{£880,000}{£8\,\text{million}} = £0.11$

> **Top tips.** Under the current system customers are charged the list price of the drugs plus a charge for selling and distribution overheads based on the annual selling and distribution costs and the annual total list price of the drugs ordered. Every order will have a surcharge of £0.11 per £1 of list price of drugs supplied, for selling and distribution overheads.

Charge for selling and distribution overheads

Order A   £1,200 × £0.11 = £132
Order B   £900 × £0.11 = £99

(ii)   Activity based costing approach

> **Top tips**. There are four components to the total selling and distribution overheads.
>
> Applying the correct cost driver to each of the overheads is the trickiest part of the question and the one that presented most problems to candidates.
>
> In allocating delivery overhead costs you need to take into account the number of packages each vehicle can take when filled to capacity.

			Cost driver	**Per invoice**
Invoice processing £280,000	75% related to invoice lines of 75% × £280,000 = 210,000		Invoice lines 28,000	$\dfrac{210,000}{28,000}$ = £7.50
	25% related to number of invoices 25% × £280,000 = 700		Invoices 8,000	$\dfrac{70,000}{8,000}$ = £8.75

Delivery costs £180,000	£40,000	Delivery journeys 1,000	$\dfrac{£40,000}{1,000}$ = £40 per journey
	£140,000	Delivery distance 350,000 miles	$\dfrac{£140,000}{350,000}$ = £0.40 per mile

Packing   £32 large
          £25 small

Other overheads   £200,000   By number of orders = $\dfrac{£200,000}{8,000}$ = £25 per order

Overhead costs – Order A

	£
Invoice costs	
One invoice per order 1 × £8.75 = 8.75	8.75
Two invoice lines 2 × £7.50 = £7.50	15.00
Packing costs – small package	25.00
Delivery costs per journey 8 miles × £0.40 per mile	3.20
per package £40/12	3.33
Other overhead costs per order	25.00
	80.28

Overhead costs – Order B

	£
Invoice costs	
For one invoice 1 × £8.75	8.75
Eight invoice lines 8 × £7.50	60.00
Packaging costs – large package	32.00
Delivery costs per journey 40 miles × £0.40	16.00
per package 1 × £40/6	6.67
Other overhead costs per order	25.00
	148.42

(b)

> **Top tips.** Start by setting out clearly presented and appropriate report headings.
>
> Answer the two parts of the question (i) (strengths and weaknesses of proposed ABC) and (ii) (recommendations to management of F plc) separately under two distinct headings. The answer to both parts must be specific to the circumstances of F plc.
>
> **Easy marks.** Clearly presented report headings would earn an easy mark.
>
> **Examiner's comments.** The examiner commented that whereas the standard of answers to part (i) was reasonable, candidates showed a lack of ideas for part (ii).

REPORT

To: Management of F plc
Subject: Relative merits of activity-based costing and recommendation
From: Management Accountant
Date: XX December 20X5

(i)   Assessment of strengths and weaknesses of the proposed activity based costing for F plc.

Strengths of ABC

ABC is appropriate where there is a high proportion of overhead costs. For F plc the overheads to be apportioned amount to more than 10% of the total list price of drugs.

- ABC gives a **better understanding** of what drives overhead costs.

- By adopting ABC, F plc will be able to **set prices that relate more closely** to actual overheads consumed.

- ABC helps **identify possible loss making orders** enabling F plc to decide an appropriate strategy.

> Alternative strengths that you might have explained in your answer
>
> - ABC may **help control overhead** costs by identifying where these are incurred and thus leading to appropriate action to reduce these.
>
> - Surcharges on list price could be **justified** in a rational way to customers if questioned.
>
> - ABC should provide a **better decision making** tool in terms of:
>   - which orders to be accepted
>   - outsourcing decisions

Weaknesses

- ABC is a **costly** approach and the expense of identifying cost pools and appropriate cost drivers may exceed the expected benefits.

- There is still a portion of overhead costs which are **allocated on the old basis**, ie number of orders. Further work may be necessary and care must be exercised when making decisions based on these data. The extra work required may be too expensive for the benefits involved.

> Alternative weaknesses that you might have explained in your answer
>
> - The activity data may still be **too aggregate** to reveal a detailed enough pattern of cost behaviour.

(ii) Recommendations to the directors of F plc

The current approach is simple and relatively inexpensive to operate. The charge for overheads though, **does not reflect the actual costs** incurred by each order.

A pricing policy that recovers overheads based on this simple approach is satisfactory where all output can be sold. However, it does not reflect the fact that **some orders** such as those with many different products and those delivered over a long distance are **more expensive** than orders with few products delivered over shorter distances.

Practicality of ABC as a pricing system

The new activity based costing recognises this fact, but it is probably **too complex** to be practicable as a pricing system.

Reflect key cost drivers in price

It is recommended that F develops a pricing structure that would enable the key **cost drivers** to be reflected in the charge over and above the list price.

Outsourcing or higher charges

The company may consider several options in respect of the **high costs of long distance deliveries**. For example, deliveries may be undertaken only within a certain radius. Long distance ones may be outsourced, or an extra high charge imposed.

The extra cost of multiple invoice lines needs further investigation. Customers could be informed of an additional charge relating to multiple orders.

F plc could, however, consider whether new systems or procedures could reduce these administrative costs.

(c) Product range and diversity

(i) Impact of range of products

If an organisation produces only a small number of products, product mix decisions for example can be made on a relevant cost basis. If a **vast number of products** are produced, however, the number of individual products and the number of combinations of products would make relevant cost analysis impossible. A general-purpose activity-based system is required that reports long-run product costs. The product costs reported are not designed to be used directly for decision making; instead they should provide attention-directing information and highlight problem areas that need more detailed analysis and the attention of management.

With the current focus on satisfying the customer, many organisations produce a **huge range of diverse products**. ABC is useful if increased product diversity means that an organisation produces **both high-volume standard products and low-volume variant products**. A more sophisticated costing system is required because, as the level of diversity increases, so does the level of distortion reporting by absorption costing systems (which tend to allocate too high a proportion of overheads to high-volume products and too low a proportion of overheads to low-volume products).

(ii) Impact of customer base

Likewise, if an organisation's **customer base is wide**, ABC can provide information for customer profitability analysis. Costs such as those associated with travelling to call on a customer, after-sales service and special delivery methods are revealed, thereby assisting with the identification of profit-making/loss-making customers.

31 Section C: Bottlenecks

Text references. Bottleneck resources are covered in Chapter 10.

Top tips. This question may well have thrown you simply because it mentions throughput accounting. But it's actually very straightforward.

Indeed part (a), a simple limiting factor exercise, should have presented you with no problems.

As you will see in the layout of our workings to part (b)(i), you can adopt the same approach as taken in (a) when dealing with a TA environment. You had to remember to deduct the 'variable' costs from the total throughput contribution, but otherwise there were eight very easy marks available for part (b)(i).

Easy marks. You should have got the full three marks for part (b)(ii) (provided you could remember how to calculate a TA ratio!).

The message underlying this question has to be the importance of attempting (with confidence) questions on trickier/obscure parts of the syllabus as they can be more straightforward than those on the traditionally popular areas such as budgeting.

(a)   We need to carry out **limiting factor analysis**.

Step 1   Establish scarce resources, if any

We are told that one of the production operations is the bottleneck, limiting production/sales.

Step 2   Rank products on the basis of contribution per unit of the limiting factor

	A £	B £
Direct material cost	2	40
Variable production overhead cost	28	4
	30	44
Selling price	60	70
Contribution per unit	30	26
Bottleneck hours per unit	0.02	0.015
Contribution per bottleneck hour	£1,500	£1,733
Ranking	2	1

Step 3   Determine profit-maximising product mix

Product	Demand	Hours required	Hours available		Units of production
B	45,000 × 1.2 = 54,000 (× 0.015)	810	810	(÷ 0.015)	54,000
A	120,000 × 1.2 = 144,000 (× 0.02)	2,880	2,265 (bal)	(÷ 0.02)	113,250
		3,690	3,075		

Maximum profit calculation

Product	Units	Contribution per unit	Total contribution £
A	113,250	× £30	3,397,500
B	54,000	× £26	1,404,000
			4,801,500
Less: fixed production overhead			1,470,000
Maximum net profit			3,331,500

(b)   (i)   Throughput return per production hour of the bottleneck resource = (selling price − material cost)/hours on the bottleneck resource

Step 1   Rank products on the basis of throughput return per bottleneck hour

	A £	B £
Selling price	60	70
Material cost	2	40
Throughput return	58	30
Bottleneck hours per unit	0.02	0.015
Return per bottleneck hour	£2,900	£2,000
Ranking	1	2

Step 2   Determine profit-maximising product mix

Product	Demand	Hours required	Hours available		Units of production
A	144,000	2,880	2,880	(÷ 0.02)	144,000
B	54,000	810	195 (bal)	(÷ 0.015)	13,000
		3,690	3,075		

Maximum profit calculation

Product	Units	Throughput return per unit	Total return £
A	144,000	× £58	8,352,000
B	13,000	× £30	390,000
Total throughput return			8,742,000
Less: overhead costs			
shown as variable in (a) ((120,000 × £28) + (45,000 × £4))			(3,540,000)
Fixed			(1,470,000)
Maximum net profit			3,732,000

(ii)   TA ratio = throughput return per hour/conversion cost per hour

Conversion cost per hour = overhead costs/bottleneck hours
= £(3,540,000 + 1,470,000)/3,075
= £1,629.27

∴ TA ratio for B = £2,000/ £1,629.27 = 1.2275

(iii)   <u>The meaning of the TA ratio</u>

In a throughput accounting environment, a product is worth producing and selling if its throughput return per time period is greater than the production cost per time period. This can be measured by the throughput accounting (TA) ratio. If the ratio is greater than 1, the return exceeds the cost and the product should be produced.

<u>TA as a control device</u>

Efforts should be made to improve the size of the TA ratio as follows.

(1)   **Improving throughput (£) per unit** by increasing selling price or reducing material cost per unit. Product B has a very high material cost element (£40).

(2)   **Improving the throughput return per hour** by reducing the time spent on the bottleneck resource. If product B spent 0.012 hours instead of 0.015 hours on the bottleneck resource, say, its TA ratio would improve.

The organisation's overall position can be improved by reducing conversion costs and/or by reducing or eliminating the impact of any bottlenecks.

Product B's TA ratio, at 1.2275, is **greater than 1** and so the product is worth producing. Product A's ratio is 1.780 (£2,900/£1,629.27), however, and hence priority should be given to product A.

32   Section C: ZW plc and Z Ltd

Text references. JIT is covered in Chapter 9. Backflush costing is covered in Chapter 10.

Top tips. In part (b) ensure that you do not just describe the feature of JIT but discuss the change in working practices required for Z Ltd. Remember to use a report format.

Easy marks. Correct definitions of backflush costing and a JIT system would have earned you easy marks.

(a)   (i)   **Backflush costing** is 'A method of costing, associated with a JIT production system, which applies cost to the output of a process. Costs do not mirror the flow of products through the production process, but are attached to the output produced (finished goods inventory and cost of sales), on the assumption that such backflushed costs are a realistic measure of the actual costs incurred.'

(CIMA *Official Terminology*)

Backflush costing is **appropriate** for organisations trying to keep **inventories to the very minimum**. In such circumstances, the **recording** of every little increase in inventory value, as each nut and bolt is added, is simply an expensive and **non-value-added activity** that should be **eliminated**.

Disadvantages of backflush costing

- **It is only appropriate for JIT operations** where production and sales volumes are approximately equal.

- It is claimed that it **should not be used for external reporting** purposes. If, however, **inventories are low** or are practically **unchanged** from one accounting period to the next, operating income and inventory valuations derived from backflush accounting will **not be materially different from the results using the conventional systems**. Hence, in such circumstances, backflush accounting is acceptable for external financial reporting.

- It is **vital** that adequate production controls exist so that **cost control during the production process is maintained**.

Advantages of backflush costing

- It is much **simpler**, as there is no separate accounting for WIP.

- Even the **finished goods** account is **unnecessary**, as we demonstrated in the first example above.

- The number of **accounting entries should be greatly reduced**, as are the supporting vouchers, documents and so on.

- The system should **discourage** managers from **producing simply for inventory** since working on material does not add value until the final product is completed or sold.

(ii)

DEBIT	Conversion costs	£88,200	
CREDIT	Expense payables		£88,200

Being the actual conversion costs incurred (W1)

DEBIT	Raw materials	£78,400	
CREDIT	Payables		£78,400

Being the raw materials received (W2)

DEBIT	Cost of sales	£161,500	
CREDIT	Finished goods inventory		£161,500

Being the standard cost of goods sold (W3)

DEBIT	Finished goods inventory	£166,600	
CREDIT	Raw materials		£78,400
CREDIT	Conversion costs		£88,200

Being the transfer to finished goods (W4)

The finished goods inventory is = £5,100 = (300 × £170)

Workings

1   980 units × £90 = £88,200
2   980 units × £80 = £78,400
3   950 units × £170 = £161,500
4   980 units × £170 = £166,600

(b) **To:** Board of Directors
From: Management Accountant   Date: 26 June 20X6
Subject: JIT accounting system

(i) <u>Key features of a JIT system</u>

In a JIT system **items are received from a supplier** just as they are required by the production process. There is, therefore, no inventory held and this results in significantly lower stockholding costs. A JIT system normally extends to work-in-progress and finished goods as well as raw materials. For a JIT system to be effective, Z Ltd needs to ensure that suppliers are reliable both in terms of quantity, quality and timing of deliveries. In addition, good communication between different parts of the organisation and between the organisation and its suppliers and customers is essential.

(ii) <u>Changes in working practices</u>

If Z Ltd were to adopt a JIT system they would probably need to **reduce the number of their raw material suppliers** and may need to concentrate on those that are the most reliable and located closer to Z Ltd, enabling them to respond quickly to the company's needs.

Z Ltd would need to ensure that there is **good co-ordination of activities** between the different parts of the production process so as to ensure that the items are produced as required by customers. **Internal communications** between production and sales department will have to be improved so that the production department are fully aware of the customers' requirements and delivery dates.

Z Ltd would need to ensure that there is **100% quality** throughout its production processes as there would be no stock of materials to use in an emergency. For this reason Z Ltd will need to introduce a number of quality control measures such as control checks on raw materials, production processes and finished items.

Z Ltd's agreement with its material suppliers should focus much more on **material quality**, **delivery reliability and flexibility rather than price**. It is likely, therefore, that as a consequence of adopting JIT, the price paid for materials will be greater than that currently being paid.

33 Section A: Budgeting and forecasting

1   B   Zero-based budgeting techniques re-evaluate all activities from scratch each time a budget is prepared.

Option C describes an incremental budgeting process.

2
	£
40% of May sales for cash (40% × £55,000)	22,000
70% of April credit sales less 2% discount (70% × 60% × £70,000 × 98%)	28,812
27% of March credit sales (27% × 60% × £60,000)	9,720
	60,532

3   B   Trend value   = 345.12 – (1.35 × 16) = 323.52

Forecast sales = trend + seasonal component
= 323.52 – 23.62
= 299.9
= 300 (to the nearest whole unit)

If you selected **option A** you reduced the trend figure by 23.62 per cent, instead of subtracting 23.62 as an absolute figure.

If you selected **option C** you forgot to adjust the trend for the seasonal variation.

If you selected **option D** you added the seasonal component instead of subtracting it.

4   A   A regression equation is worthless unless a sufficiently large sample is used to determine it. In practice, samples of ten or more are acceptable.

If you chose **option B**, you forgot that forecasting for values of x outside the range of original data leads to unreliable estimates because there is no evidence that the same regression relationship holds for such values.

If you chose **option C**, you didn't realise that working to a high number of decimal places gives spurious accuracy.

If you chose **option D**, you obviously thought that a correlation coefficient close to 0 indicates a strong linear relationship between x and y. The coefficient must be close to +1 or −1 for such an indication, however.

Top tips. Make sure you allow for defective units and calculate the allowance for defective units as 10% of all units produced and **not** as 10% of satisfactory units.

Make sure you calculate the correct figure for raw materials usage, and do not forget to adjust at the end for the budgeted increase in raw materials inventory.

5

	Units
Budgeted sales	18,000
Add closing inventory of finished goods	11,400
Less opening inventory of finished goods	(15,000)
Budgeted production of completed units	14,400
Allowance for defective units (10% of output = $^1/_9$ of input)	1,600
Production budget	16,000

	kg
Raw materials usage budget (16,000 × 6kg)	96,000
Add closing inventory of raw materials	24,400
Less opening inventory of raw materials	(21,000)
Raw materials purchases budget	99,400

6   Adjust price levels to a common basis, say index level 100.

	Volume Units	Total cost £	Cost at price level index = 100 £
High level	160,000	2,770,000 × $(^{100}/_{100})$	2,770,000
Low level	110,000	2,092,800 × $(^{100}/_{109})$	1,920,000
	50,000		850,000

$$\therefore \text{Variable cost per unit} = \frac{£850,000}{50,000} = £17$$

Now calculate the fixed costs.

	£
Total cost of 160,000 units (index 100)	2,770,000
Variable cost of 160,000 units (× £17)	2,720,000
Fixed costs (index 100)	50,000

Costs in year 3 at index 100

	£'000
Variable costs (120,000 × £17)	2,040
Fixed costs	50
	2,090

Costs in year 3 at index 112   = £2,090,000 × $(^{112}/_{100})$
                                       = £2,340,800

7   Expected sales = ((27 × 12) − 24) × 1.35 = 405 units

Top tips. Ensure you do not reduce the deseasonalised sales by 35 per cent, instead of increasing by 35 per cent.

---

8   Orders are estimated as follows, using the given formula which combines regression analysis and a time series model.

Number of orders   = (100,000 + 240 × 30) × Index value
                     = (100,000 + 240 × 30) × 1.08
                     = 115,776

The overhead cost was represented by

y   = £10,000 + £0.25 X where X = number of orders = 115,776
     = £10,000 + (£0.25 × 115,776) = £39,000 to the nearest £1,000.

34   Section B: X plc

> **Text references**. Budgeting and forecasting are covered in Chapters 13 and 14.
>
> **Top tips**. The important part to consider in part (a) is the inventory. You need to remember that production = sales + closing inventory – opening inventory. You may find it easier to think that you need to produce enough to cope with the sales and the closing inventory but you get a head start from the opening inventory.
>
> **Easy marks**. Prepare a template for the production budget and the materials purchases budget. You can then slot in the figures as you calculate them from the information provided.
>
> **Examiner's comments**. The examiner commented that many students seemed poorly prepared for the narrative sections and many failed to make reference to the scenario presented.

(a)   (i)   <u>Production budget in units</u>

	Q1	Q2	Q3	Q4	Total
Budgeted sales	2,250	2,050	1,650	2,050	8,000
Closing inventories (30% of next quarter's sales)	615	495	615	375	375
Opening inventory	(675)	(615)	(495)	(615)	(675)
(Decrease)/increase in inventory	(60)	(120)	120	(240)	(300)
Production	2,190	1,930	1,770	1,810	7,700

(ii)

	Q1	Q2	Q3	Q4	Total
Production units	2,190	1,930	1,770	1,810	
	kg	kg	kg	kg	
Materials					
Opening inventory (3 kg × 45% × current quarter's production)	(2,957)	(2,606)	(2,390)	(2,444)	(2,012)
Usage (3 kg per unit of current production)	6,570	5,790	5,310	5,430	23,100
Closing inventory (45% × next quarter's usage)	2,606	2,390	2,444	2,012	2,957
	6,219	5,574	5,364	4,998	22,155
Cost in £	43,533	39,018	37,548	34,986	155,085

> **Top tips**. Read the question carefully. You are being asked to **discuss** the **impact** of material A being in short supply **not just on budget preparation**, but also on **other areas**. Consider **alternative sources** or **substitute products**. Where these are not available X plc will need to start with the production budget as material A will be the principal budget factor. X plc will also need to maximise contribution per unit of limiting factor.

(b) Material A which may be in short supply during the year is referred to as the **principal budget factor, key or limiting budget factor**. It is the factor that limits the activities of the organisation. The scarcity of material A will mean that there is a limit to how many units can be produced.

The company could try to obtain **alternative supplies** or **substitute products**. If this is not possible, the impact this will have is that production will be limited by the supply of material A and therefore, once this has been identified, the production budget has to be prepared before all others. In addition, to make use of limited resources the company will have to concentrate production on the product that **maximises contribution per limiting factor**.

(c) **Incremental budgeting** is based on the **previous period's budget**, adjusted for current period changes – for example, X plc's material purchases budget may be increased by 4% to account for inflation of material prices. The main disadvantage of incremental budgeting is that any inefficiencies in the previous year's budget remain in the current year. Any **budgetary slack** already built into the budget will be maintained. This can lead to wasteful spending as managers strive to hit their inefficient targets to justify their inclusion in the first place.

Zero based budgeting (ZBB) builds the budget from zero and justifies each item of cost from scratch. This requires **detailed analysis of a company's activities**, and leads to the identification of inefficient activities, thus preventing the inclusion of budgetary slack. It should also encourage more efficient spending – ie only on activities that have been fully justified.

Furthermore, by forcing a detailed budget review, ZBB will help X plc by better reflecting the changing external environment. Incremental budgeting is very inward-looking and unresponsive to external factors.

(d) Sales forecasting

Sales forecasting techniques include asking sales personnel, market research, and using mathematical models and techniques

- **Sales personnel** They can be asked to provide estimates, particularly in the light of increasing competition for product W.

- **Market research** Especially relevant for new products or services.

- **Mathematical models** Set up so that repetitive computer simulations can be run which permit managers to review the results that would be obtained in various circumstances.

The sales budget is frequently the first budget prepared since sales is usually the principal factor, but before the sales budget can be prepared a sales forecast has to be made. Sales forecasting is complex and difficult and involves the consideration of a number of factors including the following.

- The economic environment
- The results of market research
- Competition, particularly for product W.
- Changing consumer taste and increasing awareness of energy consumption issues
- New legislation, or changing government subsidies for insulating products
- Pricing policies and discounts offered

As well as bearing in mind those factors, management can use a number of forecasting methods, often combining them to reduce the level of uncertainty.

(e) The **linear regression method** determines the line of best fit. Plotting historical data on a line can reveal a trend or long-term relationship. This relationship may need to be adjusted for variations such as cyclical, seasonal, long-term trend or random variations. Once these are adjusted for, the line of best fit can be used to forecast future values. It should be noted, however, that linear regression analysis is based on the assumption that the past is a good indication of what will happen in the future.

Using linear regression to forecast sales may be useful to X plc as a base. However, as changes are expected in the market, this should be used with caution as past data may not be the best predictor for the future.

(f) Forecasting problems

All forecasts are subject to error, but the likely errors vary from case to case.

- The further into the future the forecast is for, the more unreliable it is likely to be, particularly since X plc is facing increased competition.
- The less data available on which to base the forecast, the less reliable the forecast.

- The pattern of trend and seasonal variations may not continue in the future.
- Random variations may upset the pattern of trend and seasonal variation.

There are a number of changes that also may make it difficult for X plc to forecast future events.

- **Political and economic changes**   Changes in interest rates, exchange rates or inflation can mean that future sales and costs are difficult to forecast. In particular the restricted supply of X plc's specialised materials might cause rapid cost inflation.

- **Environmental changes**   Global warming and milder winters in the UK might affect the demand for X plc's insulating products.

- **Technological changes**   These may mean that the past is not a reliable indication of likely future events. New and improved insulating products developed by competitors might erode the demand for X plc's products.

- **Social changes**   Alterations in taste, fashion and the social acceptability of products can cause forecasting difficulties. Some of the materials used by X plc might be discovered to have detrimental effects on health. This would affect the forecast demand.

35 Section C: Cash budget

> **Text references**. Breakeven and margin of safety are covered in Chapter 6a. Budgets are covered in Chapter 13.
>
> **Top tips**. Part (a) is fairly straightforward. In part (b) don't forget to label the axes on your graph. In part (c) make sure you lay out the budget and then put all your workings underneath. This makes it easier for the marker to see what you have done. Cross reference your workings to the budget as we have done in the answer below.
>
> **Easy marks**. To get the easy marks, make sure that you manage your time. Try to be methodical with your workings and move on if you run out of time for any part of the question.

(a)   Fixed costs   = depreciation + fixed expenses + loan interest
         = (£2.70 × 860,000) + (£3.20 × 860,000) + (£10,000,000 × 9%)
         = £2,322,000 + £2,752,000 + £900,000
         = £5,974,000

Contribution per unit

	£
Sales price	30.00
Raw materials	(9.50)
Production wages	(8.20)
Variable expenses	(1.10)
Variable selling costs	(1.60)
Bad debt (30 × 2%)	(0.60)
	9.00

Breakeven point   = Fixed costs/Contribution per unit
                = £5,974,000/£9.00
                = 663,778 units

Margin of safety   = Budgeted sales volume – breakeven sales volume
                = 810,000 – 663,778
                = 146,222 units

(b)   If price falls to £7·50 the budgeted profit would rise to £3,231,000

      If price rises to £11·50 the budgeted profit falls to a loss of £9,000

(c)

	Period 1 £'000	Period 2 £'000
Sales (W1)	5,144	5,314
Raw materials (W2)	(2,139)	(2,201)
Production wages (W3)	(1,720)	(1,722)
Variable production expenses	(231)	(231)
Variable selling expenses	(240)	(320)
Fixed production expenses (W4)	(1,376)	
Interest (W5)	0	(450)
Cash flow	(562)	390
Opening balance	76	(486)
Closing balance	(486)	(96)

Workings

1   Sales

	Period 1 £'000	Period 2 £'000
Sales	4,500	6,000
Bad debts @ 2%	(90)	(120)
	4,410	5,880
Opening tr receivables	2,430	1,696
Closing tr receivables*	(1,696)	(2,262)
Receipts	5,144	5,314

* Revised sales × 5/13 = 1,696

2   Materials

	Period 1 £'000	Period 2 £'000
Production (210,000 × £9.50)	1,995	1,995
Closing inventory	921*	1,125*
Opening inventory	(710)	(921)
Purchases	2,206	2,199
Opening payables	612	679
Closing payables	(679)**	(677)
Paid	2,139	2,201

* 1,995 × 6/13 and 220 × £9.50 × 7/13

** 2,206 × 4/13

3   Production wages

	Period 1 £'000	Period 2 £'000
Production (210 ×£8.20/unit)	1,722	1,722
Opening unpaid wages	130	132
Closing unpaid wages	(132)	(132)
Paid	1,720	1,722

BPP
LEARNING MEDIA

4   Fixed production expenses = 860,000 units × £3.20 = £2,752,000
    Paid in period 1 = £2,752,000/2 = £1,376,000

5   Interest payment
    £10,000,000 × 9% = £900,000.
    Paid in period 2 = £900,000/2 = £450,000

36   Section C: Zap plc

Text references. Budgets and principal budget factors are covered in Chapter 13.

Top tips. You could have wasted quite a lot of time if you did not think very carefully about what you were doing in advance. You were given demand information in terms of Product A and Product B but capacity information in terms of product A only so you had to convert all the information into machine hours.

To determine how many of each product you could produce, you had to look at how many sets of one unit of each product (which uses six machine hours) could be produced in the available time.

Easy marks. To get the easy marks, make sure that you manage your time. Remember that the first 50% of the marks on each question are the easiest to get. Instead of running over the time limit for a part of a question, move onto the next one.

(a)   What is the principal budget factor?

Known as the key budget factor or limiting budget factor, this is the factor which, at any given time, effectively **limits the activities of an organisation**. The principal budget factor is usually sales demand: a company is usually restricted from making and selling more of its products because there would be no sales demand for the increased output at a price which would be acceptable/profitable for the company. The principal budget factor may also be machine capacity, distribution and selling resources, the availability of key raw materials or the availability of cash.

The importance of the principal budget factor

Once this factor is identified then the rest of the budget can be prepared. For example, if sales are the principal budget factor then the production budget can only be prepared after the sales budget is complete.

Sales forecasting

There are two basic approaches to sales forecasting.

(i)   Use of internal estimates

In-house sales staff can forecast future sales using their experience and knowledge and by considering the following factors.

(1)   Past sales patterns
(2)   Economic environment
(3)   Results of market research
(4)   Anticipated advertising
(5)   Competition
(6)   Changing consumer taste
(7)   New legislation
(8)   Distribution and quality of sales outlets and personnel

(ii)   Statistical techniques

Such an approach is most appropriate if past sales patterns given some indication of future sales patterns (that is, extrapolation is valid). The techniques include regression analysis by the least squares method in combination with moving averages analysis.

Obviously both approaches can be used in conjunction with each other. Statistical forecasts can be considered and adjusted by sales personnel based on their knowledge and consideration of factors (1) to (8) listed above.

(b) (i)

	Demand Units of A	Demand Units of B	Demand Hrs*	Capacity Hrs
July	2,400	2,000	12,800	4,000
August	2,400	2,000	12,800	2,000
September	2,400	2,000	12,800	8,000
October – December	3,000	6,000	30,000	24,000
January – March	4,800	6,000	33,600	24,000
April – June	9,000	6,000	42,000	24,000
	24,000	24,000	144,000	86,000

There is a shortfall of 144,000 – 86,000 = 58,000 machine hours.

* (2 × demand for A in units) + (4 × demand for B in units)

(ii)   To prepare the budgets we produce the **maximum number of Product A** with the hours available and then use the **remaining hours to produce Product B**. In July, for example, we have 4,000 hours so we can produce only 4,000 ÷ 2 = 2,000 units of Product A whereas in September we can produce 2,400 units of Product A, using 4,800 of the 8,000 hours. The remaining 3,200 can be used to make 3,200 ÷ 4 hrs = 800 units of Product B. Likewise, in October, November and December, the demand for Product A can be met, leaving 8,000 – 2,000 = 6,000 hours to produce 6,000 ÷ 4 = 1,500 units of product B.

Production and sales budgets

July – December 20X8

	Product A Units	Product B Units
July	2,000	–
August	1,000	–
September	2,400	800
October	1,000	1,500
November	1,000	1,500
December	1,000	1,500
	8,400	5,300

(iii) We have to sell **equal quantities** of each product and so for each Product A we have to produce one unit of Product B, which takes six hours in total. We therefore need to **divide up the available hours into groups of six hours** to determine what we can produce. In July, for example, the available capacity is 4,000 hours and so we can produce (4,000 ÷ 6) 666 groups of products, where the products in each group take six hours in total (and where the products are one Product A and one Product B). We can't produce 667 groups because that would take 4,002 hours.

	Product A				Product B			
	Inventory b/f Units	Production Units	Sales (W4) Units	Inv c/f Units	Inv b/f Units	Production Units	Sales (W4) Units	Inv c/f Units
July	–	666 (W1)	666	–	–	666 (W1)	666	–
Aug	–	333 (W2)	333	–	–	333 (W2)	333	–
Sept	–	1,333 (W3)	1,333	–	–	1,333 (W3)	1,333	–
Oct	–	1,333 (W3)	1,000	333	–	1,333 (W3)	1,000	333
Nov	333	1,333 (W3)	1,000	666	333	1,333 (W3)	1,000	666
Dec	666	1,333 (W3)	1,000	999	999	1,333 (W3)	1,000	999
			5,332				5,332	

Workings

1   4,000 ÷ 6 = 666
2   2,000 ÷ 6 = 333
3   8,000 ÷ 6 = 1,333
4   Limited by demand each month

37 List price

Text references. ABB and ZBB are covered in Chapter 13.

Top tips. You will produce a much better answer to part (b)(ii) if you use your answer to part (b)(i) to illustrate the points that you make. The question prompts you to do this in part (b) but it is a good technique to use even if you are not specifically instructed to refer back to earlier parts.

Easy marks. Part (a) is fairly straightforward. Part (b)(i) is not difficult but requires a methodical approach with clear workings underneath.

(a)   Zero based budgeting (ZBB)

ZBB **rejects** the **assumption** inherent in traditional incremental budgeting that the current period's activities will continue at the same level or volume next period, and that the **next period's budget can be based on the current period's costs plus an extra amount for inflation**.

It involves preparing a budget for each cost centre from a zero base. The expenditure for every activity and task therefore has to be **justified in its entirety** in order to be included in the next period's budget.

Activity based budgeting (ABB)

At its **simplest**, ABB is merely the **use of costs determined using activity based costing as a basis for preparing budgets**.

More **formally**, ABB involves defining the activities that underlie the financial figures in each function and **using the level of activity to decide how much resource should be allocated to that function, how well it is being managed and to explain variances from budget**.

Similarities between ZBB and ABB

Both ZBB and ABB require managers to perform a critical assessment of the various tasks and activities carried out within an organisation in order to determine whether or not they should be continued.

In **ABB, different activity levels** can be used to provide the **foundation for base and incremental decision packages** (descriptions of specific organisational activities), which are **used in ZBB to rank activities** in order of priority against other activities.

It is worth noting that some writers treat **ABB** as more of a **philosophy** than a technique and attribute to it all the good features of a number of 'new' or not so new ideas **including ZBB**.

Difference between ZBB and ABB

ABB considers all of an organisation's activities whereas ZBB tends to focus on discretionary costs such as advertising and training.

(b)   (i)   Cash flow forecast

	Sept £'000	Oct £'000	Nov £'000	Dec £'000	Jan £'000	Feb £'000
Receipts						
Credit sales (60% of last month's sales)	30.00	28.80	24.00	27.00	26.40	25.20
Cash sales (38% (40% × 0.95) of this month's sales)	18.24	15.20	17.10	16.72	15.96	19.00
Non-current asset disposal	–	8.00	–	–	–	–
	48.24	52.00	41.10	43.72	42.36	44.20
Payments						
Purchases (W1)	18.80	19.60	17.60	17.00	19.80	17.20
Wages (W2)	6.80	6.00	6.50	6.40	6.20	7.00
Fixed costs (less depn.)	6.00	6.00	6.00	6.00	6.00	6.00
Capital expenditure	15.00	–	10.00	–	–	4.00
Corporation tax	–	–	44.00	–	–	–
	46.60	31.60	84.10	29.40	32.00	34.20
Net cash flow	1.64	20.40	(43.00)	14.32	10.36	10.00
Opening balance	5.00	6.64	27.04	(15.96)	(1.64)	8.72
Closing balance	6.64	27.04	(15.96)	(1.64)	8.72	18.72

Workings

1 Purchases payment month

	Jul £'000	Aug £'000	Sept £'000	Oct £'000	Nov £'000	Dec £'000
Closing stock required (following month sales × 0.5 × 0.4)	10.0	9.6	8.0	9.0	8.8	8.4
(additional safety inventory)	–	–	–	–	2.0	2.0
Sales at cost (× 40%)	17.6	20.0	19.2	16.0	18.0	17.6
	27.6	29.6	27.2	25.0	28.8	28.0
Less opening inventory	8.8	10.0	9.6	8.0	9.0	10.8
Purchases	18.8	19.6	17.6	17.0	19.8	17.2
Payment month	Sept	Oct	Nov	Dec	Jan	Feb

2 Wages

	Sept £'000	Oct £'000	Nov £'000	Dec £'000	Jan £'000	Feb £'000
Fixed sum	2.0	2.0	2.0	2.0	2.0	2.0
10% of sales	4.8	4.0	4.5	4.4	4.2	5.0
	6.8	6.0	6.5	6.4	6.2	7.0

(ii) **Spreadsheets** can **assist cash forecast preparation** in a number of ways.

(1) The basic **calculation** function is performed **automatically**, thus saving time in calculating and re-calculating. In (i) the percentages credit and cash sales would be calculated using a formula.

(2) In a spreadsheet, the model can be separated into **input areas** and **display areas**. The cash budget would pick up information from input areas that contain the underlying relationships. For example the monthly purchase would be calculated as in (i) and the figure inserted into the cash budget as a cash payment two months later.

(3) The model would **display** the results of the calculations as shown in (i). This could be in whatever level of detail was required by the user. **Graphics** would also be used to aid presentation.

(4) **Changes** to a cash flow forecast could also be **made easily** on a spreadsheet. Use of a spreadsheet would mean changes in data such as additional capital expenditure could be incorporated and all totals changed automatically. Likewise extra rows or columns could be incorporated, if further types of expenditure had to be added, or the model extended over additional months (if for instance a rolling budget was being used).

(5) Spreadsheets can also be used to **forecast** cash movements, in **'what if' analysis situations**. Management can enter different assumptions or situations, for example adding safety inventory, or assessing the effect of an increase in sales, and the spreadsheet be adjusted easily.

(6) Further columns can be added to the spreadsheet to **compare actual results with forecast**. Alternatively as actual results are known, the spreadsheet can be amended to incorporate these, and hence **revised forecasts** made of cash balances in the periods to come.

(7) Once the basic model has been set up, it can be used with suitable amendments for **fresh forecasts in future periods.**

38 Section A: Project appraisal, DCF, tax and inflation

1   B   Net present value is the appraisal method to adopt when appraising mutually exclusive projects.

2   C   The NPV approach is superior if discount rates are expected to vary over the life of the project. Variable discount rates can be incorporated easily into NPV calculations, but not into IRR calculations.

        Option A is false because the methods only give the same accept or reject decision when the cash flows are conventional. When the cash flow patterns are non-conventional, there may be several IRRs that decision makers must be aware of to avoid making the wrong decision.

        Option B is false because NPV is technically superior to IRR and easier to calculate.

        Option D is false because NPV is dissimilar to accounting ROCE. However, IRR can be confused with ROCE since both measures are expressed in percentage terms.

3   D   The present value of £5,000 in perpetuity is calculated as £5,000/0.1.

        If you selected **option A**, you might have calculated £5,000 × 10%.

        If you selected **option B**, you might have calculated £5,000 × 110%.

        If you selected **option C**, you might have calculated £5,000/110%.

4   A   **I** is not a disadvantage because the fact that it tends to bias in favour of short-term projects means that it tends to minimise both financial and business risk.

        II is untrue. It is simple to calculate the simple to understand, which may be important when management resources are limited.

        III is not a disadvantage because it helps to identify those projects which generate additional cash for investment quickly.

5

> **Top tips.** There are two possible approaches to answering this question.

Year	Annual cash flow inflated		Discount factor	PV
		£	8%	£
0		(50,000)	1.000	(50,000)
1	(4,000 × £5 × 1.03)	20,600	0.926	19,076
2	(4,000 × £5 × 1.03²)	21,218	0.857	18,184
3	(4,000 × £5 × 1.03³)	21,855	0.794	17,353
				4,613

<u>Alternative approach</u>

Here we discount using the real rate.

(1 + money rate) = (1 + real rate) × (1 + inflation rate)

∴ 1.08/1.03 = 1 + real rate

∴ Real rate = 4.85%

Year	Annual cash flow	Discount factor		PV
	£	4.85%		£
0	(50,000)	1.000		(50,000)
1	20,000	1/1.0485	0.954	19,080
2	20,000	1/1.0485²	0.910	18,200
3	20,000	1/1.0485³	0.868	17,360
				4,640

6   C   The rate required is the IRR (the rate at which the project breaks even).

Let the rate = r

∴£50,000 = PV of (4,000 × £5) for years 1 to 3 at rate r

∴£50,000 = (cumulative PV factor for years 1 to 3 at rate r) × £20,000

∴£50,000/£20,000 = cumulative PV factor for years 1 to 3 at rate r

∴2.5 = cumulative PV factor for years 1 to 3 at rate r

In cumulative PV tables, this corresponds to a rate of approximately 9.7% over three years.

> **Top tips.** Because we are asked to give an answer to the nearest 0.5%, we need to assume that the PV factors behave in a linear fashion so as to determine a more accurate rate than 9% or 10%.

r	PV factor
9%	2.531
10%	2.487
	0.044

∴r = 9% + ((2.531 − 2.5)/0.044)% = 9.7%

This 9.7% is the real cost of capital (because we did not inflate the cash flows).

Now (1 + money rate) = (1 + real rate) × (1 + inflation rate)

∴Money rate = (1.097 × 1.04) − 1 = 0.14088
= 14.1%

7   WDA in year 1 = £100,000 × 25% = £25,000

Tax saved in year 2 = £25,000 × 50% × 30% = £3,750

Reducing balance of asset at beginning of year 2 = £100,000 − £25,000 = £75,000

∴ WDA in year 2 = £75,000 × 25% = £18,750

Tax saved in year 2 = £18,750 × 50% × 30% = £2,813

	Cash flows
	£
Annual cash inflow	20,000
Tax on inflow *	(6,000)
Tax saved (year 1)	3,750
(year 2)	2,813
	20,563
× 8% discount factor for year 2	× 0.857
PV	17,622

*£3,000 of this relates to year 1 annual cash inflow, £3,000 to year 2 annual cash inflow.

8

	Tax saved	Yr 1	Yr 2	Benefit received Yr 3	Yr 4	Yr 5
	£	£	£	£	£	£
Purchase price	80,000					
Yr 1 WDA	20,000	6,000	3,000	3,000		
	60,000					
Yr 2 WDA	15,000	4,500		2,250	2,250	
	45,000					
Yr 3 WDA	11,250	3,375			1,687.50	1,687.50
	33,750					
Yr 4 sales price	20,000					
Balancing allowance	13,750	4,125			2,062.50	2,062.50
					3,937.50	3,750.00

39 Section B: Project appraisal, DCF, tax and inflation

> **Text references.** Project appraisal, DCF, tax and inflation are covered in Chapters 15 to 17.
>
> **Top tips.** It is important to relate your answers to (a), (b) and (c) specifically to the scenario described. Do not provide only a general discussion of NPV and PCAs.
>
> **Easy marks.** You should not experience too many difficulties in calculating NPVs and payback periods. Lay out your workings neatly so that the marker can easily see what you have done.

(a) Difficulties associated with the net present value method when appraising a major IT investment include the following.

- Investment in tangible manufacturing equipment will more than likely give rise to specific outflows of cash. **Cash flows** from an IT project are **less likely to be as easily identifiable or measurable**. Estimates of the financial benefits to be received, for example, can only be 'guesstimates'. Probabilities could be used to incorporate uncertainty into the appraisal process.

- The **estimation of the future life** of an IT investment is made **difficult** by the **rapid rate of technological change** in this area. Benefits may materialise over the long term, outside the time period considered.

- It is difficult to determine the appropriate cost of capital for discounting purposes. A **higher discount factor** could be used to reflect the risk associated with an IT project.

- It is possible that a **negative NPV** will be generated from an IT project such as that currently being considered. The decision should be based on management's assessment of whether the negative NPV is a price worth paying for the intangible benefits of the system (enhanced corporate image, for example).

(b) Given that JLX is a manufacturing organisation and therefore likely to make capital expenditure for new machinery, say, on a fairly regular basis, the claimed benefits of the use of PCA could be significant.

(i) **Learning aspect**. PCA should highlight areas where improvements can be made in methods that should help to achieve better results in general from capital investment. This is particularly applicable if investments have similar characteristics, which could well be the case in the manufacturing environment within which JLX operates.

(ii) **Improved forecasting**. PCA might identify weaknesses in the forecasting and estimating techniques used to provide information for NPV calculations, and so should help to improve the discipline and quality of forecasting for future investments.

(iii) Behavioural implications

(1) Following from (ii) above, PCA could highlight the fact that ambitious managers are being overoptimistic in their forecasting in order to be associated with high-profile projects.

(2) The 'threat' of a PCA should motivate managers to work to achieve the benefits promised from the project.

(3) PCA should also help to identify those managers who have been good performers and those who have been poor performers.

(iv) **Improved efficiency**. If the appraisal takes place before the end of the project's life, and it finds that the benefits have been less than expected because of management inefficiency, steps can be taken to improve efficiency.

(v) **Discontinuance**. Following on from (iv) above, the appraisal could alternatively highlight those projects which should be discontinued.

(c) If an organisation operates a system of PCA, all projects should be submitted to scrutiny.

(i) Analysis of a successful project should highlight **the reason why the project was successful.** This knowledge can then be applied to future projects to increase their chances of success.

(ii) Some projects may appear to be **performing poorly** but are actually **relatively successful given actual circumstances**. For example, the occurrence of unexpected events such as the terrorist attack in New York in September 2001 can have a significant unforeseen impact on projects. Yet projects might be performing satisfactorily given actual operating conditions.

(iii)   Likewise, an **apparently successful project** might only **be performing well because of differences between predicted and actual circumstances.** The recent favourable trading conditions experienced by JLX could well be the reason for the success of PRO35.

The application of a PCA will therefore ensure that **apparent success** does not lead to **complacency** and that **apparent failure** does not lead to management **aversion to risk, lack of motivation** and to 'punishment' for not achieving expected returns.

(d)   (i)   The **payback** method looks at **how long it takes for a project's net cash inflows to equal the initial investment.** For investment A, it is clear that the project pays back sometime during year 4.

Therefore payback   = 3 + ((400 − (100 + 120+140))/120)
                     = 3+ 40/120
                     = 3.33 years

(ii)   The **discounted payback** period is the **time it takes for a project's cumulative NPV to become positive**.

With a cost of capital of 10% and the cash flows shown below, we can calculate a discounted payback period.

Year	Cash flow £'000	Discount factor 10%	Present value £'000	Cumulative NPV £'000
0	(450)	1.000	(450)	(450)
1	130	0.909	118	(332)
2	130	0.826	107	(225)
3	130	0.751	98	(127)
4	130	0.683	89	(38)
5	150	0.621	93	55

The DPP is during year 5.

DPP   = 4 + (38/93)
         = 4.41 years

(e)   (i)   Calculation of net present value at a discount rate of 10%.

Year	Cash flow £'000	Discount factor 10%	Present value £'000
0	(350)	1.000	(350.00)
1	50	0.909	45.45
2	110	0.826	90.86
3	130	0.751	97.63
4	150	0.683	102.45
5	100	0.621	62.10
			48.49

The NPV is £49,000 (to the nearest £'000)

(ii)   The IRR defines the DCF rate of return at which a project's NPV is zero. At 10%, the project has a positive NPV of £49,000. Therefore use a higher discount factor to calculate a negative NPV for the project.

Choose a discount rate of say 15%.

Year	Cash flow £'000	Discount factor 15%	Present value £'000
0	(350)	1.000	(350)
1	50	0.870	44
2	110	0.756	83
3	130	0.658	86
4	150	0.572	86
5	100	0.497	50
		NPV =	(1)

So IRR $= 10 + \left[\dfrac{49}{49+1} \times (15-10) \right]\% = 14.9\%$, say 15%.

(f)   (i)

Average annual profit   = sum of cash flows/5
                        = $170,000/5
                        = $34,000

Average investment   = ($200,000 + $0)/2
                        = $100,000

ARR   = ($34,000/$100,000) × 100%
                        = 34%

(ii)

Year	Cash flow $	DF at 20%	PV $
0	(200,000)	1.000	(200,000)
1	80,000	0.833	66,640
2	90,000	0.694	62,460
3	100,000	0.579	57,900
4	60,000	0.482	28,920
5	40,000	0.402	16,080
			NPV = 32,000

So IRR $= 10 + \left[\dfrac{87,980}{87,980 - 32,000} \times (20 - 10) \right]\% = 25.71\%$, say 26%

40   Section C: Household products

Marking scheme

		Marks
(a)	Sales values	2
	Production costs	3
	Non-production costs	1
	Tax saved on capital allowances	3
	Tax cash flows	3
	Machine purchase and resale value	1
	Discounting and calculating NPV	2
		$\overline{15}$
(b)	Discounting correctly at a lower discount rate	3
	Calculating IRR	1
		$\overline{4}$
(c)	Explanation of treatment of inflation	3
	Description of alternative method	3
		$\overline{6}$

(a) Net present value

	20X8 $	20X9 $	20Y0 $	20Y1 $	20Y2 $	20Y3 $	20Y4 $
Sales (W1)	–	578,448	613,267	662,095	675,944	722,692	–
Production costs (W2)	–	(364,560)	(388,080)	(418,598)	(433,693)	(464,567)	–
Non-production costs (W2)	–	(82,400)	(84,872)	(87,418)	(90,041)	(92,742)	–
Taxable cash-flow	–	131,488	140,315	156,079	152,210	165,383	–
Tax at 30%:							
Current year	–	(19,723)	(21,047)	(23,412)	(22,832)	(24,807)	–
Following year	–	–	(19,723)	(21,047)	(23,412)	(22,832)	(24,807)
Machinery:							
Purchase	(500,000)	–	–	–	–	–	–
Sale	–	–	–	–	–	100,000	–
Tax savings (W3)	–	15,000	27,000	21,600	17,280	23,400	15,720
Post-tax cash flow	(500,000)	126,765	126,545	133,220	123,246	241,144	(9,087)
Discount factor	1.000	0.877	0.769	0.675	0.592	0.519	0.456
Present value	(500,000)	111,173	97,313	89,924	72,962	125,154	(4,144)

Net present value = $(7,618) or $(8,000) to nearest $'000

Workings

1   Sales

Year

20X8 $540,000

20X9 $540,000 $\times \dfrac{103}{100} \times 1.04 \quad = \$578,448$

20Y0 $540,000 $\times \dfrac{105}{100} \times (1.04)^2 \quad = \$613,267$

20Y1 $540,000 $\times \dfrac{109}{100} \times (1.04)^3 \quad = \$662,095$

20Y2 $540,000 $\times \dfrac{107}{100} \times (1.04)^4 \quad = \$675,944$

20Y3 $540,000 $\times \dfrac{110}{100} \times (1.04)^5 \quad = \$722,692$

2 Costs

Production costs

	20X9 $	20Y0 $	20Y1 $	20Y2 $	20Y3 $
Variable prodn cost					
20X8 costs	240,000	240,000	240,000	240,000	240,000
× Volume increase	$\frac{103}{100}$	$\frac{105}{100}$	$\frac{109}{100}$	$\frac{107}{100}$	$\frac{110}{100}$
× Inflation		$(1.05)^2$	$(1.05)^3$	$(1.05)^4$	$(1.05)^5$
Total variable prodn cost	259,560	277,830	302,835	312,142	336,938
Fixed overhead					
Previous year's figure	100,000	105,000	110,250	115,763	121,551
Inflation at 5%	5,000	5,250	5,513	5,788	6,078
Total fixed overhead	105,000	110,250	115,763	121,551	127,629
Total production costs	364,560	388,080	418,598	433,693	464,567

Note. Fixed overhead excludes depreciation

Non-production costs

	20X9 $	20Y0 $	20Y1 $	20Y2 $	20Y3 $
Previous year's cost	80,000	82,400	84,872	87,418	90,041
Inflation at 3%	2,400	2,472	2,546	2,623	2,701
Total for the year	82,400	84,872	87,418	90,041	92,742

3 Taxation

Year	WDA (20%)	Tax saved at 30%
Purchase price	$500,000	
20X9	$\frac{(100,000)}{400,000}$	30,000
20Y0	$\frac{(80,000)}{320,000}$	24,000
20Y1	$\frac{64,000}{256,000}$	19,200
20Y2	$\frac{(51,200)}{204,800}$	15,360
20Y3 Sale	(100,000)	
Balancing allowance	104,800	31,440

Schedule of tax savings

	Total saving $	20X9 $	20Y0 $	20Y1 $	20Y2 $	20Y3 $	20Y4 $
20X9	30,000	15,000	15,000	–	–	–	–
20Y0	24,000	–	12,000	12,000	–	–	–
20Y1	19,200	–	–	9,600	9,600	–	–
20Y2	15,360	–	–	–	7,680	7,680	–
Balancing allowance	31,440	–	–	–	–	15,720	15,720
		15,000	27,000	21,600	17,280	23,400	15,720

(b)   Internal rate of return

Try a lower discount rate to obtain a positive NPV (say 12%).

	20X8 $	20X9 $	20Y0 $	20Y1 $	20Y2 $	20Y3 $	20Y4 $
Cashflow	(500,000)	126,765	126,545	133,220	123,246	241,144	(9,087)
Discount factor	1.000	0.893	0.797	0.712	0.636	0.567	0.507
Present value	(500,000)	113,201	100,856	94,853	78,384	136,729	(4,607)

Net Present Value = $19,416

Use interpolation to find IRR.

$$\text{IRR} = A + \left[\frac{P}{P+N} \times (B-A) \right] \%$$

$$= 12 + \left[\frac{19,416}{19,416 + 7,618} \times (14 - 12) \right] \%$$

$$= 13.44\% \approx 13\%$$

(c)   Inflation was included in the NPV calculation as the given discount rate was a **money cost of capital**. As the money cost of capital includes the effects of inflation, the cash flows must also be inflated.

An alternative method would be to **ignore inflation** when calculating cash flows and discount at the **real discount rate**, which can be calculated using the following formula:

$$(1 + \text{real cost of capital}) = \frac{(1 + \text{money cost of capital})}{(1 + \text{inflation rate})}$$

41   Section C: X

> **Text reference.** This question covers material found in Chapters 13 and 14.
>
> **Top tips.**
>
> In part (a), there are a few things that you need to remember to do. These include:
>
> (i)   Adjusting the draft statement for the receivables and payables figures to arrive at a true cash flow in each year.
>
> (ii)   Making sure that you adjust for the depreciation on the investment when calculating cash flows.
>
> (iii) Ensuring that you get the correct profit figures for calculating tax. These are not the same as the cash flows calculated.
>
> (iv)   Allocating the correct timing on the tax payments as there will be a payment due in the year after the investment finishes.
>
> You should also note that there are no writing down allowances available on the investment.
>
> Part (b) wants you to mention money cash flows, and what effect this may have on the detail and type of information needed. You also need to discuss what discount factor is appropriate when inflation is included in cash flows.
>
> **Easy marks.** Use lots of workings to break up your calculations especially in part(a) where there are quite a few adjustments to make. Using $'000 rather than $ saves a bit of time when doing calculations.
>
> **Examiner's comments.** The examiner commented that many candidates were unable to explain clearly the terms 'money rate' and 'real rate'. Being unable to explain such fundamental terms will lose you easy marks.
>
> **Further question practice.** If you struggle to explain the money rate and the real rate you should try Question 42(c) next.

(a) NPV of investment proposal

	Y0 $'000	Y1 $'000	Y2 $'000	Y3 $'000	Y4 $'000
Investment	(200)	–	–	50.0	
Annual cash flows					
Sales (W1)		210.0	340	275.0	25.0
Production costs (W2)		(138.0)	(219)	(167.0)	(8.0)
Net pre-tax cash flow	(200)	72.0	121.0	158.0	17.0
Taxation (W3)	0	(12.9)	(32.1)	(34.8)	(15.6)
Net post-tax cash flow	(200)	59.1	88.9	123.2	1.4
Discount factor	1.000	0.943	0.890	0.840	0.792
PV	(200)	55.73	79.12	103.49	1.11
NPV	**39.45**				

Workings

1

	Y1 $'000	Y2 $'000	Y3 $'000	Y4 $'000
Sales				
Per statement	230	350	270	
Receivables				
Plus opening	0	20	30	25
Less closing	(20)	(30)	(25)	0
	(20)	(10)	5	25
Cash flow sales	210	340	275	25

2

	Y1 $'000	Y2 $'000	Y3 $'000	Y4 $'000
Production costs				
Per statement	194	272	216	
Less depreciation (W)	(50)	(50)	(50)	
	144	222	166	
Payables				
Plus opening	0	6	9	8
Less closing	(6)	(9)	(8)	0
	(6)	(3)	1	8
Cash flow costs	138	219	167	8

Working for depreciation

$$\frac{(\text{Cost of investment less residual value})}{\text{Life}} = \$'000\ \frac{(200-50)}{3} = \$50{,}000\ pa$$

3

	Y1 $'000	Y2 $'000	Y3 $'000	Y4 $'000
Tax				
Profit from main statement	36.0	78.0	54.0	
Adjusted for depreciation	50.0	50.0	50.0	
Profit for tax purposes	86.0	128.0	104.0	
At 30% (Note)	25.8	38.4	31.2	
Payable	12.9	12.9		
		19.2	19.2	
	0.0	0.0	15.6	15.6
Total tax payable	12.9	32.1	34.8	15.6

Note. The company is liable to pay corporation tax on its accounting profits adjusted for various tax-related amendments. So we need to take the figures from the financial statement and adjust for depreciation only.

(b) **Inflation** would affect the investment in a variety of ways.

(i) Cash flows would have to be inflated **where inflation applied** so each relevant cash flow for the investment would be inflated over three years. Rates of inflation may vary depending on the particular cash flow so these might have to be broken down further. These cash flows would be **money cash flows**.

(ii) Where **receipts and payments** relate to a previous year's sales and costs, these need to be inflated at the previous year's rate .

(iii) The discount factor or cost of capital would be at a **money rate**. This is expressed as follows

$$(1 + \text{money rate}) = (1 + \text{real rate}) \times (1 + \text{inflation rate})$$

(c)

> **Top tips.** It is vital in a question such as this, that requires lots of calculations, to show all your workings in case you make an arithmetical mistake. As there was no residual value, the balancing allowance is simply the brought forward written down value at the beginning of year 4.
>
> **Easy marks.** Calculate WDAs first on the purchased machine. You could save a bit of time by using cumulative PV factors for years 1 to 3 on the lease option where cashflows are identical.

Lease v purchase

R Ltd should lease the machine as this option has the least negative NPV.

Lease option

Time	Cash outflow £'000	Tax savings (W) £'000	Net cash flow £'000	Discount factor 12%	PV £'000
0	300	45	(255)	1.000	(255,000)
1	300	90	(210)	0.893	(187,530)
2	300	90	(210)	0.797	(167,370)
3	300	90	(210)	0.712	(149,520)
4	–	45	45	0.636	28,620
					(730,800)

Working

Tax savings

	Year 0 £'000	Year 1 £'000	Year 2 £'000	Year 3 £'000	Year 4 £'000
Saving on year 0 payment	45	45			
Saving on year 1 payment		45	45		
Saving on year 2 payment			45	45	
Saving on year 3 payment				45	45
	45	90	90	90	45

Purchase option

Year	Cash flow £'000	Tax benefit (W) £'000	Discount factor 12%	PV £
0	(1,000,000)		1.000	(1,000,000)
1		37,500	0.893	33,488
2		65,625	0.797	52,303
3		49,219	0.712	35,044
4		84,375	0.636	53,663
5		63,282	0.567	35,881
				(789,621)

Working

WDAs

	Reducing Balance £	Tax saved £	Year 1 £	Year 2 £	Year 3 £	Year 4 £	Year 5 £
					Benefit received		
Purchase price	1,000,000						
Yr 1 WDA (25%)	250,000	75,000	37,500	37,500			
Value at start of yr 2	750,000						
Yr 2 WDA (25%)	187,500	56,250		28,125	28,125		
Value at start of yr 3	562,500						
Yr 3 WDA (25%)	140,625	42,188			21,094	21,094	
Value at start of yr 4	421,875						
Disposal value							
Balancing allowance	421,875	126,563				63,281	63,282
			37,500	65,625	49,219	84,375	63,282

42 Section C: JK plc

Text reference. The information to answer this question can be found in Chapters 13 and 14 of the Study Text.

Top tips. This question is asking you to evaluate an investment using **long -term decision making techniques.** This is a good question if you love calculations. **The actual calculations aren't difficult but there are lots of them.**

In part (a) you are asked to assess whether the investment is financially worthwhile. You should be familiar with NPV by now. You need to read the question closely to extract the information you need to perform your calculations. Split up the calculations into workings for tax, tax depreciation and the variable costs and revenues. This will help you manage the sheer volume of calculations needed.

Remember with the tax cash flows that 50% is paid or received in **the year after the year the profit arises.** This means that the cash flows will extend beyond Year 4. Don't forget to **advise** the company on whether the investment is worthwhile.

In part (b), you are asked to calculate the IRR of the investment. You will need to use the IRR formula and that is one you need to learn! The formula requires two NPVs so you will need to calculate the NPV of the net cash flows from part(a) at a different rate.

Easy marks. Set out a proforma for calculating the NPV in part (a). The fixed costs can be input straight into the main proforma calculation, but remember to inflate them. Keep your workings neat and the marker will be able to do their job more easily!

You can choose to do part (c) separately as this is a discrete question and could get you a few marks straight away.

(a)　Projected cash flows for a computer controlled production facility

	Year 0 £'000	Year 1 £'000	Year 2 £'000	Year 3 £'000	Year 4 £'000	Year 5 £'000
Sales (W1)		120,000	132,300	145,530	150,012	
Variable costs						
Production costs (W2)		(75,000)	(85,050)	(96,250)	(102,060)	
Selling/distribution costs(W3)		(10,000)	(11,130)	(12,320)	(12,852)	
Fixed costs(W4)						
Production costs		(4,000)	(4,320)	(4,666)	(5,039)	
Selling/distribution costs		(2,000)	(2,120)	(2,247)	(2,382)	
Administration costs		(1,000)	(1,050)	(1,103)	(1,158)	
Total costs		(92,000)	(103,670)	(116,586)	(123,491)	
Net cash inflow before tax		28,000	28,630	28,944	26,521	
Tax due on net cash flow (W5)		(4,200)	(8,494)	(8,637)	(8,319)	(3,978)
Tax saved (via WDA) (W6)		1,875	3,281	2,461	4,069	3,014
Capital cost (W7)	(50,000)				1,000	
Net cash inflow after tax	(50,000)	25,675	23,417	22,768	23,271	(964)
Discount factor at 12%	× 1.000	× 0.893	× 0.797	× 0.712	× 0.636	× 0.567
PV of cash out flow	(50,000)	22,928	18,663	16,211	14,800	(547)

NPV of cash flow = £22,055,000

Based on a positive NPV of £22.055 million the investment is worthwhile and should be undertaken.

Workings

1　Sales revenue

	Year 1	Year 2	Year 3	Year 4
Sales units ('000)	100	105	110	108
Sales price/unit (£)	1,200	1,260	1,323	1,389
Sales revenue (£'000)	120,000	132,300	145,530	150,012

Note. The sales price/unit is inflated by 5% pa.

2　Production costs

	Year 1	Year 2	Year 3	Year 4
Sales units ('000)	100	105	110	108
Variable cost price/unit (£)	750	810	875	945
Production costs (£'000)	75,000	85,050	96,250	102,060

Note. The variable production cost/unit is inflated by 8% pa

3　Selling and distribution costs

	Year 1	Year 2	Year 3	Year 4
Sales units ('000)	100	105	110	108
Variable cost price/unit (£)	100	106	112	119
Selling and distribution costs (£'000)	10,000	11,130	12,320	12,852

Note. The selling and distribution cost /unit is inflated by 6% pa

4　Fixed costs

These are inflated in accordance with the question as follows:

(a)　production costs are inflated by 8% pa
(b)　selling and distribution costs are inflated by 6% pa
(c)　administration costs are inflated by 5% pa

5   Tax on net cash flows

	Year 1 £'000	Year 2 £'000	Year 3 £'000	Year 4 £'000	Year 5 £'000
Net cash inflow before tax	28,000	28,630	28,944	26,521	
Tax at 30%	8,400	8,589	8,683	7,956	
Due 50% in year and 50% in the following year	4,200	4,200			
	0	4,294	4,295		
			4,342	4,341	
				3,978	3,978
Tax due on net cash flow (W5)	4,200	8,494	8,637	8,319	3,978

6   Tax depreciation

Year		£'000
0	Purchase	50,000
1	WDA	12,500
	Value at start of year 2	37,500
2	WDA	9,375
	Value at start of year 3	28,125
3	WDA	7,031
	Value at start of year 4	21,094
4	Sale	1,000
	Balancing allowance	20,094

Year of Claim	Allowance £'000	Tax saved £'000	Year 1 £'000	Year 2 £'000	Year 3 £'000	Year 4 £'000	Year 5 £'000
1	12,500	3,750	1,875	1,875			
2	9,375	2,813		1,406	1,407		
3	7,031	2,109			1,054	1,055	
4	20,094	6,028	–	–	–	3,014	3,014
5			1,875	3,281	2,461	4,069	3,014

7   Treatment of receipt on sale in Year 4

The receipt on sale of the machine is a capital receipt and would not be taxed. Capital allowances are claimed instead.

> **Top tip.** Remember that where discount rates are not found in your tables, you can calculate these by taking the formula $1/(1+r)^n$ where n = 1,2 or 3 in this situation and r is the rate you wish to use to discount the cash flows. In this case we are using 35%.

(b)   Internal rate of return of the investment

Cost of capital

We need to calculate the IRR of the project. We know that the NPV using a discount rate of 12% is £22.055 million.

As the NPV is fairly high at a rate of 12%, the rate to produce a negative NPV will need to be well in excess of 12%.

Let's try 35%.

Year	Net cash flow £'000	Discount factor @ 35%	Present value £'000
0	(50,000)	1.000	(50,000)
1	25,675	0.741	19,025
2	23,416	0.549	12,855
3	22,769	0.406	9,244
4	23,270	0.301	7,004
5	(964)	0.223	(215)
			(2,087)

Then calculate the IRR of the project.

$$IRR = 12\% + \left[\frac{22,055}{22,055+2,087} \times (35-12)\right]\% = \mathbf{33.01\%}$$

(c) <u>Real rate of return and money rate of return</u>

The money rate or nominal rate measures the return in terms of the unit of currency that is, (usually due to inflation) falling in value.

The **real rate** measures the return in **constant price level** terms.

The two rates of return and the inflation rate are linked by an equation.

(1+ money rate of return) = (1 + real rate of return) × (1 + rate of inflation)

Money cash flows should be discounted at a money discount rate.

Real cash flows (ie adjusted for inflation) should be discounted at a real discount rate.

We must decide **which rate** to use for discounting, the **money rate** or the **real rate**. The rule is as follows.

(i) If the cash flows are expressed in terms of the **actual number of pounds** that will be received or paid on the various future dates, we **use the money rate for discounting**.

(ii) If the cash flows are expressed in terms of the value of the pound at time 0 (that is, in constant price level terms), we use the real rate.

The **cash flows** calculated in part (a) are expressed **in terms of the actual number of pounds** that will be received or paid at the relevant dates. We should, therefore, **discount** them using a **money rate of return**.

43 Section A: Further aspects of investment decision making

1 Project 4 has the lowest annualised equivalent and so should be rejected.

Project	1	2	3	4
Investment (£)	66,000	72,000	60,000	43,000
Life (years)	3	6	8	4
Annual receipts (£)	31,000	20,000	16,000	17,000
Cumulative discount factor	2.577	4.623	5.747	3.312
NPV (£)	13,887	20,460	31,952	13,304
Annualised equivalent (£)	5,389	4,426	5,560	4,017

2 The initial investment can rise by £246,000 before the project breaks even and so it may increase by (246,000/714,000) × 100% = 34%.

3 Lowest annualised equivalent cost is over a two-year replacement cycle.

Year	0	1	2	3	4
Discount factor	1.000	0.926	0.857	0.794	0.735
Outflows (£)	(28,000)	(12,000)	(14,000)	(15,000)	(17,000)
PV of outflows (£)	(28,000)	(11,112)	(11,998)	(11,910)	(12,495)
Year-end disposal value (£)		20,000	18,000	12,000	6,000
PV of disposal value (£)		18,520	15,426	9,528	4,410
NPV of replacement at year-end (£)		(20,592)	(35,684)	(53,492)	(71,105)
Cumulative 8% discount factor (£)		0.926	1.783	2.577	3.312
Annualised equivalent (£)		(22,238)	(20,013)	(20,757)	(21,469)

4 **False.** The cost of capital can increase by ((17 − 10)/10) × 100% = 70%.

5   C

		£
Annual cash flow		320,000
add fixed costs		160,000
Annual contribution		480,000

Contribution per unit = £120

∴ **Annual sales volume** = £480,000/£120 = 4,000 units

Permissible fall in present value of revenue =	£244,170
PV of revenue (4,000 × £180 × 3.791)	÷ £2,729,520
Percentage change in selling price = 244,170/£2,729,520	= 8.9 %

6   EV of year 1 cash flow = 0.2 × £10,000 + 0.5 × £7,000 + 0.3 × £6,400 = £7,420

EV of year 2 cash flow = 0.2 × £12,000 + 0.5 × £8,000 + 0.3 × £7,200 = £8,560

EV of year 3 cash flow = 0.2 × £9,000 + 0.5 × £7,600 + 0.3 × £6,200 = £7,460

Year	Cash flow	Discount factor	PV
	£	10%	£
0	(20,000)	1.000	(20,000.00)
1	7,420	0.909	6,744.78
2	8,560	0.826	7,070.56
3	7,460	0.751	5,602.46
			(582.20)

44   Section B: Further aspects of investment decision making

> **Text references.** Further aspects of investment decision making are covered in Chapter 18.
>
> **Top tips.** Parts (a) to (c) demonstrate that as well as being able to perform techniques, you also need to be able to discuss them and consider their advantages and disadvantages.

(a)   Profitability index

The **profitability index** (PI) is the ratio of the **present value** (PV) of the project's **future cash flows** (not including capital investment) **divided by** the **PV** of the **total capital outlays**.

$$\text{Profitability index} = \frac{\text{Present value of cash inflows}}{\text{Present value of capital outlays}}$$

This ratio measures the PV of future cash flows per £1 of investment, and so indicates **which investments** make the **best use** of the limited resources available.

Assumptions

The profitability index is based upon the following assumptions.

(i)   If a project is not accepted and undertaken during the period of capital rationing, the **opportunity** to undertake it is **lost**. It cannot be postponed until a subsequent period when no capital rationing exists.

(ii)   There is **complete certainty** about the outcome of each project, so that the choice between projects is not affected by considerations of risk.

(iii)   Projects are **divisible**, so that it is possible to undertake x% of a given project and earn x% of the expected return on that project.

In a capital rationing situation, the project with the **highest PI** will be selected first, and projects will continue to be selected on this basis until the supply of capital is used up.

(b)   Limitations of the PI approach in a capital rationing situation

(i)   The technique has little use when the projects are indivisible because it cannot be used to find the **best combination** of projects that will maximise the NPV.

(ii)   It does not take account of differing levels of **risk** between projects. This must be dealt with separately, for example by adjusting the discount rates.

(iii)   It does not take into account the **relative strategic importance** of the different projects and the degree to which they fit with the company's wider strategic objectives.

(iv)   It ignores the **pattern** of **cash flows** associated with the different projects. This is because it is essentially a **single period model**. However, the speed with which a project starts to generate a positive cash flow may be important to the company's subsequent investment decisions.

(v)   As with the internal rate of return method of project appraisal, this technique ignores the **relative size** of the different projects. A project that generates a **large overall return**, albeit over a longer period, may be **more valuable** to the company than one which shows a **high PI**, but a relatively **small absolute return**.

(c)

> **Examiner's comments.** To score highly, candidates needed to relate sensitivity analysis to the actual scenario given.

Sensitivity analysis is one method of analysing the risk surrounding a capital expenditure project and enables an assessment to be made of **how responsive** the project's NPV is to changes in the variables that are used to calculate that NPV.

The manager could use sensitivity analysis to look at **how sensitive the project's NPV is to changes in the different variables** (sales, costs, cost of capital etc) affecting the project. This analysis would identify those variables where the change is least before the NPV becomes negative and so need more regular monitoring.

(d)

> **Top tips.** The cost of capital above which the project is not viable is the IRR of the project. We therefore need to calculate the IRR to determine by how much the cost of capital can change before the project is no longer viable. Since tax is paid in the same year that cash flows arise there is no need to phase the cash payments for tax. The final pre-tax NPV can simply be reduced by 20%.

We know that the NPV using a discount rate of 7% is $1.018m.

To find IRR, we need to find another NPV at a **higher rate** than 7% and then use the IRR formula. Try to use a rate that is included in the present value tables provided in the exam so that you can obtain discount factors quickly.

Let's try a rate of 20%.

Year	Net cash flow $'000	Discount factor @ 20%	Present value $'000
1	1,350	0.833	1,125
2	1,800	0.694	1,249
3	1,150	0.579	666
			3,040

Tax is paid at 20% so the net PV after tax is $3,040,000 × 80% = $2,432,000.

Post tax NPV less initial investment   = $'000(2,432-2,000)

$$= \$432,000$$

Then calculate the IRR of the project.

$$IRR = 7 + \left[\frac{1,018}{1,018 - 432} \times (20 - 7) \right]\% = 29.58\%$$

The cost of capital can therefore increase by 29.58 – 7 = 22.58 percentage points.

or: $\dfrac{22.58}{7} = 323\%$

> **Top tips.** You are asked to compare the NPVs for three possible replacement cycles. So you are looking at comparing investments with unequal lives. Therefore you will need to use **annualised equivalents** here to be able to rank the investments.
>
> **Easy marks.** You should be able to calculate present values easily for all three investment cycles as there are few costs and no tricky adjustments such as tax or inflation involved.

(e)   Optimum replacement cycle

Year	Cost	Cash flow $	DF	PV $
0	Purchase cost	400,000	1.000	400,000
1	Operating costs	300,000	0.926	
1	Trade-in value	(240,000)		
		60,000	0.926	55,560
				PV = 455,560

Therefore the **annualised equivalent cost** for a replacement cycle of one year is:

$455,560/0.926 = $491,965.

Year	Cost	Cash flow $	DF	PV $
0	Purchase cost	400,000	1.000	400,000
1	Operating costs	300,000	0.926	277,800
2		400,000		
2	Trade-in value	(150,000)		
		250,000	0.857	214,250
				PV = 892,050

Therefore the **annualised equivalent cost** for a replacement cycle of two years is:

$892,050/(0.926 + 0.857) = $500,308.

Year	Cost	Cash flow $	DF	PV $
0	Purchase cost	400,000	1.000	400,000
1	Operating costs	300,000	0.926	277,800
2		400,000	0.857	342,800
3		600,000		
3	Trade-in value	(80,000)		
		520,000	0.794	412,880
				PV = 1,433,480

Therefore the **annualised equivalent cost** for a replacement cycle of three years is:

$1,433,480/(0.926 + 0.857+0.794) = $556,259.

When we compare the three cycles we can see that the **lowest annualised equivalent cost** is that for a yearly replacement cycle at $491,965.

(f)

> **Top tips.** Your P1 syllabus specifically mentions non-financial considerations in project appraisal. This question asks you for general considerations but you should be prepared, if necessary, to relate your discussion to a particular scenario that might be provided in the exam.

Non-financial considerations cannot be easily quantified and it can be difficult to include them in decision data. However they can have a significant impact and any decision support information provided to managers should incorporate non-financial considerations.

Examples of non-financial considerations that might be relevant to a particular project are as follows.

- **The impact on the company's image.** Certain projects might be worthwhile from a financial point of view but they might not fit well with the image that the company has built for itself and could damage the company's reputation.

- **The impact on employee morale.** For example a labour-saving investment project might have a favourable financial impact. However if staff are made redundant it would be important to consider the impact on the morale of the remaining staff who might feel that their jobs are also under threat.

- **The impact on working conditions and the health and safety of employees.** A project designed to improve staff working conditions might not be financially worthwhile but the non-financial benefits of improved employee safety should also be taken into account.

- **The impact on the community.** Projects such as building works and investments that result in the loss of jobs or the creation of new ones will have an impact on the local community which might not be quantifiable in financial terms.

- **The impact on the environment.** For example a project to develop products or services that create environmentally-harmful waste could have an impact on the environment that might not be quantifiable in financial terms. This could also impact on the company's reputation and image, as mentioned above.

- **Ethical issues.** A viable and legal proposed investment project might contravene the ethics and code of conduct required by the organisation's various stakeholders.

45 Section C: Airport

Text references. Taking account of tax and inflation is covered in Chapter 17.

Top tips. Part (a) will need methodical workings. Layout a proforma for your NPV calculation and put your workings on a separate page. Make sure you calculate the contribution from customers rather than wasting time calculating the revenue and then the variable costs. Part (b) is worth a hefty 9 marks so keep an eye on the time to make sure that you can answer it. Use headings and leave spaces between your paragraphs.

Easy marks. Even if you don't get all of this question completely correct, there are easy marks for correctly for calculating salaries, the additional overheads and the WDA and balancing allowance. You should be getting most of the marks available in part (b) as it is fairly straightforward.

Marking scheme

		Marks
(a)	Restaurant contribution	2
	Cold food outlet opportunity cost	3
	Other relevant cash flows	3
	Non-inclusion of irrelevant cash flows	2
	Tax calculations and phasing of cash flows	4
	Discounting	2
		16
(b)	1 mark per relevant point made	9
		25

(a) Net present value

	Year 0	Year 1	Year 2	Year 3	Year 4	Year 5
	$	$	$	$	$	$
Contribution (W1)		720,000	792,000	871,200	958,320	
Salaries (W2)		(80,000)	(80,000)	(100,000)	(100,000)	
Overheads (W3)		(70,000)	(70,000)	(70,000)	(70,000)	
Opportunity cost (W4)		(432,000)	(475,200)	(522,720)	(574,992)	
Taxable cashflow		138,000	166,800	178,480	213,328	
Tax at 30%:						
Current year		(20,700)	(25,020)	(26,772)	(31,999)	
Following year			(20,700)	(25,020)	(26,772)	(31,999)
Fitting:						
Purchase	(350,000)					
Sale					30,000	
Tax saving (W5)		13,125	22,969	17,227	25,031	17,648
Net cash inflow after tax	(350,000)	130,425	144,049	143,915	209,588	(14,351)
Discount factor at 8%	1	0.926	0.857	0.794	0.735	0.681
PV	(350,000)	120,774	123,450	114,268	154,047	(9,773)

NPV = $152,766

Workings

1 Contribution from customers

Year		$
1	($9.00-$5.00) × 360 days × 500 customers	720,000
2	720,000 × 1.1	792,000
3	792,000 × 1.1	871,200
4	871,000 × 1.1	958,320

2 Staff salaries

Year		$
1	4 × $20,000	80,000
2	4 × $20,000	80,000
3	5 × $20,000	100,000
4	5 × $20,000	100,000

3 Overheads. The only extra overheads which occur as a result of the new restaurant are:

Electricity	$40,000
Advertising	$20,000
Audit	$10,000
	$70,000

4 Contribution lost if restaurant opened

Year		$
1	$2.50 × 1,200 × 360 × 40%	432,000
2	432,000 × 110%	475,200
3	475,200 × 110%	522,720
4	522,720 × 110%	574,992

5   WDAs and balancing charges/allowances

		Reducing balance
Year		£
0	Purchase	350,000
1	WDA (25%)	(87,500)
	Value at start of Year 2	262,500
2	WDA	(65,625)
	Value at start of Year 3	196,875
3	WDA	(49,219)
	Value at start of Year 4	147,656
4	Sales price	30,000
	Balancing allowance	117,656

Year of claim	Allowance	Tax saved	Yr 1	Yr 2	Tax Saving Yr 3	Yr 4	Yr 5
	$	$	$	$	$	$	£
1	87,500	26,250	13,125	13,125			
2	65,625	19,688		9,844	9,844		
3	49,219	14,766			7,383	7,383	
4	117,656	35,297				17,648	17,648
	320,000		13,125	22,969	17,227	25,031	17,648

(b)   Expected NPV

The NPV method of project appraisal takes account of the **time value of money**. It does this by **discounting cash flows** to obtain today's value, known as the present value. The NPV method compares the present value of all the cash inflows from a project with the present value of all the cash outflows of a project. If the net present value (the inflows minus the outflows) is **positive** then the project should be **accepted**.

Projects A, B and C all have positive NPVs so are all acceptable. Project B and C have the higher NPV so are more preferable than Project A.

However the NPV calculation **does not take into account the range of outcomes** that could result from the projects.

Standard deviation of expected NPV

The standard deviation measures the **spread of data** around the expected NPV. It is a measure of **risk** because the **more spread out** the possible incomes are, the **more risky** the project is. The standard deviation is calculated in relation to the expected NPV so we can compare Projects B and C. We need to calculate the **coefficient of variation**, however, to compare Project A.

Project B has a higher standard deviation than Project C therefore **Project B is more risky than Project C.**

	A	B	C
Standard deviation	$10,000	$50,000	$30,000
EV NPV	$150,000	$180,000	$180,000
Coefficient of variation	0.067	0.278	0.167

Project A has a **lower coefficient of variation** than Project C and so it is **less risky**.

IRR

The IRR method of project appraisal is to calculate the exact discount factor rate of return which the project is expected to achieve, in other words, the **rate at which the NPV is zero**. If the expected rate of return (the IRR yield) **exceeds a target rate of return**, the project would be **worth undertaking** (ignoring risk and uncertainty factors).

Project C has the lowest IRR but the **NPV method is considered to be superior to the IRR** method so the company decision should be **based on NPV in situations where the NPV result and the IRR result conflict.**

<u>Factors to consider</u>

<u>Risk and return</u>

There is usually a **greater risk** involved with projects which have a **higher return**. The manager needs to decide on his or her attitude to risk and this will influence which project the manager chooses. For example a risk seeker will opt for Project B as it has the potential to generate higher returns.

<u>Length of the project</u>

The NPV method does not consider the **length of the project**. The longer the project takes, the more **uncertain the future cash flows**. The payback method could be used to assess this.

46 Section C: Projects One and Two

> **Text references**. Taking account of tax and inflation is covered in Chapter 17.
>
> **Top tips**. Part (a) will need methodical workings. Layout a proforma for your NPV calculation and put your workings on a separate page. Make sure that you inflate the revenue and operating costs at 8% and 6% respectively. For (a)(ii) remember to use a report format. Part (b) is not as difficult as it might first look. If you find it easier, think about how much you would have to save each month (as an annuity) to obtain £250,000 after 10 years.
>
> **Easy marks**. Even if you don't get all of this question completely correct, there are easy marks for correctly inflating the revenue and operating costs and for calculating the WDA and balancing allowance.

(a) (i) Accounting rate of return $= \dfrac{\text{Average annual profit from investment}}{\text{Average investment}} = 100$

Average annual profit

	Year 1 £'000	Year 2 £'000	Year 3 £'000	Year 4 £'000	Year 5 £'000	Total £'000
Tax profit (from NPV calculation below)	81.600	189.940	189.867	208.286	162.641	
Less depreciation	(90.000)	(90.000)	(90.000)	(900.000)	(90.000)	
	(8.400)	99.940	99.867	118.286	72.641	382.334

Average annual profit = £382,334/5 = £76,467

Average investment $= \dfrac{\text{Initial investment} + \text{residual value}}{2}$

$= (£500,000 + £50,000)/2 = £275,000$

∴ APR = £76,467/£275,000

$= 27.8\%$

Net present value

	Year 0	Year 1	Year 2	Year 3	Year 4	Year 5	Year 6
	£'000	£'000	£'000	£'000	£'000	£'000	£'000
Revenue (W1)		399.600	583.200	642.453	700.652	697.931	
Operating costs (W2)		(318.000)	(393.260)	(452.586)	(492.366)	(535.290)	
Tax profit		81.600	189.940	189.867	208.286	162.641	
Tax due (30% in arrears)			(24.480)	(56.982)	(56.960)	(62.486)	(48.792)
Tax saved (W3)			37.5	28.125	21.094	15.820	32.461
Capital cost	(500)					50	
Net cash inflow after tax	(500)	81.600			172.42	165.975	(16.331)
Discount factor at 12%	1	0.893	0.797	0.712	0.636	0.567	0.507
PV	(500)	72.869	161.759	114.639	109.659	94.108	(8.280)

NPV = £44,754

Workings

1   *Revenue*

Year		£'000
1	370×1.08	399.600
2	500×1.08^2	583.200
3	510×1.08^3	642.453
4	515×1.08^4	700.652
5	475×1.08^5	697.931

2   *Operating costs*

Year		£'000
1	300×1.06	318.000
2	350×1.06^2	393.260
3	380×1.06^3	452.586
4	390×1.06^4	492.366
5	400×1.06^5	535.290

3   *WDAs and balancing charges/allowances*

Year		Reducing balance £
0	Purchase	500,000
1	WDA (25%)	(125,000)
	Value at start of Year 2	375,000
2	WDA	(93,750)
	Value at start of Year 3	281,250
3	WDA	(70,313)
	Value at start of Year 4	210,937
4	WDA	(52,734)
	Value at start of Year 5	158,203
5	Sale	50,000
	Balancing allowance	108,203

Year of claim	Allowance £	Tax saved £	Yr 2 £	Yr 3 £	Tax Saving Yr 4 £	Yr 5 £	Yr 6 £
1	125,000	37,500	37,500				
2	93,750	28,125		28,125			
3	70,313	21,094			21,094		
4	52,734	15,820				15,820	
5	108,203	32,461					32,461
	450,000		37,500	28,125	21,094	15,820	32,461

(ii)   REPORT

To: Board of Directors

From: Management accountant

Date: 18th February 2010

Subject: Project one and two

Accounting rate of return

The ARR is based on the ratio of average accounting profit from an investment to the average capital employed. A project should be **undertaken** if its estimated ARR is **greater** than our **target ARR** of 30%.

On the **basis of ARR** alone, **Project One** would be **accepted** and **Project Two** would be **rejected**.

Advantages and disadvantages

The advantages of ARR are that is it **quick** and **easy to calculate** and to **understand**. In addition it incorporates profit flows from the **entire life** of the project. (Some appraisal methods do not)

A serious drawback of the ARR is that it does not take account of the **timings of the profits** from the project, nor the **time value of money**. It is based on **accounting profits** which are subject to a number of different accounting treatments.

Net present value (NPV)

The NPV is the sum of the present value of all cash inflows of a project and all cash outflows of a project taking account of the time value of money. If the **NPV** is **positive** then the **project** should be **accepted**.

In this case both projects have a position NPV but Project Two has the higher NPV. Therefore, based on NPV alone, Project Two should be accepted.

Advantages and disadvantages

The main advantage of the NPV method is that it takes the time value of money into account.

Some of the problems associated with the NPV method include the **difficulty** in **deciding** on an **appropriate discount rate** and the difficulty in **explaining** the method **to non-financial mangers**. The NPV method also fails to highlight how **quickly** the **original investment** is **recouped**.

Non-financial factors

Possible considerations include:

Impact on the environment

It may be that one of the machines is not as environmentally friendly as the other. This could affect an organisation's image and reputation and hence its long term growth and survival prospects.

Technical compatibility

It may be that one machine fits better with existing operations than the other. Or it may be that one machine is less likely to become obsolete.

The business needs to consider obsolescence in case repairs and maintenance are needed in the future. They do not want to be left needing a replacement part for example, which is no longer available.

(b)   Annuity × 6.710* = £250,000

$$\therefore \frac{£250,000}{6.710} = \text{monthly repayment}$$

$$= £37,258$$

Payments are made at the end if each year so if there are just over 4 years left to run then there will be five payments outstanding.

£37,258 + (£37,258 × 3.312**) = £160,656

* Cumulative discount factor for 10 years at 8%.

** Cumulative discount factor for 4 years at 8%

47 Section C: Restaurant

Text reference. Chapter 16 covers net present value (NPV) and internal rate of return (IRR). Sensitivity analysis is covered in Chapter 18.

Top tips. Use the proforma layout for NPV calculations as this helps to ensure you do not miss anything out.

In the NPV calculation, make sure you only use the incremental costs and revenues rather than using total figures as you will end up with a very large (and inaccurate) NPV. Note that cost inflation and selling price inflation are different figures so be careful to use the correct one. Note also that the discount rate is the money cost of capital which suggests that cash flows must be adjusted to include the effects of inflation. Inflation starts in 20X9 so make sure you inflate sales and costs in this year.

The investment takes place at the beginning of year 1 which is equivalent to the end of year 0. Timing of capital allowances is always an issue – if you are not sure when the tax benefits should be claimed, just make an assumption and stick with it (make sure your assumptions are clearly indicated in your answer).

Make sure all workings are labelled. Not only is it easier for the marker when marking your script, it also makes it easier for you to find the relevant numbers when you are slotting them into your NPV proforma.

Part (b) is a straightforward IRR calculation. Don't worry if you think you've made mistakes in your NPV calculation in part (a) – you will be marked on your technique using the figures you have calculated. Remember to interpret your result rather than just calculating the number. This solution uses interpolation to find IRR – you can just as easily use extrapolation.

The sensitivity analysis in part (c) might throw you slightly as it is in terms of percentage capacity utilisation. The present value on the bottom line of the sensitivity formula should contain only those costs that vary directly with capacity.

Easy marks. If you are comfortable with NPV there are a number of easy marks to be gained in part (a). The IRR calculation is also straightforward if you remember the formula.

Examiners' comments. The examiner commented that the presentation and neatness of answers was poor. In many cases workings were not referred to and were difficult to decipher. Remember that clear workings make it easier for you as well as for the marker.

The examiner also commented that only a small percentage of candidates attempted to interpret the IRR in part (b), thus forgoing easy marks.

Further question practice. If you struggled with the application of an incremental approach in this question you should try Question 48 next.

Marking scheme

		Marks
(a)	Correct sales figures	2
	Extra food and drink costs	4
	Extra staff costs	1
	Extra other costs	1
	Inflation adjusted incremental costs	1
	Taxation on profits	2
	Tax benefit of capital allowances	2
	Calculation of NPV and recommendation	1
		14
(b)	IRR calculation	3
	Recommendation based on calculated IRR	3
		6
(c)	Identification of cash flows affected by capacity utilisation	3
	Calculation of sensitivity	2
		5

(a)   Net present value

Year		0	20X9	20Y0	20Y1	20Y2	20Y3
		£'000	£'000	£'000	£'000	£'000	£'000
Sales	(W1)		101.97	105.03	108.18	111.43	
Costs	(W2)		(86.70)	(90.17)	(93.78)	(97.53)	
Operating cash flows			15.27	14.86	14.40	13.90	
Taxation at 20%				(3.05)	(2.97)	(2.88)	(2.78)
Initial investment		(40)					
Tax benefits of capital allowances	(W3)			6.40	0.32	0.26	1.02
Net cash flow		(40)	15.27	18.21	11.75	11.28	(1.76)
8% discount factors		1.000	0.926	0.857	0.794	0.735	0.681
Present value		(40)	14.14	15.61	9.33	8.29	(1.20)

Net present value = £6.17 (that is, £6,170)

Recommendation

The expansion project is worthwhile as the restaurant company will be £6,170 better off if the project is implemented.

Workings

(1)   Sales

Food and drink sales will increase by 30% in real terms due to the 30% increase in capacity. Total extra sales will increase by 3% per annum.

	20X9	20Y0	20Y1	20Y2
	£000	£000	£000	£000
Extra food sales (180 × 30%)	54	54	54	54
Extra drink sales (150 × 30%)	45	45	45	45
Extra sales (£330 × 30%)	99	99	99	99
Inflated at 3%	101.97	105.03	108.18	111.43

(2)   Costs (all figures are in £000)

(i)   Food and drink costs

$$\text{Food costs as percentage of food sales} = \frac{125}{180} \times 100 = 69\%$$

Extra food costs = extra sales × 69% = £54 × 69% = £37.26

Drink costs as percentage of drink sales $= \dfrac{70}{-150} \times 100 = 47\%$

Extra drink costs = extra drink sales × 47% = £45 × 47% = £21.15

Total increase in food and drink costs = £37.26 + £21.15 = £58.41

    (ii)   <u>Staff costs</u>

Increase in staff costs = 20% of £55 = £11

    (iii)   <u>Other costs</u>

Current variable element = 30% of £45 = £13.5 (= 4% of current sales figure of £330)

Increase in variable cost due to capacity increase = 4% of £99 = £3.96

Total increase in other costs = £3.96 + £10 = £13.96

    (iv)   <u>Total incremental costs adjusted for inflation</u>

Total incremental costs = £58.41 + £11 + £13.96 = £83.37

Inflation adjustments:

20X9	£83.37 × 1.04	£86.70
20Y0	£83.37 × 1.04^2	£90.17
20Y1	£83.37 × 1.04^3	£93.78
20Y2	£83.37 × 1.04^4	£97.53

(3)   <u>Capital allowances</u>

Year	*Cost/WDV* £'000	*Tax benefit at 20%* £'000	*Year of benefit*
20X9	40.00		
100% allowance	(30.00)	6.00	20Y0
Tax WDV	10.00		
20% cap. all.	(2.00)	0.40	20Y0
	8.00		
20Y0 20% cap. all.	(1.60)	0.32	20Y1
Tax WDV	6.40		
20Y1 20% cap. all.	(1.28)	0.26	20Y2
Tax WDV	5.12		
20Y2 20% cap. all.	(1.02)	0.20	20Y3
Tax WDV	4.10		
Resale value	Nil		
Balancing allowance	4.10	0.82	20Y3

(b)   <u>Internal rate of return (IRR)</u>

$$IRR = a + \dfrac{NPVa}{NPVa - NPVb} \times (b - a)$$

Calculate NPV using a higher discount rate to obtain a value close to 0.

Try 16%

NPV = £(0.39)

$$IRR = 8 + \dfrac{6.17}{(6.17 + 0.39)} \times (16 - 8) = 15.52\%$$

The IRR is the discount rate at which NPV = 0. The IRR is **considerably higher** than the company's discount rate therefore, **unless the company's required rate of return increased substantially, the expansion project is likely to remain profitable.**

The problem with IRR being so high compared with the company's discount rate is that it **makes the assumption of being able to reinvest funds at the IRR very unlikely**. The IRR result should therefore be interpreted with caution.

(c) <u>Sensitivity analysis</u>

The present value of the cash inflows can fall by £6,170 before the expansion project breaks even.

Sensitivity of project to changes in capacity = NPV of project ÷ PV of cash flows directly affected by capacity

<u>Cash flows directly affected by capacity</u>

	20X9 £'000	20Y0 £'000	20Y1 £'000	20Y2 £'000
Sales revenue	101.97	105.03	108.18	111.43
Food and drink costs	(60.75)	(63.18)	(65.71)	(68.34)
Variable 'other' costs	(4.11)	(4.27)	(4.44)	(4.62)
Net relevant cash flow	37.11	37.58	38.03	38.47
Discount factor 8%	0.926	0.857	0.794	0.735
Present value	34.36	32.21	30.20	28.28

Total present value = £125.05

$$\text{Sensitivity of project to changes in capacity} = \frac{6.170}{125.05} \times 100 = 4.9\%$$

This means that capacity could fall by 4.9% before the project breaks even.

48 Section C: H plc

Text references. Taking account of taxation in investment appraisal is covered in Chapter 17. Throughput accounting is covered in Chapter 10.

Top tips. Use an incremental approach, ie calculate the extra contribution that will arise from the additional capacity. Although it will be possible to produce 500 units per hour with the new machine, remember to check that the sales demand exists for this number of units.

The £20,000 removal costs for the old machine can be added to the machine cost to calculate the tax deprecation allowances.

Easy marks. Prepare the pro forma columnar layout for your workings of the tax calculations and the final net present value calculations and slot the figures in as you produce them. Use plenty of space and present clear working so that the marker can see what you have done.

Marking scheme

			Marks
(a)		Revised weekly sales volume	3
		Incremental contribution	2
		Tax deprecation allowances	3
		Other tax cash flows	2
		Acquisition/disposal cash flows	2
		Discounting	1
		Net present value	2
			15
(b)		Explanation of TA	1.5
		Explanation of TA ratio	1.5
			3
(c)	(i)	IRR calculation	3
	(ii)	Sensitivity calculation	4
			7

(a) Initial workings

1 Tax cash flows

	£	Tax @ 30% £	Year 1 £	Year 2 £	Year 3 £	Year 4 £	Year 5 £
Machine cost	520,000						
WDA year 1, 25%	130,000	39,000	19,500	19,500			
	390,000						
WDA year 2, 25%	97,500	29,250		14,625	14,625		
	292,500						
WDA year 3, 25%	73,125	21,938			10,969	10,969	
	219,375						
Sale for scrap, year 4	50,000						
Balancing allowance	169,375	50,813				25,406	25,406
Tax payable on contribution (working 2)			(40,320)	(80,640)	(80,640)	(40,320)	
Tax relief on training costs (£5,000 × 30% × 0.5)			750	750			
Total tax recoverable/(payable)			(20,070)	(45,765)	(55,046)	(3,945)	25,406

2 Incremental contribution

Demand per week	12,000	units
Demand per working hour (12,000/40)	300	units
Current capacity per hour	200	units
Incremental units per hour (300 – 200)	100	units
Contribution per unit	£1.40	
Hours available (40 hours × 48 weeks)	1,920	
Incremental contribution per annum (100 × £1.40 × 1,920)	£268,800	
Tax at 30%	£80,640	

Cash flows from machine

Year	Acquisition /disposal £	Contribution (W2) £	Tax (W1) £	Total cash flow £	Discount factor	Present value £
0	(525,000)*			(525,000)	1.000	(525,000)
1		268,800	(20,070)	248,730	0.909	226,096
2		268,800	(45,765)	223,035	0.826	184,227
3		268,800	(55,046)	213,754	0.751	160,529
4	50,000		(3,945)	46,055	0.683	31,456
5			25,406	25,406	0.621	15,777
Net present value						93,085

* £500,000 + £20,000 + £5,000 training costs

(b) Throughput accounting

Throughput accounting is a management accounting system that focuses on ways in which return per scarce resource can be achieved.

Throughput accounting focuses on throughput contribution ie sales revenue less direct material costs and assumes that other costs are fixed.

As the only costs that throughput accounting considers variable are materials, it is known as 'supervariable costing'.

Throughput accounting ratio

Products can be ranked according to the throughput accounting ratio.

$$\text{TA ratio} = \frac{\text{throughput contribution or value added per time period}}{\text{conversion cost per time period}}$$

The **higher** the ratio, the more **profitable** the company. A profitable product should have a ratio **greater than one**. If it is less than one then the organisation is **losing money** every time the product is produced.

(c)   (i)   <u>IRR calculation</u>

Step 1 **By trial and error, find a discount factor at which NPV < 0.**

$$\text{Try } 20\%: NPV = (15,000) + \left[(30,000 - 22,500) \times 2.106 \right]$$

$$= (15,000) + 15,795$$

$$= 795$$

$$\text{Try } 25\%: NPV = (15,000) + \left[(30,000 - 22,500) \times \frac{1 - (1 + 0.25)^{-3}}{0.25} \right]$$

$$= (15,000) + \left[(30,000 - 22,500) \times 1.952 \right]$$

$$= (360)$$

Step 2 **Calculate IRR**

$$IRR = 10 + \frac{3,652.50}{(3,652.50 + 360)} \times (25 - 10)$$

$$= 23.65\% \text{ (to 2 decimal places)}.$$

(ii)   **Sensitivity of investment to changes in annual cash inflows:**

The present value of the cash inflows can fall by $3,652.50 before the project breaks even.

Current present value of cash inflows = $30,000 × 2.487

$$= \$74,610$$

∴ The % by which the current present value can fall $= \dfrac{3,652.50}{74,610} \times 100$

$$= 4.90\% \text{ (to two decimal places)}.$$

49 Section C: Print Co

Text references. The answer to this question draws very much on material from Chapters 17 and 18 of your Study Text.

Top tips. Look at the incremental contribution from the new machine. Note the residual value of the new machine and adjustments to WDAs required on both the old and new machines.

Examiner's comments. A good attempt was made by most students at part (a) but the standard of layout and presentation was often poor as was any reference to workings.

Part (b). This was very poorly answered. Many students showed that they had an incomplete understanding of sensitivity analysis.

Common errors noted by the examiner include:

- Not appreciating that the calculations needed the additional contribution (£896k) and not the new contribution (£2,496k)
- Incorrect phasing of tax relief and tax on the incremental contribution
- Incorrect calculation of the balancing charge
- Not discounting the contribution figures
- Not using the answer to part (a) as the numerator in the sensitivity tests

Further question practice. If you struggled to deal with the taxation aspects and the required sensitivity analysis you should try Question 52 next.

(a) Workings

1 Tax depreciation on the new machine

	£'000	Tax at 30% £'000	Year 1 £'000	Year 2 £'000	Year 3 £'000	Year 4 £'000	Year 5 £'000	Year £'000
Machine cost	3,000							
Year 1 WDA at 25%	(750	225	112	113				
	2,250							
Year 2 WDA at 25%	(563	169		84	85			
	1,687							
Year 3 WDA at 25%	(422	127			63	64		
	1,265							
Year 4 WDA at 25%	(316	95				47	48	
	949							
Year 5 Disposal	(300							
Balancing allowance	649	195					97	98
			112	197	148	111	145	98

2 Balancing charge on old machine

		£'000	Tax at 30% £'000	Year 1 £'000	Year 2 £'000
Year 0 TWDV (tax written down value)		250			
Disposal		(400)			
		150	45	22	23

> **Easy marks.** Split the question into manageable chunks. Do the tax WDA parts first, then calculate the incremental contribution. The examiner gives eight marks for these two calculations.

3 Increased contribution from the new machine

(a) New sales £4m × 1.2 = £4.8m

(b) Reduced UNIT variable costs = 0.60 × 0.80 = 0.48 of sales

(c) Therefore new contribution = £4.8m × 0.52 = £2.496m

(d) Existing contribution = £4m × 0.4 = £1.6m

Therefore incremental contribution = £0.896m

4 **Tax** on this will be 30% × £0.896m × 50% year 1 to year 6

> **Top tips.** The examiner is asking for a sensitivity analysis on the annual contribution and the rate of corporation tax. Consider calculating the NPV on the tax cash flows separately and then add together for the final assessment of NPV. This means it is easier to pick out what figures you need for your answer to part (b).

5 NPV of cash flows

	0 £'000	1 £'000	2 £'000	3 £'000	4 £'000	5 £'000	6 £'000
				Year			
Capital cost	(3,000)						
Increased contribution	–	896	896	896	896	896	–
Sales proceeds	400	–	–	–	–	300	–
Tax:							
Contribution (W3)	–	(134)	(268)	(268)	(268)	(268)	(134)
Old machine (W2)	–	(23)	(22)	–	–	–	–
New machine (W1)	–	112	197	148	111	145	98
Net cash flow	(2,600)	851	803	776	739	1,073	(36)
Discount factor							
14% (after tax rate)	1.000	0.877	0.769	0.675	0.592	0.519	0.456
Present value	(2,600)	746	618	524	437	557	(16)

NPV = £266,000

The overall investment **NPV** is **positive**, therefore the investment is **worthwhile**.

(b) **Sensitivity analysis enables an analysis of risk in a capital expenditure project by testing the responsiveness of the NPV to changes in the variables that are used to calculate the NPV.**

The variables that are most sensitive are those critical to the project's outcome. These variables are those where the change in the variable is smallest. This sensitivity is measured by:

$$\frac{\text{NPV of the project}}{\text{PV of the cash flow affected}}$$

By analysing these variables managers can review the risks posed by an existing cost structure and allows them to consider alternative structures.

(i) <u>Contribution</u>

> **Top tips.** Note that the question asks for change in the annual contribution, which is different from the incremental contribution used in part (a).

	1 $'000	2 $'000	3 $'000	4 $'000	5 $'000	6 $'000
Pre tax contribution	2,496	2,496	2,496	2,496	2,496	–
Tax at 30% (see below)	(374.4)	(748.8)	(748.8)	(748.8)	(748.8)	(374.4)
	2,121.6	1,747.2	1,747.2	1,747.2	1,747.2	(374.4)
Discount factor (14%)	0.877	0.769	0.675	0.592	0.519	0.456
Present value	1,860.6	1,343.6	1,179.4	1,034.3	906.8	(170.7)

NPV = $6,154

(Tax per annum = $2,496 × 0.3 = $748.8. 50% is paid in the same year and 50% in the next year)

Sensitivity of this factor: $\dfrac{\text{NPV of project}}{\text{PV of affected cash flow}} = \dfrac{266}{6,154} = \underline{4.3\%}$

So a reduction of 4.3% in the contribution would make the project NPV zero.

(ii) <u>PV of corporation tax on profits</u>

	1 $'000	2 $'000	3 $'000	4 $'000	5 $'000	6 $'000
Tax:						
Contribution	(134)	(268)	(268)	(268)	(268)	(134)
Old machine	(23)	(22)	–	–	–	–
New machine	112	197	148	111	145	98
	(45)	(93)	(120)	(157)	(123)	(36)
Discount factor	0.877	0.769	0.675	0.592	0.519	0.456
Present value	39.5	71.5	81.0	92.9	63.8	16.4

Total present value = $365.1

$\dfrac{\text{NPV of project}}{\text{PV of affected cash flow}} = \dfrac{266}{365} = \underline{72.9\%}$

So tax rates would have to increase by nearly 73% to make the NPV zero. Thus the project is more sensitive to changes in contribution than it is to changes in the rate of tax.

50 Section C: CH Ltd

Text references. Look at Chapter 17 if you get stuck on inflating the cash flows or need help with the calculation of tax benefits. Chapter 18 covers sensitivity analysis.

Top tips. The costs and benefits given in the question are at current prices which means a real rate should be applied to them for discounting purposes. Such an approach does not allow for the benefit of the lag in the payment of taxation. You therefore need to inflate the values given so that they represent the actual number of pounds that will be received or paid, and then apply the money rate, as this takes account of this time lag of taxation. We have provided the alternative approach to discounting using the real rate of 10%, in case that is the method you adopted.

Because part (b) so clearly requires sensitivity analysis of contribution, if you are planning your answer carefully you should aim to calculate the PV of the sensitive variable (contribution) separately in part (a) so that you can use your answer in part (b). In our alternative approach to (a) we dealt with them together to show the appropriate method if you did not deal with them separately.

Because we are using the nominal rate of 15.5% you cannot use PV tables and so have to determine the discount factors using $(1/(1.155)^n)$ and your calculator.

Easy marks. Part (c) of the question examines the preparation of project cash flows that take account of taxation and inflation. It was a fairly straightforward DCF/tax scenario except for one small point: the disposal value of £55,000 was a current value; the actual disposal value at year 5 needed to be included in the analysis. This part of the question is 'stand alone', in that it is unaffected by parts (a) and (b). If you have practised capital allowance workings then it might be better to tackle this part first before you make any attempt at the more complex and unfamiliar parts (a) and (b).

Don't worry if your answer is slightly different due to the approach to rounding that you have adopted.

(a) As explained in top tips, we need to inflate the cash flows and use the nominal rate of 15.5%. And we are dealing with contribution separately, as discussed in top tips.

Step 1 Calculate the PV of non-contribution items

Inflated fixed cost = £90,000 × 1.05^n (when n is for years 1 to 5)

Inflated disposal value = £55,000 × 1.05^5

Time	Cash Flows £	Tax benefits (W) £	Net cash flow £	Discount factor 15.5%	PV £
0 Investment	(550,000)	–	(550,000)	1.000	(550,000)
1 Fixed costs	(94,500)	14,175	(80,325)	0.866	(69,561)
2 Fixed costs	(99,225)	29,059	(70,166)	0.750	(52,625)
3 Fixed costs	(104,186)	30,512	(73,674)	0.649	(47,814)
4 Fixed costs	(109,396)	32,037	(77,359)	0.562	(43,476)
5 Fixed costs	(114,865)	33,640	(81,225)	0.487	(39,557)
5 Disposal value	70,195		70,195	0.487	(34,185)
6 Fixed costs	–	17,230	17,230	0.421	7,254
					(761,594)

Working

Tax effect of fixed costs

Year	Cash flow £	Tax saved (30%) £	Yr 1 £	Yr 2 £	Benefit Yr 3 £	Yr 4 £	Yr 5 £	Yr 6 £
1	94,500	28,350	14,175	14,175				
2	99,225	29,768		14,884	14,884			
3	104,186	31,256			15,628	15,628		
4	109,396	32,819				16,409	16,410	
5	114,865	34,460					17,230	17,230
			14,175	29,059	30,512	32,037	33,640	17,230

Step 2 Calculate annual contribution

Estimated annual sales revenue = (£800,000 × 0.25) + (£560,000 × 0.5) +
(£448,000 × 0.25) = £592,000

Contribution/ sales ratio = 55%

∴Annual contribution = 0.55 × £592,000 = £325,600

Inflated contribution = £325,600 × 1.05^n (where n is for years 1 to 5)

Step 3 Calculate the PV of contribution

Year	Inflated contribution £	Tax payment (W) £	Net cash flow £	Discount factor 15.5%	PV £
1	341,880	(51,282)	290,598	0.866	251,658
2	358,974	(105,128)	253,846	0.750	190,385
3	376,923	(110,384)	266,539	0.649	172,984
4	395,769	(115,904)	279,865	0.562	157,284
5	415,557	(121,699)	293,858	0.487	143,109
6		(62,334)	(62,334)	0.421	(26,243)
					889,177

Working

Year	Cash flow £	Tax saved (30%) £	Yr 1 £	Yr 2 £	Yr 3 £	Yr 4 £	Yr 5 £	Yr 6 £
1	341,880	102,564	51,282	51,282				
2	358,974	107,692		53,846	53,846			
3	376,923	113,077			56,538	56,539		
4	395,769	118,731				59,365	59,366	
5	415,557	124,667					62,333	62,334
			51,282	105,128	110,384	115,904	121,699	62,334

Tax payments

Step 4 Determine overall NPV

NPV= £(889,177 – 761,594) = £127,583

The project should be undertaken as it results in a positive NPV.

Alternative approach

(a) **Step 1 Work out the real rate.**

(1 + money rate) = (1 + real rate) × (1 + inflation rate)

∴ 1.155 = (1 + real rate) × 1.05

∴Real rate = (1.155/1.05) – 1 = 10%

Step 2 Work out the annual cash flows.

Estimated annual sales revenue = (£800,000 × 0.25) + (£560,000 × 0.5) +
£448,000 × 0.25)

= £592,000

Contribution/sales ratio = 55%

∴Annual contribution = 0.55 × £592,000 = £325,600

Step 3 Work out the tax effects.

Expected profit (cash flow) = Annual contribution – fixed costs

Year	Cash inflow £	Tax at 30% £	Year 1 £	Year 2 £	Year 3 £	Year 4 £	Year 5 £	Year 6 £
1	235,600	70,680	35,340	35,340				
2	235,600	70,680		35,340	35,340			
3	235,600	70,680			35,340	35,340		
4	235,600	70,680				35,340	35,340	
5	235,600	70,680					35,340	35,340
			35,340	70,680	70,680	70,680	70,680	35,340

Tax payments

Alternative approach continued

Step 4 **Perform DCF analysis.**

Year	Cash flow £	Discount factor 10%	PV £
0	(550,000) investment	1.000	(550,000)
1-5	235,600 inflow	3.791	893,160
1	(35,340) tax	0.909	(32,124)
2-5	(70,680) tax	2.882 *	(203,700)
5	55,000 disposal	0.621	34,155
6	(35,340) tax	0.564	(19,932)
			121,559

* 3.791 – 0.909

The project should be undertaken as it results in a positive NPV.

(b)   NPV of after-tax contribution = £889,177 and overall NPV = £127,583

∴ The PV of after-tax contribution could fall by £127,583 before the recommendation above changes.

This represents a (127,583/889,177)×100%   = 14.3% fall

(c)   Tax implications

	Reducing balance £	Tax saved £	Year 1 £	Year 2 £	Benefit received Year 3 £	Year 4 £	Year 5 £	Year 6 £
Purchase price	550,000							
Yr 1 WDA (25%)	(137,500)	41,250	20,625	20,625				
Value at start of Yr 2	412,500							
Yr 2 WDA (25%)	(103,125)	30,938		15,469	15,469			
Value at start of Yr 3	309,375							
Yr 3 WDA (25%)	(77,344)	23,203			11,602	11,601		
Value at start of Yr 4	232,031							
Yr 4 WDA (25%)	(58,008)	17,402				8,701	8,701	
Value at start of Yr 5	174,023							
Yr 5 scrap proceeds	(70,195)*							
Balancing allowance	103,828	31,148					15,574	15,574
			20,625	36,094	27,071	20,302	24,275	15,574

* The **disposal value** of 10% of initial expenditure (£55,000) is a current price. The actual disposal value therefore needs to be **inflated** to determine the actual tax effects. WDAs are based on current prices.

∴ Disposal value = £55,000 × 1.05^5 = £70,195

NPV implications

We **discount at the money rate** as we are **dealing with actual cash flows**.

Year	Cashflow £	Discount factor 15.5%	PV £
1	20,625	0.866	17,861
2	36,094	0.750	27,071
3	27,071	0.649	17,569
4	20,302	0.562	11,410
5	24,275	0.487	11,822
6	15,574	0.421	6,557
		NPV	92,290

The NPV of the project would therefore **increase** by £92,290 **due to savings from tax implications**.

51   Section C: A Company

Text references. Asset replacement and sensitivity analysis are covered in Chapter 18.

Top tips. Part (a) Remember to split the calculation into manageable elements so do the tax depreciation on the purchase separately, then fit this into the calculation for the purchase NPV.

You can use annuities instead of individual discount factors to save a bit of time where cash flows are identical in later years. Part (d) The examiner remarked that many candidates completely ignored the tax implications in their answers despite this being noted in the scenario. So don't lose marks by not reading the question carefully.

In sensitivity analysis of a project being appraised using DCF, the assessment of sensitivity is always based on the NPV of the project and how this is affected by changes. So remember the simple formula to calculate

sensitivity in a variable: $\dfrac{\text{NPV of project}}{\text{PV of cashflow affected}} \times 100\%$.

In Part (d)(ii) we have shown two alternative approaches to calculating an IRR. Our first approach uses the BPP P1 Text formula for deriving an IRR (based on using a higher discount rate to determine a negative NPV). Our second approach shows that adopted in the CIMA model answer, which is based on using another positive NPV to determine the IRR, and involves subtracting the NPV at the higher rate of return from the NPV at the lower rate of return. Either method will earn you full marks as long as you apply your chosen method correctly.

Easy marks. Calculate WDAs first and slot these into your main workings. Remember to use proformas to set out your workings. You should have absolutely no problems in calculating the PV of sales in part (d)(i) and the second IRR needed in part (d)(ii).

Examiner's comments.

Common errors noted by the examiner include:

- Calculating an incorrect figure for the balancing allowance on the purchase option
- Calculating incorrect figures for the tax savings on both the purchase and the lease option
- Showing no tax relief for the initial lease payment

(a)   **Purchase**

	Year 0 £	Year 1 £	Year 2 £	Year 3 £	Year 4 £
Initial investment	(15,000)	–	–	–	–
Tax saved (W)		563	985	937	516
Trade in value				5,000	
	(15,000)	563	985	5,937	516
Discount rate at 15%	× 1.000	× 0.870	× 0.756	× 0.658	× 0.572
PV	(15,000)	490	745	3,907	295

NPV = £(9,563)

Working

Tax depreciation and tax saved

	£	Tax at 30% £	Year 1 £	Year 2 £	Year 3 £	Year 4 £
Machine cost	15,000					
Year 1 – WDA at 25%	(3,750)	1,125	563	563		
	11,250					
Year 2 – WDA at 25%	(2,813)	844		422	422	
	8,437					
Year 3						
Disposal	(5,000)					
Balancing allowance	3,437	1,031			515	516
Tax saved			563	985	937	516

Lease

Note: You are told that an initial payment is made for the lease. It is assumed that this was made at the end of year 0, which means that tax allowances were claimed immediately. In an exam, always state your assumptions on such issues if the question does not make it 100% clear.

	Year 0 £	Year 1 £	Year 2 £	Year 3 £	Year 4 £
Payment	(1,250)	(4,992)	(4,992)	(4,992)	–
Tax deduction at 30%	188	187	749	749	
		749	748	748	748
	(1,062)	(4,056)	(3,495)	(3,495)	748
Discount rate at 15%	× 1.000	× 0.870	× 0.756	× 0.658	× 0.572
PV	(1,062)	(3,529)	(2,642)	(2,300)	428

NPV = £ (9,105)

As it is less costly to lease the vehicle, the company should adopt this approach (a saving of (9,563 – 9,105) = £458).

(b)

	Replace after 1 year		Replace after 2 year		Replace after 3 year	
Year	Cash Flow $	PV @ 12% $	Cash flow $	PV @ 12% $	Cash flow $	PV @ 12% $
0	(14,000)	(14,000)	(14,000)	(14,000)	(14,000)	(14,000)
1	4,000*	3,572	(6,000)	(5,358)	(6,000)	(5,358)
2			(1,000)*	(797)	(8,000)	(6,376)
3					(4,500)*	(3,204)
PV over one cycle		(10,428)		(20,155)		(28,938)
Cumulative PV factor		÷0.893		÷1.690		÷2.402
Annualised equivalent cost		($11,677)		($11,926)		($12,047)

* Resale value – running costs

Year 1 10,000 - 5,000 - 1,000 = 4,000
Year 2 7,000 – 6,000 – 2,000 = (1,000)
Year 3 5,000 – 6,500 – 3,000 = (4,500)

The optimum replacement policy is the one with the lowest equivalent annual cost so the ovens should be replaced every year.

(c)   Inflation

We have ignored the effect of inflation in this solution. A zero rate of inflation is an unrealistic assumption.

Type of oven

We have assumed that the same type of oven will be available every year. Again, this may be an unrealistic assumption. Technology changes frequently and it is more likely that the ovens will be upgraded over the three years.

(d)   (i)   Sensitivity   = ($1.018m/$10,023.6m(w)) × 100%
            = 10.16%

Working

The PV of sales

Year	Cash flow $'000	Tax at 20% $'000	Net cash after tax $'000	Discount factor (7%)	Present value $'000
1	4,200	840	3,360	0.935	3,141.6
2	4,900	980	3,920	0.873	3,422.2
3	5,300	1,060	4,240	0.816	3,459.8
					10,023.6

(ii)   We need to calculate the **IRR of the project**. We know that the NPV using a discount rate of 7% is $1.018m.

To find IRR, we need to find another NPV at a **higher rate** than 7% and then use the IRR formula. Try to use a rate that is included in the present value tables provided in the exam so that you can obtain discount factors quickly.

Let's try a rate of 20%.

Year	Net cash flow $'000	Discount factor @ 20%	Present value $'000
1	1,350	0.833	1,125
2	1,800	0.694	1,249
3	1,150	0.579	666
			3,040

Tax is paid at 20% so the net PV after tax is $3,040,000 × 80% = $2,432,000.

Post tax NPV less initial investment   = $'000(2,432-2,000)

= $432,000

Then calculate the IRR of the project.

$$IRR = 7 + \left[\frac{1,018}{1,018 - 432} \times (20-7) \right]\% = 29.58\%$$

The cost of capital can therefore increase by 29.58 – 7 = 22.58 percentage points.

or: $\dfrac{22.58}{7} = 323\%$

Top tips. The mark allocation in part (d) was two marks for calculating the sensitivity of the project to changes in the selling price and three marks for the longer calculation of the sensitivity of the project to changes in the cost of capital.

---

52 Section C: SS Ltd

Text reference. You will find most of the information to answer this question in Chapters 15 to 18.

Top tips. You may have missed that fact that the annual maintenance costs are paid in advance. The first cash flow relating to maintenance therefore occurs at time 0 but we have assumed that the tax implications are first accounted for at time 1, so that the tax cash flows occur in time 1 and time 2. You may have taken the view that the cash flow occurs at time 0, and the tax is accounted for in time 0 too and so we have set out an alternative solution to cover this option.

Hopefully you noticed that because the two alternatives had different lives, they could not be compared directly and so annualised equivalents have to be calculated.

If you had read through the question before starting it you might have picked up on the fact that you would need the cash flows (including those due to tax) relating to contribution in part (c) and so it would have been a good idea to show these separately in part (a) to save you time later.

Easy marks. Part (a) required a fairly straightforward DCF analysis involving taxation. We recommend you lay out your answer in a series of tables as we have done so that both you and the marker can keep track of your workings.

(a)   <u>Recommendation</u>

The figures in the table below can be found in the workings that follow.

	NPV	Years	12% disc factor for 3/5 years	**Annualised** equivalent
Alternative 1	£48,308	3	2.402	£20,112
Alternative 2	£102,257	5	3.605	£28,365

SS Ltd should therefore **invest in alternative 2** as this maximises the return on the investment.

<u>Alternative 1</u>

Step 1 WDAs and balancing charges/allowances

Year		Reducing balance £
0	Purchase	100,000
1	WDA	(25,000)
	Value at start of year 2	75,000
2	WDA	(18,750)
	Value at start of year 3	56,250
3	Sale for scrap	(5,000)
	Balancing allowance	51,250

<u>Tax savings/payments due to WDA</u>

Yr of claim	Allowance £	Tax saved £	Tax saving Yr 1 £	Yr 2 £	Yr 3 £	Yr 4 £
1	25,000	7,500	3,750	3,750		
2	18,750	5,625		2,812	2,813	
3	51,250	15,375			7,687	7,688
			3,750	6,562	10,500	7,688

Step 2 Other tax flows

Yr for tax purposes	Cash flow £	Tax (due)/saved £	Tax (payment)/saving Yr 1 £	Yr 2 £	Yr 3 £	Yr 4 £
1	(24,000)	7,200	3,600	3,600		
	100,000	(30,000)	(15,000)	(15,000)		
2	(24,000)	7,200		3,600	3,600	
	100,000	(30,000)		(15,000)	(15,000)	
3	(24,000)	7,200			3,600	3,600
	100,000	(30,000)			(15,000)	(15,000)
			(11,400)	(22,800)	(22,800)	(11,400)

Step 3 Calculate NPV

Year	Server £	Other cash flows £	Tax (payment)/ saving on other cash flows £	Tax saved on capital allowances £	Net cash flow £	Discount factor 12%	PV of cash flow £
0	(100,000)	(24,000)			(124,000)	1.000	(124,000)
1		76,000*	(11,400)	3,750	68,350	0.893	61,037
2		76,000*	(22,800)	6,562	59,762	0.797	47,630
3	5,000	100,000	(22,800)	10,500	92,700	0.712	66,002
4			(11,400)	7,688	(3,712)	0.636	(2,361)
							48,308

*£((24,000) + 100,000)

Alternative solution

Other tax flows

Yr of claim	Cash flow	Tax (due)/saved	Tax (payment)/saving Yr 0	Yr 1	Yr 2	Yr 3	Yr 4
	£	£	£	£	£	£	£
0	(24,000)	7,200	3,600	3,600			
1	(24,000)	7,200		3,600	3,600		
	100,000	(30,000)		(15,000)	(15,000)		
2	(24,000)	7,200			3,600	3,600	
	100,000	(30,000)			(15,000)	(15,000)	
3	100,000	(30,000)				(15,000)	(15,000)
			3,600	(7,800)	(22,800)	(26,400)	(15,000)

Calculate NPV

Year	Server £	Other cash flows £	Tax (payment)/ saving on other cash flows £	Tax saved on capital allowances £	Net cash flow £	Discount factor 12%	PV of cash flow £
0	(100,000)	(24,000)	3,600		(120,400)	1.000	(120,400)
1		76,000*	(7,800)	3,750	71,950	0.893	64,251
2		76,000*	(22,800)	6,562	59,762	0.797	47,630
3	5,000	100,000	(26,400)	10,500	89,100	0.712	63,439
4			(15,000)	7,688	(7,312)	0.636	(4,650)
							50,270

*£((24,000) + 100,000)

Alternative 2

Step 1 WDAs and balancing charges/allowances

Year		Reducing balance £
0	Purchase	100,000
1	WDA	(25,000)
	Value at start of year 2	75,000
2	WDA	(18,750)
	Value at start of year 3	56,250
3	WDA	(14,063)
	Value at start of year 4	42,187
4	WDA	(10,547)
	Value at start of year 5	31,640
5	Sale for scrap	(3,000)
	Balancing allowance	28,640

Tax savings/payments of WDA

Yr of claim	Allowance	Tax saved	Tax saving Yr 1	Yr 2	Yr 3	Yr 4	Yr 5	Yr 6
	£	£	£	£	£	£	£	£
1	25,000	7,500	3,750	3,750				
2	18,750	5,625		2,812	2,813			
3	14,063	4,219			2,109	2,110		
4	10,547	3,164				1,582	1,582	
5	28,640	8,592					4,296	4,296
			3,750	6,562	4,922	3,692	5,878	4,296

Step 2 Other tax flows

Yr for tax purposes	Cash flow	Tax (due) /saved	Yr 1	Yr 2	Yr 3	Yr 4	Yr 5	Yr 6
					Tax (payment)/saving			
	£	£	£	£	£	£	£	£
1	75,000*	(22,500)	(11,250)	(11,250)				
2	75,000	(22,500)		(11,250)	(11,250)			
3	75,000	(22,500)			(11,250)	(11,250)		
4	75,000	(22,500)				(11,250)	(11,250)	
5	75,000	(22,500)					(11,250)	(11,250)
			(11,250)	(22,500)	(22,500)	(22,500)	(22,500)	(11,250)

*£((30,000) + 105,000) = £75,000

Step 3 Calculate NPV

Year	Server	Other cash flows	Tax (payment)/ saving on other cash flows	Tax saved on capital allowances	Net cash flow	Discount factor	PV of cash flow
	£	£	£	£	£	12%	£
0	(100,000)	(30,000)			(130,000)	1.000	(130,000)
1		75,000	(11,250)	3,750	67,500	0.893	60,278
2		75,000	(22,500)	6,562	59,062	0.797	47,072
3		75,000	(22,500)	4,922	57,422	0.712	40,884
4		75,000	(22,500)	3,692	56,192	0.636	35,738
5	3,000	105,000	(22,500)	5,878	91,378	0.567	51,811
6			(11,250)	4,296	(6,954)	0.507	(3,526)
							102,257

Alternative solution

Other tax flows

Yr of claim	Cash flow	Tax (due) /saved	Yr 0	Yr 1	Yr 2	Yr 3	Yr 4	Yr 5	Yr 6
					Tax (payment)/saving				
	£	£	£	£	£	£	£		
0	(30,000)	9,000	4,500	4,500					
1	75,000*	(22,500)		(11,250)	(11,250)				
2	75,000	(22,500)			(11,250)	(11,250)			
3	75,000	(22,500)				(11,250)	(11,250)		
4	75,000	(22,500)					(11,250)	(11,250)	
5	105,000	(31,500)						(15,750)	(15,750)
			4,500	(6,750)	(22,500)	(22,500)	(22,500)	(27,000)	(15,750)

*£((30,000) + 105,000) = £75,000

Alternative solution continued

Calculate NPV

Year	Server £	Other cash flows £	Tax (payment)/ saving on other cash flows £	Tax saved on capital allowances £	Net cash flow £	Discount factor 12%	PV of cash flow £
0	(100,000)	(30,000)	4,500		(125,500)	1.000	(125,500)
1		75,000	(6,750)	3,750	72,000	0.893	64,296
2		75,000	(22,500)	6,562	59,062	0.797	47,072
3		75,000	(22,500)	4,922	57,422	0.712	40,884
4		75,000	(22,500)	3,692	56,192	0.636	35,738
5	3,000	105,000	(27,000)	5,878	86,878	0.567	49,260
6			(15,750)	4,296	(11,454)	0.507	(5,807)
							105,943

(b)   **Sensitivity analysis** is a term used to describe any **technique** whereby **decision options are tested for their vulnerability to changes in any variable**.

It can be used to **analyse the risk** surrounding a capital investment and enables an assessment to be made of **how responsive the investment's NPV is to changes in the variables that are used to calculate that NPV**.

The **basic approach** involves **calculating an NPV under alternative assumptions** (for example different sales volumes, different costs of capital) to **determine how sensitive it is to changing conditions**, thereby indicating those variables to which the NPV is most sensitive (most critical) and the **extent to which those variables may change** before the investment decision would change (ie a positive NPV becomes a negative NPV).

Once these **critical variables** have been identified, **management** should **review** them to assess whether or not there is a strong possibility of events occurring which will lead to a change in the investment decision. Management should also pay particular **attention to controlling** those variables to which the NPV is particularly sensitive, once the decision has been taken to proceed with the investment.

Sensitivity analysis can also be applied to an investment's accounting rate of return or its payback in much the same way.

The approach does have **limitations**, however.

(i)   It requires that changes in each key variable are isolated but management is likely to be more interested in the combination of the effects of changes in two or more key variables. Looking at factors in isolation is unrealistic since they are often interdependent.

(ii)   It does not examine the probability that any particular variation in costs or revenues might occur.

(c)

Year	Contribution £	Tax due £	Cash flow £	Discount factor 12%	Present value £
1	100,000	(15,000)	85,000	0.893	75,905
2	100,000	(30,000)	70,000	0.797	55,790
3	100,000	(30,000)	70,000	0.712	49,840
4		(15,000)	(15,000)	0.636	(9,540)
					171,995

The annualised equivalent of the contribution is £171,995/discount factor for 12% over 3 years = £171,995/2.402 = £71,605

The difference between the overall annualised equivalents of alternatives 1 and 2 as calculated in (a) is £(20,112 – 28,365) = £8,253.

So if the AE of contribution from alternative 1 increases by more than £8,253 to £(71,605 + 8,253) = £79,858 (an increase of (8,253/71,605) × 100% = 11.5%, alternative 1 will become the better option.

53   Section A: Dealing with uncertainty in analysis

1   EV = (500 × 0.5) + (600 × 0.1) + (400 × (1 – 0.5 – 0.1))= 470

2   Perfect information is calculated by taking the difference between the EV of the best decision option (predicted on the basis of the perfect information) and the highest EV of profit if the perfect information is not available.

3   D   **A** is not a drawback because the expected value averages out losses and profits according to their probabilities and so does not concentrate on avoiding losses.

   B is not a drawback because the expected value averages all the outcomes of a particular course of action and so is not solely concerned with the highest profit.

   C is not a drawback because, as far as is practical, the expected value will take into account all outcomes, though the importance it then allocates to them does depend on the likelihood of occurrence.

   D is a drawback because the calculation of expected value rates losses at their numerical value but in some circumstances making a loss might be disastrous to the decision maker, out of all proportion to the actual sum involved.

4   C   A profit of £1,000 and a loss of £3,000 are less than or equal to a profit of £1,000 and so the overall probability of a profit of £1,000 or less is 0.3 + 0.21 = 0.51.

   If you chose **option A**, you do not appear to have taken the loss of £3,000 into account.

   If you chose **option B** you have worked out the probability of there being a profit greater than £1,000.

   If you chose **option D** you do not appear to have taken the profit of £1,000 into account.

5   B   **A**: The EV at E is £1,700,000, whereas the EV at F is £1,600,000. Cost of sales should be minimised, so decision 4 would be chosen.

   B: The EV at C would be £1,600,000 (the *lower* of £1,700,000 and £1,600,000) while the EV at D is £920,000 and so the EV at B is (£1,600,000 × 0.5) + (£920,000 × 0.5) = £1,260,000.

   C: The EV of decision 1 is £1,260,000, whereas the known value of decision 2 is £1,200,000. The lower figure is taken because the figures relate to cost of sales.

   D: The EV at D = (£1,400,000 × 0.2) + (£800,000 × 0.8) = £920,000

6   EV of L = £'000 (0.2 × £500 + 0.5 × £470 + 0.3 × £550) = £500,000
   EV of M = £'000 (0.2 × £400 + 0.5 × £550 + 0.3 × £570) = £526,000
   EV of N = £'000 (0.2 × £450 + 0.5 × £400 + 0.3 × £475) = £432,500
   EV of O = £'000 (0.2 × £360 + 0.5 × £400 + 0.3 × £420) = £398,000
   EV of P = £'000 (0.2 × £600 + 0.5 × £500 + 0.3 × £425) = £497,500

   Project M should be undertaken as it has the highest EV.

7   Value of perfect information = EV with perfect information – EV without information

   With no information, EV would be £526,000

   <u>With perfect information</u>

Forecast market conditions	*Probability*	*Project chosen*	*Net cash inflow* £'000	*EV of inflow* £'000
Poor	0.2	P	600	120
Good	0.5	M	550	275
Excellent	0.3	M	570	171
EV with perfect information				566

   ∴ Value of perfect information = £'000 (566 – 526)
                                   = £40,000

8     $Y_x = aX^b$
     a = 22 minutes
     b = log 0.8/log2 = – 0.3219

     If X = 4, Y_4 = 22 × $4^{-0.3219}$ = 14.08 mins
     ∴ Time taken for four units = 4 × 14.08 = 56.32 mins

     If X = 3, Y_3 = 22 × $3^{-0.3219}$ = 15.45 mins

     ∴ Time taken for three units = 3 × 15.45 mins = 46.35 mins

     ∴ Time taken for fourth unit = (56.32 – 46.35) mins = 9.97 minutes

9 $Y = aX^{-0.415}$

  a = 6 hours

  If the cumulative number of assignments (X) = 7, the cumulative average time per assignment (Y)
                        = 6 × $7^{-0.415}$

  ∴ Total time for seven assignments = 7 × 6 × $7^{-0.415}$ = 18.73 hours
  If the cumulative number of assignments (X) = 6, the cumulative average time per assignment (Y)
                         = 6 × $6^{-0.415}$

  ∴ Total time for 6 assignments = 6 × 6 × $6^{-0.415}$ = 17.11 hours
  ∴ Time for seventh assignment = 18.73 – 17.11 = 1.62 hours

54 Section B: Dealing with uncertainty in analysis

> **Text references.** Risk and uncertainty are covered in Chapter 19.
>
> **Top tips.** If you are struggling to provide a clear explantion of a decision rule, such as the maximum basis in part (d) then make up some simple figures as a demonstration. Then the marker is able to see that you do understand how the rule is applied.
>
> **Easy marks.** Question involving probabilities often require a large number of fairly simple calculations. Think about the layout of your answer before you begin and use neat, clear tabulations so that the marker is able to award you marks for the method that you use and for the interim calculations.

(a) Expected Value of Total Costs

  = Expected Value of Variable Costs + Expected Value of Fixed Costs.

Variable Costs	Probability	Expected Value	Fixed Costs	Probability	Expected Value
$560,000	0.3	$168,000	$440,000	0.15	$66,000
$780,000	0.5	$390,000	$640,000	0.55	$352,000
$950,000	0.2	$190,000	$760,000	0.30	$228,000
		$748,000			$646,000

  Expected Value of Total Costs = $748,000 + $646,000

            = $1,394,000

  Standard Deviation:

  Step 1 **Produce a 2-way data table showing all possible combinations of Fixed and Variable Costs, and thus all possible outcomes for Total Costs:**

Fixed Costs	Variable Costs		
	$560,000	$780,000	$950,000
$440,000	1,000,000	1,220,000	1,390,000
$640,000	1,200,000	1,420,000	1,590,000
$760,000	1,320,000	1,540,000	1,710,000

Step 2 Calculate $\Sigma\left(x-\bar{x}\right)^2$ $\left(\text{where } \bar{x} = \$1,394,000\right)$

x ($'000)	$\left(x-\bar{x}\right)^2$ ($'000)
1,000	155,236
1,200	37,636
1,220	30,276
1,320	5,476
1,390	16
1,420	676
1,540	21,316
1,590	38,416
1,710	99,856
	388,904

Step 3 Calculate standard deviation (where n=9)

$$SD = \sqrt{\frac{388,904}{9}}$$

$$= 207.874 \text{ or } \underline{\$207,874}$$

(b) (i) <u>Explanation of expected net present value and standard deviation</u>

Expected net present value (ENPV). This measures the sum of the possible range of outcomes for each campaign multiplied by their probabilities. It does not tell management about the range of values however which would allow them to assess the likelihood of profit or loss. **Standard deviation (SD)**. Risk can be measured by the possible range of outcomes around the ENPV of the campaigns. One way of doing this is by calculating the SD of the ENPV. Managers can then assess the campaigns looking at the riskiness as well as the single measure of ENPV.

(ii) <u>How would the company use this data to choose between investments?</u>

One way of ranking the three campaigns is to compare their ENPVs and choose the campaign with the highest ENPV. This means that campaign K should be chosen with a ENPV of $800,000. Management may be **risk averse** in which case they would choose a campaign where the SD is smaller. This risk profile would be satisfied by choosing campaign J with a SD of $35,000. A more risk seeking management might opt for a campaign where the SD was higher but the outcomes were also higher. They would opt for campaign K which has a SD of $105,000 but also a higher ENPV. Management **would not opt for campaign** L as the ENPV is lower than campaign K and the SD is higher than campaign J.

(c) The decision rule in **minimax regret** considers the extent to which we might come to regret an action we had chosen.

Regret for any combination of action and circumstances	=	Payoff for **best** action in those circumstances	–	Payoff of the action **actually taken** in those circumstances

An alternative term for regret is **opportunity loss**. We may apply the rule by considering the maximum opportunity loss associated with each course of action and choosing the course which offers the smallest maximum. If we choose an action which turns out not to be the best in the actual circumstances, we have lost an opportunity to make the extra profit we could have made by choosing the best action.

Here is a payoff table for the decisions that the baker can make.

		Batches baked		
		10	11	12
	10	500	480	460
Batches sold	11	500	550	530
	12	500	550	600
Best outcome		500	550	600

		Batches baked		
		10	11	12
	10	None	(20)*	(40)
Batches sold	11	(50)**	None	(20)
	12	(100)***	(50)	None
Max regret		100	50	40

* 500-480
** 550-500
***600-500

Best outcome: choose outcome with the minimum regret

Minimum regret is 40, which means that 12 batches should be baked.

(d) (i) Expected values are a weighted average result

The calculation of an expected value (EV) produces a **weighted average** result of all possible outcomes, where each outcome is weighted by the probability of its occurrence. This is a valuable measure where **outcomes will occur many times over**, such as the number of customers arriving each day over a period of three months.

The limitation of expected values in a once-only decision

However the use of expected values is of **limited usefulness for a once-only decision,** perhaps where the decision is based on the prediction of the number of customers arriving on a particular day. This is because the EV **does not take account of the range of possible outcomes** that could occur on a particular day. If there is a wide range of possible outcomes then actual outcome could be very different from the EV on a particular day.

Therefore for a once-only decision with a wide range of possible outcomes it is probably preferable to apply other techniques to analyse the uncertainty involved.

(ii) The maximin basis

The maximin basis is short for 'maximising the minimum possible outcome'. This means that the decision maker will select the option that has the **best outcome even if the worst situation arises**. For example with the maximin rule option B would be selected from the following range of options.

	Option A	Option B	Option C
	Profit/(loss)	Profit/(loss)	Profit/(loss)
	£000	£000	£000
Best possible outcome	600	280	450
Worst possible outcome	(120)	80	(10)

Option B has the highest result if the worst possible outcome occurs. Thus a risk averse manager would select this option to avoid what might be disastrous consequences from the low outcomes for A and C, even though both these options offer the possibility of higher returns.

(e)

Demand (a)	Probability (b)	Revenue (a) × £45	Variable cost per unit (c)	Probability (d)	Total variable costs (a) × (c)	Contribution	Joint probability (b) × (d)
Units		£'000	£		£'000	£'000	
100,000	0.45	4,500	20	0.40	2,000	2,500	0.18
100,000	0.45	4,500	18	0.60	1,800	2,700*	0.27
120,000	0.55	5,400	20	0.40	2,400	3,000*	0.22
120,000	0.55	5,400	18	0.60	2,160	3,240*	0.33
							1.00

* Contribution higher than current level of contribution of £90,000 × £(50 – 21) = £2,610,000

∴ Probability = 0.27 + 0.22 + 0.33 = 0.82

(f)   EV of profit   = EV of contribution – fixed costs

                            = £'000 ((0.18 × 2,500) + (0.27 × 2,700) + (0.22 × 3,000) + (0.33 × 3,240))

                            – £1,200,000

                            = £1,708,200

55 Section C: Theatre

Text references. The information to answer this question can be found in Chapter 19 of the Study Text.

Top tips. The calculation in part (a) involves **two** variables, audience size and the contribution from confectionery sales. So you need to set out your calculations in a table like the one we have used. Remember that the probabilities used should add up to 1. If they don't you have missed something out.

Part (b) asks you to use a **two-way data table** to show the profit values that could arise. If you don't know what two variables to use think what factors in the scenario affect profit. Of course the relevant factors will be the fee, the audience size and the confectionery sales. The price of the ticket is fixed. Remember that the question asks for **profit** so you will need to deduct the fee of $10,000 from each possible total revenue. Take this information from the table in part (a).

Part (c) wants you to combine your answer from part (b) with the probabilities given to evaluate financial risks including **the probability of making a profit.** Set out your workings like we have done below so you can easily distinguish the probabilities asked for.

Easy marks. Setting out your workings in tables as in our suggested answer will ensure that you don't miss vital information and lose marks through carelessness. The two-way data table should be easy enough to draw up.

Examiners' comments. The examiner commented that in many cases correct figures were not supported by meaningful explanations. Remember that you will often be required to explain the meaning of the results of your calculations. Revising only how to perform the calculations is completing only a part of the task.

Further question practice. If you struggled with producing a two-way data table and calculating the value of perfect information in this question, you should try question 60 next.

Marking scheme

		Marks
(a)	Expected value of confectionery sales per person	1
	Expected value of total income	2
	Expected profit	1
	Clear advice	1
		5
(b)	Correct structure of two way data table	2
	Correct outcome values	3
		5
(c)	Comment on range of possible outcomes	2
	Probability of breaking even and making profit	2
	Expected values for each outcome	2
	Discussion of skewed distribution and risk	3
		9
(d)	Maximum expected value with perfect information	4
	Value of perfect information	2
		6

(a) Expected audience size:

Audience size	Probability	EV
300	0.5	150
400	0.3	120
500	0.2	100
		370

Expected value of confectionery sales

Contribution/person	Probability	EV
$3	0.3	0.90
$5	0.5	2.50
$10	0.2	2.00
		5.40

Expected spend per person
= Ticket price + EV of confectionery sales
= $25 + 5.40
= $30.40

Expected total spend
= $30.40 × expected number of people
= $30.40 × 370
= $11,248

Expected profit
= $11,248 – fixed costs of $10,000
= $1,248

As the theatre is expected to make a profit of $1,248, it is financially worthwhile to engage MS for the concert.

(b) Two-way data table for profit values

Two-way data table showing profit for a range of audience size based on $25 ticket per head, and confectionery sales.

		Audience size		
		300	400	500
		$'000	$'000	$'000
	$3/head	(1,600)	1,200	4,000
Confectionery sales	$5/head	(1,000)	2,000	5,000
	$10/head	500	4,000	7,500

(c) Using the two-way data table

If a probability distribution can be applied to either or both of the variables in our data table, a revised table can be prepared to provide improved management information.

Table of total contributions

The shaded area on this table shows the possible total contributions and the associated joint probabilities. We have also calculated the EV for each outcome. (This will be used in part (d) of the question when we calculate the value of perfect information.)

Audience size			300	400	500
Probability			0.5	0.3	0.2

Contribution from confectionery sales	Probability	EV			
$3	0.3		$(1,600)k	$1,200k	$4,000k
			0.15	0.09	0.06
		EV	(240)	108	240
$5	0.5		$(1,000)k	$2,000k	$5,000k
			0.25	0.15	0.10
		EV	(250)	300	500
$10	0.2		$500k	$4,000k	$7,500k
			0.10	0.06	0.04
		EV	50	240	300

We have taken the data from the table in part (b) and applied the probabilities given in the question to each possible combination of audience size and confectionery contribution. This table shows us some useful information.

Thus, taking the combinations where the outcome is negative and adding the associated probabilities we can work out the likelihood of making a loss. This is 0.15 + 0.25 = 0.40 or 40% and **so the probability of breaking even and making a profit is 60%.**

It is also possible for management to see that the distribution of possible outcomes is skewed, since the probability of earning a profit higher than the expected value of $1,248 is 41% (0.15 + 0.06 + 0.06 + 0.10 + 0.04).

Looking at the range and distribution of possible outcomes in this way enables management to understand better the risk associated with the decision they are making.

(d)

> **Top tips.** The requirements of Part (d) are a bit unclear. When a decision is made involving perfect information, the best decision option will always be chosen. The best decision option is not known but is calculated by taking the best outcome for a variety of decisions, then calculate their EVs and compare with the EV without perfect information. In our case that has already been calculated in part(a) as $1,248.
>
> With perfect information, the theatre would not engage MS if 300 people attend and the contribution was $3 or $5 from confectionery. This would be the best outcome and **one that is not already known**. Look back at the two-way data table you have drawn up in part(c). This should provide you with the information you need.
>
> So to do this, you would need to add up the combinations of confectionery sales and audience size that result in a profit and use their EVs to get the value of perfect information based on profit.

Maximum price for perfect information that management should pay

Using the table above:

Audience size		300	400	500
Probability		0.5	0.3	0.2
Contribution from confectionery sales	Probability	EV	EV	EV
$3	0.3	0*	108	240
$5	0.5	0*	300	500
$10	0.2	50	240	300

* These EVs are entered as 0 rather than the negative contributions shown in the box above as the business would not run the concerts with negative contributions and would therefore avoid losses.

Total EV =	$1,738
Less: EV of contribution	
From part (a)	(1,248)
Value of perfect information	$ 490

56 Section C: Health Clinic

Text references. You can refer to Chapter 19 for help in drawing up the decision tree and EVs.

Top tips. Part (a) requires a decision tree so you need to consider the alternative decisions and plot these based on the levels of demand for each alternative and for the three years.

Remember that a **decision point** (eg to launch or not to launch) **is shown as a square. The outcomes** from this decision are **shown with their probabilities** [these must always add up to 1!] and any values which are attached. **Outcomes are shown as circles.**

The examiner gave one mark for identifying the three alternatives, two marks for plotting year 1 outcomes and three marks for plotting the outcomes of the rest of the project.

Easy marks. If you feel a bit unsteady start with part (c), where you should be able to pick up a couple of marks. In theory there should be some easy marks to be had on part (a), as no analysis is required on the decision tree – you simply have to draw it. Just using the correct symbols and drawing it from left to right - starting with the decision being considered and then the options arising from this – will get you some marks.

Examiner's comments. Part (a) was, on the whole, badly answered and few candidates showed a good knowledge of decision trees.

Part (b) could be answered in a variety of ways but candidates often just presented a page of figures without any clear analysis.

Part (c) was often answered generally, without reference to the scenario in the question.

Further question practice. If you struggle to draw the decision tree you should try Question 58 next.

(a)   <u>Decision tree</u>

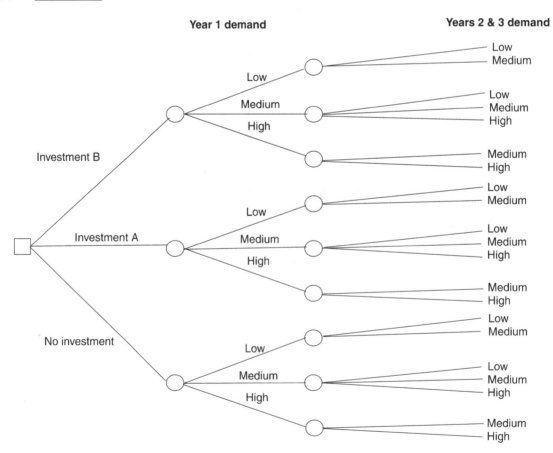

(b)

> **Top tips.** Part (b) carries 15 marks so represents the bulk of marks on this question. You need to cost out the three alternatives using the cost data in the question and determine expected values for the three levels of demand. See our table below for a suggested layout to this part of the question. A clear table of workings is vital in these Section C questions.
>
> Let's have a look at a couple of the tricky bits. You may find it difficult to understand where the probabilities for years 2 and 3 come from. Let's take the probability for a low outcome. In years 2 and 3 there are three probabilities of a low demand, 40%, 30% and 0%. However these follow three possible outcomes in year 1 being 30%, 50% and 20%. So the combinations are:
>
> Low outcome year 1, low outcome years 2 and 3 gives 30% x 40% = 12%
>
> Medium outcome year 1, low outcome years 2 and 3 gives 50% x 30% = 15%
>
> High outcome year 1, low outcome years 2 and 3 gives 20% x 0% = 0%
>
> The total of course is 27%. Try this for yourself with the other outcomes for years 2 and 3.
>
> Secondly, with the investment decision for Facility A, although there is no capacity to meet demand at the high level, remember that this demand is still an outcome and may need to be met. So you need to use the figures for the cost of providing additional facilities on a yearly contract basis (which is how the demand would be met). Therefore the cost at the high level of demand would be £150,000 + £350,000 = £500,000.
>
> Finally, remember to multiply the EV for years 2 and 3 in the table by two as there are two years. The examiner remarked that candidates' answers to this part of the question were better than answers to part (a). Five marks were awarded for identifying the costs under each alternative, three marks each for the probability of each outcome and expected cost of each outcome and the balance for stating the investment required.

Investment decision

Facility A

Demand	Probability	Year 1 Cost £'000	EV £'000	Probability	Years 2 and 3 Cost £'000	EV £'000	Total £'000
Low	0.3	250	75	0.27	250	67.50	
Medium	0.5	350	175	0.44	350	154.00	
High	0.2	500	100	0.29	500	145.00	
						366.50	
			350	Multiply EV by 2, as this EV occurs in both years		733.00	1,083
					Investment		500
					Total PV of cost		1,583

Facility B

Demand	Probability	Year 1 Cost £'000	EV £'000	Probability	Years 2 & 3 Cost £'000	EV £'000	Total £'000
Low	0.3	300	90	0.27	300	81	
Medium	0.5	350	175	0.44	350	154	
High	0.2	400	80	0.29	400	116	
						351	
			345	Multiply EV by 2, as this EV occurs in both years		702	1,047
					Investment		800
					Total PV of cost		1,847

No further investment

Demand	Probability	Year 1 Cost £'000	EV £'000	Probability	Years 2 & 3 Cost £'000	EV £'000	Total £'000
Low	0.3	300	90	0.27	300	81.00	
Medium	0.5	400	200	0.44	400	176.00	
High	0.2	550	110	0.29	550	159.50	
						416.50	
			400		X 2 years	833	1,233
					Investment		
					Total PV of cost		1,233

On the basis of the calculations shown above, the **decision** that should be made is **not to invest** but to take on additional facilities on a yearly contract basis as this option has the **lowest PV of cost**.

Top tips. Part (c) requires you to briefly list and discuss non-financial factors for four marks so a couple of well made points should suffice. However, remember that the examiner remarked that most candidates gave general answers and did not apply their analysis to the scenario.

(c)   In the context of this organisation, which is a **not for profit** organisation, the manager must consider the **objectives** of the organisation and how these all balance with each other.

One important objective is the **service** provided by the clinic. For instance, does it aim to offer **free treatment** to anyone who turns up, whatever the cost? If this were the overriding objective then Facility B would be the better choice despite the calculations made above, as this enables all levels of demand to be met.

The manager may call upon the **additional facilities** as a top-up should levels of demand exceed those catered for by other means. If this is the case, this would allow **greater flexibility but with a loss of control**. This could mean problems with **quality and reliability** with if services are outside management's control.

Furthermore, if the **yearly contract** was chosen, this could have an **adverse motivational effect** on employees. They may regard this as short-termism (ie that the clinic considers short-term cost objectives above longer-term operations and investment).

57 Section C: MP Organisation

Text references. Refer to Chapters 16 and 19 to help answer this question.

Top tips. There are two parts to this question. Part (a) requires you to calculate NPVs based on a range of outcomes which means you need to take the PV for cost and revenues based on the expected costs and revenues and flex these for the anticipated variations in sales and costs.

In part (a), nine marks were available for calculating the PV of relevant production costs, non-production costs and revenues at the three levels of sales demand.

Another four marks could be earned for drawing up a table of the combinations of revenues and costs and NPV.

The remaining marks were available for discussion and recommendations. In part (b), five marks each were possible for discussing probabilities and simulation as techniques applied to problem solving of this type.

Easy marks. It is easiest to approach the question this way so you can draw up a table as we have done below with all of the possible combinations. There are nine in all which you would expect with three possible levels of sales and three possible levels of costs.

Remember to discuss your findings and make a recommendation to MP.

The second part of the question requires a written answer on expected NPVs and simulation as these are used in estimating probabilities. You will find it easier if you use illustrations from your calculations in part (a) to explain how ENPV and simulation models work.

See that the question requires two formats – in part (a), it requires a calculation and in part (b), it requires notes. Always look at what the required output is and tailor your approach to that.

(a)   Projected cash flows – project at 100% revenues and costs

	Year 0 $'000	Year 1 $'000	Year 2 $'000	Year 3 $'000	Year 4 $'000	Year 5 $'000	Total PV $'000
Sales (W1)		100	150	112.50	50	30	
Discount factor at 15%		x 0.870	x 0.756	x 0.658	x 0.572	x 0.497	
PV of cash in flow		87	113	74	29	15	318
Certain costs							
Fixed costs (director's fees)	(100)						
Advertising and PR	(15)	(10)	(10)	(5)	(5)	(5)	
	(115)	(10)	(10)	(5)	(5)	(5)	
Discount factor at 15%	x 1.000	x 0.870	x 0.756	x 0.658	x 0.572	x 0.497	
PV of cash out flow	(115)	(9)	(8)	(3)	(3)	(2)	(140)
Uncertain costs (W2)	(120)						
Discount at 15%	x 1.000						
PV of cash flow	(120)						(120)
NPV of cash flow							58

Workings

(1)   Sales

Year	Gross revenue $'000		MP's revenue $'000
1	400	× 25%	100
2	600	× 25%	150
3	450	× 25%	112.5
4	50	× 100%	50
5	30	× 100%	30

(2)   Uncertain costs

	$'000
Set design	10
Costumes and wardrobe	20
Actors' fees	50
Musician/songwriter for sound track	5
Camera and equipment hire	20
Actors' travel and accommodation costs	10
Other production costs	5
	120

Projected cash flows – project with varying revenues and costs

	$'000	$'000	$'000	$'000	$'000	$'000	$'000	$'000	$'000
Present value at	100%	100%	100%	120%	120%	120%	80%	80%	80%
Sales	318	318	318	382	382	382	254	254	254
Costs									
Certain	(140)	(140)	(140)	(140)	(140)	(140)	(140)	(140)	(140)
Uncertain									
90%	(108)			(108)			(108)		
100%		(120)			(120)			(120)	
110%	–	–	(132)	–	–	(132)	–	–	(132)
NPV of cash flow	70	58	46	134	122	110	6	(6)	(18)

This analysis shows that there are a range of possible NPVs depending on the combination of expected sales and cost increases or decreases. The range is between a negative NPV of $18,000 which is definitely not acceptable to a positive NPV of $134,000 which would be acceptable. So the most likely, optimistic and pessimistic cost and revenue values are as follows.

Outcome	NPV
	$000
pessimistic	(18)
optimistic	134
most likely	58

It is also possible to use sensitivity analysis to look at the cashflows that are most vulnerable to change and that would need to change the least to make the NPV reduce to zero.

(b)   Notes for the management meeting on expected NPV and simulation

Notes

(i)   The easiest way to explain expected NPVs (ENPVs) is to show an example of how these are calculated using the film project as our example. What ENPVs show is the expected NPV where a range of outcomes exist that have known probabilities. Therefore it measures risk which can be quantified rather than uncertainty which cannot.

Thus, taking our earlier example.

Sales revenue		318	254	382
Probability		0.5	0.1	0.4
Costs	Probability			
260	0.6	58[1]	(6)[1]	122[1]
248	0.3	70[2]	6[2]	134[2]
272	0.1	46[3]	(18)[3]	110[3]
	EV[4]	30.20	(0.36)	49.76

Expected NPV = $79.600

Workings

(1)   When costs = 260 and
  (a)   Sales = 318 :   Contribution = 58   (318 – 260)
  (b)   Sales = 254 :   Contribution = (6)   (254 – 260)
  (c)   Sales = 382 :   Contribution = 122   (382 – 260)

(2)   When costs = 248 and
  (a)   Sales = 318 :   Contribution = 70
  (b)   Sales = 254 :   Contribution = 6
  (c)   Sales = 382 :   Contribution = 134

(3)   When costs = 272 and
  (a)   Sales = 318 :   Contribution = 46
  (b)   Sale = 254 :   Contribution = (18)
  (c)   Sales = 382 :   Contribution = 110

(4)   Expected value = Σ(contribution × probability of sales revenue × probability of costs)

(i)	$(58 \times 0.5 \times 0.6) + (70 \times 0.5 \times 0.3) + (46 \times 0.5 \times 0.1)$ =	30.20
(ii)	$((6) \times 0.1 \times 0.6) + (6 \times 0.1 \times 0.3) + ((18) \times 0.1 \times 0.1)$ =	(0.36)
(iii)	$(122 \times 0.4 \times 0.6) + (134 \times 0.4 \times 0.3) + (110 \times 0.4 \times 0.1)$ =	49.76
	Expected NPV =	79.60

Of course with other probabilities the ENPV would be quite different and so it does depend very much on the expected probabilities assigned to each outcome.

(ii)   Simulation models can be used to assess risk using random numbers assigned to probabilities. These are particularly suitable where there are many variables with uncertain outcomes. Continuing with our example:

Sales revenue has three possible outcomes based on probabilities of say 50%, 10% and 40%.

Sales revenue PV $'000	Probability (say)	Assign random numbers
254	0.10	00–09
318	0.50	10–59
382	0.40	60–99

A random number generator could give numbers say 19007174604721296802. These would then be matched to the random numbers assigned to each probability and values assigned to PV based on this.

Likewise, costs have three possible outcomes being $248k, $260k and $272k. In the same way probabilities could have random numbers assigned and so combinations of both sales and costs generated for cash flow outcomes.

Costs PV $'000	Probability (say)	Assign random numbers
248	0.30	00 – 29
260	0.60	30 – 89
272	0.10	90 – 99

As the random numbers generated give 10 possible outcomes, this gives ten periods of sales and costs on which to base data. Thus

Random number	Sales revenue PV $'000	Costs PV $'000	NPV $'000
19	318	248	70
00	254	248	6
71	382	260	122
74	382	260	122
60	382	260	122
47	318	260	58
21	318	248	70
29	318	260	58
68	382	260	122
02	254	248	6

58 Section C: RY Ltd

Text reference. You will find most of the information to answer this question in Chapter 19.

Top tips. In (b)(i), we do not need to apply the probabilities relating to demand levels as we know that the market is pessimistic and hence we know what the demand will be at the three prices.

Part (b)(ii) is tricky. It requires you to calculate the value of perfect information. In other words, you need to work out the difference between the EV as calculated in (a) when no information about the state of the market is known, and the EV the organisation could expect to earn if accurate information about the state of the market were available. The latter requires you to calculate an EV for each market state on the assumption that that market will occur and hence the price charged should be the one that maximises contribution given that market state. The probabilities of each market state occurring are then applied, the EVs summed and an overall EV determined.

Bear in mind that you would not be penalised in part (b) for the use of incorrect probabilities derived in part (a).

Easy marks. The decision tree in part (a) was not difficult to draw. Remember you need to start with a decision. Each alternative set of probabilities should sum to 1.

(a)

Price	Demand		Variable cost	Contribution	Combined probability	EV of contribution
			£5	£6,000*	0.2 × 0.6 = 0.12	£720.00**
		80 / 0.2	0.6			
			£6	£5,920	0.2 × 0.4 = 0.08	£473.60
			0.4			
			£5	£7,500	0.6 × 0.6 = 0.36	£2,700.00**
		100 / 0.6	0.6			
			£6	£7,400	0.6 × 0.4 = 0.24	£1,776.00
			0.4			
			£5	£11,250	0.2 × 0.6 = 0.12	£1,350.00
		150 / 0.2	0.6			
			£6	£11,100	0.2 × 0.4 = 0.08	£888.00
			0.4			
£80					EV of contribution from price of £80	£7,907.60
			£5	£5,100	0.2 × 0.6 = 0.12	£612.00
		60 / 0.2	0.6			
			£6	£5,040	0.2 × 0.4 = 0.08	£403.20
			0.4			
			£5	£7,650	0.6 × 0.6 = 0.36	£2,754.00
£90		90 / 0.6	0.6			
			£6	£7,560	0.6 × 0.4 = 0.24	£1,814.40
			0.4			
			£5	£12,750	0.2 × 0.6 = 0.12	£1,530.00
		150 / 0.2	0.6			
			£6	£12,600	0.2 × 0.4 = 0.08	£1,008.00
			0.4			
					EV of contribution from price of £90	£8,121.60
			£5	£2,850	0.2 × 0.6 = 0.12	£342.00
£100		30 / 0.2	0.6			
			£6	£2,820	0.2 × 0.4 = 0.08	£225.60
			0.4			
			£5	£7,600	0.6 × 0.6 = 0.36	£2,736.00
		80 / 0.6	0.6			
			£6	£7,520	0.6 × 0.4 = 0.24	£1,804.80
			0.4			
			£5	£11,400	0.2 × 0.6 = 0.12	£1,368.00
		120 / 0.2	0.6			
			£6	£11,280	0.2 × 0.4 = 0.08	£902.40
			0.4			
					EV of contribution from price of £90	£7,378.80

* £(80 - 5) × 80
** £6,000 × 0.12

The optimum selling price is £90 as this results in the highest EV of contribution.

(b) (i) <u>EVs if the market is pessimistic</u>

Price	Demand	EV of contribution
£80	80	(£80 – £(£5 × 0.6 + £6 × 0.4)) × 80 = £5,968
£90	60	(£90 – £(£5 × 0.6 + £6 × 0.4)) × 60 = £5,076
£100	30	(£100 – £(£5 × 0.6 + £6 × 0.4)) × 30 = £2,838

RY Ltd should choose a price of £80 as this produces the highest EV of contribution if the market is known to be pessimistic.

(ii) To work out how much RY Ltd should pay for the further analysis, we need to determine the difference in the EV of contribution with the analysis, and the EV of contribution without the analysis.

We worked out the EV without the analysis (ie selecting the highest EV of contribution) in (a) as £8,121.60. This is not necessarily the best decision in all future conditions, however.

With the analysis, we can select the best decision option as future conditions are known with certainty.

Forecast demand	Probability	Price chosen £	Contribution £	EV of contribution £
Pessimistic	0.2	80 (from (b)(i))	5,968	1,193.60
Most likely	0.6	90 (W1)	7,614	4,568.40
Optimistic	0.2	90 (W2)	12,690	2,538.00
EV of contribution with perfect information (ie the analysis)				8,300.00

The maximum price is therefore the difference between the EV without the analysis of £8,121.60 and the EV if the future state of the market is known (£8,300), which is £178.40

Workings

1   EVs if the most likely state is known to occur

Price	Demand	EV of contribution
£80	100	(£80 – £(£5 × 0.6 + £6 × 0.4)) × 100 = £7,460
£90	90	(£90 – £(£5 × 0.6 + £6 × 0.4)) × 90 = £7,614
£100	80	(£100 – £(£5 × 0.6 + £6 × 0.4)) × 80 = £7,568

A price of £90 would be chosen.

2   EVs if the optimistic state is known to occur

Price	Demand	EV of contribution
£80	150	(£80 – £(£5 × 0.6 + £6 × 0.4)) × 150 = £11,190
£90	150	(£90 – £(£5 × 0.6 + £6 × 0.4)) × 150 = £12,690
£100	120	(£100 – £(£5 × 0.6 + £6 × 0.4)) × 120 = £11,352

A price of £90 would be chosen.

(c)   By basing the decision on EV calculations, a price of £90 would be charged as this results in the highest EV of contribution of £8,121.60, and hence an EV of profit after fixed costs of £(8,121.60 – 4,422) = £3,699.60.

There are a number of **disadvantages** with such an approach.

(i)   Depending on the state of the market and the outcome of negotiations with the airports, if a price of £90 is charged, the contribution could vary from £5,040 to £12,750. The outcome of £8,121.60 contribution is not guaranteed. This is the average outcome that occurs only if the probabilities used in the calculation are correct and the decision is made many times over. The use of an EV therefore **ignores that range of possible values** that could occur.

(ii)   The use of the EV approach leads to the choice of a price of £90. The **worst possible outcome** if a price of £80 is charged is £5,920 with a probability of 0.08 whereas the worst outcome if a price of £90 is charged (£5,040 also with probability of 0.08) is lower.

(iii)   The **actions of competitors** can seriously undermine the accuracy of the demand data. Two other companies control a vast proportion of the market, and it is difficult to imagine that they would not retaliate were RY Ltd to offer the new route.

59 Section C: Purchase options

> **Text references.** Chapter 19 is the place to go if you want help with probabilities.
>
> **Top tips.** In (a), for each purchase option you need to calculate the unit contribution at each selling price, then total contribution at each forecast level, and then, taking probability into account, expected profit.
>
> Under purchase option 2 you need to check whether material requirements exceed 50,000 kg. If not, excess material will have to be purchased, but can then be sold on.
>
> Likewise, under purchase option 3 you need to check whether material requirements exceed 70,000 kg.
>
> In (b) you need to calculate the difference between profit expected with no knowledge (your answer to (a)) and the profit expected if the company knew what demand was going to be.
>
> **Easy marks.** The calculation of the value of perfect information in part (b) is a 'standard' calculation using figures that you have already calculated in part (a). Lay out your pro forma for the calculation and then slot in your data from your answer to (a). Even if your figures from (a) are incorrect you will earn full marks if you use them correctly.

(a)   Purchase option 1

	£			£		
Selling price	15			20		
Variable manufacturing costs	3			3		
'Contribution' to material and fixed costs	12			17		
Materials (£3 × 3 kg)	9			9		
Contribution	3			8		
Sales ('000)	36	28	18	28	23	13
	£'000	£'000	£'000	£'000	£'000	£'000
Contribution	108.0	84.0	54.0	224.0	184.0	104.0
Fixed costs	65.0	65.0	65.0	136.0	136.0	136.0
Conditional profit	43.0	19.0	(11.0)	88.0	48.0	(32.0)
Probability	0.3	0.5	0.2	0.3	0.5	0.2
	12.9	9.5	(2.2)	26.4	24.0	(6.4)
Expected profit (£'000)		20.2			44.0	

Purchase option 2

	£			£		
'Contribution' from above	12.00			17.00		
Materials (£2.75 × 3)	8.25			8.25		
Contribution	3.75			8.75		
Sales ('000)	36	28	18	28	23	13
	£'000	£'000	£'000	£'000	£'000	£'000
Contribution	135.0	105.0	67.5	245.0	201.250	113.75
Fixed costs	65.0	65.0	65.0	136.0	136.000	136.00
Purchase of excess material Less £1 revenue	–	–	–	–	–	*19.25
Conditional profit	70.0	40.0	2.5	109.0	65.250	(41.50)
Probability	0.3	0.5	0.2	0.3	0.500	0.20
	21.0	20.0	0.5	32.7	32.625	(8.30)
Expected profit (£'000)		41.5			57.025	

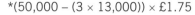 *(50,000 – (3 × 13,000)) × £1.75

Purchase option 3

		£			£	
'Contribution' from above		12.00			17.00	
Materials £2.50 × 3		7.50			7.50	
Contribution		4.50			9.50	

Sales ('000)	36	28	18	28	23	13
	£'000	£'000	£'000	£'000	£'000	£'000
Contribution	162.0	126.0	81.0	266.0	218.5	123.5
Purchase of excess material Less £1 revenue	–	–	*24.0	–	**1.5	***46.5
Fixed costs	65.0	65.0	65.0	136.0	136.0	136.0
Conditional profit	97.0	61.0	(8.0)	130.0	81.0	(59.0)
Probability	0.3	0.5	0.2	0.3	0.5	0.2
	29.1	30.5	(1.6)	39.0	40.5	(11.8)
Expected profit (£'000)		58.0			67.7	

*	(70,000 – (3 × 18)) × £1.50
**	(70,000 – (3 × 23)) × £1.50
***	(70,000 – (3 × 13)) × £1.50

Optimum expected profit = £67,700 and so the company should use a **selling price of £20 and purchase a minimum quantity of 70,000 kg at a price of £2.50 per kg.**

(b)

	£'000
If demand is optimistic, best expected profit =	39.0
If demand is most likely, best expected profit =	40.5
If demand is pessimistic, best expected profit =	0.5
Total expected profit with perfect knowledge	80.0
Expected profit without information	67.7
Maximum price to pay for perfect information	12.3

60 Section C: Tourist hotel

Text references: Decision trees are covered in Chapter 19.

Top tips: Always draw decision trees with a pencil initially, and use a ruler to make the tree as neat as possible. This is a challenging question for the marks available, so try to gain as many marks as possible through clear labelling of the tree. Remember to answer the question – it is really easy to get so involved in drawing the tree that you forget what the question actually asked. Part (c)(i) is a straightforward explanation of the figures in the two way table.

Part (c)(ii) requires more calculation but you should be able to get the figures straight from the data in part (c). Remember the probabilities should add up to 1!

Easy marks: There are three easy marks to be gained in part (b) if you have an appreciation of the limitations of decision trees. In part (c) set out a table to calculate EVs.

Examiner's comments. This question was generally answered poorly. The decision trees were poorly drawn, making the marking task very difficult. There was a lack of understanding of multiple probabilities. Most candidates failed to discuss the limitations of using a decision tree in part (b), but simply discussed weather conditions and the hotel trade. For part (c)

- Poorly tabulated tables
- Incorrect interpretation of tables
- Poor advice on how the information from the table would be useful to the recipient

(a)

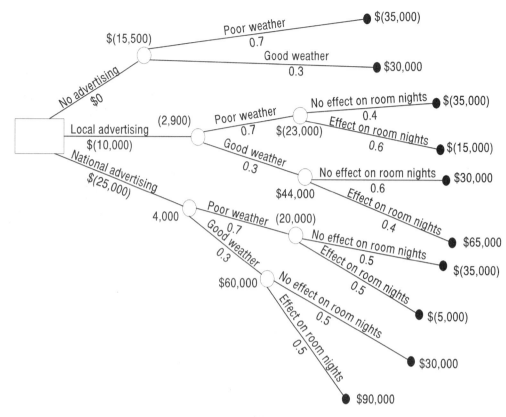

The expected outcomes for each level of advertising are:

No advertising: $(15,500) ie $(35,000) × 0.7 + $30,000 × 0.30

Local advertising: $(2,900) – 10,000 = $(12,900)

National advertising: $4,000 – 25,000 = $(21,000)

(Obtained by working backwards – ie rollback – through the decision tree to calculate expected values)

The best course of action for the hotel owner would be to advertise locally, as the results in the lowest expected losses. This of course assumes that the high season will generate sufficient earnings to make it worthwhile for the hotel owner to remain in business.

(b) **Limitations of decision trees in solving this problem:**

The tree starts to get very complex as more and more possible outcomes are added. This makes drawing the tree very time consuming and increases the likelihood of mistakes, which could lead to an incorrect decision being made.

Decision trees oversimplify scenarios. In reality, weather can take many forms, not just 'poor' and 'good'. Advertising might have different effects in different weeks – there will be some weeks when people will just not want to stay in hotels; others where, regardless of advertising and weather, demand will be greater. It would be dangerous to assume that the hotel industry can be simplified to this extent.

(c) (i) The data table shows the effect on the relevant cost of $10,860 of changes in the hotel cost and/or fuel cost.

There are a range of outcomes from a minimum relevant cost of $9,560 if hotel costs fall to $4,000 and fuel costs to $1,200. This is calculated as $10,860 + $1,500 from the table. A maximum relevant cost of $12,360 applies if fuel costs increase to $2,000 and hotel costs to $6,000.

(ii) **Adjustment to relevant cost**

		Fuel ($)		
		1,200	1,500	2,000
Hotel	4,000	(1,300)	(1,000)	(500)
($)	5,000	(300)	–	500
	6,000	700	1,000	1,500

Joint probability

		Fuel ($)		
		1,200	1,500	2,000
Hotel	4,000	0.02	0.10	0.08
($)	5,000	0.05	0.25	0.20
	6,000	0.03	0.15	0.12

Expected value of costs

		Fuel ($)		
		1,200	1,500	2,000
Hotel	4,000	(26)	(100)	(40)
($)	5,000	(15)	–	100
	6,000	21	150	180

Expected value of costs = sum of (joint probability × cost)

= $270

This means that the expected value of the total hotel and fuel costs is $270 higher then initially expected and hence relevant cost is likely to be $270 higher.

However, the use of expected values does not distinguish between the outcomes of individual variances such as downside variances – for example, when the hotel and fuel costs are $1,500 more and there is a 12% likelihood of this outcome.

Alternative solution

The information contained in the individual tables can be combined into one table as follows:

Hotel	Fuel	Probability	Adjustment to relevant cost	EV of costs
$	$		$	$
4,000	1,200	0.02	(1,300)	(26)
4,000	1,500	0.10	(1,000)	(100)
4,000	2,000	0.08	(500)	(40)
5,000	1,200	0.05	(300)	(15)
5,000	1,500	0.25	–	–
5,000	2,000	0.20	500	100
6,000	1,200	0.03	700	21
6,000	1,500	0.15	1,000	150
6,000	2,000	0.12	1,500	180
		1.00		270

61   Section A: Mixed objective test question bank 1

> **Top tips** The examiner always mentions that some candidates do not attempt all of the multiple-choice questions. If you are given a choice of answers you must write one of them down, even if it is a guess!

1   C   Zero based budgeting requires that each cost element be **specifically justified**. In practice, managers can start from their **current** level of expenditure and work downwards **questioning** what would happen if current expenditure were **removed** from the budget. In this way, **every aspect** of the budget is examined in terms of its **costs** and **benefits.**

      Functional budgets (option B) can be prepared using a zero-based approach but they might also be prepared using an incremental approach, whereby the previous year's results are used as a base.

2   D

	Patients	$
High	8,400	45,660
Low	5,000	37,500
	3,400	8,160

∴ variable cost per patient = $8,160/3,400 = $2.40/patient
∴ fixed cost   = 45,660 – (8,400 × $2.40) = $25,500
∴ y   = 25,500+2.4x

3   B   The sales profit volume variance measures the change in profit caused by the sales volume differing from budget, at the standard gross profit margin per unit.

4   B   Actual input = 2,200 + 2,750 = 4,950 litres

      Standard mix of actual input:

	Litres
Liquid X 5/11 × 4,950 litres	2,250
Liquid Y 6/11 × 4,950 litres	2,700
	4,950

	Should mix Actual qty Std mix	Did mix Actual qty Actual mix	Difference Litres	Std price $	Variance $
X	2,250	2,200	50 litres (F)	16	800 (F)
Y	2,700	2,750	50 litres (A)	25	1,250 (A)
					450 (A)

5   D   Each litre of output requires

5/10 litres X costing $16	= $8
6/10 litres Y costing $25	= $15
1.1 litres of output	= $23

4,950 litres should have yielded (÷1.1 litres)	4,500 litres
But did yield	4,800 litres
Yield variance in litres	300 (F)
× std cost per litre of output	× $23
Yield variance in $	$6,900 (F)

6

Year	Cost savings $'000	Cumulative cost savings $'000
1	35	35
2	45	80
3	55	135

Payback is between 2 and 3 years.

$$\text{Payback} = 2 + \frac{(100-80)}{55} = \textbf{2.4 years}$$

7   Rank in terms of profitability index

Investment	Profitability index	Ranking
J	$\dfrac{(650,000+400,000)}{400,000}=2.625$	2
K	$\dfrac{(450,000+250,000)}{250,000}=2.8$	1
L	$\dfrac{(480,000+300,000)}{300,000}=2.6$	3
M	$\dfrac{(550,000+350,000)}{350,000}=2.571$	4

The correct ranking is K, J, L, M.

8   B   Increasing credit given to customers = increasing receivables. This will lengthen the working capital cycle.

9   Four factors to consider before the cause of a variance is investigated are as follows.

- The **materiality** of the variance.
- The **cost of investigation** compared with the potential benefits.
- Whether a **trend** is developing in the variance over a period.
- Any **inter-relationships** with other variances.

62 Section A: Mixed objective test question bank 2

1   B   Marginal costing will report a lower profit.

2   D

3   A

	W £ per unit	X £ per unit	Y £ per unit
Selling price	180	150	150
Less variable costs:			
Direct material	(41)	(20)	(30)
Direct labour	(30)	(20)	(50)
Variable production overheads	(24)	(16)	(20)
Contribution	85	94	50
Bottleneck minutes	7 mins	10 mins	7 mins
Contribution per bottleneck	£12.10	£9.40	£7.10
Ranking	1	2	3

4   B

	W £ per unit	X £ per unit	Y £ per unit
Selling price	180	150	150
Less direct material	(41)	(20)	(30)
Throughput contribution	139	130	120
Bottleneck minutes	7 mins	10 mins	7 mins
Per bottleneck resource	£19.9	£13	£17.1
Ranking	1	3	2

5   D   All of the statements are true.

6

Possible combinations	Total capital required $	Total NPV $
W and X	250,000	131,000
W and Y	240,000	124,000
W and Z	290,000	147,000
X and Y	290,000	143,000
X and Z	340,000	166,000
Y and Z	330,000	159,000

The combination that should be selected is X and Z as this gives the highest NPV.

7   D

				Seasonal index	Forecast units
For quarter 3	BU=4,000+(80 × 3)	=4,240		× 95% =	4,028
For quarter 4	BU=4,000+(80 × 4)	=4,320		× 120% =	5,184

The forecast increase in sales units is therefore 5,184-4,028 = 1,156 units.

8   D   Cash budgets ensure that sufficient funds will be available when they are needed to sustain an entity's activities.

9   A $EOQ = \sqrt{\dfrac{2C_0D}{C_h}}$

$= \sqrt{\dfrac{2 \times 10 \times 36,000}{2}}$

$= 600$ units

No of orders $= \dfrac{36,000}{600}$

$= 60$

10   D   The PV of sales revenue can fall by $42,500 before the project becomes unacceptable (that is, the NPV becomes zero).

$Sensitivity = \dfrac{Net\ present\ value}{PV\ of\ sales\ revenue} = \dfrac{42,500}{385,000} = 11.04\% \approx 11\%$

63   Section A: Mixed objective test question bank 3

Top tips. The examiner always mentions that some candidates do not attempt all of the multiple-choice questions. If you are given a choice of answers you must write one of them down, even if it is a guess!

1   A   The actual overheads were £481,250 and they were under absorbed by £19,250. This means that the amount that was actually absorbed is £481,250 less £19,250.

Amount absorbed = £481,250 - £19,250 = £462,000

The overhead absorption rate (OAR) $= \dfrac{Overheads\ absorbed}{Actual\ number\ of\ hours}$

$= \dfrac{£462,000}{38,500}$

$= £12/hour$

Budgeted production overheads = number of standard hours × OAR

$$= 38,000 \times £12$$

$$= £456,000$$

2   A   £60 A

Operational efficiency variance

	£'000
370 times should have taken (×12/60)	74 hours
But did take	80 hours
Operational efficiency variance in hours	$\overline{6}$ (A)
× standard rate per hour	× £10
Operational efficiency variance in £	£60 (A)

Double check:

Total operational variance

	£'000
Revised standard cost of actual number of times (12/60 × £10 × 370)	740
Actual cost	850
	$\overline{110}$ (A)

Operational rate variance

	£'000
Actual cost of actual number of times	850
Revised standard cost of actual number of hours (80 × £10)	800
	$\overline{50}$ (A)

Total = efficiency + rate = £60(A) + £50(A) = £110(A)

3   A   The first definition is of material requirements planning and the second is enterprise resource planning. You either know these definitions or you don't!

4   A   The volume variance is the under or over absorption caused by the volume of activity being different from that budgeted.

5   C   Over-absorption occurs when the overhead absorbed is greater than the actual overhead amount incurred. In other words, the actual overheads incurred are lower than the amount absorbed.

6   A   (1+ money cost of capital) = (1+ real cost of capital) (1 + inflation rate)

$$= (1 + 0.06)(1 + 0.04)$$

$$= 1.1024$$

Money cost of capital is 10.24%.

7   Payback is based on **cash flows** so no need for depreciation calculations.

The payback period will occur when cash flows = $15,000 (initial investment).

Year	Cash flow	Cumulative cash flow
1	2,500	2,500
2	3,000	5,500
3	5,500	11,000
4	4,000	15,000

The payback period is 4.0 years.

8   Accounting Rate of Return $= \dfrac{\text{Average annual profit from investment}}{\text{Average investment}} \times 100$

Profit = cash flow – depreciation

Annual depreciation $= \dfrac{\text{Initial investment - residual value}}{\text{Useful life}} = \dfrac{\$15,000 - 3,000}{5} = \$2,400$

Year	Cash flow	Depreciation	Profit
	$	$	$
1	2,500	(2,400)	100
2	3,000	(2,400)	600
3	5,500	(2,400)	3,100
4	4,000	(2,400)	1,600
5	3,000	(2,400)	600
Total profit			6,000
Total years			5
Average profit			1,200

$$\text{Average investment} = \frac{\text{Initial investment} + \text{residual value}}{2} = \frac{\$15,000 + 3,000}{2} = \$9,000$$

$$\text{ARR} = \frac{1,200}{9,000} = 13.33\%$$

9

Variable costs	Probability	Expected value
$		$
70,000	0.40	28,000
90,000	0.35	31,500
110,000	0.25	27,500
		87,000

Fixed costs	Probability	Expected value
$		$
100,000	0.35	35,000
130,000	0.45	58,500
160,000	0.20	32,000
		125,500

Expected value of total cost   = EV of variable costs + EV of fixed costs
                                     = \$87,000 + 125,500
                                     = \$212,500

10   B   GS has used long-term funding to finance all permanent assets and part of the fluctuating portion of current assets.

64   Section A: Mixed objective test question bank 4

1   D   In a standard absorption costing system, overheads are absorbed based on the standard content of the actual output.

$$\therefore \text{OAR} = \frac{\text{Budgeted overhead}}{\text{Budgeted labour hours}}$$

$$= \frac{\$450,000}{900,000}$$

$$= \$0.5 \text{ per labour hour}$$

Absorbed overheads = OAR × standard content of actual output

Standard labour hours per unit = 900,000/50,000 = 18 hours per unit

60,000 units × 18 hours = 1,080,000 standard hours

Absorbed overheads = \$1,080,000 × 0.5 = \$540,000

So overheads were over absorbed by \$540,000 − \$475,000 = \$65,000

2   (i)

	Should mix Actual quantity Standard mix	Did mix Actual quantity Actual mix	Difference	Standard price	Variance
X	640	600	40(F)	$5	$200 (F)
Y	384	380	4(F)	$6	$24 (F)
Z	256	300	44(A)	$7	$308 (A)
	1,280	1,280			$84 (A)

(W1)

(ii)   <u>Yield variance</u>

1,280 kg should have yielded (÷ 1.25 kg)	1,024 kg
But did yield	960 kg
Yield variance in kg	64 kg (A)
× standard cost per kg of output (W2)	$7.125
Yield variance in $	$456(A)

<u>Workings (1)</u>

	Standard mix of actual output	Kg
X	5/10 × 1,280 kg	640
Y	3/10 × 1,280 kg	384
Z	2/10 × 1,280 kg	256
		1,280

<u>Workings (2)</u>

Standard cost of one kg of output:

Standard cost of X for 800kg of output = 500kg @ $5 = $2,500

Standard cost of Y for 800kg of output = 300kg @ $6 = $1,800

Standard cost of Z for 800kg of output = 200kg @ $7 = $1,400

$5,700

∴ Standard cost of 1kg = ($5,700 ÷ 800) = $7.125

3   41 days

y/e 30.09.X8

Purchases = $324,444

y/e 30.09.X9 purchases = $356,900

$$20X8: 45 = \frac{\text{Average trade payables}}{\$324} \times 365$$

∴ average trade payables = $40,000

$$20X9: \text{Trade payable days} = \frac{\$40,000}{\$356,000} \times 365 = 40.91$$

Days outstanding at 30 Sept 20X9 = 41 days

4   $814

	$
Capital at maturity: 1,000 × 0.659*	659
Interest: 50 over 4 years = 50 × 3.102*	155
Market price	814

* discount rate for 4 years at 11%

5   A $(1 + \text{money rate}) = (1 + \text{real rate})(1 + \text{inflation rate})$

$$(1 + \text{real rate}) = \frac{(1+\text{money rate})}{(1+\text{inflation rate})} = \frac{(1+0.18)}{(1+0.05)} = 1.124$$

Real rate is approximately 12%

6   The present value of the direct materials can increase by $683,000 before the project breaks even.

Direct material costs may therefore increase by $\dfrac{683,000}{825,000} \times 100$

$$= 82.79\%$$

7   **Step 1**   **Cost driver is number of batches, therefore calculate number of batches for each product and in total.**

	X	Y	Z	Total
Number of batches				
$= \dfrac{\text{Production units}}{\text{Batch size}}$	$\dfrac{15}{2.5}$	$\dfrac{25}{5}$	$\dfrac{20}{4}$	
	= 6	= 5	= 5	16

Step 2   **Calculate machine set-up costs attributable to product Y using number of batches as the allocation basis.**

	Y
Machine set up costs	$\dfrac{5}{16} \times 600,000$
	$= £187,500$

Step 3   **Calculate the machine set-up costs that would be attributable to each unit of Product Y:**

Machine set up costs	=	£187,500
Production units	=	25,000
Machine set-up costs per unit	=	£7.50

65 Section A: Mixed objective test question bank 5

1   B   First we need to calculate the number of units of inventory left at the end of October.

Closing inventory units   = Opening inventory units + units produced – units sold
                      = 0 + 4,000 – 3,600
                      = 400

The value of inventory using marginal costing is:

	$
Direct material	20,000
Direct labour	6,300
Variable production overhead	4,700
	31,000

∴ cost per unit = $31,000/4,000 = $7.75

∴400 units cost 400   × $7.75 = $3,100

2   D   Using throughput accounting we include the cost of the materials only.

400 × ($20,000/4,000) = $2,000

3   C   The entity will have **more** cash available but may have damaged its creditworthiness.

4   C   A production budget is calculated as sales plus closing inventory less opening inventory.

        30,000 units + (1.35 × 3,500 units) – 3,500 units   = 30,000 + 4,725 – 3,500

                                                   = 31,225 units

5   D   £490,000 F

Fixed overhead expenditure variance

	£'000
Budgeted fixed overhead expenditure	2,500
Actual fixed overhead expenditure	2,010
	490 (F)

6   C   £300,000 A

Fixed overhead volume variance

	£'000
Actual production at standard rate	
440,000 × (1,000,000/500,000) × (2,500,000/1,000,000)	2,200
Budgeted production at standard rate 500,000 × 2 × 2.5	2,500
	300 (A)

7   **Step 1**   **As payback is calculated using cash flows, we have to convert profits into cash flows by adding back depreciations.**

$$\text{Depreciation per annum} = \frac{\text{Cost - Residual Value}}{\text{Expected useful life}}$$

$$= \frac{400,000 - 50,000}{5}$$

$$= \$70,000$$

Year	Profit	Depreciation	Cash flow
	$	$	$
1	175,000	70,000	245,000
2	225,000	70,000	295,000
3	340,000	70,000	410,000
4	165,000	70,000	235,000
5	125,000	70,000.	195,000

    Step 2   **Calculate payback period using the cash flows calculated in Step 1 above.**

Year	Cash flow	Cumulative cash flow
	$	$
0	(400,000)	(400,000)
1	245,000	(155,000)
2	295,000	140,000

Payback is between one and two years. Use interpolation to obtain a more accurate answer:

$$\text{Payback} = 1 + \frac{155,000}{295,000} \text{ years}$$

      = 1.5 years (to nearest 0.1 years)

8   (1 + money rate) = (1 + real rate) × (1 + inflation rate)

$$\left(1 + \text{real rate}\right) = \frac{\left(1 + \text{money rate}\right)}{\left(1 + \text{inflation rate}\right)}$$

$$\left(1 + \text{real rate}\right) = \frac{\left(1 + 0.2\right)}{\left(1 + 0.08\right)}$$

(1 + real rate) = 1.1111

∴ Annual real percentage = 11.11%

9   0.78   The labour hours are restricted to 12,000pa and each unit takes 45 minutes. The maximum number of units that can be produced is therefore:

12,000/0.75 = 16,000 units

Throughput accounting ratio = (sales – material costs) per time period/conversion cost per time period

= [16,000 × (12-5)]/144,000

= 112,000/144,000

= 0.78

A profitable product should have a ratio greater than one. This product has a ratio of 0.78 so the organisation is losing money every time it is produced.

66   Section A: Mixed objective test question bank 6

1   C   The interest yield is the **gross yield** divided by the **market value of the stock** expressed as a percentage, in this case $(11,000 × 10\%) ÷ 10,000$.

2   A   OAR = £300,000/220,000 = £1.50/unit

		£'000
OAR × output achieved = £1.50 × 200,000 =		300
Actual overhead		260
		40

Actual overheads were £40,000 less than absorbed overheads so overheads were overabsorbed.

3   C   360,000 units

Fixed overhead total variance

	£'000
Fixed overhead incurred	1,950
	X
Fixed overhead absorbed (1,500/300 × actual production)	150 (A)

So X = 1,950,000 – 150,000 = 1,800,000

∴ 1,500,000/300,000 × actual production = 1,800,000

∴ actual production = 360,000 units

4   C   A basic standard is one which is kept unaltered over a long period of time and may be out of date. They are used to show changes in efficiency or performance over a long period of time.

5   C   Use the high/low method:

	Volume	£
Highest activity level	6,500	33,000
Lowest activity level	4,500	29,000
	2,000	4,000

∴ Variable cost of 2,000 units is £4,000

∴ Variable cost per unit = $\dfrac{£4,000}{2,000}$ = £2

∴ Variable cost of 4,500 units = 4,500 × £2
= £9,000

∴ Fixed cost = total cost – variable cost (of 4,500 units)
= £(29,000 – 9,000) = £20,000

∴ Budget cost for 5,750 units = fixed cost + variable cost of 5,750 units
= £(20,000 + (5,750 × £2)) = £31,500

6   41.2%

     Using the formula $(100/98.5)^{(365/16)} - 1$

     $= 41.2\%$

7

Project	Investment required	Present value of cash inflows*	NPV	Profitability index (PI)**	Ranking as per NPV	Ranking as per PI
	$'000	$'000	$'000			
J	400	431	31	1.08	=2	3
K	500	543	43	1.09	1	2
L	300	331	31	1.10	=2	1

However, only $1 million is available for capital investment.

* NPV + initial investment
** PV of cash inflows/PV of total capital outlay

As projects are divisible, it is possible to invest fully in projects L and K, with the remaining balance of $200,000 being invested in J (so one half of the full investment would be made to earn one half of the NPV).

Project	Priority	Outlay	NPV
		$'000	$'000
L	1st	300	31
K	2nd	500	43
J (balance)	3rd	200	(½ of $31,000) 15
		1,000	89

8   **We know that at a discount rate of 15%, the NPV of K is $43,000.** This is **fairly close to zero**. It is also **positive**, which means that the **internal rate of return** is **more than 15%.** As a guess, it might be worth trying 20% next, to see what the NPV is.

Try 20%

Year	Cash flow	Discount factor	PV of cash flow
	$'000	20%	$'000
0	(500)	1.000	(500)
1	70	0.833	58
2	90	0.694	62
3	630	0.579	365
		NPV	(15)

This is fairly close to zero and negative. The internal rate of return is therefore greater than 15% but less than 20%.

Note. If the first NPV is positive, choose a higher rate for the next calculation to get a negative NPV. If the first NPV is negative, choose a lower rate for the next calculation.

So IRR $= 15 + \left[\dfrac{43}{43+15} \times (20-15) \right] \% = 18.71\%.$

Note. Depending on the degree of accuracy in your calculations, there would be a range of acceptable answers to 2 decimal places.

9   Clearly this is a **payback** calculation. The payback period is how long it takes a **project's net cash inflows to equal the initial investment**. So set out the cumulative cash inflows in a table. These are the cash benefits of the time saved in using the new computer system.

Year	Cash benefit	Cumulative Benefit
	$'000	$'000
1	20	20
2	30	50
3	50	100
4	50	150
5	50	200

The original investment is $80,000 so the payback takes place somewhere between the second and third years of the project. The question asks for a payback period to one decimal place of one year so is 2 years +((80-50)/(100-50) x 12 months) = 2.6 years.

67   Section A: Mixed objective test question bank 7

1   D

Selling price £/unit	Probability	Unit var cost £	Probability	Combined probability	Monthly Contribution* £	Expected Value** £
20	0.25	8	0.20	0.050	12,000	600
	0.25	10	0.50	0.125	10,000	1,250
	0.25	12	0.30	0.075	8,000	600
25	0.40	8	0.20	0.080	17,000	1,360
	0.40	10	0.50	0.200	15,000	3,000
	0.40	12	0.30	0.120	13,000	1,560
30	0.35	8	0.20	0.070	22,000	1,540
	0.35	10	0.50	0.175	20,000	3,500
	0.35	12	0.30	0.105	18,000	1,890
				1.000		15,300

*(selling price – variable cost) × 1,000

** monthly contribution × combined probability

The **expected value** of contribution is £15,300. Note contribution excludes fixed costs.

2   C   The probability of monthly contribution > £13,500 = 0.08 + 0.2 + 0.07 +0.175 + 0.105
= 0.63

3   C   The profitability index is stated as the NPV of a project/initial outlay.

Taking data from the question:

NPV = $140,500 and initial outlay = $500,000. Therefore the profitability index is

$140,500/$500,000 = 0.281 which is closest to 0.28.

4   C   Use the standard sensitivity formula. This measures sensitivity of cash flows as:

NPV of a project/PV of the cashflow affected × 100%

Substituting data from the question.

NPV = $320,000 and PV of sales revenue = $630,000.

$320,000/$630,000 × 100% = 50.79% which is closest to 51%.

5   10.5%

Taking 10% as the discount factor:

100 × 0.467	46.70
7 × 5.335	37.35
	84.05

Taking 11% as the discount factor:

100 × 0.434	43.40
7 × 5.146	36.02
	79.42

Extrapolating:

$$10\% + \left(\frac{84.05 - 82.00}{84.05 - 79.42}\right) = 10\% + \left(\frac{2.05}{4.63}\right) = 10.44\%$$

This can be rounded to 10.5%.

6   C   Non-current assets are not a part of working capital. Receivables would increase and thus working capital would increase.

7   $Y = Ax^{0.6}$

Therefore, June + July = $1,500 \times 2^{0.6}$
= 2,274 units

Therefore, July = 2,274 – 1,500
= 774 units

June + July + August = $1,500 \times 3^{0.6}$
= 2,900 units

Therefore, August = 2,900 – 2,274
= 626 units

	Monthly sales units	Cumulative sales units
June	1,500	1,500
July	774	2,274
August	626	2,900

8   Return per hour = (Sales revenue-material costs)/Hour

	Sales revenue $	Material cost $	Sales less materials	Return per hour
A	200	41	159	(× (60/12)) $795
B	150	20	130	(× (60/10)) $780
C	150	30	120	(× (60/7)) $1,029

68   Section A: Mixed objective test question bank 8

1   A   The company will be retaining the majority of its delivery vehicles, and it is safe to assume that reasonably priced contracted-out alternatives are available. This sale should not damage the long-term profitability of the company.

B is not correct. It can be assumed that the blending of pigments to go into the china products is a core activity of the business. This plant should not be sold in these circumstances.

C is not correct. Such a patent is likely to be a key to securing the long-term future profitability of the company. It should not be sold to meet short-term needs.

D is not the most appropriate option. A 60% stake constitutes a controlling interest in a company. It could therefore be unsafe to sell this shareholding.

2   C   The question is asking you to rank products when there is a scarcity of capital i.e. **capital rationing** is required. You need to use the **profitability index** to rank the projects here. Make sure that you read the entire question so you are aware that, for instance, the projects are divisible.

	Investment required $'000	NPV $'000	PV of cash inflows (W1) $'000	Profitability index (PI)(W2)	Ranking from PI
Project					
J	400	125	525	1.313	3
K	350	105	455	1.300	5
L	450	140	590	1.311	4
M	500	160	660	1.320	1
N	600	190	790	1.317	2

Therefore based on the PI ranking, should choose to invest $500,000 in M with the balance of $500,000 in N.

Workings

1   The PV of cash inflows is the NPV plus the investment required.
2   The PI is simply the PV of cash inflows/the investment required.

3   B   Definitions I and II are correct.

4   B $\text{Sensitivity} = \dfrac{\text{NPV of project}}{\text{PV of cashflow affected}} \times 100\%$

                  $= (\$160{,}000/(\$50{,}000 \times 3.605^{*})) \times 100\%$

                  $= 88.77\%$

                  *discount factor over five years at 12%

5   B $(70{,}000 + 10{,}000)/(88{,}000 + 7{,}000) = 0.84$

6   (i)   £55,000 A

           Sales price variance

	£'000
Sales revenue from 110,000 units should have been (× £10)	1,100
But was	1,045
	55 (A)

    (ii)   £20,000 F

           Sales volume variance = 100,000 units – 110,000 units

                             = 10,000 units (F)

           Sales volume profit variance = 10,000 units × standard gross profit margin per unit

                                    = 10,000 × (£10-£8)

                                    = £20,000 (F)

7   The labour rate variance is calculated as:

    Actual hours worked at actual rate – actual hours worked at standard rate

    or actual hours worked × (actual rate – standard rate)

    = actual hours worked × (actual rate – £12) = £45,000 (A)

> **Top tips**. As we have two unknowns in this relationship, we need to look at the efficiency variance to find the actual hours worked.

Labour efficiency variance:

(Actual hours worked – 11,500 units × 5 hrs) × £12 = £30,000 (A)

(Actual hours worked – 57,500) × 12 = 30,000 (A)

$$\text{Actual hours worked} - 57{,}500 = \frac{30{,}000}{12} = 2{,}500$$

Actual hours worked = 60,000

60,000 × (actual rate – £12) = 45,000

Therefore, (actual rate × 60,000) – 720,000 = 45,000

$$\text{Actual rate} = \frac{45{,}000 + 720{,}000}{60{,}000} = £12.75$$

8   £110,784

		Month 1 £	Month 2 £	Month 3 £	Month 4 £
Sales		90,000	105,000	120,000	108,000
Cash	20%	18,000	21,000	24,000	21,600
Credit	80%	72,000	84,000	96,000	86,400
Within one month	40%		28,800	33,600	38,400
less discount	1.5%		(432)	(504)	(576)
			28,368	33,096	37,824
Within two months	30%			21,600	25,200
Within three months	28%				20,160
Outstanding receivables					6,000
Total receipts		18,000	49,368	78,696	110,784

69 Section A: Mixed objective test question bank 9

1   B   £41,000 Favourable

Actual quantity sold × (actual price − standard price)

8,200 units × (£31 − £26) = £41,000 (F)

2   A   £6,000 Adverse

Sales volume profit variance = (8,700 − 8,200) × standard gross profit margin per unit (W)

Working

	£	£
Selling price per unit		26
Less: Variable cost per unit	10	
Fixed overhead per unit		
$\dfrac{34,800}{8,700} =$	4	
		14
		12

500 units × £12 = £6,000 Adverse

3   A   £2,000 adverse

> **Top tips**. The fixed overhead volume variance is a measure of the over or under absorption of fixed
> overhead costs caused by actual production volume differing from that budgeted. It is calculated as the
> difference between actual and budgeted production/volume multiplied by the standard absorption rate per
> unit.

500 units × £4* = £2,000 adverse

The variance is adverse as fewer units have been produced.

* Calculated in 2 above.

4   B   The receivables are unlikely to be sold at a profit to the selling company.

5   (i)   Material price planning variance:
(Revised standard cost − original standard cost) × actual materials
(4.50 − 4.10) × 1,600 units × 7kg = £4,480 (A)

(ii)   Actual quantity should have been 11,200 but was 12,000
Operational material usage variance:
Standard quantity − actual quantity) × revised standard
(11,200 − 12,000) × £4.50 = £3,600 (A)

6

		EV $'000
Project L	(500 × 0.2 + 470 × 0.5 + 550 × 0.3)	500.0
Project M	(400 × 0.2 + 550 × 0.5 + 570 × 0.3)	526.0
Project N	(450 × 0.2 + 400 × 0.5 + 475 × 0.3)	432.5
Project O	(360 × 0.2 + 400 × 0.5 + 420 × 0.3)	398.0
Project P	(600 × 0.2 + 500 × 0.5 + 425 × 0.3)	497.5

Project M has the highest EV of expected cash flows and should therefore be undertaken.

7

Market condition	Probability	Project chosen	Net cash inflow $'000	EV of net cash inflow $'000
Poor	0.2	P	600	120
Good	0.5	M	550	275
Excellent	0.3	M	570	171
EV of net cash inflows with perfect information				566
EV of net cash inflows without perfect information (from question 1.4 above)				526
Value of perfect information				40

8   The ranking of the products for best use of the bottleneck is W, Y, X.

Throughput accounting approach

	W £	X £	Y £
Selling price	200	150	150
Direct material	(41)	(20)	(30)
Throughput	159	(130)	(120)
Throughput per minute on bottleneck	159/9 = 17.67	130/10 = 13	120/7 = 17.14
	1	3	2

9   This question wants you to use the present value of a perpetuity to calculate the PV of the rental income. The formula for the PV of a perpetuity is $1/r$ where r is the discount rate. You need to learn this formula, as it is not given in the exam.

So for the rental income this is £80,000/0.08 = £1,000,000.

Therefore the NPV of the investment = £1,000,000 – £850,000 = £150,000.

70   Section A: Mixed objective test question bank 10

1   B $30,000 Adverse

	$
Materials price planning variance	
Original standard cost of standard usage for actual output ($4.00 × 3 kg × 10,000) =	120,000
Revised standard cost of standard usage for actual output ($5.00 × 3kg × 10,000) =	150,000
	30,000 A

2   D $10,000 Adverse

	kg
Materials operational usage variance	
Actual production 10,000 units should use 3 kg per unit	30,000 kg
10,000 units did use	32,000 kg
	2,000 kg

2,000kg at standard revised cost of $5 per kg = $10,000

3   B $6,400 Favourable

	$
Operational price variance	
Actual purchases 32,000kg did cost	153,600
32,000kg should cost at revised standard cost of $5/kg	160,000
	6,400 F

4   B   £1,700,000 and £50,000

	£	£
DR Cost of goods sold	1,700,000	
CR Conversion costs		840,000
CR Materials (remaining balance)		860,000

Being the 'backflush' at standard cost

	£	£
DR Conversion costs	890,000	
CR Cash		890,000

Being the actual conversion cost incurred (assumes cash paid but does not affect the backflush)

	£	£
DR Cost of goods sold	50,000	
CR Conversion costs		50,000

Being the balancing figure on the conversion cost account (£890,000 - £840,000)

5   D   130

> The index values for a multiplicative model with four seasons add to 400, therefore:
>
> 80 (Q1) + 80 (Q2) + 110 (Q3) +130 (Q4) = 400

6   This requires you to run through the different combinations of selling price and variable cost that will give a contribution exceeding $20,000/week or $20 per unit.

Clearly at a selling price of $40/unit all contributions of 1,000 units will be less than $20,000. So you should be able to eliminate a few combinations using this basic logic.

Thus the combinations of selling price and variable cost that give at least $20,000 and the probability resulting:

Sale price (unit)	Variable cost	Probability
$	$	
50	20	0.45 × 0.55
60	30	0.25 × 0.25
60	20	0.25 × 0.55
		44.75%

7

	W	X	Y
	£ per unit	£ per unit	£ per unit
Selling price	200.0	183	175
Direct material	(50.0)	(40)	(35)
Direct labour	(30.0)	(35)	(30)
Overheads re: inspecting etc	(33.6)	(33.6)	(31.11)
Overheads re: production schedule	(36.0)	(26.0)	(25.00)
	50.4	48.4	53.89

Workings

1   Total number of purchase requisitions
    1,200 + 1,800 + 2,000 = 5,000

Receiving/inspecting quality assurance attributable to each product

W: $\dfrac{1,200}{5,000} \times 1,400,000 = £336,000$

X: $\dfrac{1,800}{5,000} \times 1,400,000 = £504,000$

Y: $\dfrac{2,000}{5,000} \times 1,400,000 = £560,000$

2   Receiving/inspecting quality assurance attributable to each product on a per unit basis.

W: $\dfrac{£336,000}{10,000} = £33.6$

X: $\dfrac{£504,000}{15,000} = £33.6$

Y: $\dfrac{£560,000}{18,000} = £31.11$

3   Production scheduling/machine set up costs attributable to each product

240 + 260 + 300 = 800

W: $\dfrac{240}{800} \times £1,200,000 = £360,000$

$$X: \quad \frac{260}{800} \times £1,200,000 = £390,000$$

$$Y: \quad \frac{300}{800} \times £1,200,000 = £450,000$$

On a per unit basis

$$W: \frac{360,000}{10,000} = £36 \quad X: \frac{390,000}{15,000} = £26 \quad Y: \frac{450,000}{18,000} = £25$$

8

		1 year		2 years		3 years		4 years	
Year	Disc factors	Cash flow	PV	Cash flow	PV	Cash flow	PV	Cash flow	PV
	12%	£'000	£'000	£'999	£'000	£'000	£'000	£'000	£'000
0	1.000	(220)	(220.000)	(220)	(220.000)	(220)	(220.000)	(220)	(220.000)
1	0.893	11	9.823	(110)	(98.230)	(110)	(98.230)	(110)	(98.230)
2	0.797			(44)	(35.068)	(132)	(105.204)	(132)	(105.204)
3	0.712					(88)	(62.656)	(154)	(109.648)
4	0.636							(110)	(69.960)
PV of cost after one replacement cycle			(210.177)		(353.298)		(486.090)		(603.042)
Cumulative PV factor			0.893		1.690		2.402		3.037
Annualised equivalent cost			£235,000		£209,000		£202,000		£199,000

The supermarket should replace its vehicles every four years, since this results in the lowest annualised equivalent cost.

71 Section A: Mixed objective test question bank 11

1   A   The budgeted value of the fixed overheads and the standard fixed overheads absorbed by actual production.

2   B   £6,750

Marginal cost = total cost – fixed production overheads – selling costs
= £101,800 – £22,500 – £6,000 – £19,300
= £54,000

Marginal cost per unit = £54,000/2,000
= £27

Units left at month end = 2,000 – 1,750 = 250
Valued at £27/unit = 250 × £27
= £6,750

3   B   £4,000

Materials cost = £32,000
∴ Throughput cost per unit = £32,000/2,000
= £16
∴ Closing inventory value = £16 × 250
= £4,000

4   C   £1,194 favourable

When x = 3,900 y   = £2,000 + (£0.0003 × 3,900²)
                        = £6,563

Adjusting for inflation gives £6,563 × 102%
                        = £6,694.26

	£
Operating cost should have been	6,694.26
But was	5,500.00
	1,194.26 (F)

5   A   5.0%

Assume that revenue = $100

	Original $		Revised $	
Revenue	100	× 80%	80	
Variable costs	80	× 80%	64	
Fixed costs	12		12	(Fixed remain the same)
Profit	8		4	(Balancing figure)

$$\frac{\text{Revised profit}}{\text{Revised revenue}} \times 100\% = \frac{4}{80} \times 100\% = 5\%$$

6   B   Overheads will always be over absorbed when actual overheads incurred are lower than the overheads absorbed.

7   £27.99

	£	
Materials	18.00	
Labour	3.20	(£64,000/8,000 hrs × 0.4)
Set-up costs	5.00	(£22,000/44) × (200/100)/200
Quality testing	0.85	(£6,800/160) × (200/100) × 2/200
General overheads	0.94	(£18,800/8,000) × 0.4
	27.99	

8   £2,222 under absorbed

	Assembly £	Finishing £	Maintenance £	Stores £
Overheads	200,000	160,000	60,000	80,000
Reapportion stores	44,000	36,000	–	(80,000)
	244,000	196,000	60,000	–
Reapportion maintenance	24,000	24,000	(60,000)	12,000
	268,000	220,000	–	12,000
Reapportion stores	6,600	5,400		(12,000)
	274,600	225,400		

$$\text{OAR} = \frac{£274,600}{10,000} = £27.46$$

	£
Absorbed in assembly: 10,800 × £27.46 =	296,568
Actual overhead	298,790
Under-absorption	2,222

72   Section A: Mixed objective test question bank 12

1   C   A basic standard is a standard which is kept unchanged over period of time.

2   C

	$
Sales revenue from 85,000 units should have been (× $11)	935,000
But was (× $14)	1,190,000
	255,000 (F)

3   A

Should have sold	90,000 units
But did sell	85,000 units
	5,000 units (A)
× standard profit*	× $2
	$10,000 (A)

* Fixed prod^n o/h per unit $= \$400,000/80,000$
                                 $= \$5$
Variable cost per unit $= \underline{\$4}$
Total cost per unit $= \underline{\$9}$
∴ Profit per unit $= \$11 - \$9 = \$2$

4   B   Inventory has decreased so marginal costing will report a higher profit than absorption costing.

Profit difference $=$ Change in inventory $\times$ fixed prod^n o/h per unit (calculated above)
$= (85,000 - 78,000) \times \$5$
$= \$35,000$

5   (i)   0.857

$$\text{TA ratio} = \frac{\text{sales - material costs}}{\text{labour + overhead}}$$

$$\text{Overhead} = \frac{\$216,000}{12,000\,\text{hours}} \times \frac{10}{60} = \$3 \text{ per unit}$$

$$\therefore \text{TA ratio} = \frac{\$8 - \$2}{\$4 + \$3}$$

$$= \$6/\$7$$

$$= 0.857$$

(ii)   A profitable product should have a ratio greater than one. This product is therefore not profitable.

6   D   10.67%   Sensitivity $= \$28,000/\$262,500$

$= 10.67\%$

7   Payback period $=$ 2 years
                      $+ \$9,000/\$19,000$
                      $=$ 2.5 years

8

	$'000
Inventory used in production	331
Adj for increase in inventory	2
Add reduction in payables	7
Forecast cash required	340

73 Section A: Mixed objective test question bank 13

1 C

Variable cost   45% (100% - 55%)
Fixed cost   25% (balancing figure)
Profit   <u>30%</u>
Revenue   100%
Fixed costs are 25% of revenue.

$$\therefore \text{ Revenue } = \frac{\$50,000}{0.25}$$
$$= \$200,000$$

2 A

	$
Revenue from 52,000 units should have been (× $25)	1,300,000
But was (× $24)	<u>1,248,000</u>
	<u>52,000</u> (A)

3 B

Should have sold	50,000 units
But did sell	<u>52,000</u> units
	2,000 units (F)
× standard profit*	<u>× $6</u>
	<u>$12,000</u> (F)

$$\text{* Fixed cost per unit } = \frac{\$250,000}{50,000} = \$5$$

Variable cost per unit   = $14

$\therefore$ Profit per unit   = $25 – $5 – $14

              = $6

4 D   Inventories have decreased so marginal costing will show a higher profit.

Profit difference   = Change in inventory × OAR

                   = 5,000 units × $8

                   = $40,000

	$
Marginal profit =	435,000
	(40,000)
Absorption profit =	<u>395,000</u>

5 A   (i) and (v) are true.

6 C   Using the high-low method we have

Cost	Units
$28,480	15,400
<u>$19,600</u>	<u>8,000</u>
8,880	7,400

Cost per unit (variable cost)   = $8,880/7,400
                                = $1.20
$\therefore$ Fixed cost   = $19,600 – (8,000 × $1.20)
                                = $10,000

For 12,000 machine hours the cost would be
$10,000 + (12,000 × $1.20)
= $24,400

7

	Cost driver rate
Purchase requisitions	£300 per requisition
Production run set-ups	£250 per set-up

Inventory acquisition overheads

$$\text{X: Cost per unit} = 4 \times \frac{£300}{2,400} = £0.50$$

$$\text{Y: Cost per unit} = 8 \times \frac{£300}{3,000} = £0.80$$

Production overheads

$$\text{X: Cost per unit} = \frac{2,400}{400} \times \frac{£250}{2,400} = £0.625$$

$$\text{Y: Cost per unit} = \frac{3,000}{1,000} \times \frac{250}{3,000} = £0.25$$

Total cost per unit

	X £	Y £
Prime cost	5.00	7.50
Acquisition overheads	0.50	0.80
Production overheads	0.625	0.25
Total cost	6.125	8.55

8   47 days

Trade receivable turnover $\frac{12}{48} \times 365 = 91.25$ days

Trade payable turnover $\frac{8}{48 \times 0.75} \times 365 = 81.11$ days

Inventory turnover
91.25 + inventory turnover – 81.11 = 57
10.14 + inventory turnover = 57
Inventory turnover = 46.86 days

74   Section A: Mixed objective test question bank (Specimen paper)

1   C

	$
Revenue W1	220,000
Variable costs W2	88,000
Fixed costs	36,000
Profit	96,000

Workings

1   Revenue $200,000 × 110% = $220,000

2   Variable costs = $100,000 × 110% × 80% = $88,000

$$\frac{96,000}{64,000} = 1.5 \qquad \therefore \text{increase} = 50\%$$

2   B   NPV = –250,000 + 500,000 – 200,000 = 50,000

$$\frac{50}{500} = 10\%$$

3   *Expected members*   *Expected variable cost per member* $
     20,000 × 0.1 =   2,000 $70 × 0.3 =   21
     30,000 × 0.6 =   18,000 $60 × 0.5 =   30
     40,000 × 0.3 =   12,000 $40 × 0.2 =   8
                            ———————   ——
                             32,000   59
                            ———————   ——

                                           $
     Sales (32,000 × $120)   3,840,000
     Variable costs (32,000 ×$59)   (1,888,000)
     Fixed costs   (1,100,000)
                                           —————————
                                            852,000
                                           —————————

4   (i)   Contribution = Selling price – variable cost

                  = $120 – $40

                  = $80

            Total contribution = 40,000 members × $80 = $3,200,000

            Profit = $3,200,000 – $1,100,000

                  = $2,100,000

     (ii)   0.1 × 0.2 = 0.02

5   In order to calculate a suitable selling price, we need to know what the bond is worth, in present value terms. We need to take the annual (discounted) interest receipts and add the (discounted) repayment after four years. This will give us the selling price. The selling price and the discounted interest and repayment will sum to zero. We therefore have the following.

Time		$	DF (11%)	DCF	
0	Selling price	(X)	1	(X)	◄——Balancing figure
1-4	Interest	50	3.102	155.10	
4	Repayment	1,000	0.659	659	
				———	
				0	

(X) + 155.10 + 659 = 0

∴ X = $814.10

GF should sell the bond for $814.10

6   Purchases = usage + closing inventory – opening inventory

     (in $'000) = $331 + $31 – $29

            = $333

     Payments to suppliers = opening payables + purchases – closing payables

                  = $47 + $333 – $40

                  = $340 (in $'000)

                  = $340,000

7   Trade payable days = $\dfrac{\text{Average trade payables}}{\text{Average daily purchases on credit terms}}$ × 365 = 45 days

     y/e 30.09.09 purchases = $324,444

     y/e 30.09.10 purchases = $356,900

$$2009 \quad 45 = \frac{\text{Average trade payables}}{\$324,444} \times 365$$

$\therefore$ Average trade payables = $40,000

$$2010 \quad \text{Trade payable days} = \frac{\$40,000}{\$356,900} \times 365 = 40.91$$

Days outstanding at 30 September 2010 = 41 days

75   Section A: Mixed objective test question bank

1   D   Increasing levels of long term borrowing

2   C

	Days
Raw material inventory turnover period	46
Finished goods inventory turnover period	43
Trade payables payment period	(67)
Work in progress inventory turnover period	32
Trade receivable collection period	54
	108

3   A

$$\frac{46,000}{250,000} \times 100\% = 18.4\%$$

4   A   Maximin = maximise the minimum achievable profit. The minimum achievable profits are when the weather is bad. The maximum profit when the weather is bad is achieved when 1,000 burgers are purchased.

5   C

Table of regrets
Number of burgers purchased

	1,000	2,000	3,000	4,000
Weather				
Bad	0	1,000	2,000	4,000
Average	4,000	1,000	0	1,000
Good	9,000	6,000	3,000	0
Maximum regret	9,000	6,000	3,000	4,000

The lowest of these four maximum regrets is 3,000 when 3,000 burgers are purchased.

6   Cost of early settlement discount is estimated using the formula

$$\left(\frac{100}{100-d}\right)^{\frac{365}{t}} - 1$$

$$= \left(\frac{100}{100-2.5}\right)^{\frac{365}{65-15}} - 1$$

$$= \left(\frac{100}{97.5}\right)^{7.3} - 1$$

$$= 20.3\%$$

7

Cash inflow	Cash outflow	Joint probability		Profit
$	$			$
120,000	(50,000)	0.3 ×0.25 =	0.075	70,000
120,000	(60,000)	0.3 × 0.35 =	0.105	60,000
120,000	(70,000)	0.3 ×0.4 =	0.12	50,000
140,000	(50,000)	0.45 ×0.25 =	0.1125	90,000
140,000	(60,000)	0.45 × 0.35 =	0.1575	80,000
140,000	(70,000)	0.45 ×0.4 =	0.18	70,000
160,000	(50,000)	0.25 ×0.25 =	0.0625	110,000
160,000	(60,000)	0.25 × 0.35 =	0.0875	100,000
160,000	(70,000)	0.25 ×0.4 =	0.1	90,000

The probabilities of each of the profits of $90,000 or greater are added together.

0.1125 + 0.0625 + 0.0875 + 0.1 = 0.3625 = 36.25%

8   This is an internal rate of return calculation. We will use 10% and 12%.

$$IRR = A + \left[\frac{P}{P-N} \times (B-A) \right]\%$$

where A is the (lower) rate of return

B is the (higher) rate of return

P is the NPV at A

N is the NPV at B

Time	Cash flows	Discount rate @ 10%	PV of cash flows	Discount rate @ 12%	PV of cash flows
	$		$		
0	(900)	1.000	(900.00)	1.000	(900.00)
1-4	80	3.170	253.60	3.037	242.96
4	1,000	0.683	683.00	0.636	636.00
			36.60		(21.04)

$$IRR = 10 + \frac{36.60}{36.60 + 21.04} \times (12-10) = 11.27\%$$

76 Section B: Mixed question bank 1

Top tips. For part (a) you should lay out your workings and assumptions carefully so that the marker can see exactly how you have apportioned the overheads.

Easy marks. The easy marks in this section are for parts (b) and (e) which require explanations of points that you should know by now. But keep your answer concise. Only five marks are available for each part so don't write pages and pages in your answer.

Examiner's comments. The examiner commented that in their answers to part (e) (i), candidates tended to discuss the weaknesses of the other three investment appraisal techniques, which was not the main thrust of the question.

(a)

	£	Basis of apportionment	Cost
Machinery costs	285,000	Per machine hr	285,000/95,000=£3/hr
Set up costs	235,000	Per production run	235,000/235=£1,000/run
Purchasing costs	300,000	Per purchase order	300,000/5,000=£60/order

		Product S		Product T
		£		£
Machinery costs	2 hours × 5,000 units × £3	30,000	20,000 units × £3	60,000
Set up costs	20 × £1,000	20,000	5 × £1,000	5,000
Purchasing costs	100 × £60	6,000	100 × £60	6,000
Total		56,000		71,000
Cost per unit:	£56,000/5,000	11.20	£71,000/20,000	3.55

(b)   What is backflush accounting?

Backflush accounting is a **method of costing** associated with a JIT production system, which **applies cost** to the **output of a process**. Costs do not mirror the flow of products through the production process, but are attached to the output when products are sold, on the assumption that such backflushed costs are a realistic measure of the actual costs incurred.

Method in traditional costing systems

Traditional costing systems use **sequential tracking** to track costs as products pass from raw materials to work in progress, to finished goods and finally to sales. So material costs are charged to **WIP** when materials are **issued** to production and labour and overhead costs are charged in a similar way as the **cost is incurred**.

Working backwards

In backflush accounting, budgeted or standard costs are used to work **backwards** to 'flush out' manufacturing costs for the finished units when they are sold.

Simplifying the costing system

The application of standard costs to finished goods or units sold **simplifies** the **costing system** and **saves** on **administrative effort**.

Inventory

The substantial reduction in inventories which is a feature of JIT, means that **inventory valuation** is **less relevant** and so the costing system can be greatly simplified. The backflush system should discourage managers from producing simply for inventory since working on material **does not add value** until the final product is **completed** or **sold.**

(c)   (i)   Product P1

Machine M1: 126 hours/0.35 = 360 units

Machine M2: 195 hours/0.6 = 325 units

Product P2

Machine M1: 126 hours/0.4 = 315 units

Machine M2: 195 hours/0.65 = 300 units

M2 is the bottleneck (as lowest throughput capacity for both products).

(ii)

	P1	P2
	$	$
Selling price	36.00	39.00
Materials	(14.20)	(16.75)
Throughput return	21.80	22.25
Conversion costs (lab + prod o/h)	9.00	11.25
Throughput accounting ratio = throughput return/conversion costs	2.42	1.98

(d)

	P1	P2
Throughput contribution	21.80	22.25
Time on bottleneck	0.60	0.65
Contribution/bottleneck hour	36.33	34.23
Rank	1st	2nd

Profit will be maximised by making as much of product P1 as possible as it has the higher contribution per bottleneck hour.

Maximum production of P1 is 325 units: M1 325 × 0.35 hours = 113.75 hours
                                            M2 325 × 0.6 hours = 195 hours

---

Top tips. To focus your answer, make sure that you specifically **compare** NPV to each of the other methods. Don't simply describe each method in isolation.

(e) (i)   **Net present value and its superiority over other investment appraisal techniques**

Net present value is generally seen as being superior to the other investment appraisal techniques mentioned at the presentation for the following reasons.

It takes into account the time value of money. This means that greater emphasis is placed on cash flows occurring at early stages in the project's life because these cash flows can then be reinvested. The accounting rate of return method and incremental profit place equal emphasis on all project returns, whenever they occur.

It considers all the cash flows, whereas the **payback method** focuses only on cash flows up to the point where the initial investment has been 'paid back'.

NPV is based on cash flows, whereas **accounting rate of return** (ARR) and **incremental profit** are based on profits which can be easily manipulated by accounting policies such as changes in depreciation methods.

(ii) The internal rate of return is the annual percentage return on an investment project. It is the discount rate at which the total of the discounted cash inflows is equal to the total of the discounted cash outflows, so that the net present value is zero.

(f) (i) $$EOQ = \sqrt{\frac{2C_oD}{C_h}}$$

$$= \sqrt{\frac{2 \times 150 \times 8,000}{2.75}}$$

$$= 934 \text{ units}$$

(ii) Total cost at order quantity of 934 units

	$
Purchase price 8,000 × $8	64,000
Order costs (8,000/934) × $150	1,285
Holding costs (934/2) × $2.75	1,285
	66,570

Total cost at order quantity of 2,000 units

	$
Purchase price 8,000 × $8 × 0.98	62,720
Order costs (8,000/2,000) × $150	600
Holding costs (2,000/2) × $2.75	2,750
	66,070

GC should accept the offer of the 2% discount as this decreases the total annual inventory cost.

77 Section B: Mixed question bank 2

> **Top tips.** Parts (a), (d) and (e) all ask for a specific number of factors so don't waste time by providing more than required.
>
> **Easy marks.** Neat workings in parts (b) and (f) will earn you marks because it is easier for the marker to follow what you have done.

(a)   Key features that are present in any organisation which is focused on TQM

(Note that other features could have been used.)

(i)   Get it right first time

One of the basic principles of TQM is that the **cost of preventing mistakes is less than the cost of correcting them** once they occur. Therefore an organisation which is focused on TQM should be aiming to get things right first time. Every mistake, delay and misunderstanding directly costs an organisation money through **wasted time and effort**.

(ii)   Continuous improvement

An organisation which is focused on TQM will believe that it is always possible to improve and so the aim should be to '**get it more right next time**.' This means that standards will be changed frequently rather than kept at a historical standard.

(iii)   Design for quality

A TQM environment aims to get it right first time and this means that **quality**, not faults, must be designed into the organisation's products and operations from the outset. Quality control must happen at the various stages in the process of designing the product or service. Good quality products or services also means that customers are more likely to be satisfied.

(b)

> **Examiner's comments.** Part (b) was badly answered because the information in the question was not used correctly. For example the collection of cash from customers was calculated incorrectly and the amount receivable was often shown in the wrong month.

Cash receipts for January to March 20X9

Month	January	February	March
	$'000	$'000	$'000
Cash receipts	440	474	416

Workings

January receipts	$'000
Cash sales to public 1/7 × 400	57
January credit sales 10% × 6/7 × 400	34
December credit sales 25% × 6/7 × 550	118
November credit sales 63% × 6/7 × 428	231
Total January cash receipts	440

February receipts	$'000
Cash sales to public 1/7 × 400	57
February credit sales 10% × 6/7 × 400	34
January credit sales 25% × 6/7 × 400	86
December credit sales 63% × 6/7 × 550	297
Total February cash receipts	474

March receipts	$'000
Cash sales to public 1/7 × 500	71
March credit sales 10% × 6/7 × 500	43
February credit sales 25% × 6/7 × 400	86
January credit sales 63% × 6/7 × 400	216
Total March cash receipts	416

(c)

> **Examiner's comments.** A significant number of candidates were able to correctly calculate the rate of interest being offered but came to the incorrect conclusion, assuming that it would cost DN more to accept the offer as the rate was higher than the overdraft.

We will calculate the value of the discount using the formula

$$\frac{100^{\frac{365}{t}}}{(100-d)} - 1$$

This gives us 100/98 to the power of 365/30, minus 1

100/98 = 1.0204
365/30 = 12.1667

1.0204 ^ 12.1667 = 1.2786

Minus 1 gives 27.86%

The discount is therefore worth 27.86%

It is therefore to DN's advantage to pay 30 days earlier and obtain the discount, unless it has other investment opportunities yielding more than 27.86%. As it is only paying 10% on its overdraft, it would even be advantageous to borrow on overdraft, if necessary, in order to pay this supplier in 10 days.

(d)   Just-in-time aims for zero inventory and perfect quality and operates by demand-pull. It consists of JIT production and JIT purchasing.

JIT production is a system driven by demand for finished products. Work in progress is only processed through a stage of production when it is needed by the next stage. The result is **minimal** (or in some cases non-existent) **inventories of work in progress and finished goods.**

JIT purchasing seeks to match the usage of materials with the delivery of materials from external suppliers. This means that **material inventories** can be kept at **near-zero levels.**

Timing of supplier deliveries

For JIT purchasing to be successful, the organisation must have confidence that the **supplier** will **deliver on time**. This is vital because in a JIT environment there will be no inventory to fall back on if the supplier fails to deliver.

Quality of supplier deliveries

Another requirement for JIT to be successful is that suppliers will deliver **materials of 100% quality**, that there will be no rejects, returns and hence **no consequent production delays**. Once again this is vital in a JIT environment because there will be no inventory to fall back on.

(e)   (i)   Undertaking a post-completion audit for an investment project

A post-completion audit involves **comparing the actual results of the project with the estimated results** that were included in the investment appraisal. The comparison exercise should use the **same method of appraisal** as that used in making the investment decision. Where possible, actual cash flows to date plus estimated cash flows to the end of the project's life should be compared with the cash flows incorporated in the original appraisal. The ability to carry out such a comparison will depend on the ease and cost of estimating future cash flows, however. If **actual plus forecast flows are different (unfavourably)** from those estimated, an **investigation** will be required.

(ii) <u>Possible drawbacks of undertaking a post-completion audit (PCA)</u>

As well as being **expensive** and **time consuming**, a PCA also suffers from a number of other problems.

- It may **not be possible to identify separately** those **costs** and **benefits** associated with the Intranet project.

- The exercise may lead **managers** to become **over cautious** and **unnecessarily risk averse** if they are unfairly punished for worse than expected outcomes.

- The **strategic effects** of a capital investment project may **take years to materialise** and it may never be possible to identify or quantify them effectively.

(f) <u>Rate per cost driver</u>

Machining $\dfrac{£35,750}{12,500}$ machine hours = £2.86 per machine hour

Set-up costs $\dfrac{£5,250}{10}$ production runs = £525 per run

Materials handling $\dfrac{£17,500}{40}$ materials deliveries = £437.50 per delivery

Packing costs $\dfrac{£22,500}{15}$ deliveries to customers = £1,500 per delivery

<u>Product Y overhead costs</u>

		£
Machining	2,000 machine hours × £2.86	5,720.00
Set-up costs	2 production runs × £525	1,050.00
Materials handling	19 deliveries × £437.50	8,312.50
Packing costs	5 customer deliveries × £1,500	7,500.00
		22,582.50

Overhead cost per unit = $\dfrac{£22,582.50}{200 \text{ units}}$ = £112.91

78 Section B: Mixed question bank 3

Top tips. Part (a) is fairly straightforward if you set out your workings clearly and remember how to calculate production and purchases. For part (b), learn a pro forma for marginal and absorption costing profit statements before you go into the exam. This will save you wasting valuable exam time in thinking about how to lay out your profit statements. Part (d) specifically asks for examples so don't forget to mention these.

Easy marks. In part (b)(iii) you can pick up at least one mark for explaining the reason why the profits will be different even if you cannot reconcile your own profit figures. You have to answer all parts of all questions so always attempt each part. It is easier to pick up the first few marks in each part than it is to earn the last few available marks.

Examiner's comments. Very few candidates managed to calculate the correct marginal and absorption costing profits in part (b).

(a) The production requirements are as follows.

	Quarter 1 Units	Quarter 2 Units
Opening inventory	(5,500)	(5,400)
Closing inventory (45% × 12,000) and (40%×14,000)	5,400	5,600
Sales	10,000	12,000
Production	9,900	12,200

Raw materials purchases budget:

	Kg
Opening inventory	(4,500)
Closing inventory (25% × 12,200 × 1.5kg)	4,575
Production (9,900 × 1.5kg)	14,850
Purchases = 14,925kg × £6 = £89,550	14,925

(b) (i) £92,000

Profit for quarter 3 using marginal costing

	£	£
Sales (14,000 × £40)		560,000
Opening inventory (5,600 × (£9+£8))	95,200	
Variable production cost (12,600 × (£9+£8))	214,200	
Less value of closing inventory (4200 × (£9+£8))	(71,400)	
Variable cost of sales		(238,000)
Contribution		322,000
Less fixed costs (W1)		(230,000)
Profit		92,000

Workings

(1)

	Quarter 3 Units
Opening inventory	(5,600)
Closing inventory	4,200
Sales	14,000
Production	12,600

(ii) £71,000

Profit for quarter 3 using absorption costing

	£	£
Sales (14,000 × £40)		560,000
Opening inventory (5,600 × (£9+£8+£15))	179,200	
Full production cost (12,600 × (£9+£8+£15))	403,200	
Less value of closing inventory (4200 × (£9+£8+£15))	(134,400)	
Full production cost of sales		(448,000)
Adjustment for over-absorbed overhead (W2)		9,000
Gross profit		121,000
Administration costs		(50,000)
Net profit		71,000

Workings

(2)

	Quarter 3 £
Fixed production cost absorbed (12,600 × £15)	189,000
Fixed production cost incurred (£720,000/4)	180,000
Over-absorbed fixed production cost	9,000

(iii) In quarter 3 the level of inventory was reduced from 5,600 units to 4,200 units. When changes in inventory occur, marginal and absorption costing systems will report different profit figures. This difference is equal to the change in inventory volume multiplied by the fixed production overhead rate per unit.

The difference in profits is £92,000-£71,000=£21,000

This is equal to (5,600-4,200) × £15 = £21,000

(c)

MEMORANDUM

To: Production Director
From: Management accountant
Date: 19 November 20X7
Re: Investment appraisal policy

1   Introduction

1.1   Thank you for your letter of 16 November in which you suggested that, since cash flow and profit are the same thing in the long run, we should always adopt courses of action which maximise accounting profit.

2   Advantages of using profit

2.1   **Profit** is a more widely known and understood concept than discounted cash flow (DCF) analysis and it is perfectly **understandable** that **non-financial specialists** should be more ready to **accept decisions based on a concept with which they have familiarity**. **DCF analysis** is, however, the more usual **and correct approach to take when appraising investments**.

3   The unsuitability of profit

3.1   **Profit** has a number of **features which make it unsuitable as an appraisal measure**. For example, due to **different accounting conventions** that organisations might adopt, such as the depreciation method or inventory valuation method, it is a **subjective** measure.

4   The advantages of DCF

4.1   DCF analysis, on the other hand, takes account of actual cash flows, the timing of those cash flows and the time value of money (the idea that £1 received now is worth more than £1 received in the future), all of which are vital components of the investment appraisal method adopted by an organisation.

4.2   **Although profit and cash flow might be the same in the long run, the timing of the short-term differences can have an impact on the acceptability of an investment** and so DCF analysis rather than measures of profit should be used to appraise investments.

5   DCF and our company

5.1   The company uses the net present value (NPV) approach to DCF analysis. This means that we require the net cash flows from an investment project to produce a return greater than the company's cost of capital.

6   I hope you have found this explanation useful but if you do require any further information please do not hesitate to contact me.

Signed: Management accountant

(d)   Internalised environmental costs

Internalised environmental costs are **incurred within the organisation**. They can be identified from the accounting records, can be **quantified and valued in monetary terms** and can often be traced to individual products and services, perhaps using an activity based costing system.

Two examples of internalised environmental costs are the cost of environmental certification and waste disposal costs.

Externalised environmental impacts

Externalised environmental impacts are the **effects that the organisation's activities have on the external environment.** Not all externalised environmental impacts result in the organisation itself incurring a cost that can be quantified and recorded in the costing system. However environmental costing is concerned with monitoring an organisation's external environmental impact, even if not all impacts can be quantified in financial terms. Such impacts might also be **traced to individual products and services** to assess the effect on the external environment of the manufacturing of specific products and the provision of individual services.

As part of its environmental costing system an organisation might **develop measures** to ensure that external standards concerning the impact of the organisation on the external environment are adhered to.

Two examples of externalised environmental impacts are carbon emissions and resource consumption.

(e)   <u>Features of an overdraft</u>

An **overdraft** is a negative balance on a current account at a bank. This constitutes borrowing and, because the balance will vary daily, the **interest** on the borrowing is normally computed on a **daily basis** at an **agreed rate**. A **maximum limit** to the overdraft is agreed with the bank and above this limit penalty **charges** will apply. In theory, the overdraft can be **cancelled immediately** if the bank is not happy with the company's **creditworthiness**. An overdraft can be **unsecured**, or **secured** on company assets or the personal assets of the proprietors.

The major advantage of an overdraft is that the company only pays interest when the overdraft is being used, in contrast to a bank loan.

<u>Importance of overdraft</u>

The overdraft is a key source of finance for working capital because of its **flexibility:** the finance varies automatically up to the agreed limit, enabling the company to handle peaks and troughs in cash flows without incurring excess interest charges. The potential disadvantage for an expanding company is that the **overdraft limit** may have to be **frequently renegotiated**. There is also a tendency for expanding companies to ignore the need to underpin their growth with longer term finance.

(f)   Since we are given a money cost of capital, the actual money cash flows must be used in the appraisal:

Yr	Investment £	Fixed costs £	Contribution £	Net cash flow £	14% factor	Present value £
0	(700,000)			(700,000)	1.000	(700,000)
1		(200,000)	620,000	420,000	0.877	368,340
2	+ 5%	(210,000) (+ 7%)	663,400	453,400	0.769	348,665
3	+ 5%	(220,500) (+ 7%)	709,838	489,338	0.675	330,303
4	+ 5%	(231,525) (+ 7%)	759,527	528,002	0.592	312,577
				Net present value		659,885

= £660,000 to the nearest £'000

79   Section B: Mixed question bank 4

(a)   (i)   Budgeted profit using absorption costing.

> **Top tips.** The difference in budgeted profit reported by the two costing systems (absorption and marginal) results from the fixed production overhead that is carried forward in inventory under the absorption costing system.
>
> When inventory levels are increasing, absorption costing will report a higher profit than marginal costing.
>
> The way to approach the question is to multiply the budgeted increase in inventory by the fixed overhead absorbed in that inventory.

Overhead absorption rate = $\dfrac{\text{Fixed production overhead costs}}{\text{Number of units produced}}$ = $\dfrac{\$12,800}{2,000}$ = \$6.40 per unit.

Profit under absorption costing = Profit under marginal costing + increase in inventory × overhead absorption rate

= \$5,700 + (600 × \$6.40) = \$9,540

(ii)   Marginal costing is more useful to management as a tool for decision making as it **focuses on variable costs** and the more relevant and **controllable** measure of **contribution**. Fixed costs are treated as period costs as these do not change with volume of output. When sales increase, the cost of sales rises only by the variable costs. Therefore contribution (sales less variable costs) is a more useful tool for **planning, control and decision making**.

Marginal costing is also is a more useful tool for determining rewards to management. A system of rewards based on absorption costing would have encouraged inventory building.

(b)

> **Top tips.** Don't be thrown by the fact that this question relates to a hospital environment. The application of standard costing to service industries is part of the syllabus and was frequently examined under the previous syllabus. There are a number of ways of approaching and presenting the answer. As long as you follow a methodical and logical approach you cannot go wrong. Start from the standard cost and work backwards to the actual cost. Remember that you are asked to calculate five variances in the reconciliation of actual and budgeted profit margins.
>
> We are told that the daily rates for nursing pay, space and food and hospital overheads were as expected. Therefore, the variances from standard cost will relate to the **length of stay** in hospital and the **drugs** and **specific materials** variances.
>
> First identify the variance that reflects the 3-day stay as compared to the standard 2-day procedure.
>
> The next variance to calculate relates to the drugs and specific materials relating to the individual patient.
>
> The last variance relates to the ratio of 0.9 nurses instead of the standard ratio of 0.75. This is again, another adverse variance as it implies that more staff time is spent than originally budgeted.

	£	£
Total standard cost for 2-day procedure		1,165
Variances relating to extra day in hospital		
1. Nursing costs: 1 extra day ×0.75 × £320 per day	240 (A)	
2. Space and food costs: 1 extra day × £175 per day	175 (A)	
3. Hospital overheads: 1 extra day at £110 per day	110 (A)	
		525
Standard cost for 3-day stay		1,690
4. Variance relating to drug and specific materials		
(£320 – £115)	205 (A)	
5. Variance relating to staff: patient ratio		
3 days × (0.9 – 0.75) × £320	144 (A)	
		349
Actual cost		2,039

(c)

> **Top tips.** A trend in variances is easier to appreciate and interpret when variances are calculated as percentages and presented graphically.
>
> The price and usage variances are given but it is important to calculate the percentages correctly.
>
> The percentage usage variance should be based on the standard cost of output. The percentage price variance should be based on the standard cost of actual purchases.

	February	*March*	*April*
Output (units)	11,000	5,100	9,100
× std cost per unit	£12	£12	£12
	£	£	£
Standard cost of actual output	132,000	61,200	109,200
Usage variance (as given)	15,970	5,950	8,400
Standard cost of actual purchases	147,970	67,150	117,600
Usage % variance	$\dfrac{15,970}{132,000} \times 100$	$\dfrac{5,950}{61,200} \times 100$	$\dfrac{8,400}{109,200} \times 100$
	12.1%	9.7%	7.7%
Price % variance	$\dfrac{12,300}{147,970} \times 100$	$\dfrac{4,500}{67,150} \times 100$	$\dfrac{8,400}{117,600} \times 100$
	8.3%	6.7%	5.3%

Percentage chart from February to April

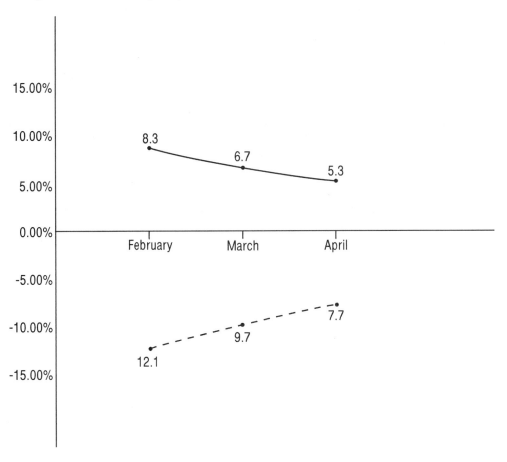

(d)

(i)   Standard costing and variance analysis concentrate on only a narrow range of costs and does not give sufficient attention to issues such as quality and customer satisfaction.

(ii)   Standard costing systems were developed when the business environment was more stable and less prone to change. The current business environment is more dynamic and it is not possible to assume stable conditions.

(iii)   Standard costing systems assume that performance to standard is acceptable. Today's business environment is more focused on continuous improvement.

Alternative suggestions

(iv)   Many of the variances in a standard costing system focus on the control of short term variable costs. In most modern manufacturing environments, the majority of costs, including direct labour costs, tend to be fixed in the short run.

(v)   Most standard costing systems produce control statements weekly or monthly. The manager in the modern business environment needs much more prompt control information to function efficiently in a dynamic business environment.

(e)

> **Top tips.** Don't simply discuss MC and TA, each in isolation. The question asks you to **compare** and **contrast** them so make sure that your answer does this.

The underlying concepts between marginal costing (MC) and throughput accounting (TA) are the same in that **both are based on the concept of contribution and consider variable costs only**. The concept of contribution is not the same under the two concepts. This is because **TA and MC define variable costs in different ways**. Throughput accounting takes a more extreme view than MC and considers only direct materials as variable costs. This is based on the idea that labour costs are not variable in the short term and are therefore ignored when calculating contribution. Throughput accounting is therefore often referred to as **'super variable costing'**.

TA is based on the underlying concepts of the 'Theory of constraints' that seeks to maximise throughput by identifying binding constraints in a production system. To achieve evenness of production the 'Theory of constraints' aims to identify and remove bottlenecks where possible. Output through the binding constraint should never be delayed or held up or sales will be lost. To avoid this happening, a buffer inventory should be kept prior to the binding constraint.

(f)   The detection of false claims: performance measure

$$\frac{\text{False claims}}{\text{Total claims}} \times 100$$

Relevant benchmarking

The percentage of false claims to total claims is compared to previous periods within the same company and with data from other organisations within the industry. Data may be from industry groups or trade journals. Best practice should be identified and used to establish targets.

Speed of processing claims: performance measure

- Time from receipt to settlement
- Complaints from policy holders

Compare to previous records and industry groups and trade journals.

80   Section B: Mixed question bank 5

(a)

> **Top tips.** Remember to apply your discussion in part (ii) to the specific scenario wherever possible.

(i)   The principle behind zero-based budgeting (ZBB) is that the budget for each cost centre should be prepared from scratch. Every item of expenditure **must be justified** as though the activities ware taking place for the first time. Without approval the budget allowance is zero.

ZBB rejects the assumption inherent in incremental budgeting that this year's activities will continue at the same volume next year, and that next year's budget can be based on this year's costs plus an extra amount for expansion and inflation.

(ii)   • The major problem we can expect to arise when implementing this approach is the **volume of extra management time** and **paperwork** required

   • The application of zero based budgeting may **require management** skills which a smaller company such as J Limited might **not possess**. Managers will have to be **trained** in zero based budgeting techniques

   • J Limited may not have the **systems capable** of providing the information required to implement the ZBB approach

   • It will be difficult to **rank activities** which appear **equally vital**. It will be especially difficult to rank activities with a **qualitative** rather than **quantitative** benefits

One way of obtaining the benefits of ZBB and overcoming some of the drawbacks of it is to apply it **selectively** throughout the organisation. It could be applied to **several departments** in **one budget period** and several **others** the **next budget period**. In this way all activities could be **scrutinised** over a period of time.

(b)

> **Top tips**. It is important not to reproduce what you know about McDonaldisation but to relate it to the specific industry and situation presented. You are asked to explain how McDonaldisation will impact on budget cost and preparation control within UV Limited given that the latter provides standard meals at fixed prices as well as customised meals at specially negotiated prices.
>
> **Easy marks.** Read the question carefully and earn marks by showing an appreciation of the application of McDonaldisation in both lines of the company's business.
>
> **Examiner's comments.** The examiner complained that candidates wrote lengthy answers about McDonaldisation without relating their comments either to the scenario provided or the question asked.

The term **McDonaldisation** refers to the **standardisation** followed by the American hamburger chain in the provision of its services, which is now being applied to many sectors of society.

UV Limited provides **standardised meals** at **fixed prices** as well as requirements at negotiated prices. The McDonaldisation approach to UV Limited will assist in both lines of business in budget **planning** and **cost control** in the following ways:

McDonaldisation will provide:

Calculability

Each meal is identical and standardised thus **eliminating** the **human element**. Each meal is a **measurable standard cost** unit for which a standard cost can be established and the actual cost can be measured for cost control purposes. Even for **customised** orders a standard unit cost can be established for each **component** of the meal as a **measurable cost unit**, referred to as a **composite cost unit**. The standard cost established should also provide for variations to help budget for customised meals.

Cost control

Control over the service provided is achieved by **reducing the human influence** which can lead to **variation** in **output and quality**. Although the elimination of the human influence is **more difficult** where contracts are individually negotiated, this can still follow the same principles to a **certain extent**. Standard cost units may be established for **each component** of the meal and then **provision** may be made for a certain degree of variation to accommodate customised meals. A reasonable amount of control may be exercised in this way although normally the concept of McDonaldisation would not be applied to customised meals.

(c)

> **Top tips**. When there is idle time, remember to base the efficiency variance and the mix variance (which is a part of the efficiency variance) on the active hours only.

Idle time variance

	hrs
Hours paid for	55
Hours worked	45
Idle time	10 (A)

At standard cost of junior consultant £60/hr = £600(A)

Labour mix variance

	Actual mix	Standard mix (4:6)	Variance	Standard contribution per hour	Variance £
Senior consultant	50	38	12A	£100	1,200 A
Junior consultant	45	57	12F	£60	720 F
	95	95			480 A

Labour efficiency variance

		Actual production for one job			Standard cost/hr	Variance
		Should take	Did take	Variance	£	£
Senior consultant		40 hours	50 hours	10 (A)	100	1,000 A
Junior consultant		60 hours	45 hours(worked)	15 (F)	60	900 F
				5 (F)		100 A

(d)   (i)   The suggested method of dealing with the impact of taxation is not acceptable for the following reasons.

- The process of discounting takes account of the **timing of cash flows** in order to allow for the **time value of money.** Tax is not always paid in cash in the same period that the profits are earned. There will usually be a time lag so that at least part of the cash flow arising from taxation occurs the year after the profit is earned. This **time delay** will affect the present value of the cash flows arising from taxation and must be taken into account in the calculations.

- The tax relief for the depreciation charge (the **capital allowance**) is not all received in the year in which the expenditure is incurred. The capital allowances are **received in stages** throughout the project's life. Once again this impacts upon the timing of cash flows and hence on the present value of the cash flows arsing from the effects of taxation.

(ii)   There will be a balancing charge on the sale of the machine of £(450,000 – (1,200,000 – 950,000)) = £200,000. This will give rise to a tax payment of 30% × £200,000 = £60,000.

(e)

> **Top tip.** Depending on the degree of accuracy required, a quick way of determining the IRR when the cash flow is the same each year is to first divide the initial outlay by the annual cash inflow (£75,000/£25,000 = 3.0). Looking along the 5 year line in cumulative present value tables, the closest figure to 3.000 is 2.991 in the 20% column. Hence the IRR is close to 20%. If greater accuracy is required then you can use 20% as one of the discount rates in your interpolation calculations, as we have done in our answer below.
>
> **Easy marks.** Neat workings will enable the marker to see what you have done and award marks for the method you use.

(i)

Year	Cash flow £	Discount factor 20%	PV at 20% £	Discount factor 10%	PV at 10% £
0	(75,000)	1.000	(75,000)	1.000	(75,000)
1-5	25,000	2.991	74,775	3.791	94,775
			(225)		19,775

$$\therefore IRR = 10\% + \left(\frac{19,775}{19,775+225} \times 10\% \right)$$

$$= 19.8875\%$$

(ii)

Year	Cash flow £	Discount factor 15%	PV £
0	(75,000)	1.000	(75,000)
1-5	25,000	3.352	83,800
			8,800

PV of annual labour cost savings over 5 years at 15% = £20,000 × 3.352 = £67,040

∴ PV of annual labour cost savings could fall by £8,800 before project ceased to be viable = (£8,800/£67,040) × 100% = 13.13%

(f)

(i) $EOQ = \sqrt{\dfrac{2CoD}{Ch}}$

$= \sqrt{\dfrac{2 \times 25 \times 65,000}{3}}$

= 1,041 units

(ii)   Total cost at order quantity 1,041 units

	$
Purchase price 65,000 × $10	650,000
Order costs 65,000/1,041 × $25	1,561
Holding costs 1,041/2 × $3	1,562
	653,123

Total cost at order quantity of 2,000 units

	$
Purchase price 65,000 × $10 × 98%	637,000
Order costs 65,000/2,000 × $25	813
Holding costs 2,000/2 × $3	3,000
	640,813

BF should accept the offer of the 2% discount as this decreases the total annual inventory cost.

81   Section B: Mixed question bank 6

(a)   **Throughput accounting** was developed from the **Theory of Constraints**, formulated in the United States to help managers **improve profitability** where an organisation faces **constraints** or **bottlenecks** which **limit production**.

Profit oriented goals

The philosophy behind Throughput accounting is that profitability is determined by the rate at which sales are made and this depends on how quickly **goods** can be **produced** to **satisfy demand**. Since the goal of a profit-oriented organisation is to **make money**, goods must be sold for that goal to be achieved. Throughput accounting is consistent with a JIT environment. **Producing output** just to add to work-in-progress or **finished goods** creates **no profit** and so should not be encouraged. Until the output is sold, no **value** is added and no profit earned.

Fixed vs variable costs

Throughput accounting (TA) views most **factory costs** with the **exception of material** costs as **fixed**. Because TA differentiates between fixed and variable costs it views even direct labour costs as fixed in the short term. This is because employees are not usually paid piece work and are not laid off when there is no work and so **labour costs** are **not considered** to be truly **variable**. Marginal costing however, considers labour costs to be variable.

Buffer inventory

The theory of constraints (TOC) observes that the **production rate** of the entire factory is set at the **rate of the bottleneck resource**. In order to **maximise throughput**, a **buffer inventory** is required **prior** to the **bottleneck** procedure or resource so that the production process is not delayed.

Limitations of TA

Throughput accounting is suitable for very **short-term** decision making as it ignores more traditional techniques which would help recover all costs.

Throughput accounting also **assumes** that all factory costs other than material costs are **fixed** when this **may not be true in all cases**, such as overtime.

(b)

> **Top tips.** Five marks are available for an explanation of five separate acronyms. You merely need to demonstrate that you know what is meant by each one, but it is not sufficient merely to interpret the acronym.

MRP stands for materials requirement planning. This is a **materials scheduling software** specifying material requirements and routings based on **required outputs**, **inventory policy** and **lead times**.

MRP II stands for manufacturing resource planning. It is similar to MRP but **extends** to **staff** and **equipment** scheduling with particular **focus** on **capacity levels**.

ERP stands for enterprise resource planning. It is a **software package** that **integrates** all **information** flowing **through the company** (financial, accounting, human resources, supply chain and customer).

OPT stands for optimised production technology. The objective of OPT is to **identify** and **remove** or optimise the **use of resources** to ensure that there is no unnecessary build up of inventory.

JIT stands for Just-in-Time. This is an approach to production that seeks to **minimise** or **eliminate** the **holding of inventory**. Items are produced for immediate sale and production is normally in response to customer demand and not for inventory build up.

(c)   Changes in the modern business environment that have led to the need for ABC to replace traditional absorption costing.

- Higher proportion of overheads in relation to direct material and labour costs

   In a highly **automated**, **sophisticated** and **competitive** modern environment **overheads** (such as set-up, inspection, research and development, market research, marketing, distribution and advertising costs) represent a **very high proportion of total costs**, often higher than direct costs.

- Increasing product diversity

   In a world of constant product **innovation** there is likely to be a **range of products** of varying degrees of complexity and sophistication. These are likely to consume overheads at **different rates** and it is therefore important that these are absorbed into products accurately.

- Increased competition, leading to the need for more accurate cost information and realistic pricing

   Increased competition leading to the need to **control costs** therefore requiring more **detailed** information about what drives these costs.

(d)   (i)   Investigation of variances

   Factors to consider before deciding whether to investigate a variance:

   - Materiality – a small variance may not be worthy of investigation.

   - Controllability – the variance may not be controllable, even once the cause is established.

   - Variance trend – a variance that is becoming increasingly larger may be worthy of investigation even before it reaches predetermined units.

   - Cost of an investigation

   - Interrelationship of variances

> **Top tips.** By assuming that variances that occur are normally distributed around this average, a variance will be investigated if it is more than a distance from the expected average than the estimated normal distribution suggests is likely if the process is in control. (Note that such a variance would be deemed significant.)
>
> A 95% or 0.05 significant level rule would state that variances should be investigated if they exceed 1.96 standard deviations from the standard.
>
> A 99% or 0.01 significance level rule would state that variances should be investigated if they exceed 2.58 standard deviations from the standard. This is less stringent than a 0.05 significant level rule.
>
> For simplicity, 1.96 and 2.58 standard deviations can be rounded up to 2 and 3 standard deviations respectively.

(ii)   Variance = £26,800 – £22,000 = £4,800

Standard deviation = 2,000

Variance is equal to $\dfrac{£4,800}{2000}$ = 2.04 standard deviations

A 95% or 0.05 significance level rule would mean that this variance should be investigated.

(e)   In a **TQM** environment there are likely to be **minimal labour rate variances** if the workforce are paid a guaranteed weekly wage. Fixed price contracts, with suppliers guaranteeing levels of quality, are often a feature, especially if a JIT system is also in place, and so there are likely to be **few, if any, material price and usage variances**.

So can standard costing and TQM exist together?

- Predetermined standards **conflict** with the **TQM philosophy** of **continual improvement**. Continual improvements should alter quantities of inputs, prices and so on, whereas standard costing is best used in a stable, standardised, repetitive environment.

- Standard costs often **incorporate** a **planned level of scrap** in material standards. This is at **odds** with the TQM aim of **'zero defects'** and there is **no motivation** to **'get it right first time'**.

- Standard costing systems make **individual managers** responsible for the variances relating to their part of the organisation's activities. A **TQM programme**, on the other hand, aims to make **all personnel aware of**, and responsible for, the importance of supplying the customer with a **quality product**.

On the other hand, variance analysis can be used to **enhance product quality** and to keep track of quality control information. This is because variance analysis **measures both the planned use of resources** and the **actual use** of resources in order to compare the two.

As variance analysis is generally expressed in terms of purely quantitative measures, such as quantity of raw materials used and price per unit of quantity, some adaptions will be needed, for example.

- It should be possible to provide **financial measures for the cost of poor quality**. These can include direct costs such as the wages of inspection and quality control staff, the cost of time in rectifying the defects, and the cost of the materials used in rectification.
- Measures could be built into materials price and variance analysis, so that the **materials price variance** as currently reported includes a **factor reflecting the quality of materials purchased**.

(f)

> **Top tips.** Read the question carefully to avoid wasting time in part (ii) by calculating the cash flows for all four years of the project's life.

(i) $$(1 + \text{money or nominal rate}) = (1 + \text{real rate}) \times (1 + \text{inflation rate})$$

$$(1 + 0.07) = (1 + r) \times (1 + 0.04)$$

$$r = \frac{1.07}{1.04} - 1$$

$$= 0.0288$$

$$= 2.88\%$$

(ii)   Year 3 cash inflow

= £130,000 × 1.04³
= £146,232

Present value at discount rate of 7%   = £146,232 × 0.816
= £119,326

82   Section B: Mixed question bank 7

(a)   Whereas it is acknowledged that budgets which are **easily attainable** are **not good motivators**, budgets which are too tight and practically unattainable will cease to be motivational. It is important for the review co-ordinator to ensure that the **right balance is achieved**. In preparing budgets there is always an element of uncertainty and budgets are normally developed around a set of forecasts. The finance department will expect the budget to be based on realistic forecasts whereas management will set tight targets to increase motivation. This is where the conflict arises.

(b)   **Incremental budgeting** is based on the **previous period's budget**, adjusted for current period changes – for example, a cost budget may be increased by 4% to account for inflation of material prices. The main disadvantage of incremental budgeting is that any inefficiencies in the previous year's budget remain in the current year. Any budgetary slack already built into the budget will be maintained. This can lead to **wasteful spending** as managers strive to hit their inefficient targets to justify their inclusion in the first place.

Zero based budgeting (ZBB) builds the budget from zero and **justifies each item of cost from scratch**. This requires detailed analysis of a company's activities, and leads to the identification of inefficient activities, thus preventing the inclusion of budgetary slack. It should also **encourage more efficient spending** – ie only on activities that have been fully justified.

(c)   (i)   <u>Idle time variance</u>

10 hours × £80 = £800 (A)

<u>Labour mix variance</u>

Total actual hours = 60+80 = 140 (excludes idle time hours)

Standard mix of actual input

	Hrs
Senior hours (5/14 × 140) =	50
Junior hours (9/14 × 140) =	90
	140

	Should mix Actual hrs Std mix	Did mix Actual hrs Actual mix	Difference	× Std price	Variance
Senior	50	60	10 (A)	£120	£1,200 (A)
Junior	90	80	10 (F)	£80	£800 (F)
					£400 (A)

(ii)   Mix and yield variances are only appropriate when proportions of work are changeable and controllable, for example, if the work of the senior consultant could be done by the junior consultant and vice versa. This is not the case in this example.

(d)   (i)   <u>Materials usage planning variance</u>

Orig std kg for actual output (6kg × 380)	2,280 kg
Revised std kg for actual output (6.75kg × 380)	2,565 kg
Material usage planning variance in kg	285 (A)
× original standard rate per kg	× £12
	£3,420 (A)

(ii)   <u>Operational materials price variance</u>

	£
Revised std price of actual kg (2,500kg × £12)	30,000
Actual price of actual kg	29,000
Price variance	1,000 (F)

(iii)   <u>Operational materials usage variance</u>

380 units should use (× 6.75kg)	2,565 kg
But did use	2,500 kg
Usage variance in kg	65 (F)
× revised std cost per kg	£12
	£780 (F)

(e)   (i)   Fixed production overhead absorption rate = $40,000/2,000 = $20 per unit

Fixed production overhead absorbed = 1,800 × $20 = $36,000

Actual fixed production overhead = $39,000

Under absorption = $39,000 - $36,000 = $3,000

(ii)   Absorption costing profit statement

	$
Revenue	85,000
Cost of sales	(59,500)*
Underabsorbed o/h	(3,000)
Gross profit	22,500
Var selling and admin costs	(5,100)
Fixed selling and admin costs	(10,000)
Profit	7,400

* ($30,000/2,000 × 1,700) + (20 × 1,700) = $59,500

(iii)   Marginal costing profit statement

	$
Revenue	85,000
Variable cost of sales	(30,600)
Contribution	54,400
Fixed production overheads	(39,000)
Fixed selling and admin costs	(10,000)
Profit	5,400

(f)   Total investment lasts 2.5 years. Interest is payable twice a year = 5 periods.

$((1+ 0.02)^5 - 1) \times 100 = 10.408\%$

Balance in account = $50,000 × 1.02^5 = $55,204

83 Section B: Mixed question bank 8

(a) (i) Debtor days $= \dfrac{\text{Average trade receivables}}{\text{Credit sales for the year}} \times 365$

	£
UK customers: £2,100,000 × 40% × $\frac{10}{365}$ =	23,014
UK customers: £2,100,000 × 60% × $\frac{30}{365}$ =	103,562
Overseas customers: £900,000 × 80% × $\frac{60}{365}$ =	118,356
	244,932

Debtor days $= \dfrac{£244,932}{£3,000,000} \times 365 = 29.8$ days

	£
(ii) UK customers: £2,100,000 × 15% × $\frac{30}{365}$ =	25,890
Overseas customers: £900,000 × 80% × $\frac{60}{365}$ =	118,356
	144,246

Debtor days $= \dfrac{£144,246}{£3,000,000} \times 365 = 17.5$ days

(b) Non-financial considerations

Advantage – Time

The **managers** of the business **do not have** to spend their **time** on the problems of slow paying receivables. They can concentrate on other areas of the business.

Advantage – Expertise

The business can make use of the **receivables management expertise** that the factor has. For example, the factor may be able to perform **better credit checks** than the business.

Disadvantage – Customer perception

Customers will be making payments direct to the factor which is likely to present a **negative picture** of the firm.

Disadvantage – Reputation

Factoring may indicate that the firm is in **need of rapid cash**, raising **questions** about its **financial stability**.

Disadvantage – Working methods

The factor may attempt to influence the way that the company does business. For example, they may wish to 'vet' any potential new customers.

(c)

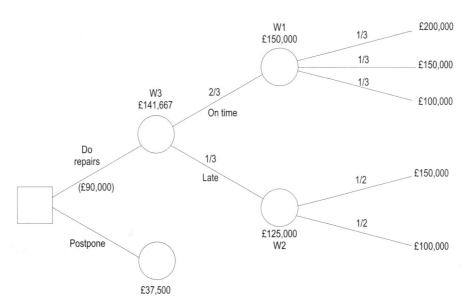

Expected value with repairs = £141,667 – £90,000

$\qquad\qquad\qquad\qquad\quad$ = £51,667

Without repairs $\qquad\qquad\quad$ = £37,500

As the expected value with repairs is higher, the repairs should be done now.

Workings

1 $\quad$ (£200,000 × 1/3) + (£150,000 × 1/3) + (£100,000 × 1/3) = £150,000

2 $\quad$ (£150,000 × 1/2) + (£100,000 × 1/2) = £125,000

3 $\quad$ (£150,000 × 2/3) + (£125,000 × 1/3) = £141,667

(d) $\quad$ S = 134.23 + 7.945Q

$\qquad\qquad\qquad\qquad\qquad\qquad\qquad\qquad$ *Burgers '000*

2010 Q2: 134.23 + (7.945 × 7(W1)) × 0.75 $\quad$ = $\qquad$ 142

2010 Q3: 134.23 + (7.945 × 8 (W1)) × 1 $\qquad$ = $\qquad$ 198

2010 Q4: 134.23 + (7.945 × 9 (W1)) × 1.50 $\quad$ = $\qquad$ 309

Working

Quarter numbers are as follows

	2007				*2008*				*2009*				*2010*		
Q1	Q2	Q3	Q4	Q1	Q2	Q3	Q4	Q1	Q2	Q3	Q4	Q1	Q2	Q3	Q4
–6	–5	–4	–3	–2	–1	0	1	2	3	4	5	6	**7**	**8**	**9**

(e) $\quad$ **Motivation** and **morale** of employees are **affected** by the control system (including the budget) operating within the workplace. If such a system has been **poorly implemented**, employees may **react adversely**. For example, if standards are set which even the most conscientious employee fails to reach, they will be **demotivated** and may give up working as hard as 'there doesn't seem to be any point'.

$\qquad$ If budgeting is done well, it can provide a **useful psychological incentive** by giving employees a realistic but challenging target of efficiency. For control purposes, budgets must **strike a balance** between striving for **perfection** and **motivating** employees.

(f)   Environmental internal failure costs

These are the costs of activities that must be undertaken when contaminants and waste have been created by a business but not released into the environment.

Example

Examples include maintaining pollution equipment and recycling scrap.

Environmental external failure costs

These are the costs which arise when a business releases waste into the environment. A business can harm its reputation by doing this.

Example

Examples include cleaning up oil spills or decontaminating land.

84 Section B: Mixed question bank 9

(a)   (i)

Customer	Balance	Up to 30 days	Up to 60 days	Up to 90 days	Over 90 days
J	701	145	438*	0	118**

*135 + 232 + 71 = 438

**125 + 181 + 92 + 287 – 217 – 63 – 287 = 118

(ii)   Decision-making

The age analysis of receivables may be used to help decide **what action to take** about older debts. Old debts could be **investigated, chased up** or **written off**. If there is a persistent problem, the credit controller might have to insist on a **refusal of credit**

Control and targets

The age analysis can be used to monitor the efficiency of the cash collection and to ensure that collection is kept under control and that targets are met.

(b)   (i) $EOQ = \sqrt{\dfrac{2C_oD}{C_h}}$

$= \sqrt{\dfrac{2 \times 150 \times 64,000}{1.20}}$

$= \sqrt{16,000,000}$

$\therefore Q = 4,000$

Holding cost + ordering cost $= QC_h/2 + C_oD/Q$

$= \dfrac{4,000 \times 1.20}{2} + \dfrac{150 \times 64,000}{4,000}$

$= \$2,400 \times \$2,400$

$= \$4,800$

(ii)   If delivery can take up to three weeks then three weeks' worth of raw material should be kept available, just in case.

Annual usage = 64,000 units

Three weeks' worth = 64,000 units × 3/52 = 3,693 units

(c)   Integration of resource needs

MRPII plans production jobs and also calculates **resource needs** such as labour and machine hours. It therefore attempts to **integrate materials** requirement **planning**, factory capacity planning and purchasing into a **single complete** manufacturing **control system**.

Computerised sharing of information

Most MRPII systems are a collection of **computer programs** that permit the **sharing** of **information** between **departments** in an organisation. This means that purchasing and production departments can produce a planned schedule of all requirements and track orders through the manufacturing process.

EOQ v MRPII

The company currently uses **EOQ** but this model **assumes** that **demand is constant** throughout the year and normally materials are only re-ordered when inventory falls to an agreed level. This could mean that a company could either be holding too little or too much inventory at any given point.

An MRPII system incorporates an MRP system where information from a master production schedule detailing the finished goods quantities and timings is used to **work backwards** to determine the **requirements** for parts and materials.

Minimising inventory levels

The MRPII system aims to ensure that the resources are delivered **only when they are needed**. Raw materials are therefore kept to a minimum to reduce costs.

(d)   Strategy

The organisation's overall strategy and any actual or likely changes in that **strategy** will be **taken into account** because ABB attempts to manage the business as the **sum of its interrelated parts.** It does this by ensuring that resources are allocated within a budget to the activities that are integral to meeting company objectives.

Emphasis on outputs

Traditional accounting tends to focus on the **nature of the costs** being incurred (the input side) and traditional budgeting tends to mirror this by only making adjustments to the budget for expected changes to these inputs. This means that potentially any errors or inefficiencies within the current budgeting system will be perpetuated.

ABB emphasizes the activities that are being achieved (the outputs) and only includes in the budgets resources that are required to fulfil these activities.

Value and non-value adding activities

The more detailed scrutiny of ABB will provide management with **better information** about the costs of their different activities. This will permit the company to **identify any non-value adding activities** and therefore make more informed decisions about which activities to undertake.

Focus on whole of activity

The focus is on the **whole of an activity**, not just its separate parts and so there is **more likelihood** of getting it **right first time**. For example, what is the use of being able to produce goods in time for their despatch date if the budget provides insufficient resources for the distribution manager who has to deliver them.

(e)

	Quarter 3
Production (Units)	23,000
Budgeted production costs	$
Direct materials (W1)	262,200
Production labour (W2)	219,000
Production overheads (W3)	278,000
	759,200

Workings

1   Direct material cost per unit $= \dfrac{\$180,000}{15,000}$ or $\dfrac{\$240,000}{20,000}$ $= \$12/\text{unit}$

For quarter 3: 23,000 units $\times$ \$12 = \$276,000

This will attract a 5% discount so the cost will be \$276,000 $\times$ 95% = \$262,200

2   High low method

Units	Labour $
20,000	195,000
15,000	155,000
5,000	40,000

Variable element = \$40,000/5,000

= \$8/unit

Fixed element: $(15,000 \times \$8)$ + FC   = \$155,000

$\therefore$ FC   = \$155,000 – \$120,000

= \$35,000

Production labour cost for 23,000 units   = \$35,000 + ($8 $\times$ 23,000)

= \$219,000

3   High low method

Units	Overhead $
20,000	240,000
15,000	210,000
5,000	30,000

Variable element   = \$30,000/5,000

= \$6/unit

Fixed element: $(15,000 \times \$6)$ + FC   = \$210,000

$\therefore$ FC   = \$210,000 – \$90,000

= \$120,000

Production overhead cost for 23,000 units   = \$120,000 + ($6 $\times$ 23,000)

= \$258,000

Add \$20,000 per quarter as levels > 22,000 units = \$278,000

(f)

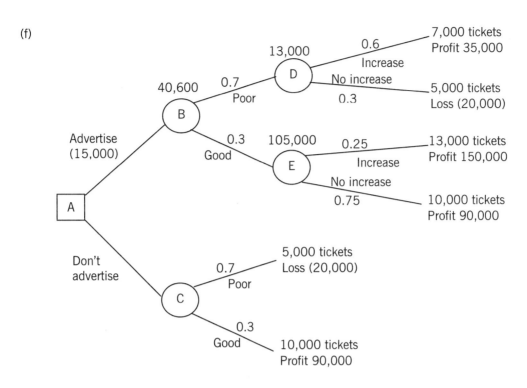

Outcome E (150,000 x 0.25) + (90,000 x 0.75)   =   105,000
Outcome D (35,000 x 0.6) + ((20,000) x 0.3)   =   13,000
Outcome B (105,000 x 0.3) + (13,000 x 0.7)   =   40,600
Outcome C (90,000 x 0.3) + ((20,000) X 0.7)   =   13,000

Decision A   Advertise (40,600 – 15,000)   =   25,600
             Don't advertise   =   13,000

As the expected value with an advertisement is higher, the advertisement should go ahead.

MOCK EXAMS

300

CIMA
Paper P1 (Operational)
Performance Operations

Mock Exam 1

Question Paper	
Time allowed	**3 hours**
This paper is divided into three sections	
Section A	**EIGHT objective test questions**
Section B	**SIX short answer questions**
Section C	**TWO scenario questions**

DO NOT OPEN THIS PAPER UNTIL YOU ARE READY TO START UNDER EXAMINATION CONDITIONS

SECTION A – 20 marks

Answer ALL sub-questions

Questions 1 to 5 are worth 2 marks each (10 marks in total)

Questions 6 to 8 are worth 10 marks in total

Question 1

1   K Ltd are considering an investment of £1,300,000. The company requires a minimum real rate of return of 10% under the present and anticipated conditions. Inflation is expected to be 3% per annum over the life of the investment and all costs and revenues are expected to increase in line with inflation. Which of the following is the most appropriate approach to take to a DCF appraisal?

   A   Increase costs and revenues at 3% per annum and discount at 10%
   B   Make no adjustment to the cash flows for inflation and discount at 10%
   C   Increase the cash flows by 3% per annum and discount at 13%
   D   Make no adjustment to the cash flows for inflation and discount at 13%   **(2 marks)**

2   M plc uses time series analysis and regression techniques to estimate future sales demand. Using these techniques, it has derived the following trend equation:

   $y = 10,000 + 4,200x$

   where y is the total sales units; and
          x is the time period

   It has also derived the following seasonal variation index values for each of the quarters using the multiplicative (proportional) seasonal variation model:

Quarter	Index value
1	120
2	80
3	95
4	105

   The total sales units that will be forecast for time period 33, which is the first quarter of year 9, are

   A   138,720
   B   148,720
   C   176,320
   D   178,320   **(2 marks)**

3   Nile Limited is preparing its sales budget for 20X4. The sales manager estimates that sales will be 120,000 units if the Summer is rainy, and 80,000 units if the Summer is dry. The probability of a dry Summer is 0.4.

   What is the expected value for sales volume for 20X4?

   A   96,000 units
   B   100,000 units
   C   104,000 units
   D   120,000 units   **(2 marks)**

The following data relate to sub-questions 4 and 5 below

McRon plc is a fast food manufacturer who blends ingredient X in the processing of its main product the big Ron.
The standard cost for 1 kg of big Ron is:

	£
0.2kg of X at £0.80 per kg	0.16

Actual data for April 20X3 were as follows

Output of the big Ron (000s kgs)	2,800	kg
Ingredient X used (000s kgs)	600	kg
Cost (£'000)	534	

A worldwide shortage in X meant that the standard was revised to a more realistic one of £0.85 per kg.

4   The planning price variance for ingredient X to be reported for April 20X3 is:

    A   £28,000 (A)
    B   £28,000 (F)
    C   £30,000 (A)
    D   £30,000 (F)   **(2 marks)**

5   The operating price variance for ingredient X to be reported for April 20X3 is:

    A   £54,000 (F)
    B   £54,000 (A)
    C   £24,000 (F)
    D   £24,000 (A)   **(2 marks)**

6   Standard cost data for ED Ltd's single product is as follows.

	£ per unit
Direct labour, 1 hour at £7 per hour	7
Variable production overhead	3
Fixed production overhead	4

The fixed production overhead absorption rate is based on budgeted monthly production of 2,000 units.
Overheads are assumed to be related to direct labour hours of active working.

Actual results for June

Production output	1,800 units

	£
Direct wages paid – 1,600 hours	12,000
Variable production overhead	6,000
Fixed production overhead	8,200

A machine breakdown resulted in 200 hours of idle time during June.

What is the variable overhead efficiency variance?   **(3 marks)**

7   Standard cost data for ED Ltd's single product is as follows.

	£ per unit
Direct labour, 1 hour at £7 per hour	7
Variable production overhead	3
Fixed production overhead	4

The fixed production overhead absorption rate is based on budgeted monthly production of 2,000 units. Overheads are assumed to be related to direct labour hours of active working.

Actual results for June

Production output	1,800 units

	£
Direct wages paid – 1,600 hours	12,000
Variable production overhead	6,000
Fixed production overhead	8,200

A machine breakdown resulted in 200 hours of idle time during June.

What are the overhead expenditure variances?   **(3 marks)**

8   A bond has a current market price of $83. It will repay it face value of $100 in seven years' time and has a coupon rate of 4%.

If the bond is purchased at $83 and held, what is its yield to maturity?   **(4 marks)**

                                                           (Total = 20 marks)

SECTION B – 30 marks

Answer ALL six sub-questions. Each sub-question is worth five marks

---

Question 2

(a)	Briefly explain total quality management (TQM).	**(5 marks)**
(b)	State the differences between incremental and zero based budgeting techniques.	**(5 marks)**

(c) Fixed overhead absorption rates are often calculated using a single measure of activity. It is suggested that fixed overhead costs should be attributed to cost units using multiple measures of activity (activity based costing).

Explain 'activity based costing' and how it may provide useful information to managers.

(Your answer should refer to both the setting of cost driver rates and subsequent overhead cost control.)

(5 marks)

(d) Explain the importance of life-cycle assessment in an environmental costing system that is focused on reducing the environmental costs associated with a product.　**(5 marks)**

(e) The production director has stated, 'A post-completion appraisal cannot reverse the decision to incur capital expenditure because the expenditure has already taken place. Therefore there appraisals are of no value and are a waste of management time'.

Prepare a response to the director that explains the benefits of undertaking a post-completion appraisal.

(5 marks)

(f) Many statistical and accounting techniques are based on extrapolations of past performance into the future in order to provide information for planning and decision making.

Required

Discuss the problems of extrapolating past performance into the future.　**(5 marks)**

(Total = 30 marks)

SECTION C – 50 marks

Answer both questions

Question 3

JK plc operates a chain of fast-food restaurants. The company uses a standard marginal costing system to monitor the costs incurred in its outlets. The standard cost of one of its most popular meals is as follows.

		£ per meal
Ingredients	(1.08 units)	1.18
Labour	(1.5 minutes)	0.15
Variable conversion costs	(1.5 minutes)	0.06
The standard selling price of this meal is:		1.99

In one of its outlets, which has budgeted sales and production activity level of 50,000 such meals, the number of such meals that were produced and sold during April 20X3 was 49,700. The actual cost data was as follows.

		£
Ingredients	(55,000 units)	58,450
Labour	(1,200 hours)	6,800
Variable conversion costs	(1,200 hours)	3,250
The actual revenue from the sale of the meals was:		96,480

Required

(a)   Calculate the following.

    (i)   The total budgeted contribution for April 20X3

    (ii)   The total actual contribution for April 20X3 **(3 marks)**

(b)   Present a statement that reconciles the budgeted and actual contribution for April 20X3. Show all variances to the nearest £1. **(15 marks)**

(c)   Briefly state why a marginal costing approach to variance analysis is more appropriate in environments such as that of JK plc, where there are a number of different items being produced and sold. **(4 marks)**

(d)   Consider the outlet's results for April and May 20X3. Use the TA ratio to assess whether performance has improved. Comment on the result.

	April 20X3		May 20X3	
	£	£	£	£
Sales		96,480		108,860
Cost of sales				
Opening inventory	5,000		3,800	
Ingredients	58,450		66,295	
Labour	6,800		7,936	
Variable conversion costs	3,250		4,510	
	73,500		82,121	
Closing inventory	(3,380)		4,640	
		(70,120)		77,481
		26,360		31,379

(3 marks)

(Total = 25 marks)

Question 4

NP plc is considering investing in a project named Fantazia, which is a pleasure park consisting of a covered dome and external fun rides. The cost of the dome, which is a covered frame that can be dismantled and erected elsewhere or stored, is £20 million. NP plc is considering two sites for the dome: London or Manchester. The cost of acquiring the land and installing the equipment is expected to be £20 million for the London site and £9 million for the Manchester site.

A market research survey shows that if Fantazia were to be situated in London, there is a 0.5 chance of getting 1.2 million visitors a year for the next four years and a 0.5 chance of getting only 0.8 million visitors a year. Each visitor to the London site is expected to spend £25 on average. This comprises a £10 entrance fee which includes access to the fun rides, £10 on souvenir merchandise and £5 on food and drink.

If Fantazia were to be situated in Manchester, there is a 0.4 chance of getting 1.2 million visitors a year for the next four years and a 0.6 chance of getting only 0.8 million visitors. Each visitor to the Manchester site is expected to spend £23 on average. This comprises £9 entrance fee, £10 on merchandise and £4 on food and drink.

The average cost of servicing each visitor (that is, providing rides, merchandise and food and drink) at both sites is estimated to be £10.

After four years, the dome could be kept in operation for a further four years or dismantled. If the dome is kept on the same site, it is estimated that visitor numbers will fall by 0.1 million a year. This means that London would have a 0.5 chance of 1.1 million visitors and a 0.5 chance of 0.7 million visitors in each of years 5 to 8, and Manchester a 0.4 chance of 1.1 million visitors and a 0.6 chance of 0.7 million visitors.

If the dome were to be dismantled after four years, it could be stored at a cost of £0.5 million a year, sold for £4 million or transferred to the other site. The number of visitors and revenue received at this site would be as predicted for years 1 to 4.

The cost of dismantling the dome and equipment would be £3 million and the cost of moving and re-erecting it would be £9 million.

The purchase or sale price of the land at the end of year 4 would be: London £14 million and Manchester £10 million. At the end of year 8, the dome's resale value would be zero and all land values would be as four years previously.

The final cost of dismantling the dome and equipment would be £2 million.

NP plc uses a discount rate of 10% when evaluating all projects.

Required

(a) Assuming that NP plc intends to terminate the Fantazia project *after four years:*

  (i) draw a decision tree to show the options open to NP plc for years 1 to 4; **(4 marks)**

  (ii) calculate which option would generate the highest net present value. (Use either the decision tree or another method.) **(5 marks)**

(b) Assuming that NP plc chose the most advantageous option for years 1 to 4, determined in your answer to (a)(ii) above,

  (i) draw a decision tree for years 5 to 8, showing the options open to NP plc if Fantazia is not terminated after 4 years; **(5 marks)**

  (ii) calculate which of these options generates the highest net present value over years 5 to 8. **(6 marks)**

(c) Advise the company which options it should select in order to maximise net present value over the full eight years of the project. State what that net present value would be . **(5 marks)**

(Total = 25 marks)

Answers

**DO NOT TURN THIS PAGE UNTIL YOU HAVE
COMPLETED THE MOCK EXAM**

A plan of attack

As you turned the page to start this exam, any one of a number of things could have been going through your mind. Some of them may have been quite sensible, some of them may not.

The main thing to do is take a deep breath and do not panic. It's best to sort a plan of attack before the actual exam so that when the invigilator tells you that you can begin and the adrenaline kicks in you are using every minute of the three hours wisely.

Paper format

This paper has three sections and you must answer all of the questions. The first section contains eight objective test questions. The second has six short questions. The third section has two longer questions.

Section A – 20 marks
Section B – 30 marks
Section C – 50 marks

Reading time/order of questions

However you find the paper, it is important to make good use of your reading time. We recommend that you spend some of it reviewing the Section B questions. We would advise you to look carefully through the Section B questions and plan your answer to them. Remember to allocate your time correctly. That is 54 minutes for the 30 marks of Section B , 36 minutes for the OTs of Section A and 90 minutes for the section C questions.

You then have a **choice.** An approach that has worked well with students in the past is the following**.**

- Read through and answer Section B, which you have planned in your reading time, before moving on to Section A
- Go through Section C, answering first the question you have feel most confident about.

Time spent at the start of each question confirming the requirements and producing a plan for the answers is time well spent.

When reviewing the requirements look at how many marks have been allocated to each part. This will give you an idea of how detailed your answer must be.

Doing the exam

Actually doing the exam is a personal experience. There is not a single *right way.* If you submit complete answers to all questions your approach obviously works.

One approach

The possible pitfall of doing Section B before Section A would be getting sucked too deeply into Section B and leaving insufficient time for Sections A and C.

A quick look at the Section B question would tell me that:

- Part (a) specifically requests a **brief** explanation so I would be concise and be sure to watch the clock and not overrun with my answer.
- Part (b) asks me to state the difference between ZBB and incremental budgeting so I would try to save time by identifying opportunities to integrate the mention of any differences into my discussion of each technique.
- Part (c) has two clear parts to the requirement ('explain' and 'how') so I would address both these parts separately and concisely.
- Part (d) requires me to think about environmental costs that are incurred or decided upon before, during and after the production and sale of the product.
- Part (e) is best approached by quickly describing a PCA and then addressing the comment made.
- Part (f) asks me to discuss the problems so I will state each point, then **discuss why** I think it is a problem with extrapolation.

If you do decide to start with Section B rather than the Section A objective test questions make sure you do not overrun your 54 minutes.

Having worked your way through Section B, taking no more than nine minutes per question, you should now allocate 36 minutes to answer the Section A questions.

For the Section C questions you must proceed in a methodical way. Set out your format and then work through the question requirements, doing neat, readable calculations and filling out the figures. Even if you do not finish, you will get marks for what you have done, so do the easy bits first and do not spend longer than 45 minutes on Question 3 and 45 minutes on Question 4.

Time allocation

Be disciplined. Allocate your time according to the marks available but never go over the time allocation. The last few marks in a question are the hardest to earn.

Be sure to follow the requirements. If a comparison of two techniques is required then make sure you provide the comparison rather than describe each technique in isolation.

Answer all of the question. Having a go at every part of every question will put you in a better position to pass. However difficult that last part of the question seems at first there are marks to be earned.

If you have time left at the end of the exam ensure that you have attempted every part of every question. If you have, then scan through and ensure you complete any part of an answer you left earlier. Use the full three hours working towards a pass.

Marking the exam

When you mark your exam, be honest. Don't be too harsh though. Give yourself credit for the things you did well, but don't kid yourself with 'I would have done that in the real exam'. It may be worth your while making two lists; strengths and weaknesses.

Strengths will be areas of the syllabus you are confident with and also good exam technique.

Weaknesses will be holes in your knowledge and poor exam technique (maybe you ran out of time and couldn't answer all the requirements of the last question).

Making this list will help you focus your last days of revision on the areas which require attention whilst reminding you of the areas you excel in.

SECTION A

Question 1

1   B   If the cash flows are expressed in constant price level terms, the real rate of 10% is used as the discount factor.

Option A is incorrect because the cash flows would take account of inflation but the discount rate would not.

Option C is incorrect because the money discount rate has been estimated (by addition). The correct money rate is found by

(1 + money rate)   =   (1 + real rate) × (1 + inflation rate)
                   =   1.10 × 1.03
                   =   1.133

The money rate of 13.3% should be used to discount the inflated cash flows.

Option D is incorrect because the real cash flow, expressed in terms of constant price levels, would be discounted at an incorrect money rate.

Note. The question does not state that the cash flows are expressed in constant price level terms, but option B is the only correct answer however the cash flows are expressed.

2   D   For time period 33, x = 33

∴ If y = 10,000 + 4,200x, then y = 148,600

Time period 33 is a first quarter and so the seasonal variation index value is 120.

∴ Forecast = 148,600 × 1.2 = 178,320

3   C   If the probability of a dry summer is 0.4 the probability of a wet summer is 0.6. Therefore the expected value for sales is calculated as (0.6 × 120,000) + (0.4 × 80,000) = 104,000 units.

4   A   £28,000 A

Planning price variance

	£'000
Revised standard cost (2,800,000 × 0.2 kg × £0.85 per kg)	476
Original standard cost (2,800,000 × 0.2 kg × £0.80 per kg)	448
	28 (A)

5   D   £24,000 A

Operating price variance

	£'000
600,000 kg did cost	534
But should have cost (600,000 kg × £0.85)	510
	24 (A)

6

1,800 units should take (× 1 hour)	1,800 hours
but did take (active hours only (1,600 – 200))	1,400 hours
	400 hours (F)
× standard variable overhead rate per hour	× £3
Variable overhead efficiency variance	£1,200 (F)

7

	£
Variable overhead cost of 1,400 active hours should be (× £3)	4,200
but was	6,000
Variable overhead expenditure variance	1,800 (A)

	£
Budgeted fixed production o/hd expenditure (2,000 units × £4)	8,000
Actual fixed production o/hd expenditure	8,200
Fixed production overhead expenditure variance	200 (A)

8   Using rates of 7% and 9% from the tables:

$(4 \times 5.389) + (100 \times 0.623) = 21.556 + 62.3 = 83.856$

$(4 \times 5.033) + (100 \times 0.547) = 20.132 + 54.7 = 74.832$

$$7 + \left(\frac{83.856 - 83.000}{83.856 - 74.832} \times 2\right) = 7 + \left(\frac{0.856}{9.024} \times 2\right) = 7.19\%$$

SECTION B

Question 2

Marking scheme

		Marks
(a)	Discussion of general TQM philosophy	3
	TQM techniques	2
		5
(b)	Explanation of incremental budgeting	1
	Explanation of zero base budgeting	1
	One mark for each specific difference, to a max of	2
	Disadvantages of each method	1
		5
(c)	Discussion of cost drivers	1
	Application of ABC	2
	Benefits/usefulness of ABC informtion	2
		5
(d)	Environmental costs/costing	1
	Design stage	2
	Costs during production	1
	End of life costs	1
		5
(e)	Brief explanation of PCA	1
	One mark per benefit, to a max of	4
		5
(f)	Up to two marks for each problem discussed, to a max of	5

(a) The **aim** of total quality management (**TQM**) is that **all products produced/services provided meet or exceed customer expectations**.

It provides a **philosophy** of business behaviour, incorporating principles such as **employee involvement and empowerment**, a **customer focus**, and **continuous improvement** (the belief that it is always possible to improve, no matter how high the level of quality may already be) at all levels and in all areas.

It is also a collection of related **techniques** aimed at improving quality and **getting things right first time**, on the basis that the cost of correcting mistakes is greater than the cost of preventing them from happening in the first place. These **techniques** include quality control procedures in all areas and monitoring customer reaction.

(b) Incremental budgeting – what is it?

Incremental budgeting is the **traditional** approach to budgeting and involves basing the budget on **the current year's results plus an extra amount for estimated growth** or **inflation next year**. The approach is concerned mainly with the **increments** in costs and revenues which will occur in the coming period and hence incremental budgets are fairly **easy** and **cheap** to prepare.

When to use it

It is a **reasonable** procedure **if** current operations are as **effective, efficient** and **economical as they can be**. It is also appropriate for budgeting for costs such as staff salaries, which may be estimated on the basis of current salaries plus an increment for inflation.

Disadvantages

In general, however, it is an **inefficient** form of budgeting as it encourages **slack** and **wasteful spending** to creep into budgets. **Past inefficiencies** are **perpetuated** since the relationship between costs, benefits and objectives is rarely subjected to close scrutiny.

Zero based budgeting (ZBB) – what is it?

In contrast, ZBB does not use the previous year's results as a base. Instead, ZBB starts from the **premise** that the **budget for next year is zero** (the budget process starts from a zero base), and that **every part of every process** and cost has to be fully **justified** in order to be included in the budget, **as if it were being included for the first time**. Thus existing activities have to be justified in exactly the same way as new proposals, with all unnecessary costs stripped out.

Once budgets for individual activities have been prepared, they can be **compared** and **ranked on the basis of the benefit** they bring to the organisation, which can be a **lengthy** process. The final budget is then prepared by **allocating the available resources** on the **basis of the ranking** of the activities.

Disadvantages

ZBB therefore requires a detailed consideration of the business and its method of operating, so it is more **time consuming** and **expensive** than incremental budgeting.

(c)   CIMA *Official Terminology* defines activity based costing (ABC) as an approach to costing and monitoring of activities that 'involves tracing resource consumption and costing final outputs. Resources are assigned to activities and activities to cost objects based on consumption estimates'.

Stages of ABC

Activity based costing involves four major stages.

(i)   Identification of an organisation's major activities

(ii)   Identification of cost drivers, factors which determine the size of costs of an activity

Costs that vary with production volume such as power costs should be traced to products using production volume-related cost drivers such as direct labour hours. Overheads that do not vary with output but with some other activity should be traced using transaction-based cost drivers, such as number of production runs or number of orders received.

(iii)   Collection of the costs of activity into cost pools

(iv)   Charging of the costs of activity to products on the basis of their usage of the activity

Focus of ABC

ABC thus focuses on cost behaviour. It is also concerned with all overhead costs, including non-factory floor activities such as product design, quality control and customer service.

Benefits of ABC

The principal benefits of ABC are as follows.

(i)   It **produces information based on activities**; this will be useful for management control purposes as management is seeking to manage activities. This represents a (non-financial) measure of the performance of service departments which may otherwise be difficult to cost. It also can indicate what activities do not add value to the product.

(ii)   **ABC gives management better information** about cost behaviour, particularly about those costs which do not vary with production but with other activities. Thus ABC leads to better monitoring of those costs.

(iii)   Use of ABC should mean **product costs** are more meaningful, with more overheads being able to be traced to products on a fair basis. Hence profitability and performance measurement will be more realistic.

(iv)   ABC provides realistic indicators of long-run variable costs, which will aid decision making.

(d)   Environmental costing

An environmental costing system focuses on environmental costs. It attempts to control these costs, often by tracing them to individual products and services and by putting in place measures to monitor the costs to attempt to reduce or even eliminate them.

Life cycle assessment

This aims to identify and reduce environmental costs associated with a product throughout the whole of its life.

Many environmental costs are built into the product at the **design stage**. It may be possible to **design out of the product** any potential harmful environmental impacts before production even commences. This can be done by considering the impact on the environment of factors such as the **materials to be used**, how they will be obtained and how they will be disposed of by the final customer, the **production process** and its resulting emissions and waste and the **process of distribution** and consequent environmental costs. The **selection of the production process** can be made with full consideration of the environmental costs associated with any process alternatives.

During the product's production internalised environmental costs such as waste disposal costs will be monitored and traced to individual products so that these **costs are more transparent** and managers are more aware of a product's impact on the environment.

After production has ceased at the end of a product's life there may still be environmental costs that should be accounted for, such as the environmental impact of disposing of redundant production machinery.

(e)   A post-completion appraisal assesses whether a capital project has been successful compared with the forecasts that were used in the original project appraisal.

Post-completion appraisal cannot reverse the decision to incur capital expenditure, because the expenditure will already have taken place, but it will have some **control value**.

(i)   The **threat** of a post-completion audit will **motivate** managers to work to achieve the promised benefits from the project.

(ii)   If the appraisal takes place before the end of the project life, and if it is found that the benefits have been less than expected, steps can be taken to **improve efficiency**. Alternatively it might highlight the fact that the project should be discontinued.

(iii)   It can help to **highlight** those **managers** that have been instrumental in making the project a **success**.

(iv)   It might **identify weaknesses** in the **forecasting and estimating techniques** used to evaluate projects and so should help to improve the discipline and quality of forecasting for future investment decisions that the company might make.

(v)   Areas where **improvements** can be made in **methods to achieve better results in general** from capital investments might be revealed.

(vi)   **Original estimates** of cash flows might be **more realistic** if managers are aware that they will be monitored, but post-completion audits should not be unfairly critical.

(f)   The **problems** of **extrapolating** past performance into the future stem from the **assumptions** made in such extrapolations.

(i)   **Environmental conditions are assumed to remain unchanged**. This can render extrapolated data invalid. For example, fluctuations in exchange rates which were not present in the past may affect costs in the future.

(ii)   **Operating conditions are assumed to remain constant.** For example, an extrapolation of costs may assume that fixed costs are constant. A change in the level of activity may cause a step in fixed costs, however, which would invalidate the extrapolation.

(iii)   **The relationship between the variables is assumed to be linear.** For example, it may be assumed that if sales volume doubles then variable cost will also double. This may have been true for activity levels experienced in the past but it may not be valid to assume that the relationship will hold for activity levels in the future.

(iv)   **It is assumed that all variables affecting past performance have been identified and that other conditions have remained constant.** The identified variables may not be the only factors affecting performance and the omission of other valid variables will affect the accuracy of the extrapolation.

These problems do not mean that the extrapolation of past performance into the future has no value. It is important that the resulting forecast is used with caution, however. Anyone relying on the forecast as the basis for decision making must be aware of its shortcomings and of any assumptions on which it is based.

SECTION C

Question 3

Marking scheme

			Marks
(a)	(i)	Budgeted contribution	2
	(ii)	Actual contribution	1
			3
(b)		Sales variances	3
		Ingredients variances	2
		Labour variances	2.5
		Variable overhead variances	2.5
		Correct use of own contribution figures from (a)	3
		Layout of reconciliation statement	2
			15
(c)		Up to two marks for each point made, to a max of	4
(d)		Calculation of TA ratio	2
		Comment on results	1
			3

(a) (i) <u>Budgeted contribution per meal</u>

	£	£
Standard selling price		1.99
Less: *Variable costs*		
Ingredients	1.18	
Labour	0.15	
Conversion costs	0.06	
		1.39
		0.60

Total budgeted contribution = budgeted contribution per meal × budgeted sales level
= £0.60 × 50,000 = £30,000

(ii)   Total actual contribution

	£	£
Revenue		96,480
Less: *Variable costs*		
Ingredients	58,450	
Labour	6,800	
Conversion costs	3,250	
		68,500
		27,980

(b)   Variances

Selling price variance

	£
Revenue from 49,700 meals should have been (× £1.99)	98,903
but was	96,480
	2,432 (A)

Sales volume variance

Budgeted sales volume	50,000 meals
Actual sales volume	49,700 meals
	300 meals (A)
× standard contribution per meal (from (a)(i))	× £0.60
	£180 (A)

Ingredients price variance

	£
55,000 units should have cost (× £1.18/1.08)	60,093
but did cost	58,450
	1,643 (F)

Ingredients usage variance

49,700 meals should have used (× 1.08)	53,676 units
but did use	55,000 units
	1,324 units (A)
× standard cost per unit	× (£1.18/1.08)
	£1,447 (A)

Labour rate variance

	£
1,200 hours should have cost (× £6*)	7,200
but did cost	6,800
	400 (F)

* Standard labour cost per 1.5 mins = £0.15

∴ Standard labour cost per hour = £0.15 × 60/1.5
= £6

Labour efficiency variance

49,700 meals should have taken (× 1.5/60 hrs)	1,242.5 hrs
but did take	1,200.0 hrs
	42.5 hrs (F)
× standard rate per hour	× £6
	£255 (F)

Variable conversion costs expenditure variance

	£
1,200 hours should have cost (× £2.40*)	2,880
but did cost	3,250
	370 (A)

* Standard cost per 1.5 mins = £0.06

∴ Standard cost per hour = £0.06 × 60/1.5 = £2.40

<u>Variable conversion costs efficiency variance</u>

49,700 meals should have taken (× 1.5/60 hrs)	1,242.5 hrs
but did take	1,200.0 hrs
	42.5 hrs (F)
× standard rate per hour	× £2.40
	£102 (F)

JK PLC
RECONCILIATION STATEMENT – BUDGET AND ACTUAL CONTRIBUTION
APRIL 20X3

		£	£
Budgeted contribution (from (a)(i))			30,000
Less: **sales variances:** Price		2,423 (A)	
Volume		180 (A)	
			2,603 (A)
Actual sales less standard cost of sales			27,397
Cost variances	£	£	
	(F)	(A)	
Ingredients price	1,643		
Ingredients usage		1,447	
Labour rate	400		
Labour efficiency	255		
Variable conversion costs expenditure		370	
Variable conversion costs efficiency	102		
	2,400	1,817	
			583 (F)
Actual contribution (from (a)(ii))			27,980

(c) <u>Reasons for the appropriateness of standard marginal costing in environments in which a number of different products are produced/sold</u>

(i)   It is argued that the **absorption** of overheads into products when absorption costing or activity based costing is used is to a **great extent arbitrary**. Any fixed overhead variances calculated for each product line could therefore be viewed as **meaningless** and this may cause managers to **distrust** all **variance** analysis information. **Marginal costing**, because it identifies only variable costs with products, **does not produce such a problem**.

(ii)   General fixed overheads are incurred **irrespective** of the **level of activity**. Management therefore need to be able to determine the contribution made towards these fixed overheads by each of the different products in order to make **appropriate production decisions**.

(iii)   A marginal costing approach allows management to **concentrate** their **control processes** on the more **controllable** costs.

(d)

	April	*May*
Throughput	96,480 – 58,450 = 38,030	108,860 – 66,295 = 42,565
Conversion costs	6,800 + 3,250 = 10,050	7,936 + 4,510 = 12,446
	$\dfrac{38,030}{10,050} = 3.78$	$\dfrac{42,565}{12,446} = 3.42$

Although profits have increased, the TA ratio has slightly deteriorated.

Question 4

Text references. Look at Chapter 19 if you need help with decision trees as these can be quite tricky to draw. Parts (a), (b) and (c) require simple NPV calculations which you can refer to in Chapter 16.

Top tips. The easiest mistake to make in part (a)(i) is to miss out the reject option at year 0: NP plc does not have to go ahead with the project. The tree is only meant to show the options open to the company in the first part of (a).

In part (a)(ii) there is no need to include any costs of dismantling, storage, moving or any sales revenue as these are common to all options. It is only the purchase/sale price of the land that varies according to location.

You needed to keep your head in part (b) so that you didn't miss any of the costs and revenues associated with each option. Allowance would be made for your decision from (a), so you would not be penalised for getting (a) incorrect. Don't forget to use PV factors for years 5-8 in (b)(ii).

In part (c) you should not have included any sale of land figures at year 4 because the project was continuing in the same place. Provided you realised that you needed to consider the eight-years-in-London option because of the narrow margin in part (b)(ii), part (c) was straightforward.

Easy marks. Use a ruler and work systematically through the information provided to draw the basic decision trees. Neat labels will be necessary to earn the marks available and a clearly drawn tree will help you to make sense of all the data when it comes to the evaluation part

Marking scheme

			Marks
(a)	(i)	Branch for London	1.5
		Branch for Manchester	1.5
		Branch for reject	1
			$\overline{4}$
	(ii)	Evaluation of London option	2
		Evaluation of Manchester option	2
		Recommendation	1
			$\overline{5}$
(b)	(i)	Branch for continuing in recommended location	1
		Branch for store	1
		Branch for sell	1
		Branch for transfer	2
			$\overline{5}$
	(ii)	Evaluation of branch for continue in recommended location	1
		Evaluation of branch for store	1
		Evaluation of branch for sell	1
		Evaluation of branch for transfer	2
		Recommendation	1
			$\overline{6}$
(c)		NPV for remaining in Manchester for eight years	2
		NPV for remaining in London for eight years	2
		Recommendation	1
			$\overline{5}$

(a)   (i)

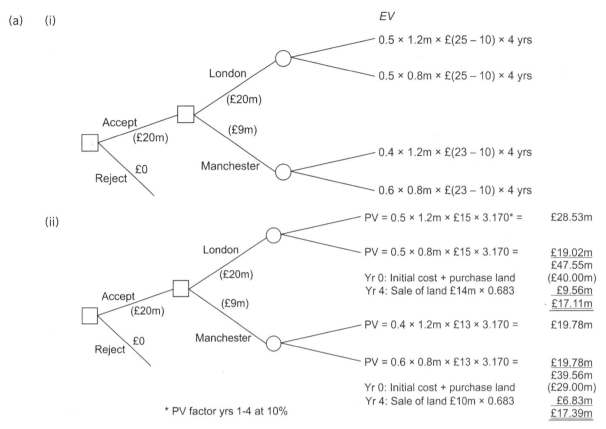

Manchester is therefore the **better** option by £0.28m.

Top tips. Alternatively you could have taken the standard approach to NPV calculations and simply tabulated the cashflows.

(b)   (i)

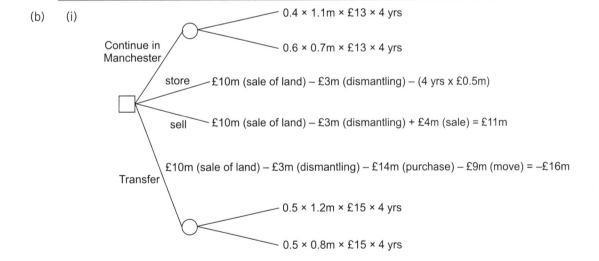

(ii)

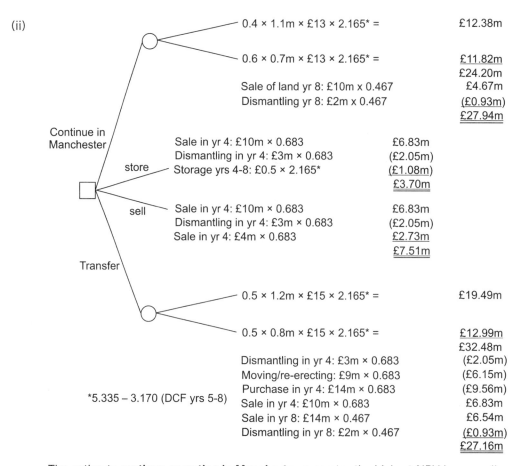

0.4 × 1.1m × £13 × 2.165* =   £12.38m

0.6 × 0.7m × £13 × 2.165* =   £11.82m
                                  £24.20m
Sale of land yr 8: £10m × 0.467   £4.67m
Dismantling yr 8: £2m × 0.467   (£0.93m)
                                  £27.94m

Continue in Manchester

store

Sale in yr 4: £10m × 0.683	£6.83m
Dismantling in yr 4: £3m × 0.683	(£2.05m)
Storage yrs 4-8: £0.5 × 2.165*	(£1.08m)
	£3.70m

sell

Sale in yr 4: £10m × 0.683	£6.83m
Dismantling in yr 4: £3m × 0.683	(£2.05m)
Sale in yr 4: £4m × 0.683	£2.73m
	£7.51m

Transfer

0.5 × 1.2m × £15 × 2.165* =   £19.49m

0.5 × 0.8m × £15 × 2.165* =   £12.99m
                                  £32.48m

*5.335 – 3.170 (DCF yrs 5-8)

Dismantling in yr 4: £3m × 0.683	(£2.05m)
Moving/re-erecting: £9m × 0.683	(£6.15m)
Purchase in yr 4: £14m × 0.683	(£9.56m)
Sale in yr 4: £10m × 0.683	£6.83m
Sale in yr 8: £14m × 0.467	£6.54m
Dismantling in yr 8: £2m × 0.467	(£0.93m)
	£27.16m

The option to **continue operating in Manchester** generates the highest NPV by a small margin.

(c)   Based on (b), the option to continue operating in Manchester for eight years should be selected.

Total NPV over eight years	NPV £m
Years 1 to 4 in Manchester *	10.56
Years 5 to 8 in Manchester ((b)(ii))	27.94
	38.50

* From (a)(ii) £(39.56 – 29.00)m = £10.56m

Given the results in (b) (where the margin is very small), the only other possible alternative could be to site the project in London for the entire eight-year period.

Total NPV over eight years		NPV £m	£m
Years 1 to 4 in London*			7.55
Years 5 to 8 in London			
Net revenue:	0.5 × 1.1m × £15 × 2.165	17.86	
	0.5 × 0.7m × £15 × 2.165	11.37	
Dismantling in yr 8:	£2m × 0.467	(0.93)	
Sale in yr 8:	£14m × 0.467	6.54	
			34.84
			42.39

∴ The **best** option is to site the **project in London** for the eight-year period.

*From (a)(ii), £(47.55 – 40)m = £7.55m

CIMA
Paper P1 (Operational)
Performance Operations

Mock Exam 2
September 2010

Question Paper	
Time allowed	**3 hours**
This paper is divided into three sections	
Section A	**EIGHT objective test questions**
Section B	**SIX short answer questions**
Section C	**TWO scenario questions**

DO NOT OPEN THIS PAPER UNTIL YOU ARE READY TO START UNDER EXAMINATION CONDITIONS

SECTION A – 20 marks

Answer ALL sub-questions

Question 1

1   Which ONE of the following is NOT considered to be a cost of holding inventory?

   A   Loss of goodwill as a result of being unable to complete customer orders due to lack of inventory
   B   Insurance cost of inventory
   C   Storage cost of inventory
   D   Interest on cash invested in inventory   **(2 marks)**

2   The following information has been calculated for a business:

   Trade receivables collection period   54 days
   Trade payables payment period   67 days

   If the working capital cycle is 102 days, the inventory turnover period is

   A   19 days
   B   115 days
   C   89 days
   D   13 days   **(2 marks)**

3   A project requires an initial investment of $200,000. It has a life of five years and generates net cash inflows in each of the five years of $55,000. The net present value of the project when discounted at the company's cost of capital of 8% is $19,615.

   The sensitivity of the investment decision to a change in the annual net cash inflow is:

   A   35.7%
   B   25.0%
   C   9.8%
   D   8.9%   **(2 marks)**

The following data are given for sub-questions 4 and 5 below

A company can choose from four mutually exclusive investment projects. The net present value of the projects will depend on market conditions.

The table below details the net present value for each possible outcome:

Market conditions   Projects

	A	B	C	D
Poor	$400,000	$700,000	$450,000	$360,000
Average	$470,000	$550,000	$500,000	$400,000
Good	$600,000	$300,000	$800,000	$550,000

4   If the company applies the maximin rule it will invest in:

   A   Project A
   B   Project B
   C   Project C
   D   Project D   **(2 marks)**

5   If the company applies the minimax regret rule it will invest in:

   A   Project A
   B   Project B
   C   Project C
   D   Project D   **(2 marks)**

6   PJ sells goods to customers on credit. It is forecast that credit sales for July will be $36,000 and that
     sales will increase by $2,000 per month for the next six months. Based on past experience PJ expects
     50% of customers to pay in the month after sale, 25% of customers to pay 2 months after sale and the
     remainder to pay 3 months after sale.

     PJ has a trade receivables balance outstanding at the beginning of July of $65,000.

     Calculate the cash that PJ will receive from credit customers during the six month period to the end of
     December.   **(3 marks)**

7   The estimated production volume of a new product for the first year is 2,000 units. The management
     accountant has produced the following table showing the possible production costs and their associated
     probabilities at this level of output.

     The probabilities of the different levels of fixed production costs and variable production costs are totally
     independent.

Total fixed production costs		Total variable production costs	
$	Probability	$	Probability
80,000	0.40	30,000	0.25
130,000	0.45	40,000	0.35
160,000	0.15	50,000	0.40

   (i)   **Calculate** the expected value of total production costs for the production of 2,000 units.

   (ii)   **Calculate** the probability of total production costs for 2,000 units being $180,000 or greater.
                                                                                                    (4 marks)

8   A $1,000 bond has a coupon rate of 10% per annum and will repay its face value in five years time.
     Similar bonds have a yield to maturity of 8% per annum.

     Calculate the current expected market value of the bond.   **(3 marks)**

                                                                                          (Total = 20 marks)

SECTION B – 30 marks

Answer ALL six sub-questions. Each sub-question is worth five marks

Question 2

(a)   JP has been offered credit terms by a supplier that will allow JP to claim a cash discount of 2.5% if payment is made within 15 days of the date of the invoice or to pay on normal credit terms within 45 days of the date of the invoice.

Required:

   (i)   Calculate, to the nearest 0.1%, the effective annual interest rate offered to JP from accepting the cash discount and paying within 15 days. You should assume a 365 day year and use compound interest methodology.   **(3 marks)**

   (ii)   State TWO other methods that the supplier could use to reduce its level of outstanding trade receivables.   **(2 marks)**

(b)   BB manufactures a range of electronic products. The supplier of component Y has informed BB that it will offer a quantity discount of 1.0% if BB places an order of 10,000 components or more at any one time.

Details of component Y are as follows:

Cost per component before discount $2.00
Annual purchases   150,000 components
Ordering costs $360 per order
Holding costs $3.00 per component per annum

Required

   (i)   Calculate the total annual cost of holding and ordering inventory of component Y using the economic order quantity and ignoring the quantity discount.   **(2 marks)**

   (ii)   Calculate whether there is a financial benefit to BB from increasing the order size to 10,000 components in order to qualify for the 1.0% quantity discount.   **(3 marks)**

(c)   Explain why a backflush cost accounting system may be considered more appropriate than a traditional cost accounting system, in a company that operates a just-in-time production and purchasing system   **(5 marks)**

(d)   XY, a not-for-profit charity organisation which is funded by public donations, is concerned that is not making the best use of its available funds. It has carried out a review of its budgeting system and is considering replacing the current system with a zero-based budgeting system.

Required

Explain the potential advantages AND disadvantages for the charity of a zero-based budgeting system.   **(5 marks)**

(e)   QR uses an activity based budgeting (ABB) system to budget product costs. It manufactures two products, product Q and product R. The budget details for these two products for the forthcoming period are as follows:

	Product Q	Product R
Budgeted production (units)	80,000	120,000
Number of machine set ups per batch	4	2
Batch size (units)	5,000	4,000

The total budgeted cost of setting up the machines is $74,400.

Required

   (i)   Calculate the budgeted machine set up cost per unit for product Q   **(3 marks)**

   (ii)   State TWO potential benefits of using an activity based budgeting system   **(2 marks)**

(f)   A university is trying to decide whether or not to advertise a new post-graduate programme. The number of students starting the programme is dependent on economic conditions. If conditions are poor it is expected that the programme will attract 40 students without advertising. There is a 60% chance that economic conditions will be poor. If conditions are good it is expected that the programme will attract only 20 students without advertising. There is a 40% chance that economic conditions will be good.

If the programme is advertised and economic conditions are poor, there is a 65% chance that the advertising will stimulate further demand and student numbers will increase to 50. If economic conditions are good there is a 25% chance the advertising will stimulate further demand and numbers will increase to 25 students.

The profit expected, before deducting the cost of advertising, at different levels of student numbers are as follows:

Number of students	Profit $
15	(10,000)
20	15,000
25	40,000
30	65,000
35	90,000
40	115,000
45	140,000
50	165,000

The cost of advertising the programme will be $15,000.

Required

Demonstrate, using a decision tree, whether the programme should be advertised.   **(5 marks)**

(Total = 30 marks)

SECTION C – 50 marks

Answer both questions

Question 3

Fx Corporation produces a single product RG. The company operates a standard absorption costing system and a just-in-time purchasing system.

Standard production cost details per unit of product RG are:

	$
Materials (5 kg at $20 per kg)	100
Labour (4 hours at $10 per hr)	40
Variable overheads (4 hours at $5 per hr)	20
Fixed overheads (4 hours at $12.50 per hr)	50
	210

Fixed and variable overheads are absorbed on the basis of labour hours.

Budget data for product RG are detailed below:

Production and sales	1,400 units
Selling price	$250 per unit
Fixed overheads	$70,000

Actual data for product RG are as follows:

Production and sales	1,600 units
Selling price	$240 per unit
Direct materials	7,300 kg costing $153,300
Direct labour	5,080 hours at $9 per hour
Variable overheads	$25,400
Fixed overheads	$74,000

Required

(a) Produce a statement that reconciles the budgeted and actual gross profit for product RG for July showing the variances in as much detail as possible. **(13 marks)**

(b) The following details have been extracted from the company's accounting records for August.

	Budget	Actual
Output of RG	800 units	890 units
Materials	4,000 kg	4,375 kg
Cost per kg	$20.00	$21.60

It has now been realised that the standard cost of per kg of the materials should have been $20.90.

Calculate the following variances for August

(i)   The total materials cost variance.
(ii) The planning variance for materials price
(iii) The operational variances for materials price and materials usage.   **(6 marks)**

(c) Discuss THREE advantages of using a standard costing system that identifies both planning and operational variances.   **(6 marks)**

(Total = 25 marks)

Question 4

The management of a hotel is considering expanding its facilities by providing a gymnasium and spa for the use of guests. It is expected that the additional facilities will result in an increase in the occupancy rate of the hotel and in the rates that can be charged for each room.

The cost of refurbishing the space, which is currently used as a library for guests, and installing the spa is estimated to be $100,000. The cost of the gymnasium equipment is expected to be $50,000. The gymnasium and spa will need to be refurbished and the equipment replaced every four years. The equipment will be sold for $15,000 cash at the end of year 4. This amount includes the effect of inflation.

The hotel's accountants have produced a feasibility report at a cost of $10,000. The key findings from their report, regarding occupancy rates and room rates are as follows:

- Current occupancy rate: 80%
- Number of rooms available: 40
- Current average room rate per night: $250

Occupancy rates following the opening of the gymnasium and spa, are expected to rise to 82% and the average room rate by 5%, excluding the effect of inflation.

The hotel is open for 360 days per year.

Other relevant information from the accountant's report is listed below:

1. **Staffing the gymnasium and spa**

   - Number of employees: 4
   - Average salary of employee: $30,000 per annum

2. **Overheads**

   - The current budgeted overhead absorption rate for the hotel is $80 per square metre per annum. The area needed for the gymnasium and spa is 400 square metres.
   - The hotel's overheads are expected to increase by $42,000 directly as a result of opening the gymnasium and spa.

3. **Inflation**

   Inflation is expected to be at a rate of 4% per annum and will apply to sales revenue, overhead costs and staff costs. The rate of 4% will apply from Year 2 to each of the subsequent years of the project.

4. **Taxation**

   The hotel's accountants have provided the following taxation information:

   - Tax depreciation available on all costs of refurbishing, installation and equipment: 25% reducing balance per annum.
   - Taxation rate: 30% of taxable profits. Half of the tax is payable in the year in which it arises, the balance is paid the following year.
   - Any losses resulting from this investment can be set against taxable profits made by the company's other business activities.

   The company uses a post-tax money cost of capital of 12% per annum to evaluate projects of this type.

Required

(a)   Calculate the net present value (NPV) of the gymnasium and spa project.   **(16 marks)**

(b)   Calculate the post-tax money cost of capital at which the hotel would be indifferent to accepting / rejecting the project.   **(4 marks)**

(c)   Discuss an alternative method for the treatment of inflation that would result in the same NVP.

   Your answer should consider the potential difficulties in using this method when taxation is involved in the project appraisal.   **(5 marks)**

(Total = 25 marks)

Answers

**DO NOT TURN THIS PAGE UNTIL YOU HAVE
COMPLETED THE MOCK EXAM**

334

A plan of attack

As you turned the page to start this exam, any one of a number of things could have been going through your mind. Some of them may have been quite sensible, some of them may not.

The main thing to do is take a deep breath and do not panic. It's best to sort a plan of attack before the actual exam so that when the invigilator tells you that you can begin and the adrenaline kicks in you are using every minute of the three hours wisely.

Paper format

This paper has three sections. All questions are compulsory. The first section contains about eight objective test questions. The second has six short questions. The third section has two longer questions.

Section A – 20 marks
Section B – 30 marks
Section C – 50 marks

Reading time/order of questions

However you find the paper, it is important to make good use of your reading time. We recommend that you spend some of it reviewing the Section B questions. We would advise you to look carefully through the Section B questions and plan your answer to them. Remember to allocate your time correctly. That is 54 minutes for the 30 marks of Section B , 36 minutes for the OTs of Section A and 90 minutes for the section C questions.

You then have a **choice**. An approach that has worked well with students in the past is the following.

- Read through and answer Section B, which you have planned in your reading time, before moving on to Section A

- Go through Section C, answering first the question you feel most confident about.

Time spent at the start of each question confirming the requirements and producing a plan for the answers is time well spent.

When reviewing the requirements look at how many marks have been allocated to each part. This will give you an idea of how detailed your answer must be.

Doing the exam

Actually doing the exam is a personal experience. There is not a single *right way.* If you submit complete answers to all questions, your approach obviously works.

One approach

The possible pitfall of doing Section B before Section A would be getting sucked too deeply into Section B and leaving insufficient time for Sections A and C.

A quick look at the Section B question would tell me that:

- Part (a)(i) specifically requests a calculation to 0.1% so I would be careful to remember this. I would be concise in part (ii) and be sure to watch the clock and not overrun with my answer.

- Part (b) again has two parts so I would watch the clock. Part (ii) asks me whether there is a financial benefit so I would calculate the financial benefit to answer this.

- Part (c) asks for an explanation so I would use short paragraphs to answer this, remembering to mention JIT as it is specifically mentioned in the question.

- Part (d) requires me to think about advantages and disadvantages so I would use headings and answer each one in turn.

- Part (e) (i) is a calculation worth only 3 marks so I would watch the clock on this and move on to part (ii) if I'm overrunning. Part (ii) says 'state' so there is no need to explain.

- Part (f) asks me to draw a decision tree. I would make sure that I make it clear whether the programme should be advertised.

If you do decide to start with Section B rather than Section A objective test questions, make sure you do not overrun your 54 minutes. Having worked your way through Section B, taking no more than nine minutes per question, you should now allocate 36 minutes to answer the Section A questions.

For the Section C questions you must proceed in a methodical way. Set out your format and then work through the question requirements, doing neat, readable calculations and filling out the figures. Even if you do not finish, you will get marks for what you have done, so do the easy bits first and divide your time evenly between the two questions.

Time allocation

Be disciplined. Allocate your time according to the marks available but never go over the time allocation. The last few marks in a question are the hardest to earn.

Be sure to follow the requirements. If four advantages are required, give four. No extra credit will be given for five. Two advantages will only get you half marks.

Answer all of the question. Having a go at all parts of every question will put you in a better position to pass. However difficult that last part of the question seems at first there are marks to be earned.

If you have time left at the end of the exam ensure that you have attempted every part of every question. If you have, then scan through and ensure you complete any part of an answer you left earlier. Use the full three hours working towards a pass.

Marking the exam

When you mark your exam, be honest. Don't be too harsh though. Give yourself credit for the things you did well, but don't kid yourself with 'I would have done that in the real exam'. It may be worth your while making two lists; strengths and weaknesses.

Strengths will be areas of the syllabus you are confident with and also good exam technique.

Weaknesses will be holes in your knowledge and poor exam technique (maybe you ran out of time and couldn't answer all the requirements of the last question).

Making this list will help you focus your last days of revision on the areas which require attention whilst reminding you of the areas you excel in.

SECTION A

Question 1

1   A   Insurance, storage and loss of interest are all costs of holding inventory. If inventory is held then customer orders will be complete and so no goodwill will be lost.

2   B

	X
Inventory turnover period	
Less trade payables payment period	(67 days)
Plus trade receivables collection period	54 days
Working capital cycle	102 days

Inventory turnover period = 102 – 54 + 67
= 115 days

3   D   Sensitivity of NPV $= \dfrac{\text{NPV of project}}{\text{PV of net cash inflow}} \times 100\%$

NPV of $55,000 for 5 years at cost of capital
= $55,000 × 3.993
= $219,615

$\therefore$ Sensitivity $= \dfrac{\$19,615}{\$219,615} \times 100\%$

= 8.9%

4   C   Maximin = maximise the minimum achievable NPV. The minimum achievable NPVs for each project are:

A	B	C	D
$400,000	$300,000	$450,000	$360,000

The maximum NPV from these is $450,000, project C.

5   C

Table of regrets
Projects

Market conditions	A	B	C	D
Poor	$300,000	0	$250,000	$340,000
Average	$80,000	0	$50,000	$150,000
Good	$200,000	$500,000	0	$250,000
Maximum regret	$300,000	$500,000	$250,000	$340,000

The lowest of these four maximum regrets is $250,000, project C.

6

	Jul $	Aug $	Sep $	Oct $	Nov $	Dec $
Sales	**36,000**	**38,000**	**40,000**	**42,000**	**44,000**	**46,000**
50% received after 1 month			18,000	19,000	20,000	21,000	22,000
25% received after 2 months				9,000	9,500	10,000	10,500
25% received after 3 months					9,000	9,500	10,000
Opening bal paid Jul, Aug, Sep	65,000					
	65,000		18,000	28,000	38,500	40,500	42,500

Total cash received = $65,000 + $18,000 + $28,000 + $38,500 + $40,500 + $42,500

= $232,500

7　(i)　$156,000

EV (fixed costs) = ($80,000 × 0.4) + ($130,000 × 0.45) + ($160,000 × 0.15)
= $32,000 + $58,500 + $24,000
= $114,500

EV (variable costs) = ($30,000 × 0.25) + ($40,000 × 0.35) + ($50,000 × 0.40)
= $7,500 + $14,000 + $20,000
= $41,500

Expected value of total cost = $114,500 + $41,500
= $156,000

(ii)　0.33

If fixed costs are $80,000 then total costs can only be

$80,000 + $30,000 = $110,000 or
$80,000 + $40,000 = $120,000 or
$80,000 + $50,000 = $130,000

If fixed costs are $130,000 then total costs can only be

$130,000 + $30,000 = $160,000 or
$130,000 + $40,000 = $170,000 or
$130,000 + $50,000 = $180,000 ≥ $180,000
Probability = 0.45 × 0.4 = 0.18

If fixed costs are $160,000 then total costs will always be $180,000 or greater.

Probability = 0.15 × 1 = 0.15

Total probability of production costs being $180,000 or greater = 0.18 + 0.15
= 0.33

8　$1,080.30

Coupon rate = interest rate

∴ interest = $1,000 × 10% = $100 per annum

Interest is received every year for 5 years so we need the cumulative present value with a discount rate of 8% (= 3.993)

The $1,000 is received after 5 years so we need the PV tables for 8% for 5 years (0.681).

The net present value = $(100 × 3.993) + $(1,000 × 0.681)
= $1,080.30

This is the market value of the bond.

Question 2

(a)　(i)　JP will make a payment 30 days earlier than normal.

Number of compounding periods = 365/30 = 12.167

$$r = \left(\frac{100}{100 - 2.5} \right)^{12.167} - 1$$

r = 1.361 - 1

∴ the interest rate is 36.1%

(ii)　• 　Invoice factoring
• 　Tighter credit control

(Alternatively you could have mentioned interest charges for late payment but the question asks for two methods so don't waste time stating any more than two.)

(b) (i) $EOQ = \sqrt{\dfrac{2C_0D}{C_h}}$

$= \sqrt{\dfrac{2 \times 150{,}000 \times 360}{3}}$

$= \sqrt{36{,}000{,}000}$

$\therefore Q = 6{,}000$

Holding cost + ordering cost $= QC_h/2 + C_0D/Q$

$= \dfrac{6{,}000 \times 3}{2} + \dfrac{360 \times 150{,}000}{6{,}000}$

$= \$9{,}000 + \$9{,}000$

$= \$18{,}000$

(ii)

Holding cost + ordering cost $= QC_h/2 + C_0D/Q$

$= \dfrac{10{,}000 \times 3}{2} + \dfrac{360 \times 150{,}000}{10{,}000}$

$= \$15{,}000 + \$5{,}400$

$= \$20{,}400$

Extra cost = $20,400 - $18,000 = $2,400.

Money saved as a result of discount = 150,000 × $2.00 × 1% = $3,000

Total net saving = $3,000 - $2,400 = $600 and so there is financial benefit from increasing the order size to 10,000.

(c) Admin savings by using standard costs

Traditional costing systems use sequential tracking to track costs sequentially as products pass from raw materials to work in progress, to finished goods and finally to sales. In backflush accounting the budgeted or standard costs are used to work backwards to flush out the manufacturing costs. The application of standard costs to finished goods simplifies the costing system and creates savings in administrative effort.

Inventory

In a JIT system very little inventory is kept in stock which makes decisions about inventory valuation unnecessary. In a backflush system, even a finished goods account is unnecessary. This simplifies the cost accounting system.

Simplification of accounts system

In a JIT system the vast majority of manufacturing costs will form part of the cost of sales and will not be deferred in closing inventory values. In such a situation the amount of work involved in tracking costs through WIP, cost of sales and finished goods is unlikely to be justified. This considerably reduces the volume of transactions recorded in the internal accounting system.

(d) <u>Advantages</u>

<u>Removing obsolete operations</u>

It is possible to identify and remove inefficient or obsolete operations.

<u>Wasteful expenditure</u>

It forces employees to avoid wasteful expenditure which can creep in due to complacency.

<u>Motivation</u>

It can increase motivation, particularly if many employees are involved in the budgeting process.

<u>Disadvantages</u>

<u>Management skills</u>

There may be a need for management skills both in constructing decision packages and in the ranking process, which the organisation does not possess. Managers may therefore need to be trained in ZBB techniques which could be time consuming and costly.

<u>Ranking</u>

The ranking process can be difficult. A large number of packages have to be ranked and it can be difficult to rank packages which appear to be equally vital. It is also difficult to rank activities which have qualitative rather than quantitative benefits, such as spending on staff welfare and working conditions.

<u>Time and paperwork</u>

Perhaps the most serious drawback is the amount of time and paperwork involved.

(e) (i)

	Product Q	Product R	Total
Number of batches	80,000/5,000 = 16	120,000/4,000 = 30	
Machine set-ups per batch	4	2	
Total number of set-ups	64	60	124
Budgeted cost of set-ups			$74,400
Budgeted cost per set up			$74,400/124 = $600

Total number of set-ups for Q = 64

Total budgeted set-up costs for Q = 64 × $600 = $38,400

$$\text{Budgeted set-up costs per unit for Q} = \frac{\$38,400}{80,000 \text{ units}} = \$0.48 \text{ per unit}$$

(ii) • The focus is on the whole activity, not just its separate parts, and so there is more likelihood of getting it right first time. For example, what is the use of being able to produce goods in time for their despatch date if the budget provides insufficient resources for the distribution manager who has to deliver them.

• Traditional accounting tends to focus on the nature of the costs being incurred (the input side) and traditional budgeting tends to mirror this. ABB emphasises the activities that are being achieved (the outputs).

(f)

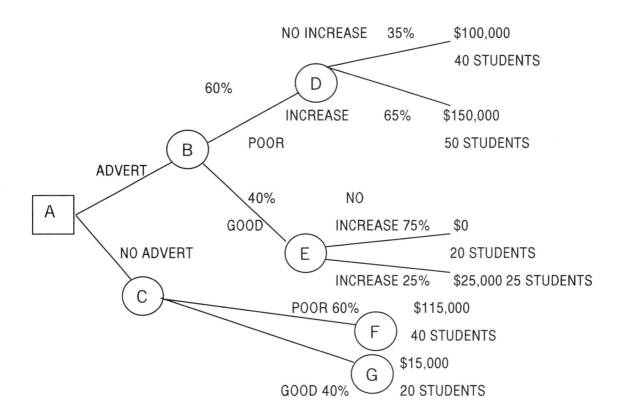

Expected value with advertisement = $21,000 + $58,500 + $0 + $2,500 = $82,000

Without advertisement = $69,000 + $6,000 = $75,000

As the expected value with an advertisement is higher, the advertisement should go ahead.

Question 3

Text references. Operating statements and mix and yield variances are covered in Chapter 8. Standard costing and new technology is covered in Chapter 7a in Section 6.2.

Top tips. For part (a) you need to organise your workings on a separate piece of paper. Don't waste too much time if your find that you reconciliation doesn't work. You will get marks for your workings and the layout of the reconciliation. For part (b) you need to remember how to set out planning and operational variances. Part (c) is asking for the advantages of a system of planning and operational variances. Write three paragraphs and give each one a heading. You can usually expect some sort of narrative question like this with variance calculations.

Easy marks. The easy marks in this question are for your variance calculations. If you have learnt the correct layout for variance calculations you should score well.

Examiner's comments. The examiner commented that parts (b) and (c) were poorly answered. If you learn the proformas for planning and operational variances (as shown in our answer to part (b)) and then practise these types of question, you will avoid the errors that other students make. The examiner also commented that some students incorrectly labelled the variances and some didn't know whether they were adverse or favourable. Make sure that this doesn't happen to you.

Marking scheme

			Marks
(a)		Budgeted gross profit	1
		Sales variances	3
		Material variances	2
		Labour variances	2
		Variable overhead variances	1
		Fixed overhead variances	3
		Actual gross profit	1
			13
(b)	(i)	Materials cost variance	1
	(ii)	Material price planning variance	2
	(iii)	Material price operational variance and usage variance	3
			6
(c)		Up to 2 marks for each reason	6
			25

(a)   Reconciliation statement

	$(F)	$(A)	$
Budgeted profit (W1)			56,000
Sales volume profit variance (W2)	8,000		
Sales price variance (W3)		16,000	
Materials price variance (W4)		7,300	
Materials usage variance (W5)	14,000		
Labour rate variance (W6)	5,080		
Labour efficiency variance (W7)	13,200		
Variable overhead expenditure variance (W8)	–		
Variable overhead efficiency variance (W9)	6,600		
Fixed overhead expenditure (W10)		4,000	
Fixed overhead volume (W11)	10,000		
	56,880	27,300	29,580
Actual profit (W12)			85,580

Workings

1

	$'000	$'000
Sales (1,400 units × $250.00)		350
Less: cost of sales		
Materials + Labour + Var o/hds (1,400 × $160.00)		(224)
Gross profit		126
Less: fixed production overheads		(70)
Budgeted profit		56

Alternatively
(Sales price per unit – total cost per unit) x budgeted sales units
($250.00 -$210.00) x 1,400 units   = $56,000

2   Sales volume profit variance

Should have sold	1,400 units
But did sell	1,600 units
Variance in units	200 units (F)
× profit ($250 – $210)	× $40
	$8,000 (F)

3   <u>Sales price variance</u>

	$
1,600 should have sold for (×$250.00)	400,000
But did sell for (× $240)	384,000
	<u>16,000</u> (A)

4   <u>Materials price variance</u>

	$
7,300kg should have cost (× $20.00)	146,000
But did cost	153,300
	<u>7,300</u> (A)

5   <u>Materials usage variance</u>

1,600 units should have used (× 5kg)	8,000 kg
But did use	7,300 kg
Variance in kg	700 kg (F)
× std cost per kg	× $20
	$14,000 (F)

6   <u>Labour rate variance</u>

	$
5,080 hours should have cost (× $10)	50,800
But did cost (× $9)	45,720
	<u>5,080</u> (F)

7   <u>Labour efficiency variance</u>

1,600 units should have taken (× 4 hours)	6,400 hours
But did take	5,080 hours
Variance in hours	1320 hours (F)
× std cost per hour	× $10
	$13,200 (F)

8   <u>Variable overhead expenditure variance</u>

	$
5,080 hours should have cost (× $5)	25,400
But did cost	25,400
	<u>0</u>

9   <u>Variable overhead efficiency variance</u>

1,600 units should have taken (× 4 hours)	6,400 hours
But did take	5,080 hours
Variance in hours	1,320 hours (F)
× std cost per hour	× $5
	$6,600 (F)

10   <u>Fixed overhead expenditure variance</u>

	$
Fixed overhead should have cost	70,000
But did cost	74,000
	<u>4,000</u> (A)

11   <u>Fixed overhead volume variance</u>

Budgeted production	1,400
Actual production	1,600
	<u>200</u> (F)
x OAR per unit ($50.00)	10,000 (F)

12

	$	$
Sales (1,600 units × $240)		384,000
Less: cost of sales		
Materials	153,300	
Labour (5,080 × $9)	45,720	
Variable overheads	25,400	(224,420)
Gross profit		159,580
Less: fixed production overheads		(74,000)
Actual profit		85,580

(b)

Total material cost variance

	$
890 units should have cost (× $20 × 5kg)	89,000
But did cost (× $21.60 × 4,375kg)	94,500
	5,500(A)

Material price planning variance

	$
Original std cost for the revised std hrs for actual output (890 × $20 × 5kg)	89,000
Revised std cost for the revised std hrs for actual output (890 × $20.90 × 5kg)	93,005
	4,005(A)

Materials usage operational variance

890 units should have used (× 5kg)	4,450 kg
But did use	4,375 kg
Variance in kg	75 kg (F)
× revised std cost per kg	× $20.90
	$1,567.50 (F)

Material price operational variance

	$
Revised std cost for the revised std kg (4,375 × $20.90)	91,437.50
Actual price of actual kg (4,375 × $21.60)	94,500.00
	3,062.50(A)

(c) Controllable v uncontrollable

The analysis highlights those variances which are **controllable** and those which are **non-controllable**. By analysing the total price variance between planning and operational, management can focus on the underlying causes of the total variances and thus identify the controllable increase in costs which could have been avoided.

Motivation

Managers' acceptance of the use of variances for performance measurement, and their motivation, is likely to increase if they know that they will **not be held responsible for poor planning** and faulty standard setting.

Improved standard setting

The planning and standard setting process should improve. Standards should be more **accurate**, **relevant** and **appropriate**.

Question 4

Marking scheme

		Marks
(a)	Current revenue	3
	Future projected revenue	2
	Incremental revenue	1
	Employee costs	1
	Overhead costs	1
	Adjusting net cash flows for inflation	1
	Residual value	1
	Tax calculations and phasing of cash flows	4
	Discounting cash flows	2
		16
(b)	Recognising need for IRR calculation	1
	Calculating NPV at higher/lower discount rate	2
	Calculating IRR	1
		4
(c)	Explanation of alternative approach	1
	Formula to calculate real cost of capital	1
	Calculation of real cost of capital	1
	Explanation of problems where taxation is involved	2
		25

(a) <u>Net present value</u>

	Year 0	Year 1	Year 2	Year 3	Year 4	Year 5
	$	$	$	$	$	
Net cash flows (W1)		57,600	59,904	62,300	64,792	
Tax at 30%:						
Current year		(8,640)	(8,986)	(9,345)	(9,719)	
Following year			(8,640)	(8,986)	(9,345)	(9,719)
Purchase	(150,000)					
Sale					15,000	
Tax saving (W2)		5,625	9,844	7,383	10,406	7,242
Net cash inflow after tax	(150,000)	54,585	52,122	51,352	71,134	(2,477)
Discount factor at 12%	1	0.893	0.797	0.712	0.636	0.567
PV	(150,000)	48,744	41,541	36,563	45,242	(1,404)

NPV = $20,686

Workings

1   Net cash flows for year 1

		$
Current revenue from rooms	40 rooms x 360 days x $250 x 80%	2,880,000
Revised revenue from rooms	40 x 360 x $250 x 105% x 82%	3,099,600
Incremental revenue		219,600
Incremental employee cost	4 x $30,000	(120,000)
Incremental overhead cost		(42,000)
Net cash flow		57,600

Net cash flows

Year		$
1		57,600
2	104% × $57,600	59,904
3	104% × $59,904	62,300
4	104% × $62,300	64,792

2   WDAs and balancing charges/allowances

		Reducing balance
Year		$
0	Purchase	150,000
1	WDA (25%)	(37,500)
	Value at start of Year 2	112,500
2	WDA	(28,125)
	Value at start of Year 3	84,375
3	WDA	(21,094)
	Value at start of Year 4	63,281
4	Sales price	(15,000)
	Balancing allowance	48,281

Year of claim	Allowance $	Tax saved $	Yr 1 $	Yr 2 $	Tax Saving Yr 3 $	Yr 4 $	Yr 5 £
1	37,500	11,250	5,625	5,625			
2	28,125	8,438		4,219	4,219		
3	21,094	6,328			3,164	3,164	
4	48,281	14,484				7,242	7,242
	135,000		5,625	9,844	7,383	10,406	7,242

(b)   We need to find the IRR as this is the point at which the NPV would be zero.

Using a discount factor of 20% we have the following.

	Year 0	Year 1	Year 2	Year 3	Year 4	Year 5
Net cash flow after tax	(150,000)	54,585	52,122	51,352	71,135	(2,477)
Discount factor	1	0.833	0.694	0.579	0.482	0.402
Present value	(150,000)	45,469	36,173	29,732	34,287	(995)

Net present value = -$5,334

$$IRR = A + \left[\frac{P}{P-N} \times (B-A) \right]\%$$

$$= 12\% + \left[\frac{20,686}{20,686 + 5,334} \times (20-12) \right]\%$$

$$= 18.36\%$$

(c) It is also possible to express the cash flows in today's value and then discount the cash flows at the real cost of capital.

(1 + money rate) = (1 + real rate) × (1 + inflation rate)

∴ the real rate $= \dfrac{1 + \text{money rate}}{1 + \text{inflation rate}} - 1$

$= 1.12/1.04 - 1$

$= 7.69\%$

The difficulties with this approach occur when there are tax implications. If tax is involved then the cash flows need to be treated separately because capital allowances are based on original cost. The residual value of equipment is given in Year 4 values and would need to be amended to present day values.

CIMA
Paper P1 (Operational)
Performance Operations

Mock Exam 3
November 2010

Question Paper	
Time allowed	**3 hours**
This paper is divided into three sections	
Section A	**EIGHT objective test questions**
Section B	**SIX short answer questions**
Section C	**TWO scenario questions**

DO NOT OPEN THIS PAPER UNTIL YOU ARE READY TO START UNDER EXAMINATION CONDITIONS

350

SECTION A – 20 marks

Answer ALL sub-questions

Question 1

1   Invoice discounting is:

    A   Reducing or discounting the amount owed by a customer in order to ensure payment
    B   Writing off a debt because the customer is not expected to pay
    C   Selling invoices to a finance company that then collects the cash from the customer
    D   Selling invoices to a finance company for less than their face value while continuing to collect the cash from the customer   **(2 marks)**

2   A project with a five year life requires an initial investment of $120,000 and generates a net present value (NPV) of $50,000 at a discount rate of 10% per annum.

The project cash flows are as follows.

	$'000 per annum
Variable material cost	30
Variable labour cost	10
Incremental fixed cost	5

The costs and activity levels are expected to remain the same for each year of the project. Ignore taxation and inflation.

The sensitivity of the investment decision to changes in the variable costs is:

    A   131.9%
    B   44.0%
    C   33.0%
    D   29.3%   **(2 marks)**

3   The data in the table below has been extracted from a company's cost accounting records. It shows the total costs and the inflation index for the periods in which the costs were incurred. Cost behaviour patterns are the same in both periods.

Output level	Total cost	Inflation index
6,000 units	$10,500	1.05
8,000 units	$13,390	1.03

The variable cost per unit, to the nearest $0.01, at an inflation index of 1.06 is:

    A $1.45
    B $1.59
    C $1.53
    D $1.50   **(2 marks)**

The following data are given for sub-questions 4 and 5 below

The budgeted selling price of one of C's range of chocolate bars was $6.00 per bar. At the beginning of the budget period market prices of cocoa increased significantly and C decided to increase the selling price of the chocolate bar by 10% for the whole period. C also decided to increase the amount spent on marketing and as a result actual sales volumes increased to 15,750 bars which was 5% above the budgeted volume. The standard contribution per bar was $2.00 however a contribution of $2.25 per bar was actually achieved.

4   The sales price variance for the period was:

    A $9,450 A
    B $9,450 F
    C $9,000 A
    D $9,000 F   **(2 marks)**

5   The sales volume contribution variance for the period was:

    A $1,500.00 F
    B $3,937.50 F
    C $3,750.00 F
    D $1,687.50 F   **(2 marks)**

6   H has a budgeted production for the next budget year of 12,000 units spread evenly over the year. It expects the same production level to continue for the next two years. Each unit uses 4kg of material.

The estimated opening raw material inventory at the start of the next budget year is 3,000kg. H's future policy will be to hold sufficient raw material inventory at the end of each month to cover 110% of the following month's production.

The budgeted material cost is $8 per kg for purchases up to 49,000kg. The excess of purchases over 49,000kg in a year will be at a cost of $7.50 per kg.

Calculate the material purchases budget for the year in $.   **(3 marks)**

7   An unquoted bond has a coupon rate of 6% per annum and will repay its face value of $100 on its maturity in 4 years' time. The yield to maturity on similar bonds is estimated to be 3% per annum. The annual interest has just been paid for the current year.

Calculate the current expected market value of the bond.   **(3 marks)**

8   A company has to choose between three mutually exclusive projects. Market research has shown that customers could react to the projects in three different ways depending on their preferences. There is a 30% chance that customers will exhibit preferences 1, a 20% chance that they will exhibit preferences 2 and a 50% chance they will exhibit preferences 3. The company uses expected value to make this type of decision.

The net present value of each of the possible outcomes is as follows:

	Probability	Project A	Project B	Project C
	$'000		$'000	$'000
Preferences 1	0.3	400	800	500
Preferences 2	0.2	500	300	600
Preferences 3	0.5	700	200	400

A market research company believes it can provide perfect information about the preferences of customers in this market.

Calculate the maximum amount that should be paid for the information from the market research company.   **(4 marks)**

(Total = 20 marks)

SECTION B – 30 marks

Answer ALL six sub-questions. Each sub-question is worth five marks

Question 2

(a) Explain the stages in the budget setting process for a company that uses a zero-based budgeting system.

(5 marks)

(b) AP sells fruit in a market where the level of demand is uncertain. AP has to order the fruit before the demand level is known.

The payoff table below shows the profits AP can expect depending on the level of order that is placed and the level of demand that occurs.

Demand level	Level of order		
	High	Medium	Low
Good	$600	$300	$100
Average	$200	$400	$100
Poor	$(100)	$300	$200

Required

(i) Identify which order level would be selected if AP applied

 a. the maximin decision criterion

 b. the maximax decision criterion **(2 marks)**

(ii) Identify, using a minimax regret table, the order level that would be selected if AP applied the minimax regret decision criterion. **(3 marks)**

(Total for sub-question (b) = 5 marks)

(c) 'Decision rules based on expected values assume that the decision maker is risk neutral'.

Required

(i) Explain the above statement **(2 marks)**

(ii) Describe TWO other attitudes to risk **(3 marks)**

(Total for sub-question (c) = 5 marks)

(d) RX has a balance outstanding on its trade receivables account at the start of the year of $83,000 after allowing for bad debts. RX forecasts sales revenue for the next year of $492,750. All sales are on credit.

Based on past experience, RX anticipates that bad debts will represent 5% of sales for the year. Trade receivable days at the end of the year are expected to be 60 days.

Required

(i) Calculate the expected receipts from customers during the year **(3 marks)**

(ii) Describe TWO methods that RX could use to reduce the possibility of bad debts occurring

(2 marks)

(Total for sub-question (d) = 5 marks)

(e) A company has forecast that it will have surplus funds to invest for a 12 month period. It is considering two investments as follows:

Investment 1

Invest in a bank deposit account that has a variable rate of interest. The current rate of interest on the account is 1.1% per quarter.

Investment 2

Buy a 12 month fixed dated government bond. The bond has a coupon rate of 2.5% payable every six months.

Required

Explain the advantages AND disadvantages to the company of each of the investments.

You should consider the return offered and the level and type of risk involved with each investment.

You should assume that there are no other investments available and that these investments are only available now. **(5 marks)**

(f)   An extract from WCC's trial balance at the end of its financial year is given below:

	$'000
Sales revenue (80% on credit)	1,400
Cost of sales	1,215
Purchases of materials (95% on credit)	915
Inventories at year end	
Raw materials	85
Finished goods	90
Trade receivables	185
Trade payables	125

Required

Calculate the length of WCC's working capital cycle to the nearest 0.1 of a day. **(5 marks)**

(Total = 30 marks)

SECTION C – 50 marks

Answer both questions

Question 3

A healthcare company specialises in hip, knee and shoulder replacement operations, known as surgical procedures. As well as providing these surgical procedures the company offers pre operation and post operation in-patient care, in a fully equipped hospital, for those patients who will be undergoing the surgical procedures.

Surgeons are paid a fixed fee for each surgical procedure they perform and an additional amount for any follow-up consultations. Post procedure follow-up consultations are only undertaken if there are any complications in relation to the surgical procedure. There is no additional fee charged to patients for any follow up consultations. All other staff are paid annual salaries.

The company's existing costing system uses a single overhead rate, based on revenue, to charge the costs of support activities to the procedures. Concern has been raised about the inaccuracy of procedure costs and the company's accountant has initiated a project to implement an activity-based costing (ABC) system.

The project team has collected the following data on each of the procedures.

Procedure information	Hip	Knee	Shoulder
Fee charged to patients per procedure	$8,000	$10,000	$6,000
Number of procedures per annum	600	800	400
Average time per procedure	2.0 hrs	1.2 hrs	1.5 hrs
Number of procedures per theatre session	2	1	4
In-patient days per procedure	3	2	1
Surgeon's fee per procedure	$1,200	$1,800	$1,500
% of procedures with complications	8%	5%	10%
Surgeon's fee per follow up consultation	$300	$300	$300
Cost of medical supplies per procedure	$400	$200	$300

The project team has obtained the following information about the support activities.

Activity	Cost driver	Overheads $'000
Theatre preparation for each session	Number of theatre preparations	864
Operating theatre usage	Procedure time	1,449
Nursing and ancillary services	In-patient days	5,428
Administration	Sales revenue	1,216
Other overheads	Number of procedures	923

Required

(a) Calculate the profit per procedure for each of the three procedures, using the current basis for charging the costs of support activities to procedures. **(5 marks)**

(b) Calculate the profit per procedure for each of the three procedures using activity-based costing. **(13 marks)**

(c) Discuss the ways in which the information obtained by the project team may be of benefit to the management of the company. **(7 marks)**

(Total = 25 marks)

Question 4

A car manufacturer has been experiencing financial difficulties over the past few years. Sales have reduced significantly as a result of the worldwide economic recession. Costs have increased due to quality issues that led to a recall of some models of its cars.

Production volume last year was 50,000 cars and it is expected that this will increase by 4% per annum each year for the next five years.

The company directors are concerned to improve profitability and are considering two potential investment projects.

Project 1 – implement a new quality control process

The company has paid a consultant process engineer $50,000 to review the company's quality processes. The consultant recommended that the company implement a new quality control process. The new process will require a machine costing $20,000,000. The machine is expected to have a useful life of five years and no residual value.

It is estimated that raw material costs will be reduced by $62 per car and that both internal and external failure costs from quality failures will be reduced by 80%.

Estimated internal and external failure costs per year without the new process, based on last year's production volume of 50,000 cars, and their associated probabilities are shown below:

Internal failure costs		External failure costs	
$	Probability	$	Probability
300,000	50%	1,300,000	60%
500,000	30%	1,900,000	30%
700,000	20%	3,000,000	10%

Internal and external failure costs are expected to increase each year in line with the number of cars produced.

The company's accountant has calculated that this investment will result in a net present value (NPV) of $1,338,000 and an internal rate of return of 10.5%.

Project 2 – in-house component manufacturing

The company could invest in new machinery to enable in-house manufacturing of a component that is currently made by outside suppliers. The new machinery is expected to cost $15,000,000 and have a useful life of five years and no residual value. Additional working capital of $1,000,000 will also be required as a result of producing the component in-house.

The price paid to the current supplier is $370 per component. It is estimated that the in-house variable cost of production will be $260 per component. Each car requires one component. Fixed production costs, including machinery depreciation, are estimated to increase by $5,000,000 per annum as a result of manufacturing the component in-house.

Depreciation is calculated on a straight line basis.

Additional Information

The company is unable to raise enough capital to carry out both projects. The company will therefore have to choose between the two alternatives.

Taxation and inflation should be ignored.

The company uses a cost of capital of 8% per annum.

Required

(a)   Calculate for Project 1 the relevant cash flows that the accountant should have used for year 1 when appraising the project.

All workings should be shown in $'000.   **(6 marks)**

(b)   Calculate for Project 2:

(i) the net present value (NPV)

(ii) the internal rate of return (IRR)

All workings should be shown in $'000   **(10 marks)**

(c)   Advise the company directors which of the two investment projects should be undertaken.   **(4 marks)**

(d)   A company is considering two alternative investment projects both of which have a positive net present value. The projects have been ranked on the basis of both net present value (NPV) and internal rate of return (IRR). The result of the ranking is shown below:

	Project A	Project B
NPV	1st	2nd
IRR	2nd	1st

Discuss potential reasons why the conflict between the NPV and IRR ranking may have arisen. **(5 marks)**

(Total = 25 marks)

Answers

DO NOT TURN THIS PAGE UNTIL YOU HAVE
COMPLETED THE MOCK EXAM

A plan of attack

As you turned the page to start this exam, any one of a number of things could have been going through your mind. Some of them may have been quite sensible, some of them may not.

The main thing to do is take a deep breath and do not panic. It's best to sort a plan of attack before the actual exam so that when the invigilator tells you that you can begin and the adrenaline kicks in you are using every minute of the three hours wisely.

Paper format

This paper has three sections. All questions are compulsory. The first section contains about eight objective test questions. The second has six short questions. The third section has two longer questions.

Section A – 20 marks
Section B – 30 marks
Section C – 50 marks

Reading time/order of questions

However you find the paper, it is important to make good use of your reading time. We recommend that you spend some of it reviewing the Section B questions. We would advise you to look carefully through the Section B questions and plan your answer to them. Remember to allocate your time correctly. That is 54 minutes for the 30 marks of Section B , 36 minutes for the OTs of Section A and 90 minutes for the section C questions.

You then have a **choice.** An approach that has worked well with students in the past is the following.

- Read through and answer Section B, which you have planned in your reading time, before moving on to Section A

- Go through Section C, answering first the question you feel most confident about.

Time spent at the start of each question confirming the requirements and producing a plan for the answers is time well spent.

When reviewing the requirements look at how many marks have been allocated to each part. This will give you an idea of how detailed your answer must be.

Doing the exam

Actually doing the exam is a personal experience. There is not a single *right way.* If you submit complete answers to all questions, your approach obviously works.

One approach

The possible pitfall of doing Section B before Section A would be getting sucked too deeply into Section B and leaving insufficient time for Sections A and C.

A quick look at the Section B question would tell me that:

- Part (a) is a fairly straightforward explanation of the stages in ZBB. I would split the stages into step 1, step 2 and so on.

- Part (b) has two parts so I would watch the clock. Part (i) just asks me to **identify** the relevant order level so I wouldn't spend too much time writing an explanation. Part (ii) asks me to use a minimax regret table to identify the correct order level so I would make sure that I draw the table.

- Part (c) also has two parts so I would be careful not to overrun on time. Part (ii) is looking for an explanation of risk averse and risk seeking.

- Part (d) asks for a calculation and a description. Part (ii) asks for two methods so I would not waste time writing on more than two methods and I would deduce that there is one mark per method.

- Part (e) will need careful reading of the requirements. The question asks for advantages and disadvantages of each method. In answering this I need to include a calculation of the return and an explanation of the risks. This is quite a lot for 5 marks so I would be careful not to spend too much time on each bit.

- Part (f) asks me to calculate the working capital cycle. It specifically says to the nearest 0.1 day so I would make sure that I did this.

If you do decide to start with Section B rather than Section A objective test questions, make sure you do not overrun your 54 minutes. Having worked your way through Section B, taking no more than nine minutes per question, you should now allocate 36 minutes to answer the Section A questions.

For the Section C questions you must proceed in a methodical way. Set out your format and then work through the question requirements, doing neat, readable calculations and filling out the figures. Even if you do not finish, you will get marks for what you have done, so do the easy bits first and divide your time evenly between the two questions.

Time allocation

Be disciplined. Allocate your time according to the marks available but never go over the time allocation. The last few marks in a question are the hardest to earn.

Be sure to follow the requirements. If four advantages are required, give four. No extra credit will be given for five. Two advantages will only get you half marks.

Answer all of the question. Having a go at all parts of every question will put you in a better position to pass. However difficult that last part of the question seems at first there are marks to be earned.

If you have time left at the end of the exam ensure that you have attempted every part of every question. If you have, then scan through and ensure you complete any part of an answer you left earlier. Use the full three hours working towards a pass.

Marking the exam

When you mark your exam, be honest. Don't be too harsh though. Give yourself credit for the things you did well, but don't kid yourself with 'I would have done that in the real exam'. It may be worth your while making two lists; strengths and weaknesses.

Strengths will be areas of the syllabus you are confident with and also good exam technique.

Weaknesses will be holes in your knowledge and poor exam technique (maybe you ran out of time and couldn't answer all the requirements of the last question).

Making this list will help you focus your last days of revision on the areas which require attention whilst reminding you of the areas you excel in.

SECTION A

Question 1

1   D   Selling invoices to a finance company for less than their face value while continuing to collect the cash from the customer.

2   C $\text{Sensitivity of investment decision} = \dfrac{\text{NPV of project}}{\text{PV of cash flow affected}} \times 100\%$

       PV of $40,000 for 5 years at 10% cost of capital
           = $40,000 × 3.791
           = $151,640

       $\therefore$ Sensitivity $= \dfrac{\$50,000}{\$151,640} \times 100\%$

           = 33.0%

3   B   Removing inflation we have $10,500/1.05 = $10,000 and $13,390/1.03 = $13,000

       We use the high low method to find the variable cost.

	Cost	Units
High	$13,000	8,000
Low	$10,000	6,000
	$3,000	2,000

       $\therefore$ Variable cost per unit $= \dfrac{\$3,000}{\$2,000} = \$1.50$ per unit

       Inflating at 1.06 gives $1.50 × 1.06 = $1.59

4   B   Sales price variance

	$
15,759 should have sold for (×$6.00)	94,500
But did sell for (× $6.00 × 1.1)	103,950
	9,450 (F)

5   A   Budgeted sales volume = 15,750/1.05 = 15,000 bars

       $\therefore$ the difference between budgeted and actual sales volume was 15,750 – 15,000 = 750 bars.

       Sales volume contribution variance   = 750 bars × standard contribution per unit

                                                = 750 bars × $2.00

                                                = $1,500 (F)

6   Purchases   = Closing inventory + production – opening inventory

   Closing inventory   = (12,000/12) × 110% × 4kg = 4,400 kg

   Production   = 12,000 units × 4 kg = 48,000 kg

   $\therefore$ Purchases   = 4,400 + 48,000 – 3,000

                     = 49,400 kg

   Cost: = (49,000kg × $8) + (400 × $7.50)

                     = $395,000

7   Coupon rate = interest rate

∴ interest = $100 × 6% = $6 per annum

Interest is received every year for 4 years so we need the cumulative present value with a discount rate of 3% (= 3.717)

The $100 is received after 4 years so we need the figure from the PV tables for 3% for 4 years (0.888).

The net present value   = $(6 × 3.717) + $(100 × 0.888) = $111.10

This is the market value of the bond.

8   EVs with no information:

		Project A		Project B		Project C	
	Probability	NPV	EV	NPV	EV	NPV	EV
		$'000	$'000	$'000	$'000	$'000	$'000
Pref 1	0.3	400	120	800	240	500	150
Pref 2	0.2	500	100	300	60	600	120
Pref 3	0.5	700	350	200	100	400	200
			570		400		470

With no information project A would be selected as it has the highest EV.

With perfect information the following projects would be chosen:

			$'000
Preference 1	Project B	EV of NPV = $800 × 0.3 =	240
Preference 2	Project C	EV of NPV = $600 × 0.2 =	120
Preference 3	Project A	EV of NPV = $700 × 0.5 =	350
		EV with perfect information	710

	$'000
EV of NPV without perfect information	570
EV of NPV with perfect information	710
Value of perfect information	140

Provided the information does not cost more than $140,000 to collect, it would be worth having.

Question 2

(a)   Stages in the ZBB process

Define decision packages, comprehensive descriptions of specific organisational activities (decision units) which management can use to evaluate the activities and rank them in order of priority against other activities. There are two types.

Mutually exclusive packages contain alternative methods of getting the same job done. The best option among the packages must be selected by comparing costs and benefits and the other packages are then discarded.

Incremental packages divide one aspect of an activity into different levels of effort. The 'base' package will describe the minimum amount of work that must be done to carry out the activity and the other packages describe what additional work could be done, at what cost and for what benefits.

Evaluate and rank each activity (decision package) on the basis of its benefit to the organisation. This can be a lengthy process. Minimum work requirements (those that are essential to get a job done) will be given high priority and so too will work which meets legal obligations. In the accounting department these would be minimum requirements to operate the payroll, payables ledger and receivables ledger systems, and to maintain and publish a satisfactory set of accounts.

 Allocate resources in the budget according to the funds available and the evaluation and ranking of the competing packages.

(b)   (i)   a. Maximin = maximise the minimum achievable profits.

	Minimum profits
High	$(100)
Medium	$300
Low	$100

The maximum of the minimum profits is $300 when a medium order is placed.

b. Maximax = maximise the maximum achievable profits

	Maximum profits
High	$600
Medium	$400
Low	$200

The maximum of the maximum achievable profits is $600 when a high order is placed.

(ii)   Re-writing information given in the question gives

	Good	Average	Poor
High	$600	$200	$(100)
Medium	$300	$400	$300
Low	$100	$100	$200

Minimax regret table

	Good	Average	Poor	Maximum	
High	$0*	$200***	$400	$400	
Medium	$300**	$0	$0	$300	(lowest maximum)
Low	$500	$300	$100	$500	

* $600 - $600   ** $600 - $300   *** $400 - $200   etc

The lowest maximum regret is with a medium order so medium would be selected if the minimax regret rule is used.

(c)   (i)   Risk neutral

The expected value is a **weighted average**, based on **probabilities**. Using probabilities means that the expected value outcome is based on what is **likely as a long-term average** and so no account is taken of whether the decision maker is risk averse or a risk seeker. Expected value decision rules assume that the decision maker is **risk neutral**, that is, **prefers the most likely outcome**.

(ii) <u>Risk seeker</u>

A risk seeker is a decision maker who is interested in the **best outcomes** no matter how **small** the **chance** that they may occur. They will choose the option which has the potential for the highest return.

<u>Risk averse</u>

A risk averse decision maker acts on the assumption that the **worst outcome might occur**. They will choose the option with the least amount of risk involved.

(d) (i) Sales revenue for the year less bad debts = $492,750 × 95% = $468,112.50

Closing receivables at year end (net of bad debts) = $468,112.50 × 60/365 = $76,950

Expected receipts = opening receivables bal + sales revenue during the year − closing receivables

= $83,000 + $468,112.50 - $76,950

= $474,162.50

(ii) <u>Chasing late payments</u>

If payments become overdue, they should be chased. Examples of procedures for chasing include instituting **reminders** or final demands, chasing payment by **telephone**, notifying the **debt collection section**, instigating **legal action** to recover the debt.

<u>Discounts</u>

Early payment can be encouraged by good administration and by **discount policies**. For example, a percentage discount could be given if payment is received by a certain date.

<u>Alternative solutions</u>

The question only asks for two methods but you may have mentioned some of the methods below.

- Establishing a credit status for new customers before giving credit, for example from a credit reference agency.

- Carrying out routine credit checks on existing customers.

- Ensuring that customers are not able to exceed their credit limit, for example by refusing the order or by contacting the customer to request some of the outstanding debt be paid first.

- Applying penalties for late payments.

(e) The interest rate on the bank deposit account is 1.1% per quarter. This is equivalent to $(1.011^4 - 1) \times 100 = 4.47\%$ per annum.

The interest rate on the bond is 2.5% every six months. This is equivalent to 2.5% × 2 = 5% per annum

<u>Deposit account</u>

<u>Advantages</u>

The deposit account is more flexible than the bonds which have a fixed date.

<u>Disadvantages</u>

The return offered is variable which means that it may change. There is also a risk to the bank itself given the banking crisis of 2008/09.

<u>Bond</u>

<u>Advantages</u>

The main advantage is that a government bond is usually considered to be risk free. The interest rate per annum is also higher than the deposit account interest. This rate will be fixed.

Disadvantages

Bonds are not as flexible because they cannot be cashed in early. It is also possible that market interest rates will rise meaning that the return on the bond could be below market rate.

(f)   68.7 days

Raw material inventory days	85/915 × 365	33.9
Finished goods inventory days	90/1215 × 365	27.0
Receivable days	185/(0.80 × 1,400) × 365	60.3
Payables days	125/(0.95 × 915) × 365	-52.5
Working capital cycle		68.7

Question 3

Text references. ABC is covered in Chapter 11.

Top tips. For part (a) you need to organise your workings separately from the profit statement. There are quite a few calculations to do for 5 marks so you need to keep an eye on the time. Part (b) also needs methodical workings and some thought over the cost drivers. For example, theatre preparation costs are driven by the number of theatre preparations so you need to consider how many theatre preparations there are for each type of procedure. For part (c), make sure you use headings and leave space between your paragraphs. Remember to compare the profits using the current method and the profits using ABC.

Easy marks. The easier marks in this question are for the discussion in part (c) of the benefit of ABC.

(a)   Single overhead rate based on revenue = Total overhead cost/fee revenue

Total overhead cost	= $864,000 + $1,449,000 + $5,428,000 + $1,216,000 + $923,000	
	= $9,880,000	
Total fee revenue	= ($8,000 × 600) + ($10,000 × 800) + ($6,000 × 400)	
	= $15,200,000	
∴ single overhead rate based on revenue	= $9,880,000/$15,200,000	
	= 0.65	

Profit statement

	Hip	Knee	Shoulder
	$	$	$
Fee	8,000	10,000	6,000
Surgeon's fee	(1,200)	(1,800)	(1,500)
Surgeon's follow up fee (W1)	(24)	(15)	(30)
Medical supplies	(400)	(200)	(300)
Overheads (W2)	(5,200)	(6,500)	(3,900)
Profit	1,176	1,485	270

Workings

1	Hip:	8% × $300	= $24 per procedure
	Knee:	5% × $300	= $15 per procedure
	Shoulder:	10% × $300	= $30 per procedure
2	Hip:	0.65 × $8,000	= $5,200 per procedure
	Knee:	0.65 × $10,000	= $6,500 per procedure
	Shoulder:	0.65 × $6,000	= $3,900 per procedure

(b)   Calculation of cost per driver

Activity	Cost driver	Overheads	No. of costs drivers	Cost/driver
		$'000		
Theatre prep	No. of preps	864	1,200 (W1)	$720/prep
Theatre usage	Procedure time	1,449	2,760 (W2)	$525/hour
Ancillary services	In-patient days	5,428	3,800 (W3)	$1,428/day
Admin	Sales revenue	1,216	15,200,000	$0.08/$
Other o/heads	No. procedures	923	1,800 (W4)	$513/procedr

Workings

1   (600/2 + 800 +400/4) = 1,200

2   (600 × 2hrs) + (800 × 1.2hrs) + (400 × 1.5hrs) = 2,760

3   (600 × 3) + (800 × 2) + (400 × 1) = 3,800

4   600 + 800 + 400 = 1,800

Calculation of overhead cost per procedure

Activity	Hip		Knee		Shoulder	
Theatre prep	$720/2	$360	$720/1	$720	$720/4	$180
Theatre usage	$525 × 2	$1,050	$525 × 1.2	$630	$525 × 1.5	$788
Ancillary services	$1,428 × 3	$4,284	$1,428 × 2	$2,856	$1,428 × 1	$1,428
Admin	$8,000 × $0.08	$640	$10,000 × $0.08	$800	$6,000 × 0.08	$480
Other o/heads		$513		$513		$513
Total		$6,847		$5,519		$3,389

Profit statement

	Hip	Knee	Shoulder
	$	$	$
Profit per current OAR	1,176	1,485	270
Add back overhead	5,200	6,500	3,900
Deduct ABC o/head	(6,847)	(5,519)	(3,389)
Profit per procedure	(471)	2,466	781

(c)   Accuracy of costs

The current method allows overheads to be related to the procedures in a rather **arbitrary way**. This means that the overhead costs attributed each procedure will not be particularly accurate. ABC focuses on what **causes costs** to increase (the cost drivers) and therefore establishes a **more accurate overhead cost per procedure**.

Profitability and cost control

The company will be able to assess the **profitability** of each procedure more **realistically**. ABC facilitates a good understanding of what drives overhead costs and so the profitability calculation of each procedure is more accurate. More accurate costs and knowledge of what drives them provide the company with information which may be used to control or reduce costs and therefore improve profitability.

Pricing and market position

Using ABC shows that the **hip procedure is actually making a loss** and that the **knee procedure** is the **most profitable** procedure. The company could consider increasing the fee for the hip procedure although this would depend on the current market prices and whether the price increase would affect the company's **market position**.

The company could also consider the possibility of no longer providing the hip service and instead providing some other more profitable service.

Activity based management

The use of ABC can encourage an activity based management system. ABM applications include the identification of value added and non-value added processes. Efficiency is measured through cost driver rates.

Question 4

> **Text references**. Relevant costs are covered in Chapter 6a. Net present value and IRR are covered in Chapter 16.
>
> **Top tips**. Remember to read the question carefully – part (a) asks for Project 1 cash flows for year 1 only. Part (b) will need methodical workings. Layout a proforma for your NPV calculation and put your workings underneath. Make sure you calculate the incremental net cash flows rather than wasting time calculating the revenue and then the costs for each year. Part (b)(ii) is asking you to calculate the IRR and should be fairly straightforward. For part (c) make it clear which Project should be chosen and why and always mention that management should consider non-financial factors as well.
>
> **Easy marks**. Parts (a), (b) and (c) have plenty of easy marks. You should find it easy to pick out the relevant costs, lay out an NPV proforma and advise which project should be undertaken.

(a)   Relevant cash flows for Project 1 for year 1

The relevant cash flows are the incremental future cash flows. The **consultant's fee** of $50,000 is a **sunk cost** and therefore not relevant. The new **machinery** cost will be in **year 0**, not in year 1 so we can ignore that.

Raw material cost reduction

Number of cars to be produced in year 1 = 50,000 × 104% = 52,000 cars

∴ cost reduction = 52,000 × $62 = **$3,224k**

Internal failure cost saving

$'000	Probability	EV	× 104%	× 80%
300	0.5	150	156	124.80
500	0.3	150	156	124.80
700	0.2	140	145.6	116.48
				366.08

Total saving = **$366k**

External failure cost saving

$'000	Probability	EV	× 104%	× 80%
1,300	0.6	780	811.2	648.96
1,900	0.3	570	592.8	474.24
3,000	0.1	300	312	249.60
				1,372.80

Total saving = **$1,373k**

Net cash flows for Year 1 = $3,224k + $366k + $1,373k

                            = **$4,963k**

(b)   (i)

Net present value

	Year 0	Year 1	Year 2	Year 3	Year 4	Year 5
	$	$	$	$	$	
Initial investment	(15,000)					
Working capital	(1,000)					1,000
Cost savings (W1)		5,720	5,949	6,187	6,434	6,691
Fixed cost (W2)		(2,000)	(2,000)	(2,000)	(2,000)	(2,000)
Net cash flow	(16,000)	3,720	3,949	4,187	4,434	5,691
Discount factor at 8%	1	0.926	0.857	0.794	0.735	0.681
PV	(16,000)	3,445	3,384	3,324	3,259	3,876

NPV = $1,288k

Workings

1

	Year 0	Year 1	Year 2	Year 3	Year 4	Year 5
Production volume (4% annual increase)	50,000	52,000	54,080	56,243	58,493	60,833
Saving per car ($370 - $260)		110	110	110	110	110
Total saving		$5,720k	$5,949k	$6,187k	$6,434	$6,691

2   Fixed costs will increase by $5,000k per annum but this includes depreciation which is not a cash flow. We therefore need to remove the depreciation charge.

Depreciation per annum = $15,000k/5 years = $3,000k per annum.

∴ Extra fixed cost per annum = $5,000k - $3,000k = $2,000k per annum.

(ii)   We need to find the IRR as this is the point at which the NPV would be zero.

Using a discount factor of 12% we have the following.

	Year 0	Year 1	Year 2	Year 3	Year 4	Year 5
Net cash flow after tax	(16,000)	3,720	3,949	4,187	4,434	5,691
Discount factor	1	0.893	0.797	0.712	0.636	0.567
Present value	(16,000)	3,322	3,147	2,981	2,820	3,227

Net present value at 12% = -$503k

Net present value at 8% = -$1,288k

$$IRR = A + \left[\frac{P}{P-N} \times (B-A) \right]\%$$

$$= 8\% + \left[\frac{1,288}{1,288+503} \times (12-8) \right]\%$$

$$= 10.9\%$$

(c)   A positive NPV means that the **present value** of the cash **inflows** from a project is **greater** than the **present value of the cash outflows**. Both projects have a positive net present value and therefore **both projects are worthwhile**. Project 1 **has the higher NPV** of $1,338k and so on the **basis of NPV** alone **Project 1 should be chosen**.

Project 1, however, requires a much **higher initial investment** ($20m instead of $16m). Management need to consider whether there is any difference in **risk** between the two projects and whether some **other investment** could be made with the $4m if Project 2 were chosen instead.

There could also be some **non-financial aspects** of the projects which management should consider before making a decision.

(d)   An assumption underlying the NPV method is that any net cash **inflows generated** during the life of the project will be **reinvested** elsewhere **at the cost of capital** (that is, the discount rate). The **IRR** method, on the other hand, **assumes** these **cash flows** can be **reinvested** elsewhere to earn a return equal to the **IRR** of the original project. This means that the **IRR** method may give **better rankings** to a project with **high early cash flows** and the **NPV method** may give a better ranking to a project with **later cash flows**.

The **IRR** is a **percentage** which means that it ignores the relative sizes of the investments and returns. The **NPV**, however, is an **absolute value**. Using the IRR method may suggest selecting a project with a lower investment where the return is relatively high compared with that initial investment. However, it may be preferable to invest a greater sum which generates a lower percentage return and a greater absolute amount.

MATHEMATICAL TABLES

374

Tables

Area under the normal curve

This table gives the area under the normal curve between the mean and the point Z standard deviations above the mean. The corresponding area for deviations below the mean can be found by symmetry.

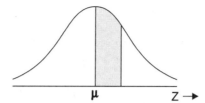

$Z = \frac{(x-\mu)}{\sigma}$	0.00	0.01	0.02	0.03	0.04	0.05	0.06	0.07	0.08	0.09
0.0	.0000	.0040	.0080	.0120	.0160	.0199	.0239	.0279	.0319	.0359
0.1	.0398	.0438	.0478	.0517	.0557	.0596	.0636	.0675	.0714	.0753
0.2	.0793	.0832	.0871	.0910	.0948	.0987	.1026	.1064	.1103	.1141
0.3	.1179	.1217	.1255	.1293	.1331	.1368	.1406	.1443	.1480	.1517
0.4	.1554	.1591	.1628	.1664	.1700	.1736	.1772	.1808	.1844	.1879
0.5	.1915	.1950	.1985	.2019	.2054	.2088	.2123	.2157	.2190	.2224
0.6	.2257	.2291	.2324	.2357	.2389	.2422	.2454	.2486	.2517	.2549
0.7	.2580	.2611	.2642	.2673	.2704	.2734	.2764	.2794	.2823	.2852
0.8	.2881	.2910	.2939	.2967	.2995	.3023	.3051	.3078	.3106	.3133
0.9	.3159	.3186	.3212	.3238	.3264	.3289	.3315	.3340	.3365	.3389
1.0	.3413	.3438	.3461	.3485	.3508	.3531	.3554	.3577	.3599	.3621
1.1	.3643	.3665	.3686	.3708	.3729	.3749	.3770	.3790	.3810	.3830
1.2	.3849	.3869	.3888	.3907	.3925	.3944	.3962	.3980	.3997	.4015
1.3	.4032	.4049	.4066	.4082	.4099	.4115	.4131	.4147	.4162	.4177
1.4	.4192	.4207	.4222	.4236	.4251	.4265	.4279	.4292	.4306	.4319
1.5	.4332	.4345	.4357	.4370	.4382	.4394	.4406	.4418	.4429	.4441
1.6	.4452	.4463	.4474	.4484	.4495	.4505	.4515	.4525	.4535	.4545
1.7	.4554	.4564	.4573	.4582	.4591	.4599	.4608	.4616	.4625	.4633
1.8	.4641	.4649	.4656	.4664	.4671	.4678	.4686	.4693	.4699	.4706
1.9	.4713	.4719	.4726	.4732	.4738	.4744	.4750	.4756	.4761	.4767
2.0	.4772	.4778	.4783	.4788	.4793	.4798	.4803	.4808	.4812	.4817
2.1	.4821	.4826	.4830	.4834	.4838	.4842	.4846	.4850	.4854	.4857
2.2	.4861	.4864	.4868	.4871	.4875	.4878	.4881	.4884	.4887	.4890
2.3	.4893	.4896	.4898	.4901	.4904	.4906	.4909	.4911	.4913	.4916
2.4	.4918	.4920	.4922	.4925	.4927	.4929	.4931	.4932	.4934	.4936
2.5	.4938	.4940	.4941	.4943	.4945	.4946	.4948	.4949	.4951	.4952
2.6	.4953	.4955	.4956	.4957	.4959	.4960	.4961	.4962	.4963	.4964
2.7	.4965	.4966	.4967	.4968	.4969	.4970	.4971	.4972	.4973	.4974
2.8	.4974	.4975	.4976	.4977	.4977	.4978	.4979	.4979	.4980	.4981
2.9	.4981	.4982	.4982	.4983	.4984	.4984	.4985	.4985	.4986	.4986
3.0	.49865	.4987	.4987	.4988	.4988	.4989	.4989	.4989	.4990	.4990
3.1	.49903	.4991	.4991	.4991	.4992	.4992	.4992	.4992	.4993	.4993
3.2	.49931	.4993	.4994	.4994	.4994	.4994	.4994	.4995	.4995	.4995
3.3	.49952	.4995	.4995	.4996	.4996	.4996	.4996	.4996	.4996	.4997
3.4	.49966	.4997	.4997	.4997	.4997	.4997	.4997	.4997	.4997	.4998
3.5	.49977									

Present value table

Present value of £1 ie $(1+r)^{-n}$ where r = interest rate, n = number of periods until payment or receipt.

Periods	Interest rates (r)									
(n)	1%	2%	3%	4%	5%	6%	7%	8%	9%	10%
1	0.990	0.980	0.971	0.962	0.952	0.943	0.935	0.926	0.917	0.909
2	0.980	0.961	0.943	0.925	0.907	0.890	0.873	0.857	0.842	0.826
3	0.971	0.942	0.915	0.889	0.864	0.840	0.816	0.794	0.772	0.751
4	0.961	0.924	0.888	0.855	0.823	0.792	0.763	0.735	0.708	0.683
5	0.951	0.906	0.863	0.822	0.784	0.747	0.713	0.681	0.650	0.621
6	0.942	0.888	0.837	0.790	0.746	0.705	0.666	0.630	0.596	0.564
7	0.933	0.871	0.813	0.760	0.711	0.665	0.623	0.583	0.547	0.513
8	0.923	0.853	0.789	0.731	0.677	0.627	0.582	0.540	0.502	0.467
9	0.914	0.837	0.766	0.703	0.645	0.592	0.544	0.500	0.460	0.424
10	0.905	0.820	0.744	0.676	0.614	0.558	0.508	0.463	0.422	0.386
11	0.896	0.804	0.722	0.650	0.585	0.527	0.475	0.429	0.388	0.350
12	0.887	0.788	0.701	0.625	0.557	0.497	0.444	0.397	0.356	0.319
13	0.879	0.773	0.681	0.601	0.530	0.469	0.415	0.368	0.326	0.290
14	0.870	0.758	0.661	0.577	0.505	0.442	0.388	0.340	0.299	0.263
15	0.861	0.743	0.642	0.555	0.481	0.417	0.362	0.315	0.275	0.239
16	0.853	0.728	0.623	0.534	0.458	0.394	0.339	0.292	0.252	0.218
17	0.844	0.714	0.605	0.513	0.436	0.371	0.317	0.270	0.231	0.198
18	0.836	0.700	0.587	0.494	0.416	0.350	0.296	0.250	0.212	0.180
19	0.828	0.686	0.570	0.475	0.396	0.331	0.277	0.232	0.194	0.164
20	0.820	0.673	0.554	0.456	0.377	0.312	0.258	0.215	0.178	0.149

Periods	Interest rates (r)									
(n)	11%	12%	13%	14%	15%	16%	17%	18%	19%	20%
1	0.901	0.893	0.885	0.877	0.870	0.862	0.855	0.847	0.840	0.833
2	0.812	0.797	0.783	0.769	0.756	0.743	0.731	0.718	0.706	0.694
3	0.731	0.712	0.693	0.675	0.658	0.641	0.624	0.609	0.593	0.579
4	0.659	0.636	0.613	0.592	0.572	0.552	0.534	0.516	0.499	0.482
5	0.593	0.567	0.543	0.519	0.497	0.476	0.456	0.437	0.419	0.402
6	0.535	0.507	0.480	0.456	0.432	0.410	0.390	0.370	0.352	0.335
7	0.482	0.452	0.425	0.400	0.376	0.354	0.333	0.314	0.296	0.279
8	0.434	0.404	0.376	0.351	0.327	0.305	0.285	0.266	0.249	0.233
9	0.391	0.361	0.333	0.308	0.284	0.263	0.243	0.225	0.209	0.194
10	0.352	0.322	0.295	0.270	0.247	0.227	0.208	0.191	0.176	0.162
11	0.317	0.287	0.261	0.237	0.215	0.195	0.178	0.162	0.148	0.135
12	0.286	0.257	0.231	0.208	0.187	0.168	0.152	0.137	0.124	0.112
13	0.258	0.229	0.204	0.182	0.163	0.145	0.130	0.116	0.104	0.093
14	0.232	0.205	0.181	0.160	0.141	0.125	0.111	0.099	0.088	0.078
15	0.209	0.183	0.160	0.140	0.123	0.108	0.095	0.084	0.074	0.065
16	0.188	0.163	0.141	0.123	0.107	0.093	0.081	0.071	0.062	0.054
17	0.170	0.146	0.125	0.108	0.093	0.080	0.069	0.060	0.052	0.045
18	0.153	0.130	0.111	0.095	0.081	0.069	0.059	0.051	0.044	0.038
19	0.138	0.116	0.098	0.083	0.070	0.060	0.051	0.043	0.037	0.031
20	0.124	0.104	0.087	0.073	0.061	0.051	0.043	0.037	0.031	0.026

Cumulative present value table

This table shows the present value of £1 per annum, receivable or payable at the end of each year for n years

$$\frac{1-(1+r)^{-n}}{r}.$$

Periods					Interest rates (r)					
(n)	1%	2%	3%	4%	5%	6%	7%	8%	9%	10%
1	0.990	0.980	0.971	0.962	0.952	0.943	0.935	0.926	0.917	0.909
2	1.970	1.942	1.913	1.886	1.859	1.833	1.808	1.783	1.759	1.736
3	2.941	2.884	2.829	2.775	2.723	2.673	2.624	2.577	2.531	2.487
4	3.902	3.808	3.717	3.630	3.546	3.465	3.387	3.312	3.240	3.170
5	4.853	4.713	4.580	4.452	4.329	4.212	4.100	3.993	3.890	3.791
6	5.795	5.601	5.417	5.242	5.076	4.917	4.767	4.623	4.486	4.355
7	6.728	6.472	6.230	6.002	5.786	5.582	5.389	5.206	5.033	4.868
8	7.652	7.325	7.020	6.733	6.463	6.210	5.971	5.747	5.535	5.335
9	8.566	8.162	7.786	7.435	7.108	6.802	6.515	6.247	5.995	5.759
10	9.471	8.983	8.530	8.111	7.722	7.360	7.024	6.710	6.418	6.145
11	10.368	9.787	9.253	8.760	8.306	7.887	7.499	7.139	6.805	6.495
12	11.255	10.575	9.954	9.385	8.863	8.384	7.943	7.536	7.161	6.814
13	12.134	11.348	10.635	9.986	9.394	8.853	8.358	7.904	7.487	7.103
14	13.004	12.106	11.296	10.563	9.899	9.295	8.745	8.244	7.786	7.367
15	13.865	12.849	11.938	11.118	10.380	9.712	9.108	8.559	8.061	7.606
16	14.718	13.578	12.561	11.652	10.838	10.106	9.447	8.851	8.313	7.824
17	15.562	14.292	13.166	12.166	11.274	10.477	9.763	9.122	8.544	8.022
18	16.398	14.992	13.754	12.659	11.690	10.828	10.059	9.372	8.756	8.201
19	17.226	15.679	14.324	13.134	12.085	11.158	10.336	9.604	8.950	8.365
20	18.046	16.351	14.878	13.590	12.462	11.470	10.594	9.818	9.129	8.514

Periods					Interest rates (r)					
(n)	11%	12%	13%	14%	15%	16%	17%	18%	19%	20%
1	0.901	0.893	0.885	0.877	0.870	0.862	0.855	0.847	0.840	0.833
2	1.713	1.690	1.668	1.647	1.626	1.605	1.585	1.566	1.547	1.528
3	2.444	2.402	2.361	2.322	2.283	2.246	2.210	2.174	2.140	2.106
4	3.102	3.037	2.974	2.914	2.855	2.798	2.743	2.690	2.639	2.589
5	3.696	3.605	3.517	3.433	3.352	3.274	3.199	3.127	3.058	2.991
6	4.231	4.111	3.998	3.889	3.784	3.685	3.589	3.498	3.410	3.326
7	4.712	4.564	4.423	4.288	4.160	4.039	3.922	3.812	3.706	3.605
8	5.146	4.968	4.799	4.639	4.487	4.344	4.207	4.078	3.954	3.837
9	5.537	5.328	5.132	4.946	4.772	4.607	4.451	4.303	4.163	4.031
10	5.889	5.650	5.426	5.216	5.019	4.833	4.659	4.494	4.339	4.192
11	6.207	5.938	5.687	5.453	5.234	5.029	4.836	4.656	4.486	4.327
12	6.492	6.194	5.918	5.660	5.421	5.197	4.988	4.793	4.611	4.439
13	6.750	6.424	6.122	5.842	5.583	5.342	5.118	4.910	4.715	4.533
14	6.982	6.628	6.302	6.002	5.724	5.468	5.229	5.008	4.802	4.611
15	7.191	6.811	6.462	6.142	5.847	5.575	5.324	5.092	4.876	4.675
16	7.379	6.974	6.604	6.265	5.954	5.668	5.405	5.162	4.938	4.730
17	7.549	7.120	6.729	6.373	6.047	5.749	5.475	5.222	4.990	4.775
18	7.702	7.250	6.840	6.467	6.128	5.818	5.534	5.273	5.033	4.812
19	7.839	7.366	6.938	6.550	6.198	5.877	5.584	5.316	5.070	4.843
20	7.963	7.469	7.025	6.623	6.259	5.929	5.628	5.353	5.101	4.870

Probability

$A \cup B$ = A **or** B. $A \cap B$ = A **and** B (overlap). P(B/A) = probability of B, **given** A.

Rules of addition

If A and B are *mutually exclusive*: $P(A \cup B) = P(A) + P(B)$
If A and B are **not** mutually exclusive: $P(A \cup B) = P(A) + P(B) - P(A \cap B)$

Rules of multiplication

If A and B are *independent*: $P(A \cap B) = P(A) * P(B)$
If A and B are **not** independent: $P(A \cap B) = P(A) * P(B/A)$

E(X) = expected value = probability * payoff

Quadratic equations

If $aX^2 + bX + c = 0$ is the general quadratic equation, then the two solutions (roots) are given by

$$X = \frac{-b \pm \sqrt{b^2 - 4ac}}{2a}$$

Descriptive statistics

Arithmetic mean

$$\bar{x} = \frac{\sum x}{n} \text{ or } \bar{x} = \frac{\sum fx}{\sum f}$$

Standard deviation

$$\sqrt{\frac{\sum(x - \bar{x})^2}{n}}$$

$$SD = \sqrt{\frac{\sum fx^2}{\sum f} - \bar{x}^2} \text{ (frequency distribution)}$$

Index numbers

Price relative = $100 * P_1/P_0$

Quantity relative = $100 * Q_1/Q_0$

Price: $\dfrac{\sum W \times P_1/P_0}{\sum W} \times 100$ where W denotes weights

Quantity: $\dfrac{\sum W \times Q_1/Q_0}{\sum W} \times 100$ where W denotes weights

Time series

Additive model: Series = Trend + Seasonal + Random

Multiplicative model: Series = Trend * Seasonal * Random

Linear regression and correlation

The linear regression equation of Y on X is given by:

$Y = a + bX$ *or*

$Y - \overline{Y} = b(X - \overline{X})$, where

$$b = \frac{\text{Covariance (XY)}}{\text{Variance (X)}} = \frac{n\sum XY - (\sum X)(\sum Y)}{n\sum X^2 - (\sum X)^2}$$

and $a = \overline{Y} - b\overline{X}$,

or solve $\sum Y = na + b\sum X$

$\qquad\quad \sum XY = a\sum X + b\sum X^2$

Coefficient of correlation (r)

$$r = \frac{\text{Covariance (XY)}}{\sqrt{\text{VAR(X).VAR(Y)}}}$$

$$= \frac{n\sum XY - (\sum X)(\sum Y)}{\sqrt{[n\sum X^2 - (\sum X)^2][n\sum Y^2 - (\sum Y)^2]}}$$

$$R(\text{rank}) = 1 - \left[\frac{6\sum d^2}{n(n^2 - 1)}\right]$$

Financial mathematics

Compound Interest (Values and Sums)

Future Value of S_1 of a sum X, invested for n periods, compounded at r% interest:

$$S = X[1 + r]^n$$

Annuity

Present value of an annuity of £1 per annum receivable or payable, for n years, commencing in one year, discounted at r% per annum:

$$PV\, s = \frac{1}{r}\left[1 - \frac{1}{[1+r]^n}\right]$$

Perpetuity

Present value of £1 per annum, payable or receivable in perpetuity, commencing in one year discounted at r% per annum

$$PV = \frac{1}{r}$$

Notes